# AFRICA IN ECONOMIC CRISIS

# AFRICA IN ECONOMIC CRISIS

## Edited by John Ravenhill

Columbia University Press

New York                    1986

**Library of Congress Cataloging-in-Publication Data**

Main entry under title:

Africa in economic crisis.

1. Africa, Sub-Saharan—Economic conditions—Addresses, essays, lectures. 2. World Bank—Africa, Sub-Saharan—Addresses, essays, lectures.
I. Ravenhill, John.
HC800.A557   1986       330.967       85–26972
ISBN 0–231–06382–2 (alk. paper)
ISBN 0–231–06383–0 (pbk.)

# Contents

# List of Tables

# List of Figures

# Preface

The harsh truth is that sub-Saharan Africa today faces a crisis of unprecedented proportions. The physical environment is deteriorating. Per capita production of food grains is falling. Population growth rates are the highest in the world and rising. National economies are in disarray. And international assistance in real terms is moving sharply downward.[1]

Robert McNamara's statement succinctly summarises the principal dimensions of Africa's economic crisis. Five years after the World Bank published *Accelerated Development in Sub-Saharan Africa*, its major study of the causes of Africa's economic problems, the region's economic situation has deteriorated further. Indeed, the rate of economic decline has gathered pace: per capita food production fell by 2 per cent per year in the period 1980–84; gross domestic product per capita fell by an average of 3.6 per cent each year in the same period. Although the response from Western publics to Africa's famines has been generous, it is clear that many Western governments, as well as private corporations, are actively delinking themselves from the continent. In 1984 a net repayment of commercial loans of more than $3 billion occurred, a sum close to half the total value of grants and loans received from multilateral and bilateral agencies. Bilateral aid to the region fell by more than $1.25 billion from 1983 to 1984 as such major donors as France, West Germany and the United Kingdom reduced their aid programmes.

The debate on appropriate measures to be taken to improve Africa's economic prospects continues to be dominated by the proposals made at the beginning of this decade in *Accelerated Development* and in the OAU's *Lagos Plan of Action*. McNamara's justification for his lecture is equally applicable to this book: 'the action proposed in the previous reports has, for the most part, not yet even been initiated; the situation is continuing to deteriorate; and the external financial flows that will be needed in the second half of this decade to support whatever structural adjustments the African governments are prepared to initiate are simply not now in prospect.'[2] As Africa's short- and medium-term economic prospects become even bleaker, the need for remedial measures assumes even greater urgency, yet the vicious downward spiral in which many African economies are enveloped makes purposive policy-making ever more difficult.

My objective in assembling this collection was to provide, first, a balanced assessment of the various proposals that have been put forward as solutions to Africa's economic problems and, secondly, to place these proposals in context through an examination both of some key issue areas, e.g. agriculture and debt, and of the recent experience of selected countries in pursuing such diverse economic strategies as self-reliance and export-led growth. On one matter there is consensus among the contributors; there are indeed 'no shortcuts to progress'. Africa faces a period of painful adjustment if a catastrophe of enormous proportions is to be avoided.

I am grateful to the University of Sydney for research and typing assistance, Mark Hayne and Barbara Page assisted in the proofreading, Liz Kirby, Senior Research Assistant in the Department of Government at Sydney, compiled the index.

J.R.
Sydney, Australia

NOTES

1. Robert S. McNamara, *The Challenge for Sub-Saharan Africa*, Sir John Crawford Memorial Lecture, 1 November 1985 (Washington, DC: World Bank, 1985) pp. 31–2.
2. Ibid., p. 3.

# Notes on the Contributors

**Caroline Addison** is a Research Officer at the Institute of Development Studies, University of Sussex. She co-edited the special issue of the Institute's *Bulletin* on the World Bank's *Accelerated Development*.

**K. Y. Amoako** is the World Bank's Resident Representative in Lusaka, Zambia. He was a member of the World Bank's African Strategy Review Group which produced the *Accelerated Development* report.

**Elliot Berg** is head of Elliot Berg Associates, a Washington, DC based consultancy firm. Formerly Professor of Economics at the University of Michigan and author of numerous articles on African development, he was the coordinator of the World Bank's African Strategy Review Group which produced the *Accelerated Development* report.

**Thomas J. Biersteker** is Associate Professor of Political Science at the University of Southern California. He is the author of *Distortion or Development?*.

**Thomas M. Callaghy** is Assistant Professor of Political Science at Columbia University. He is author of *The State–Society Struggle: Zaire in Comparative Perspective*.

**Carl K. Eicher** is Professor of Agricultural Economics at Michigan State University. His most recent book, co-edited with John M. Staatz, is *Agricultural Development in the Third World*.

**Reginald Herbold Green** is a Professorial Fellow at the Institute of Development Studies, University of Sussex, and a part-time consultant to the government of Tanzania, the World Council of Churches, SWAPO, and the SADCC. His most recent book is *Namibia*.

**E. Gyimah-Boadi** is a doctoral student in the Department of Political Science, University of California, Davis.

**Richard Higgott** is Senior Lecturer in Social and Political Theory at Murdoch University, Perth. He is the author of *Political Development Theory*.

**Steven Langdon** is a New Democratic Party member of the Canadian Parliament. He was formerly Associate Director, International Development Research Centre, Ottawa, and Assistant Professor of Economics at Carleton University. He is the author of *Multinational Corporations in the Political Economy of Kenya*.

**Stanley Please** is a Visiting Fellow at Nuffield College, Oxford. Until 1983 he was Senior Advisor to the Senior Operations Vice-President of the World Bank. He directed the World Bank team which produced *Toward Sustained Development in Sub-Saharan Africa*.

**John Ravenhill** is Senior Lecturer in Government at the University of Sydney. He is the author of *Collective Clientelism: The Lomé Conventions and North–South Relations*.

**Donald Rothchild** is Professor of Political Science at the University of California, Davis. His most recent book, co-edited with Victor A. Olorunsola, is *State versus Ethnic Claims: African Policy Dilemmas*.

**Timothy M. Shaw** is Professor of Political Science and Director of the African Studies Centre at Dalhousie University. His most recent books are: (co-edited with Olajide Aluko) *Africa Projected*, and *Towards a Political Economy for Africa*.

# List of Abbreviations

| | | | |
|---|---|---|---|
| *AD* | *Accelerated Development in Sub-Saharan Africa* | IFAD | International Fund for Agricultural Development |
| ADB | African Development Bank | IFC | International Finance Corporation (World Bank) |
| ASEAN | Association of South East Asian Nations | ILO | International Labour Organisation (UN) |
| CEAO | West African Economic Community | IMF | International Monetary Fund |
| CFA | African Financial Community | IRD | Integrated Rural Development |
| ECA | Economic Commission for Africa (UN) | ISI | Import-Substituting Industrialisation |
| ECLA | Economic Commission for Latin America (UN) | LDCs | Less Developed Countries |
| | | *LPA* | *Lagos Plan of Action* |
| ECOWAS | Economic Community of West African States | MNCs | Multinational Corporations |
| | | MSAs | Most Seriously Affected Countries |
| ECSCA | Economic Community of the States of Central Africa | MULPOC | Multilateral Programming and Operational Centres (ECA) |
| EEC | European Economic Community | NICs | Newly Industrialising Countries |
| EFF | Extended Fund Facility (IMF) | NIDL | New International Division of Labour |
| EOI | Export-Oriented Industrialisation | NIEO | New International Economic Order |
| FAO | Food and Agriculture Organisation (UN) | OAU | Organisation of African Unity |
| GATT | General Agreement on Tariffs and Trade | OECD | Organisation for Economic Cooperation and Development |
| GDP | Gross Domestic Product | OPEC | Organisation of Petroleum Exporting Countries |
| GNP | Gross National Product | PTA | Preferential Trade Area |
| GSP | Generalised System of Preferences | SADCC | Southern African Development Coordination Conference |
| IARCs | International Agricultural Research Centres | SSA | Sub-Saharan Africa |
| IBRD | International Bank for Reconstruction and Development (World Bank) | STABEX | Stabilisation of Export Earnings Scheme (Lomé Conventions) |
| ICRISAT | International Crops Research Institute for the Semi-Arid Tropics | TNCs | Transnational Corporations |
| | | UN | United Nations |
| IDA | International Development Association | UNCTAD | United Nations Conference on Trade and Development |
| IDB | Industrial Development Bank (World Bank) | USDA | United States Department of Agriculture |
| IDS | Institute of Development Studies, University of Sussex | WDR | World Development Report |

# 1 Africa's Continuing Crises: The Elusiveness of Development

## JOHN RAVENHILL

The picture that emerges from the analysis of the perspective of the African region by the year 2008 under the historical trend scenario is almost a nightmare. Poverty would reach unimaginable dimensions since rural incomes would become almost negligible relative to the cost of physical goods and services. The conditions in the urban centres would also worsen with more shanty towns, more congested roads, more beggars and more delinquents. The level of the unemployed searching desperately for the means to survive would imply increased crimes rates and misery. Against such a background of misery and social injustice, the political situation would inevitably be difficult. The very consequence of extreme poverty would be social tensions and unrest which, in turn, would result in political instability. With the continuous and cumulative financial difficulties, governments would have little choice but to yield to the often unkind designs of international monopoly capital. As a result, the very notion of national sovereignty would be at stake.

*(ECA and Africa's Development)*[1]

The history of economic development has been full of surprises. The evidence is overwhelming that, with the right combination of external assistance and domestic policies, countries can turn around, often in less than a decade.

*(Toward Sustained Development)*[2]

Sub-Saharan Africa is currently suffering an economic crisis of a magnitude unprecedented in its recent history. According to the World

Bank, 'a real possibility' exists that per capita incomes will fall below those levels which prevailed when most countries gained their independence, 25 years ago. Although impressive welfare gains have been made in the interim in areas such as health care, education, and housing, these are threatened by the continuing and deepening economic crisis. Already, as Green and Singer note, the welfare gap between Africa and other least developed countries has widened.[3] Sub-Saharan Africa is the only region in which per capita food production has declined over the last two decades. Not coincidentally, it is the region with the fastest growth of population and the only one in which rates of population growth are projected to increase during the 1980s.

Drought in eastern and southern Africa has focused world attention on the region. Such attention is welcome but can be misguided if the drought is seen as a unique problem rather than as one of the more extreme consequences of wider and deeper economic malaise. Africa's crisis is long-term, multi-sectoral, and self-reinforcing. There are no simple solutions, yet solutions must be found if the most dire predictions of the continent's future are not to be realised. The principal objectives of this book are to examine the causes of the current economic crisis and to evaluate some of the strategies that have been advocated as partial solutions (e.g. policy reform in agriculture, export-led growth, self-reliance, regional integration, etc.) Since much of the debate on the direction of Africa's future has been conducted around two sets of proposals put forward at the beginning of this decade – the Organisation of African Unity's (OAU) *Lagos Plan of Action (LPA)*, and the World Bank's *Accelerated Development in Sub-Saharan Africa (AD)* – the first part of this book appropriately focuses on these initiatives. As the authors of these chapters point out, however, the debate on strategies for Africa's future has moved beyond the initial atmosphere of confrontation that arose from what was often an overly crude juxtaposition of the two plans. This new dialogue and the emerging consensus on the nature of Africa's problems are to be welcomed: the authors of this volume hope to contribute by pointing out some of the strengths and weaknesses of the various proposals.

One of the major questions on which *LPA* and *AD* differed was on the identification of the principal causes of the current crisis. The OAU followed a typical 'dependency' approach in asserting that the origins of the current malaise lay outside the control of Africa's leaders – a legacy of integration into the world economic system on unequal terms, colonial exploitation, and the structure of the international economy which ensured continuing unequal terms of exchange with the industrialised world. The World Bank, on the other hand, placed the primary blame on the performance of African governments and heavily discounted the role of exogenous factors such as deterioration in the terms of trade. The reality of the matter undoubtedly lies between these two extremes: both internal and external factors have made significant contributions to Africa's economic crisis in the last 15 years.

Academic commentators and international agencies have been loathe to criticise the performance of African governments.[4] Many supported the right of newly-independent governments to experiment and, indeed, learn from their own mistakes. External policy advice, including that of the World Bank, had been far from infallible. Meanwhile, dependency theories, with their simple assignment of blame for the plight of the Third World on external factors, proved seductive. And, to be fair, external criticism, however constructive, was seldom welcomed by governments which appeared to be excessively preoccupied with asserting their sovereignty. To continue to deny the responsibility of African governments for the consequences of their policies is to lapse, however, into a new paternalism.

Africa's economic options are, to be sure, severely constrained by the structure of the international economy. Yet it is entirely incorrect to suggest that governments enjoy no autonomy from international forces:[5] policy choices and their implementation do matter. The outcome of the famous 'West African wager' between Nkrumah and Houphouet-Boigny is but one of the most dramatic illustrations of the consequences of different policy paths. The danger of focusing entirely on external factors is that it tends towards the assumption that Africa's problems will be resolved as soon as the world economy recovers from the second oil-induced recession. Already the data show otherwise: the rate of growth of African economies has slumped towards zero while the average for other low-income developing countries is approximately 5 per cent per annum. Clearly, as the World Bank suggests, the problem is as much one of African countries' inability to supply world markets on competitive terms as one of lagging world demand. Policy change is essential.

As is argued in Chapter 4, one of the principal weaknesses of the *LPA* was its failure to admit the need for dramatic policy change. Rather than viewing the plan as 'radical' as have some commentators, its commitment to an essential continuation of the status quo in terms of policies and priorities marks it as a profoundly conservative document. The one exception to this is the commitment in the plan to regional integration and self-reliance. But to use this as the basis for asserting that the plan makes a dramatic break with the past is to give far greater credence than is warranted to African governments' professions of faith in regionalism. Regional self-reliance has been given the same symbolic status in the 1980s as was accorded Pan Africanism in the 1960s: a concept to which lip service is paid but one which is largely ignored when it comes to policy implementation. This has already been seen in the failure of African governments to meet the plan's deadlines for trade liberalisation. The *LPA* actually has few concrete proposals for solving Africa's crises, largely being content to place the blame on external factors and to call for massive external assistance.

If Lagos erred in largely ignoring the need for domestic policy reform, the World Bank's *Accelerated Development* erred in the other direction by failing to acknowledge the important exogenous factors which have adversely affected Africa's economic growth over the last 15 years. In particular, the Bank either glossed over or attempted to deny the importance of declining terms of trade for African countries. No mention was given in *AD*, for instance, to the problems that unstable terms of trade cause for government revenue and planning, and for offering stable, remunerative prices to producers of export crops. So intent was the Bank in placing the blame for economic crisis on policy failure that at times it appeared to resort to a statistical sleight of hand – the use of weighted means which included oil-exporting countries, selective citation of data, etc. – in attempting to discount the impact of unfavourable tendencies in foreign trade.

Even by 1979, the last year for which *Accelerated Development* presents data, the median decline in net barter terms of trade for sub-Saharan Africa (SSA) as a whole for the 1970–79 period was 14.5 per cent. Prices for all major food and beverage exports except coffee and cocoa fell quite sharply during the 1970s. For Africa's principal minerals exports – copper and iron – the decline was even more precipitous (copper suffered an *annual* average fall in nominal price of 18.7 per cent for the years 1970–80). The purchasing power of exports of many countries fell significantly in this period, for example, Ethiopia, Somalia, Benin and Sierra Leone all lost over one-third of their purchasing power, Mauritania and Liberia over 40 per cent, Zaire and Zambia over 50 per cent. Subsequently, the decline has been even more pronounced. Between 1980 and 1982 alone, deterioration in the terms of trade cost sub-Saharan Africa a staggering 1.2 per cent of its total Gross Domestic Product (GDP): for low-income countries the figure was 2.4 per cent; for middle-income oil importers, 3.0 per cent. Even allowing for similar policy mistakes throughout the continent, that the crisis struck all

African countries simultaneously regardless of their different policy orientations, should have been sufficient to alert any observer to the importance of external factors. Although later Bank reports (the 1983 *Progress Report* and the 1984 *Toward Sustained Development*) note the deterioration in the external environment, neither give it detailed consideration nor discuss the policy implications for traditional agricultural exports.

Many who welcomed the Bank's emphasis on the need for internal policy reform as an essential antidote to the *LPA*'s external orientation and wishful thinking were offended by the self-righteous and sometimes unnecessarily aggressive tone of *Accelerated Development*. As several of the contributors to this volume point out, there was not even a partial admission in the Bank's report of its own policy errors and those of other donors (see, for example, Eicher's comments on the Bank's livestock projects). Although *Toward Sustained Development* does criticise the role of foreign donors in advocating inappropriate aid projects, it falls short of acknowledging policy failures on the part of the Bank.[6]

Particularly offensive was the Bank's voluntaristic conception of the African state, especially its reluctance to acknowledge the political constraints on government action. By refusing to admit that economic rationality and political rationality do not always coincide, the Bank implicitly suggested wanton stupidity in policy-making on the part of African governments. Perhaps understandably the Bank's report contains no analysis of the class interests of Africa's rulers: less excusable was the failure of *AD* to acknowledge the political imperative of satisfying urban and regional constituencies. Policy reform was portrayed as a painless political choice – as if the coincidence of urban unrest/coups with food price rises and currency devaluations had entirely escaped the notice of the Bank. One consequence of this was that, although *AD* emphasised the need for increased external assistance, insufficient attention was given to the manner in which African governments could be helped to overcome the inevitable short-term negative side-effects of policy reform. Only in the *Progress Report* and *Toward Sustained Development* are there cryptic references to barriers to policy reform, for example, *Progress Report* at p. 21 notes that 'powerful political interests have developed around existing policies, however inefficient these might be'.

These deficiencies in analysis and tone were unfortunate in that they allowed critics to divert attention from the substantive proposals for reform: some of *AD*'s least qualified statements were taken out of the context of the overall presentation and set up as straw men – which proved easy to demolish. *AD* quickly had a formidable array of critics aligned against it. African governments quite reasonably feared that their countries were to become locations for yet further externally-induced economic experimentation. Not surprisingly, they rejected the Bank's call for a reduction in the role of the state and opposed the greater conditionality implicit in the Bank's proposals for the linking of aid to policy reform. Radical critics fell into two principal camps: those who took the populist stance of opposing the Bank's proposals to extend the commercialisation of agriculture; and those who rejected the Bank's emphasis on expanding traditional agricultural exports and further integration into the world economy in favour of calls for a radical delinking from the capitalist world economy.[7] Many liberal democrats also reacted unfavourably to *AD*, perceiving it as representative of the new post-McNamara supply side orthodoxy which abandoned the Bank's focus on meeting basic human needs.[8] Some undoubtedly saw it as an opportunity to pursue personal and professional vendettas.

Fortunately, the debate on Africa's future has moved beyond the often vituperative initial response to *Accelerated Development*. Subsequent Bank reports, particularly *Toward Sustained Development*, have displayed a far greater awareness of the constraints – both internal and external – faced by African governments, and a greater sensitivity to the aspirations of the OAU as expressed in the Lagos Plan. Meanwhile, the Economic Commission for Africa (ECA) and African governments – some under external pressure which they have found very difficult to resist – have increasingly recognised the need for internal policy reform. The way has been opened for serious consideration of the issues and of the policy options available to African governments. The remainder of this chapter considers reform proposals in, first, the agricultural sector, and secondly, the industrial sector, and examines the role of the state and the political obstacles to policy reform.


AFRICAN AGRICULTURE

Development economists have long emphasised the importance of an agricultural revolution as a prerequisite for sustained economic development. Increased protectionism in industrialised countries in the last decade and the decline in the rate of growth of manufactured exports from newly industrialising countries have given rise to a renewed export pessimism. In recent years economists have turned their attention once again to the potential offered by a growth strategy based on a production revolution in domestic agriculture.[9]

Agriculture currently accounts for 72 per cent of employment in Africa and approximately 40 per cent of the value of the continent's exports. Estimates place its share of the continent's Gross Domestic Product at 33 per cent (50 per cent in low-income countries); the actual contribution is probably higher owing to difficulties in evaluating the share of the subsistence sector. Agriculture will remain the dominant source of income and employment in Africa in the foreseeable future; even in its more optimistic, 'willed', scenario, the ECA projects that this sector will still provide 53 per cent of all employment by the year 2008.[10] The sector's importance for Africa's economic future is stated succinctly by the World Bank:

> Agriculture has the potential to reverse the increasing dependence on food imports, to produce the largest increase in export earnings in the short and medium term, to provide many of the inputs for the industrial sector and much of the demand for its output, and to strengthen the domestic income and tax base to finance the education, health, and infrastructure programs that will ease the basic constraints on African development.[11]

Even those who decry Africa's dependence on primary exports cannot afford to ignore agriculture (as they have tended to do in the past); it alone has the potential to provide the surplus necessary for initiating industrial development. Unfortunately, as is discussed in Chapter 4, the Lagos Plan had very little to say about agriculture in general and export agriculture in particular, adopting the conventional dependency perspective that stresses export diversification in order to overcome the disadvantages perceived in the current international division of labour (see also Chapter 5). The World Bank's *Agenda*, on the other hand, which rightly gave priority to agricultural reforms, tends towards undue optimism regarding the prospects for traditional agricultural exports. Partly as a consequence (for example, by extrapolating from static assumptions regarding comparative advantage) it was less sympathetic than it might (and probably should) have been towards the stated Lagos objective of food self-sufficiency, and the stimulus that a revolution in food production (savings on foreign exchange, linkages to domestic industry, etc.) would provide to economic growth.

Given agriculture's dominant role in most African economies, not only the root of the continent's current crisis but also a major part of its solution must be sought in this sector. Actually gauging the nature of the agricultural problem, yet alone seeking remedies, is no easy task. As Eicher points out in Chapter 7, aggregate data on Africa's agricultural output, particularly food production, are notoriously unreliable. Production data rely heavily on official 'guestimates' of acreages planted and of yields, and/or quantities purchased by state marketing bodies. Reported declines in production thus instead may reflect the diversion of crops to non-officially-sanctioned markets through, for example, smuggling across borders or sale on parallel markets.

Not only are there problems regarding the accuracy of individual country data but much also depends on the manner in which 'average' figures are calculated. For instance, in different tables, *Toward Sustained Development* provides two substantially different 'averages' for the annual growth rate of agricultural production in the years 1970–82. The median figure for all sub-Saharan Africa is 2.1 per cent; the weighted mean is 1.4 per cent (for low-income countries the respective figures are 1.6 per cent and 0.7 per cent). Relatively poor performances by larger economies have had a negative effect on the weighted means; median statistics are not biased downwards in the same way.

Aggregate data also, of course, mask significant differences not only between individual African countries but also within them. Particular scepticism must be applied when 'average' figures for all African countries are cited. There is some evidence that the agricultural situation may not be as gloomy as 'averaged' statistics suggest, these being biased downwards by particularly poor performances of countries severely affected by drought and/or poltical unrest (e.g. Botswana, Ghana, Mozambique).[12] An optimist therefore might suggest that, barring the intervention of prolonged drought, a reversal of the recent negative trends in per capita production might be possible in a reasonably short period of time. According to World Bank data, middle-income oil importers, for example, increased their food production by an average (median) of 3.4 per cent per year in the period 1970–82, a growth rate above the median (2.9 per cent) for all Less Developed Countries (LDCs) in this category. Even Nigeria, whose agricultural policies have been much maligned, is reported to have increased its food production by 2.5 per cent p.a. in the period 1970–82 compared with an average annual increase of only 0.5 per cent in the years 1960–72.[13]

Nevertheless, these figures provide no grounds for complacency. Even if one accepts the more optimistic estimate, Nigeria's improved performance still failed to keep pace with its rate of population growth and the increased demand for higher-income foodstuffs arising from oil-induced economic growth. Africa's aggregate annual increase in food production of 1.7 per cent in the 1970–82 period was only one-half the rate of growth of its population. For the years 1980–82, only 7 of the 39 countries (Benin, Cameroon, Central African Republic, Ivory Coast, Mauritius, Rwanda, and Swaziland) for which the World Bank reported data maintained or improved on their index of food production per capita from the 1969–71 period.

That the current food crisis is indeed real and of significant magnitude is reflected in the growing volume of food imports. Whereas Africa imported an average volume of 1.96 million metric tons of agricultural products in the years 1961–63 (and, according to Eicher, was actually a net exporter of staple foodstuffs in this period),[14] by 1980–82 this figure had risen to 11.2 million metric tons at an annual value of over $6.8 billion (over one-seventh of the total value of Africa's imports in 1982). Owing to foreign exchange constraints most African countries have had to rely increasingly on food aid to meet their imported food requirements. This rose by over 75 per cent in the period 1978–82 to a total of 2.2 million metric tons. Gabon alone among the 39 countries for which the World Bank reported data was not a beneficiary of food aid in the years 1981–82. Even Kenya, long regarded as one of the continent's agricultural success stories, received an average of 140 000 metric tons of food aid in 1981 and 1982. According to the World Bank, the volume of cereal imports in 1982 implied that one in five people in Africa (equivalent to the continent's entire urban population) were dependent upon them. In some countries the figure is much higher: Elliott records that Zambia imports 40 per cent of all its foodstuffs needs.[15]

If food production in the past suffered as a result of the priority given to export crops (and here the record is far more complex than some dependency theorists have alleged),[16] this appeared not to be the case in the period 1970–82 when total agricultural output grew more slowly (1.4 per cent p.a.) than food production (1.7 per cent p.a.) (and total agricultural output per capita declined more rapidly than food production per capita). Rather than there being a zero-sum relationship. there was, in fact, a positive correlation between success in food production and in export agriculture – with the Ivory Coast, the bête noire of dependency theorists, being the prize example. The implication is that government policies have tended to have a fairly uniform (negative or positive) impact on the agricultural sector rather than discriminating for or against domestic or export production.

All of Africa's major agricultural exports, with the exceptions of tea, sugar and tobacco, registered a decline in volume in the period from 1969/72 to 1980/82. That these three exceptions are largely produced on estates or plantations may have some significance – not necessarily that this mode of production is more efficient but that plantation owners have better political access and thus have been able to achieve remunerative prices conducive to maintaining or increasing output. Since many of the export crops are perennials, production can be expected to deteriorate further before any upswing occurs. Again, however, some caution must be employed in interpreting aggregate data since the largest production declines were in oils and oilseeds, crops grown primarily in areas afflicted by drought. Trend growth rates in aggregate production can also be distorted by outliers, as appears to have occurred in the last few years in the cases of cocoa and coffee.

Whatever the long-term prospects for Africa's agricultural exports – and critics have tended to ignore the World Bank's explicit statement that its recommended agriculture-based and export-oriented development strategy 'is not a permanent course for any country'[17] – both export agriculture and food production are sorely in need of rehabilitation. If Africa's agricultural exports had maintained their share of world markets in the 1970s an additional amount in export earnings in excess of $1 billion would have been generated. Poor price prospects for the future make it unlikely that significant increases in export earnings will be achieved; nevertheless, maintenance of market shares in a growing market could ensure that total export earnings from these commodities do not decline in real terms. Similarly, maintentance of food production per capita at the levels achieved in the late 1960s would result in substantial savings on the food bill; this scarce foreign exchange could be used more productively for economic diversification.

Given the complexities of Africa's agricultural crisis, there are no simple or viable short-term solutions. Most commentators accept, however, that a major cause of the current crisis has been the inadequate incentives provided for agricultural producers and, in particular, the marked deterioration in rural–urban terms of trade that occurred in many countries during the 1970s. Much of the discussion of the World Bank's proposals in *Accelerated Development* for the agricultural sector has focused on its recommendations for changes to one aspect of the urban–rural terms of trade: pricing policy. Although these certainly were highlighted in the original report, it would be a caricature of the Bank's position to isolate them, as have some critics, from its other recommendations for reform in this sector.[18] Nevertheless, the emphasis given to pricing reform warrants that the subject be explored in greater depth.

Two major factors must be considered in examining proposals for improving the rural–urban terms of trade. First, are they politically realistic given the current structure of African politics? Second, will they produce the desired results in terms of sustained increases in aggregate agricultural production?

Bates has provided a convincing explanation of the political rationality of the anti-agricultural bias of African governments. Resources not only have been extracted from the agricultural sector for the purposes of economic diversification but also rents generated through the substitution of administration for markets. Interventionist policies, e.g. licensing, selective subsidies of inputs, etc., give rise to scarcities that generate economic and political resources used for personal enrichment and political patronage. Parastatal marketing bodies provide further patronage opportunities. Governments have found it relatively easy to exploit the agricultural sector in this manner because farmers in many countries have been a relatively ineffective political constituency compared with urban and industrial groups, whose interests in cheap food coincide with those of the government. Bates uses collective goods theory to explain why small farmers are difficult to organise and thus why they often prefer the option of 'exit' from state-controlled channels to 'voice'.[19] In sectors where there are large farms, however, particularly if owned by members of the political elite, agriculture has received far more favourable treatment, as collective goods theory would predict.[20]

For African governments, therefore, increased agricultural prices may be considered a last resort. Not only are they politically costly, in terms of offending urban and industrial constituencies, but they also provide few political benefits since prices, as public goods, generate universal benefits for all producers – political friend and foe alike. Governments will prefer to rely on imported food – made relatively inexpensive through an overvalued exchange rate or through the beneficence of food aid donors, and sometimes easier to distribute than domestic production given the port location of many of Africa's cities. Imports can be rationed which in turn produces additional rents; in contrast, increased prices to domestic producers and consumers will at best generate mixed political results.

There are, however, obvious limits to the logic of this argument, limits which may well have been reached in many parts of contemporary Africa. A first qualification is the relatively ineffective countrol that governments can exert over the marketing and thus, ultimately, the pricing, of foodstuffs. The growth of parallel markets for foodstuffs throughout Africa is testimony to the ability of producers to exit from state-controlled marketing channels. Bates, himself, notes that marketing boards for domestic foodstuffs control no more than 10–30 per cent of total production.[21] In a situation of scarcity, consumers may have no alternative but to pay the higher prices of the unofficial markets. The traditional response of governments – to depress prices through food imports – is increasingly unavailable owing to severe shortages of foreign exchange. While increased imports of food aid may provide some relief, these have failed to cover the entire import gap.

Food shortages and price hikes, of whose existence there is ample evidence in recent years, alienate those very constituencies that governments were attempting to protect and undermine the political rationality of low producer prices. In this scenario, political and economic rationality become re-united in an attempt to stimulate domestic food production through higher prices. The new political rationality would be reinforced where members of the political elite have been attracted to food production by the higher market prices – as Rothchild and Gyimah-Boadi note appears to have been the case in Ghana (see Chapter 10). Government moves in this direction would be encouraged if assistance was made available to allow a gradual phasing-in of higher domestic food prices, as has occurred in Mali under the auspices of the World Food Program.

There is a similar limit to the political rationality of utilising marketing parastatals for patronage purposes. Marketing authorities have, since their creation in the colonial period, been used as a means of extracting surplus from agriculture. Export agriculture remains the most viable short-term means of generating a surplus which can be used for economic diversification: the role of marketing authorities in extracting this surplus inevitably – and justifiably – will continue. Since independence, however, all parastatals, including marketing authorities, have also been required to play a major role in patronage politics, primarily by providing employment to secondary school graduates. Once again, a politically rational policy of creating patronage leads to the economically irrational condition of bloated public sectors. Governments have given higher priority to the agencies' patronage role than to their formal organisational goals.[22]

Marketing parastatals have played a significant role in the decline of Africa's export agriculture. Unlike food production for the domestic market, agriculturalists have few alternatives – smuggling being the obvious exception – to selling export crops through official channels. Consequently, there are few pressures on the agencies to operate efficiently. In many countries the price that producers receive is a residual one: the proceeds from sale on the world market less the marketing costs of the parastatal.[23] As marketing parastatals have become more inefficient so the producers' share of proceeds has fallen. Ultimately, this affects government revenue in two ways. Indirectly, government revenue declines as a result of reduced quantities presented for marketing: the lower price causes producers to switch to other crops, to seek alternative markets, or simply to withdraw entirely from cash crop production. Directly, government revenue will be reduced if the growing inefficiencies of marketing authorities reduce the surplus that they are able to generate (after a certain point governments are faced with the prospect that increased costs cannot be passed on to the producer). Rather than serving as agents of accumulation, marketing authorities may actually become drains on government revenue.[24]

Either way, the political patronage function of the parastatals has undermined their other purpose of extracting surplus (itself, of course, a principal source of patronage). Inefficient state organisations have also become the target for popular attack. Thus the political rationality of expanding parastatal employment has come to threaten other political objectives. There is obviously a trade-off here and individual governments will have different priorities in their expenditures. The spate of official enquiries throughout Africa into parastatals suggests, however, that the political costs of these organisations' economic activities are becoming more than many governments are willing to bear. Once again, some prospect has emerged of the re-uniting of economic and political rationality through a reform of parastatals, a reduction in the share of marketing authorities in the proceeds from export crops, and thus a possibility of raising prices paid to producers.

The bottom line for all governments is political survival. The current anti-agricultural bias on the part of African governments is not only economically irrational but has also become increasingly politically irrational. This provides a basis for anticipating policy change. But is it economically feasible for governments to raise producer prices sufficiently to induce the desired supply response?

Maintaining or increasing producer prices in real terms is made extremely difficult, even for the best-motivated government, by marked fluctuations in world market prices. Even the Ivory Coast, which consistently raised *nominal* producer prices in the 1970s, found this impossible in the years following the substantial decline in world coffee and cocoa prices after 1978. A dramatic decline in foreign exchange earnings necessitates reduced government expenditure. Since there is, for obvious political as well as economic reasons, little flexibility in many items in government accounts, e.g. government salaries, agriculture often bears the brunt of reduced expenditure through lower producer prices. Effective provision of compensatory finance offers a solution to this difficulty – providing that it is utilised to stabilise producer prices. 'Stabilisation' boards, however, often have served primarily to stabilise or increase government revenue; rather than stabilising domestic prices they have passed on cuts in world prices – but not increases – to producers.

If the problem of fluctuating export earnings can be overcome, the principal economic barrier to improved producer prices is their impact on government revenue. Here, much depends on the price elasticity of supply, and the extent to which increases in producer prices can be achieved as a result of improved efficiency in marketing. Devaluation also reduces the local budgetary costs of an increase in producer prices although it may obviously conflict with other government objectives. Estimating the price elasticity of supply for individual crops is notoriously difficult not only because of the poor quality of data on production but also as a result of the intrusion of non-price factors, e.g. availability of essential inputs, supply of consumer goods, availability and remuneration of alternative employment activities and political unrest, many of which have not been included in the econometric estimates. For countries with a history of low producer prices, data on the price elasticity of supply may be biased upwards by the local marketing of crops previously smuggled across borders – although this apparent increase in output will come at the expense of marketing authorities in other countries.[25]

Evidence abounds of a positive supply response for individual crops to increased prices. In her survey of studies of cash crop supply elasticities in Africa, Bond reports figures for long-run elasticities ranging from 0.07 for cotton in the Northern region of Uganda to 1.81 for cocoa in the Cameroon. Most of the studies cited estimated long-run supply elasticities for individual crops to be over 0.5.[26] As the World Bank itself noted in *Accelerated Development* (p. 55, *n*.14), however, whereas farmers respond strongly to changes in *relative* prices, 'the question of *aggregate* supply response is more nuanced'. Studies cited by Bond report large negative cross-elasticities between important export crops such as cocoa and coffee in West Africa. Although she concludes that there is support for the proposition that turning the terms of trade in favour of the agricultural sector does produce an increase in overall agricultural output, the elasticities of aggregate supply are much smaller than those for individual crops. Her own study of nine countries estimates an average long-run price elasticity of aggregate supply of 0.21, the individual figures ranging from 0.07 in Uganda to 0.54 in Senegal.[27] Long-run aggregate price elasticities of this magnitude indicate that governments' ability to induce increases in agricultural output through higher prices will be severely circumscribed by their repercussions for revenue and by their inflationary effects. Shapiro cites a hypothetical example where the nominal protection coefficient for export crops is 0.66. To increase producer prices by 25 per cent would necessitate a halving of the government's share (34 per cent) of income from the crop's sale. If the price elasticity of supply is 0.3, increasing producer prices by 25 per cent will yield only a 7.5 per cent (25 × 0.3 per cent) increase in overall output, with the result that government revenue would fall by about 45 per cent.[28] Government expenditure on non-agricultural sectors inevitably would suffer.

Government shares in revenue from export crops are in fact higher than that in the hypothetical example in many African countries. And reductions in the share taken by marketing authorities plus devaluation would provide governments with greater room for manoeuvre. But price increases may, at best, serve to restore past levels of production in the short term – which, to be fair, was the time perspective adopted by the World Bank in *Accelerated Development*. If Bond's estimates of long-term aggregate supply response are correct, prices would have to be raised by 15 per cent each year in real terms in order to achieve an annual growth rate of 3 per cent in agricultural output. This is highly unrealistic (particularly in an era when the world market prices for Africa's major agricultural exports are projected to decline in real terms[29]). Increased producer prices will only produce their desired effect if they are sustained in real terms over a period of years – the recent experience of Africa shows, in fact, that even when governments have substantially increased producer prices in nominal terms, gains to producers have been rapidly eroded as a result of domestic inflation (partly a reflection of the ability of other groups in society to win income increases to compensate for higher costs both of foodstuffs and of imported goods). Real price increases cannot be expected to produce the long-term increases in agricultural output necessary to provide the basis for sustained economic growth.[30]

Drawing on evidence from a wide array of developing countries, Krishna presents a powerful case for the proposition that, while rural–urban terms of trade should be kept as favourable as possible, sustained agricultural growth is more likely to be achieved if emphasis is placed on increasing investment in the agricultural sector rather than on pricing policy.[31] This is particularly relevant to Africa where most authorities conclude that post-independence growth of output has occurred almost entirely as a result of extension of the area cultivated.[32] There are obvious limits to this practice especially in the context of Africa's high rates of population growth. Yields in Africa are substantially below those of other continents and have fallen further behind as higher-income developing countries have increased their agricultural investments.[33] FAO data show that in 1977 only 1.8 per cent of Africa's land was irrigated compared with 6.1 per cent in Latin America and 28 per cent in Asia; there were only 7 tractors per 10 000 hectares in Africa in contrast to 45 in Asia and 57 in Latin America, while African farmers used only 4.4 kilos of fertiliser per hectare compared with 38.8 for their Latin American and 45.4 for their Asian counterparts.[34] In Hyden's words, African agriculture remains 'pre-scientific'.[35]

Little progress has occurred to date in transferring the successes of the Green Revolution to Africa, as Eicher notes in Chapter 7. Variability of soils and climates throughout the continent combined with the predominance of rainfed agriculture makes research and the application of improved methods and varieties more difficult than was the case in Asia. Research activities, which in general have paid little attention to food production, have been poorly coordinated and seldom conducted in an applied setting.[36] Productivity might be improved through some relatively inexpensive measures, for example, historically there has been little application of fertilisers in food crop production; FAO figures indicate increased yields of 50 per cent or more where fertiliser has been applied.[37] Similarly, a reduction in pest damage – the USDA estimates that this causes a loss of 15–25 per cent of total crop production in the field plus another 15–20 per cent in storage – should be achievable without massive capital investments or changes in the basis of production.[38] Whether, however, the smallholder mode of production, constrained by labour shortages in West Africa and by the increasing subdivision of plots as a result of population pressure in East Africa, can sustain the productivity increases necessary to effect an agricultural revolution on the continent is more questionable. Certainly, as Stryker pointed out, before its recent proclamation of faith in the progressive smallholder, the World Bank's work on the agricultural sector expressed considerable doubt on this matter.[39]

While the World Bank undoubtedly is correct in stressing that there are few alternatives to an agricultural-led growth strategy for Africa in the near future, its optimism on export agriculture has a decidedly shaky foundation. Critics have justifiably pointed to the 'fallacy of composition' problem. African countries face a relatively inelastic demand for their principal agricultural exports: if all countries followed the Bank's prescription to increase supplies then the probability would be that real prices (already projected to fall) would tumble significantly. The Bank's defence against this criticism has had two main thrusts (see Chapters 2 and 6). The first has been to assert that while the criticism is valid in principle, in practice not all African countries will follow the Bank's advice; consequently, the problem will not arise. The second argument has been that, by failing to expand its traditional agricultural exports, Africa has lost its share of world markets to higher-income developing countries such as Brazil and Malaysia in those very products in which Africa should have a comparative advantage.

Neither argument is particularly convincing. To attempt to distinguish between the Bank's examination of the situation for Africa as a whole and the fact that policy-making occurs at the individual country level (see Chapter 6) is primarily to play with words. No suggestion appears in the Bank's *Agenda* that the prescribed policies for export agriculture should be followed selectively or that success in their pursuit will be dependent on other countries failing to implement the Bank's advice. The second argument has somewhat more validity. As noted above, export earnings would have been substantially larger in the 1970s if Africa had managed to maintain its share of world markets for its traditional agricultural exports. But it is a *non sequitur* to argue that this experience suggests either that Africa will be able to increase its real export earnings in the future by expanding its production beyond current levels, or that the continent necessarily has a competitive advantage in the production of these crops.

If one accepts the World Bank's own projections that there will be little growth in consumption, unless prices are to decline significant output expansion can occur only at the expense of other producers. Viewing Africa from the perspective of a single production unit, the problem is that it already has a large share of the world market for its principal agricultural exports and, given the predominance of traditional trading patterns, it is misleading to speak of the world market as an undifferentiated whole – Africa's exports go primarily to Europe where they constitute an even larger share of imports. As Little, Scitovsky and Scott noted: 'Other things being equal, it is easier to increase exports of a particular commodity if one has a small share in the world market for it than if one has a large one.'[40] While some African countries will succeed in increasing their agricultural exports in the future this will probably occur, as in the 1970s, at the expense of others, as in the Ivory Coast supplanting Nigeria and Ghana in European cocoa imports.

Does Africa have a comparative advantage in the production of its traditional cash crops as the World Bank suggests? Please and Amoako suggest that alternative income-earning opportunities in higher-income LDCs will drive up costs of production in comparison with Africa where other uses of resources are unavailable. But, as *Accelerated Development* noted, newly-industrialising countries (NICs) have been successful in capturing some of Africa's traditional markets because of their higher productivity in agriculture, the product of significant increases in agricultural investments in recent years. Africa's labour-intensive smallholder production is not necessarily the most efficient way of producing these crops. As noted above, there are probably fairly narrow limits within which smallholder production can be improved by the application of technology, even assuming that the necessary investments will be forthcoming. Neither is it the case, given the labour surplus that characterises those NICs that have been successful in expanding agricultural exports, that labour costs in these countries (currently, in some cases, substantially below those in Africa) will necessarily rise to such an extent that Africa gains a future advantage. While countries such as Brazil and Malaysia continue to depend heavily on agricultural exports for finanacing their industrialisation, they will not willingly relinquish their improved market shares in Africa's favour (as has been seen, for example, in their behaviour in negotiations for international commodity agreements).

## AN INDUSTRIALISED FUTURE?

Pessimism regarding the prospects for traditional exports and dissatisfaction with 'the over-dependence of our continent of [*sic*] the export of basic raw minerals'[41] led the ECA and OAU to advocate greater emphasis on industrialisation as a means of stimulating economic growth. Given that trade in manufactures has been the most rapidly growing sector of world commerce, as Higgott discusses in Chapter 11, this is an entirely rational aspiration. Africa's recent record in this sector has, if anything, been even worse than that in agriculture, however. In the period 1970–82, manufacturing grew at a median rate of 3.4 per cent p.a. for SSA as a whole but the median for the 23 low-income countries was only 0.5 per cent – lower than the rate of growth of agriculture. In 1982, manufacturing in low-income SSA accounted for 6 per cent of GDP – exactly the same mean percentage as in 1960. For SSA as a whole, the mean figure was 8 per cent, up only 1 per cent from 1960. The share of manufacturing in exports declined from a weighted mean of 7 per cent in 1962 to 4 per cent in 1978; for low-income non-oil exporting countries the decline was from 9 to 6 per cent. The 1980s – proclaimed by the Lagos Plan as 'Industrial Development Decade in Africa' – have seen a negative trend towards deindustrialisation. The only sector of African economies to have experienced rapid growth has been services, which expanded at an annual median rate of 4.9 per cent in the 1970–82 period. The service sector contributes a mean of 40 per cent of GDP in SSA compared with a mean of 31 per cent for all low-income countries worldwide; for middle-income oil importers in SSA the figure is 50 per cent compared with a world mean of 42 per cent for this category of countries.

The fallacy of denying the importance of exports for Africa's economic growth is clearly illustrated by recent experience in the industrial sector. Much of the recent poor performance is closely related to the decline in agricultural export earnings which has reduced import capacity, causing severe shortages of spare parts in many industries, and eroded domestic purchasing power. Declining domestic agricultural production has also, in some countries, led to shortages of raw material inputs for processing industries. Even the drought has had unanticipated consequences for the industrial sector, for example, the low level of water in the Volta Dam is reported to have reduced electricity production to such an extent that the Alcan smelter in Ghana was severely damaged.

Much of the debate on the World Bank's proposals for this sector has been carried on in terms of the appropriateness of the 'NIC analogy' for Africa and, indeed, the Bank's understanding of the lessons of the NICs. Commentators in many cases have appeared to react more to what they perceived to be the current message of the Bank as presented in the work of such senior advisers as Bela Balassa and Anne O. Krueger[42] than to the actual contents of *Accelerated Development* itself.[43] The Report has been caricatured as advocating deprotection and deindustrialisation, and issues it raised discussed in terms of two crude dichotomies: import-substituting industrialisation (ISI) versus export-led growth; and state intervention versus market forces.

Sophisticated commentators have long accepted that ISI and export-led growth have been complementary rather than antagonistic strategies in the recent history of the NICs.[44] Indeed, if export-led growth is to be more than merely offshore assembly of components, ISI is a necessary companion to (and probably pre-requisite for) an export-led strategy. Neither is one necessarily more efficient than the other. On *a priori* grounds, arguments have been put forward that the necessity of meeting competition on world markets would bring gains in terms of X-efficiency; in reality, this is not assured in situations where domestic firms receive heavy state subsidies for their exports. As Little *et al.* noted, state promotion of export industries has been conducted in some countries as inefficiently as import substitution.[45] Nor is it the case that firms intending to produce for export will necessarily capitalise on the country's scarce factor of production (assumed to be labour) when market prices are distorted by such policies as comparatively low tariffs on capital goods imports, etc.

The World Bank itself comments in *Accelerated Development* (p. 93) that, 'Import substitution can be a sound policy, and most industrialization has started on that basis'. It states quite clearly that, 'Most African countries will still find that the majority of investment opportunities with an acceptable rate of return will be in production for the local market'. Small domestic markets, low population densities, low labour productivity, high wages, high management costs, and high capital and infrastructure costs are cited as factors which limit the potential for manufactured exports. To suggest that the Bank was advocating a growth strategy based on the export of labour-intensive manufactures is simply nonsense. To quote *Accelerated Development* once again (p. 94): 'Neither the past record nor newly uncovered special advantages suggests that concentration on exports of labor-intensive manufactures is a promising strategy for most of Africa'.

Despite the caution expressed in this statement, the Bank might well be accused of being too optimistic regarding the potential for manu-factured exports. For, as an example of potentially attractive strategies, it cites first the preferential access to the European market enjoyed by virtue of the Lomé Conventions which have, it asserts, facilitated exports of textiles and clothing by the Ivory Coast and Mauritius; and, secondly, the possibility of increased processing of raw materials prior to export. Before *Accelerated Development* had been published, however, textile and clothing exports from both Mauritius and the Ivory Coast were subject to 'voluntary' export restraints imposed by the EEC. This was a clear signal that the EEC was unwilling to provide its 'privileged partners' in Africa with special treatment as far as products which are regarded as 'sensitive' are concerned.[46] As regards increased processing of raw materials, while Africa in most cases adds less value locally to such exports than other developing countries, Table 16 in the statistical appendix to *Accelerated Development* shows how industrialised countries' tariffs escalate with greater processing. This may benefit African countries in the EEC market since Lomé provides in principle for duty-free access (assuming that tariffs are not reduced for LDC competitors by the EEC's Generalised System of Preferences (GSP) scheme), but not in other industrialised countries where effective rates of protection for processing industries are often very high. There is no mention in the Bank's report, either, of the non-tariff barriers that protect processing industries, many of which are regarded as 'sensitive'.

Again, there is a danger of an overly static presentation of the prospects for manufactured exports. While such exports are indeed subject to a similar 'fallacy of composition' to that noted for agricultural products, in this instance the market share argument works in favour of Africa.[47] With only 0.2 per cent of total world manufactured exports, African countries could, in principle, considerably expand their exports without disrupting world markets. A detailed study of trade between African, Caribbean and Pacific countries and the EEC under the Lomé Convention found, in fact, that several African countries had enjoyed success in expanding non-traditional export products.[48] Nevertheless, the rate of expansion was slower than that of other developing countries while many of the exports fell into the category of 'sensitive' products (e.g. textiles, off-season agricultural products). Realistically, it is these sensitive products that African countries can best hope to export in the near future. Their problem is that they are latecomers to international markets which in many cases are already saturated by the exports of other developing countries. Unless industrialised countries show greater willingness than at present to give priority to these newcomers, they may well find that their most promising export routes are blocked off. In any event, if African states are to successfully promote labour-intensive manufactured exports, a more efficiently-repressive state will be required – one which is capable of reducing the real costs of labour. And, as both Callaghy and Higgott point out, Africa is a relatively unattractive locus for foreign investment compared with either Asia or Latin America.

If ISI can be (and has been in the NICs) complementary to export-led industrialisation, it can nevertheless also undermine the latter strategy when the protective measures taken to promote ISI make it impossible for export industries to compete effectively. While a preoccupation with the current 'negative value added' of some import-substituting industries pays insufficient attention to the dynamic benefits of stimulating domestic industry, 'infant' industries must eventually be eased out of their protective cocoon if they are not to damage the prospects of the export sector (not only manufactures but also agriculture and minerals). Chapter 8, by Langdon, highlights two negative effects of ISI which have adversely affected the export prospects of the Kenyan textile industry: excessive product diversification leading to high-cost, short-production runs; and high-cost inputs from other protected sectors. The chapter also focuses on the political coalitions that currently sustain high tariffs and other forms of protection in Africa, and the consequent difficulties faced by reform-minded governments.

Langdon, rather surprisingly, does not discuss another serious barrier to exports: persistently over-valued exchange rates. While export subsidies can in principle compensate exporters for some of the negative effects of domestic protection (assuming that the schemes are efficiently administered which, as Langdon shows, has not been the case in Kenya), the extent of currency over-valuations in many African countries in recent years would have made effective compensation prohibitively costly. Low, for instance, estimates that the cost of subsidies sufficient to remove the anti-export bias in Kenya would have amounted to 6 per cent of total annual government revenue.[49] Again, the effect of overvalued exchange rates in 'indirectly' taxing traditional exporting sectors makes them a rational policy instrument for governments at certain stages of industrialisation.[50] But in the late 1970s the real effective exchange rates of African countries appreciated to such an extent – the IMF estimates an average of 44 per cent for the 1973–81 period – that they completely undermined the prospects for manufactured exports in many countries. There is little evidence that most African governments have begun to consider policy measures which may help reduce anti-export bias.

If the World Bank was overly optimistic regarding the prospects for exported manufactures, it was probably too pessimistic regarding ISI possibilities. Although it did comment that the majority of profitable industrial investment opportunities in Africa in the near future would lie in this sector, it also asserted (p. 93) that the first stage of import substitution had nearly been exhausted in countries such as Kenya, the Ivory Coast, and Tanzania, and for them: 'few new import substitution opportunities exist based on the internal market'. Since, as the ECA notes, as much as 35–45 per cent of the *consumer* goods market in Africa is satisfied from imports, this pessimism on ISI appears premature, to say the least. In contrast, the Lagos Plan was wildly over-optimistic regarding the prospects for a growth strategy based on import substitution and collective self-reliance.

As Shaw documents in Chapter 5, Africa's preferred development strategy, as outlined in the Lagos Plan and subsequent ECA documents, is one of collective self-reliance based on import substitution and regional integration. According to the *LPA*, increased intra-African trade will be the 'mainstay' of the new strategy; here and in the ECA's projections for Africa's future, regional integration is elevated to a categorical imperative. Unfortunately, there is nothing in Africa's post-independence experience of self-reliance and regionalism to justify an optimistic assessment of this strategy's potential. Biersteker's review of the Tanzanian experience, updated for this volume (Chapter 9), is one of the few attempts to provide a systematic examination of self-reliance in practice. No African country has more self-consciously pursued a self-reliant strategy than Tanzania. Over the years since the Arusha Declaration, its government has made errors, to be sure – and Julius Nyerere has not been afraid to admit them – but there is little reason to believe that other African countries pursuing the same strategy would have been significantly more successful.

Biersteker's chapter shows the vulnerability of countries at Tanzania's level of development to natural disasters and unfavourable external trends. Its experience is testimony to the structural constraints which limit the policy options of relatively small, open, low income economies. Indeed, as Green argues, it is probably the case that countries in the initial stages of self-reliance strategy are *more* vulnerable to exogenous disruptions.[51] Difficulties have been compounded by policy failures. Those identified by Biersteker as of principal importance – the failure of agricultural self-sufficiency and the persistent ineffectiveness of government institutions – are the very factors emphasised by the Bank in *Accelerated Development*. If these failures had not occurred then Tanzania's self-reliant strategy might have been more successful. But it is a very big 'if' – and merely exhorting countries towards greater self-reliance, as did the Lagos Plan, does little to direct attention to the sources of policy failure.

Another aspect of the rationale for collective self-reliance warrants closer attention – the assumption by proponents that South–South commerce offers a new, non-exploitative basis for trade. This issue is discussed in Chapter 4. Where South–South trade has increased in recent years it has mirrored the traditional pattern of exchange of manufactured goods for raw materials. Africa's experience of repeated breakdown of regional integration schemes provides little reason to

believe that intra-African trade imbalances will be any more acceptable
than those between African countries and the industrialised world (as
seen in Biersteker's discussion of the East African Community
experience).

Unfortunately, the Lagos Plan does not detail how its regionally-
based import-substitution industrialisation strategy would be financed
(other than appealing for massive foreign assistance). As has long been
recognised, import-substitution is import-intensive.[52] Intermediate and
capital goods will still have to be imported in the foreseeable future from
extra-regional sources – and if not paid for by exports, the objective of
self-reliance is undermined. Meanwhile, African countries will have very
little (in terms of their total external trade) to sell to each other. In 1982,
despite two decades of attempted trade diversification, Africa depended
as heavily on industrialised market economies for its exports as it did in
1960 (a weighted mean of 80 per cent of total exports compared to 79 per
cent in the earlier year). Exports to other developing countries in 1982
were marginally below those in 1960 (a fall of 1 per cent to 17 per cent).
This may be an overly static approach, but, to put the matter bluntly, the
Lagos strategy lacks an engine of development. And prospects for
successful regional cooperation are likely to be undermined by the
method advocated by the Plan – common markets – whose universal
effect in Third World regions has been to increase interstate inequalities.
While greater economic cooperation in Africa is desirable (as all
commentators, including the World Bank, agree) Lagos, whose initial
target dates for trade liberalisation have already passed, provides little
beyond a statement of faith to convince observers that it can and will be
realised.


AN OVEREXTENDED STATE?

The second dimension of the NIC analogy on which debate has focused
is the question of state intervention versus the role of the market. Again,
this is largely a false debate – both in terms of the actual NIC experience,
and with regard to the Bank's recommendations for Africa. Ruggie
again provides a succinct comment on the NIC experience: 'Any
presumed identity between an outward-oriented development strategy
and laisez-faire is fictitious, or, perhaps more accurately, ideological'.[53]
Governments in the NICs have played an active role in promoting
import substitution and exports through the manipulation of the whole
range of monetary, tariff, and fiscal devices at their disposal. But to

acknowledge the role of the state in the NICs does not in itself address the question of whether the state in most SSA countries is overextended. Critics of the Bank's recommendations in *AD* have alleged that it has advocated a dismantling of public sector involvement in productive and distributive activities. Again, the forthright manner in which the Bank presented its recommendations in *AD* undoubtedly contributed to this over-reaction. On p. 5, for instance, the Bank asserts that, 'It is now widely evident that the public sector is overextended, given the present scarcities of financial resources, skilled manpower, and organizational capacity. This has resulted in slower growth than might have been achieved with available resources, and accounts in part for the current crisis.' This was taken by some commentators as implying a simple correlation between size of government sector and rates of economic growth, a straw man which was easily demolished.[54] A more careful reading of *AD* would have revealed that it stated quite clearly, in discussing its data on government expenditure and growth rates, that it was not the ratio of government expenditure to GDP which had determined growth but 'the quality of management of the economy' (p. 36).

Elsewhere, the Bank states its faith in the greater efficiency of the private sector more explicitly: 'the greater potential for competition and the ever-present possibility of bankruptcy exercises a discipline over private business that is lacking in the public sector' (*World Development Report 1983*, p. 51). This assumes a 'pure' market, however, whose existence anywhere is questionable, least of all in contemporary Africa. Langdon's contribution (Chapter 8) shows how private firms in the Kenyan textile sector have been protected from market 'discipline' by successfully appealing for government intervention, (a) to license imports which effectively precluded competition in domestic markets, and (b) for injection of capital which saved some companies from bankruptcy. Langdon's study also shows that some subsidiaries of transnational corporations (TNCs) appeared to have little interest in running their firms at a profit; they had already obtained a handsome return on their investments through the 'predatory fraud' of selling overpriced obsolete machinery to their subsidiaries.[55]

*Accelerated Development* is in fact more cautious in its assessment of the public versus private debate. On p. 60 the Bank notes that there is no *a priori* reason why government agencies should not be able to fulfill the input supply function efficiently. However, it continues, they have often failed to do so. This would be accepted by most contemporary observers of Africa – and for the reasons that the Bank states, namely, that government agencies, besides being subject to bureaucratic rigidities, have been expected to play a number of roles that are detrimental to the efficient execution of their formal economic task. As noted above, the government has taken on the role of employer of last resort in many African countries; government employment has expanded more rapidly than the rate of growth of GNP; for instance, the 1983 *World Development Report* estimates the annual average growth rate in government employment in Zaire in the period 1976–80 to be 15 per cent. An ideological reaction against the role of foreign companies and non-citizen traders has led to an extension of government activities into areas such as retail trading where the performance of the state sector has left much to be desired.

When this issue is examined not in terms of an ideological commitment for or against state intervention, or an *a priori* belief that the private sector will necessarily be able to fulfill more efficiently the activities that the government has undertaken in some countries (e.g. transporting crops from remote areas), but in terms of the necessity of efficient provision of services whether by public sector or private means, the gap between the Bank and its more reasonable critics largely disappears. Most would agree with the Bank's assessment of the state as 'overextended', a characteristic which has caused a muddling of priorities. The following quotation from Green, for example, is almost identical to the Bank's sentiments expressed in the 1983 *World Development Report*:

> The case for change rests on the demonstrable fact that many African republic [*sic*] sectors do what they do very badly and do not seem to have clear priorities or sequences. To seek to do now what can be postponed (e.g. international airport upgrading) or what is better done by private or cooperative/local public enterprise units (e.g. retail shops, rural short distance lorry and bus transport) is disastrously expensive. This is true not simply because these activities themselves are hardly priority but even more because it means that urgent priorities (e.g. in macro economic policy and/or in national storage facilities) and key sectors in which a public enterprise role is critical (e.g. banking, external trade) are left vacant or done very badly.[56]

## POLITICAL COALITIONS FOR CHANGE?

As is abundantly clear from the discussion in this chapter, Africa's economic crisis is above all a political crisis. Four of the chapters in this volume – those by Callaghy, Higgott, Langdon, and Rothchild and Gyimah-Boadi – all focus in detail on various aspects of the current political malaise.[57] While not all of Africa is subjected to the predatory kleptocrats of Zaire's political aristocracy, discussed by Callaghy in Chapter 12, African states, besides being overextended, remain 'soft', i.e. incapable of penetrating society to implement policy reform. Hyden has likened the African state, given its lack of roots in a mature indigenous class system, to a balloon suspended in mid-air.[58] The analogy of a tumour may be more apt, given the propensity of the parasitic state to siphon off surplus from the productive sectors of the economy. Africa's political crisis is rooted in a system of clientelist politics where economic efficiency is willingly sacrificed in order to generate resources to satisfy political constituencies.

A key question for Africa's future economic prospects is how, or indeed whether, it will be possible to transform Africa's current rent-seeking states into profit-generating ones. Commentators on the NICs suggest that one of the reasons for their success has been the relative autonomy enjoyed by the state, especially its insulation from societal demands. What prospects are there for insulating the African state, and to what extent will these be changed by the repercussions for political systems of sustained economic crisis?

A logical extension of the World Bank's argument has been to assert that the political as well as the economic problems of Africa can best be solved by greater reliance on market forces. Capitalism, it is argued, ruthlessly roots out the inefficient, a market economy is more likely to attract peasant participation, while capitalism alone can create a domestic social class powerful enough to compete with international capital.[59] Nkrumah's assertion – that socialism was necessary for Africa because capitalism was too complicated – is stood on its head. While intuitively plausible, this argument discounts too heavily two vital considerations: markets do not emerge nor do they exist in a political vacuum. As Polanyi reminded us, the Western system of laissez-faire did not arise automatically but came about only through sustained state intervention.[60] To advocate capitalism as a solution to Africa's problems is merely to move the argument one step backwards to the question of how political coalitions can be constructed that will favour giving a greater role to markets.

Polanyi also demonstrated that the pure market system, given its tremendous social costs, was short-lived even in Europe. Subsequently, all 'market' systems have operated within a framework of lesser or greater state intervention. The extensive role of the state in the contemporary newly-industrialising countries in defining the con-

straints under which markets operate has already been noted. Greater
reliance on market forces in Africa will not lead to a laissez-faire system.
There is simply no guarantee that an economic system based
predominantly on private enterprise in Africa will necessarily
correspond to the alleged rationality of the market. Instead, a system
may evolve akin to the parasitic capitalism which for so long held back
economic growth in Latin America. Schatz, for instance, has termed
similar tendencies in Nigeria 'pirate capitalism'.[61]

Again the issue here is one of the degree of insulation of the state from
social groups. Where there is often not merely a close relationship
between local capitalists and the political elite but an identity – they are
one and the same, as is true to a considerable extent throughout Africa[62]
– there is a probability that state power will be used not to promote
market efficiency but to sustain oligopolistic advantages and generate
economic rents. Faith in the 'market' solution makes the major and
questionable assumption that Africa's business elite will not choose the
easier path and become rentier capitalists. Beyond a handful of
countries like Kenya and Nigeria which have nascent capitalist classes,
the prospects for successful capitalist development in Africa are even
more remote. Callaghy, in Chapter 12, presents a sophisticated analysis
of the political malaise which afflicts many such countries. In Weber's
terminology, they are patrimonial states which lack the political and
procedural predictability necessary for capitalist development.

If commentators on the NICs are agreed that an insulated state has
been a major prerequisite for their economic success, there is little
explanation of how these states were able to achieve greater insulation at
a particular point in their historical development. Two groups are often
identified as playing important roles: technocrats and military officers.
For better or worse, Africa lacks a bureaucratic equivalent of the
'Chicago Boys'. And African militaries, despite the optimism expressed
in the 1960s regarding their 'modernising' potential, remain poorly
educated, technologically backward, lacking in discipline, and as
penetrated by societal forces as all other institutions in African states.

Krueger provides a succinct argument that if wealth generation is
perceived primarily as a lottery dependent on successful rent seeking,
the market mechanism 'is bound to be suspect'. Rather than favouring a
greater reliance on market forces, a popular consensus is likely to
emerge which advocates still further intervention in the market leading
to a spiral in which further rents are generated, people become more
disillusioned, more intervention occurs, etc.[63] In the short term,
therefore, in Africa's rent-seeking states, prospects for the emergence of

domestic political groups that will insulate the state from societal pressure, undermine, in Hyden's terminology, the 'economy of affection', and thereby provide the political basis for market rationality, appear bleak.

Can external agencies serve as functional equivalents in promoting economic change in Africa? Students of such international organisations as the International Monetary Fund (IMF) have frequently noted that they may partially insulate reform-minded politicians and bureaucrats from criticism since domestic decision-makers are able to 'externalise' at least part of the responsibility for the introduction of unpopular policies. Certainly, the intention of *Accelerated Development* was to establish the principle of greater conditionality for World Bank aid. The European Community similarly has attempted to impose 'policy dialogue' on the recipients of Lomé III aid. World Bank lending for 'structural adjustment' has brought it into an even closer working relationship with the IMF; meanwhile Africa's balance of payments problems have necessitated borrowing from the Fund on ever stricter terms of conditionality.[64] International agencies thus have signalled their intention to intervene on an unprecedented scale in African decision-making; the scale of Africa's economic crisis appears to offer them the opportunity to do so. Disregarding the question of whether such intervention is desirable, can international agencies force reform in the direction that they wish?

African states appear to have been more successful in asserting autonomy from international interventions than from domestic social forces. As Callaghy shows, this has certainly been the case in Zaire where Mobutu has engaged in a game of brinkmanship which has enabled him to effectively play off competing interests among Western creditors. Here the mixed motives of different agencies are clearly illustrated as is their complete inability to effectively monitor what was happening to their funds. Conditionality has little meaning without such monitoring: in the extreme, funding could be terminated entirely but this would conflict with the desire, in the absence in the eyes of Western security interests of a feasible or acceptable alternative, for Mobutu's survival in office. Zaire may, however, be an exception, not so much because of the nature of its malaise which probably differs from many other African countries only in quantitative rather than qualitative terms, but because of the unwillingness of the West to sacrifice the present regime in the name of economic rationality.

Other governments may not be so fortunate. From the government's perspective, it may come down to a choice between the (longer term?)

costs of being denied access to international finance, and the domestic repercussions of imposing unpopular reforms. The experience to date shows little willingness on the part of domestic constituencies to accept the projection of blame for unpopular policies on to external agencies: the IMF may indeed be seen as the ultimate source of food price rises or devaluations but domestic interests have frequently vented their wrath on the only available and vulnerable target – incumbent local regimes. Even if governments come to accept the long-term equation of political rationality with economic rationality and desire to modify, for example, the more extreme examples of anti-agricultural bias in their policies, their willingness to do so will depend on a calculation of expected costs and benefits in the short term. In a situation of extreme economic crisis the latitude for creative policy-making is extremely narrow.[65]

Rothchild and Gyimah-Boadi's chapter in this volume presents an innovative analysis of the domestic political impact of economic crisis in Ghana. There has in fact been little exploration to date of the various dimensions of the political consequences of Africa's economic crisis. Famine, for instance, has led to massive numbers of refugees crossing into neighbouring territories not only placing further demands on already strained resources but also often exacerbating ethnic and regional tensions; disillusionment with central governments has led to a strengthening of the influence of traditional leaders and of syncretist religions; elsewhere, the economic crisis contributed to the decision of Mozambique to seek rapprochement with South Africa in a historical reversal of policy. The Ghanaian experience shows the tendency for a cycle to emerge in which attempts at economic rationality alternate with populism – and the vulnerability of regimes which pursue a more 'rational' approach approved by the principal international agencies.

The Busia regime was one of Africa's first political victims of IMF-inspired deflationary policies.[66] Following its overthrow the Acheampong junta's attempts to purchase approval through such populist policies as low food prices and expansion of the money supply severely exacerbated Ghana's economic problems. A period of IMF-approved stabilisation under Akuffo was brief as popular unrest inspired the first of the Rawlings interventions, a reversion to what Rothchild and Gyimah-Boadi term an 'economic populism which displayed elements of idealism and some disdain for long-term consequences'. The return to relative economic rationality under the Limann government again proved short-lived as popular discontent with the lack of tangible, short-term benefits from the austerity policies once more tempted Rawlings to intervene. In his second coming,

Rawlings has faced the problem of high expectations generated by his earlier populist intervention, policies which cannot be sustained on a longer-term basis. Inevitably his second regime has not retained the popularity enjoyed at the time of the coup. The Ghanaian experience is a perfect illustration of the difficulties of implementing reformist, economically-rational policies in contemporary Africa. While in the long-term such moves may generate political as well as economic benefits, few African governments, given their lack of autonomy from societal forces and their lack of coercive capacity, can afford to adopt this time horizon. Short-term payoffs from higher food prices, devaluation, a reduced money supply, etc., are likely merely to be popular unrest and an invitation to others to topple incumbent regimes.

Clearly, international agencies can assist reform-minded regimes by providing carrots as well as the stick. As noted in the introductory section of this chapter, a major weakness of *AD* was its relative lack of attention to the means through which African governments could be assisted in their efforts to introduce policy reforms. Although an increase in external assistance was advocated, little consideration was given to how it might best be employed. Some critics, for example Eicher in Chapter 7 of this volume, have responded by suggesting that Africa is already awash on a sea of aid which in many countries 'cannot be absorbed with integrity'. Here there is a danger of treating aid in an undifferentiated manner: when the appropriateness of different types of aid is distinguished there is a much greater consensus among commentators. Most are agreed that there has been far too great an emphasis on project aid in recent years. Proliferation of projects and donors has placed a tremendous administrative burden on overextended bureaucracies,[67] the desire of donors to have identifiable monuments to their beneficence has led to the erection of numerous 'cathedrals in the sand' (the terminology of former EEC Commissioner for Development, Edgard Pisani). In *Toward Sustained Development*, the World Bank noted (p. 38) that, 'Almost without exception, the Bank's reviews have revealed that a good deal of the pressure to undertake new investment or continue with low-priority projects derives from the inflexibility of foreign donors.' Little attention meanwhile was given to the recurrent and maintenance costs with the result that many projects rapidly fell into disuse.

Some African countries may have reached their absorptive capacities for project aid, but this is far from true as regards foreign exchange. Declining export revenue has reduced import capacity, has exacerbated budgetary deficits and inflation, and given rise to greater external indebtedness. Shortage of foreign exchange, in fact, is one of the most serious dimensions of the current economic crisis: exports from many African states currently cover less than half the value of their (severely curtailed) imports; most have foreign exchange reserves insufficient to cover even one month's imports. In the years from 1979 onwards, when Africa's crisis has been most severe, the IMF has made few low-conditionality resources available. As Helleiner points out, African countries have not received a fraction of the low-conditionality transfers to which they should have been entitled, given the declining terms of trade experienced. The IMF's Compensatory Financing Facility supplied only 4 per cent of the finance necessary to offset the impact of deteriorating terms of trade in 1980–81.[68] Transfers under the Lomé Convention's STABEX scheme have also fallen far short of recorded falls in export earnings. Besides borrowing on stricter conditions, African countries have faced more severe terms: higher interest rates, shorter loan periods, lower grant elements, etc.

Although Africa's debt problem is small in total in relation to that of Latin America (which, of course, provides African countries with less leverage against private and official creditors), it has rapidly become a major component of the current crisis. As Callaghy notes, African countries have been responsible for the majority of debt reschedulings under the Paris Club in recent years. Many of these were at best short-term 'fixes', however, with loans rolled over for a few more years but at higher interest. As a result, many African countries face severe debt-servicing requirements. According to data in *Toward Sustained Development*, debt service as a percentage of exports of goods and services for SSA as a whole amounted to a weighted mean of 12.6 per cent in 1982. For some countries, the situation was far more severe: oil-importing middle-income countries had a weighted mean debt-service ratio of 16.9 per cent; for the Ivory Coast the figure was 36.9 per cent. Since many loans, including currency purchases from the IMF, become due in the 1985–87 period, many African countries face a difficult future: 'Unless corrective measures are taken, the external resource position of sub-Saharan Africa is likely to become disastrous in the next few years' (*Toward Sustained Development*, p. 13).

To repay the debts incurred as a result of policy mistakes (often by previous regimes) or which were primarily the result of factors beyond the control of African governments, severely strains the few economic and political resources available to incumbent regimes. The World Bank has emphasised that unless sufficient external financial support is forthcoming countries which have initiated policy reform may go no further.

The priority must be to increase import capacity so that rehabilitation of manufacturing and infrastructure can begin; at the same time, imports are needed to provide the incentives for increased agricultural production. There is a demonstrable case for debt relief, at the minimum, debt rescheduling over longer periods; more effectively, debts such as some suppliers' credits might be written off. Greater compensation for fluctuating terms of trade could be made available through increasing the size of African countries' IMF quotas and further liberalising the terms of the Compensatory Financing Facility.[69]

Most donors now accept that greater priority needs to be given to programme rather than project aid. Rather than undertaking new projects, emphasis on rehabilitation of existing infrastructure is called for and the continued provision of funding for local operating costs once rehabilitation has been successfully completed. There is also a case for continued food aid. Certainly, food aid played a major role in India in the 1950s and 1960s in buying time while domestic agriculture was made more productive. In Africa, at least two major qualifications need to be made to the case for food aid: firstly, it will continue to encourage a switch from local staples to rice and wheat with the danger of a long-term dependence on crops which cannot be produced locally (to some extent probably an inevitable trend given the convenience of these foods for urban dwellers); secondly, the natural tendency, as noted above, has been for African governments to use food aid as a means of avoiding the difficult policy decision of increasing producer prices and domestic food costs. Food aid may thus be most effective when it is conditional upon domestic policy reform and is linked with other financing which enables governments to gradually phase in higher domestic food prices.

A compelling case can thus be made for the need for increased aid to assist reform-minded African governments. Increased aid may not necessarily convince governments that the short-term costs of domestic policy reform are outweighed by the possibility of long-term gains but it can, at least, help reduce these costs. Whether such aid will be forthcoming is an entirely different matter. As the World Bank itself admitted, the projections of overseas development assistance in *AD* were 'extremely unrealistic' (*Progress Report*, p. 6). The Bank has found itself unable to deliver its own commitment to increase lending to Africa by 5 per cent per annum in real terms over the 1983–87 period. As a result of deepening crisis, few African countries can now qualify for regular International Bank for Reconstruction and Development (IBRD) resources; meanwhile, the budget of its soft-loan affiliate, the International Development Association (IDA), the largest single source of development assistance for Africa, has been severely curtailed as a result of the refusal of the Reagan administration to meet its contribution. As the Bank notes in *World Development Report 1984*, the level of funding for IDA 7 represents a 25 per cent reduction in nominal terms, and 40 per cent in real terms from its predecessor; if the accesssion of China is taken into account, the reduction is 70 per cent in real per capita terms. Under IDA 7, funding for Africa will be cut by 21 per cent in real terms. The Bank's proposed new $6 billion emergency aid fund for Africa was cut back to $1.1 billion at a donor's conference in January 1985 (and some of that sum represented aid previously pledged); the United States again refused to contribute.


CONCLUSION

There is little in this chapter, or indeed this book, to give rise to optimism regarding Africa's prospects in either the short or medium term. A partial exception is the finding of Rothchild and Gyimah-Boadi that there have developed in Ghana, albeit in a climate of extreme economic hardship, an encouraging new realism among the populace, a willingness on the part of government to face the problems and take difficult decisions, a desire for decentralisation, and increasing investment in agriculture. Other authors are extremely pessimistic regarding the options available, however, on the basis of past experience: export-led manufacturing has failed for the Kenyan textile industry and appears to offer little potential elsewhere; a strategy of self-reliance has had few payoffs for Tanzania; regional cooperation, particularly in the form of common markets as advocated by the Lagos Plan, has produced a record of two decades of failed integration schemes; and the World Bank's strategy of promoting export agriculture at best will see African countries running rapidly on a treadmill in order merely to stay in place. An agriculture-led strategy may well offer the greatest potential for growth in the future but it will be one directed primarily towards the domestic market and the generation of linkages with the nascent domestic manufacturing sector.

Rather than moving forward, Africa faces the real danger of sustained regression; the World Bank continues to revise downwards its projections for Africa's future economic growth. Even under the most optimistic scenario presented in the 1984 *World Development Report* (high rates of growth in industrialised countries, lower interest rates, no resort to increased protectionism, effective policy reform in Africa), low-income Africa will experience an annual *decline* in per capita income of 0.1 per cent in the 1985–95 period. Under the most pessimistic scenario the projection is for an annual decline of 0.7 per cent – on top of annual declines of 1.0 per cent in the 1973–79 period, and 1.6 per cent in the years 1980–85.

Without policy reform in the near future, which must necessarily be accompanied by substantial external assistance if it is to be sustained, Africa will be caught in a vicious downward spiral of disintegration. The crisis has already exacerbated political instability which further undermines the prospects for rational policy-making. Current populist regimes may well be the first in a succession of governments capable of dramatic gestures but lacking either the legitimacy or coercion necessary to sustain constructive policies. Food riots, jacqueries and expulsions of minorities may become the norm – or alternate with political apathy and withdrawal from national economy and polity. For some, such tendencies may herald the revolutionary potential of the crisis. In reality, however, anomie and withdrawal rather than revolution are the more likely outcomes: revolution requires cohesive organisation, an attribute conspicuously lacking in contemporary Africa.

Response to Africa's difficulties over the last decade has been a clear signal that the world does not believe that it owes Africa anything. There is little sympathy with the demands in the Lagos Plan, which appears to be stuck in the groove of NIEO (New International Economic Order) rhetoric, for massive transfers of resources, technology, etc. In the current economic and political climate in the West, external assistance will be marginal at best. Africa faces involuntary delinking as private investors choose, as Rothchild and Gyimah-Boadi describe for Ghana, to departicipate. There is a real danger that Western governments, despairing of Africa's plight, will conclude that their few vital interests on the continent can best be secured by periodic interventions on the Shaba model.

At the present time, the most positive aspect is a new willingness on the part of key decision-makers to engage in dialogue and realistically assess the prospects for various strategies. From their initial position of antagonism resulting from the often crude juxtaposition of *Accelerated Development* and the Lagos Plan, the Bank and African governments have moved much closer together in their analysis of the nature of the contemporary crisis and potential solutions.[70] The aim of this book is to contribute to this new dialogue. If we err on the side of pessimism, this is excusable given the dimensions of Africa's difficulties. All share the hope, however, that the World Bank is correct in its assessment that the history of economic development is full of surprises and that Africa will indeed surprise the pessimists.


NOTES

1. United Nations Economic Commission for Africa, *ECA and Africa's Development, 1983–2008* (Addis Ababa: ECA, 1983) pp. 93–4.
2. World Bank, *Toward Sustained Development in Sub-Saharan Africa: A Joint Program of Action* (Washington, DC: World Bank, 1984) p. 15.
3. Reginald Herbold Green and Hans Singer, 'Sub-Saharan Africa in Depression: The Impact on the Welfare of Children', *World Development*, vol. 12 (March 1984) no. 3, p. 284.
4. It is no coincidence that one of the earliest exceptions to this focused on agricultural policies: Michael F. Lofchie, 'Political and Economic Origins of African Hunger', *Journal of Modern African Studies*, vol. 13 (December 1975) no. 4, pp. 551–67.
5. This point is developed further by Callaghy in Chapter 12 of this volume.
6. Cf. the statement by the Bank's President, A. W. Clausen: 'We have had more project failures in agriculture than in any other sector, and the failures have been concentrated in Africa'. *Poverty in the Developing Countries 1985*, Address given at the Martin Luther King, Jr, Center, Atlanta, Georgia, 11 January 1985 (Washington, DC: World Bank, 1985) p. 9.
7. For the former position see, e.g., Cheryl Payer, 'Tanzania and the World Bank', *Third World Quarterly*, vol. 5 (October 1983) no. 4, pp. 791–813; for the latter, Samir Amin, 'A Critique of the World Bank Report Entitled "Accelerated Development in Sub-Saharan Africa"', *Africa Development*, vol. 7 (1982) no. 1/2, pp. 23–9.
8. Such critics probably overestimate the extent to which the Bank became fully converted to the Basic Needs philosophy: 'The concern that the Bank might desert the poor must depart from a realization that under McNamara it never totally embraced them'. Robert L. Ayres, *Banking on the Poor* (Cambridge, Mass.: MIT Press, 1983) p. 33. See also William Ascher, 'New development approaches and the adaptability of international agencies: the case of the World Bank', *International Organizaton*, vol. 37 (Summer 1983) no. 3, pp. 415–39.
9. See, for example, Irma Adelman, 'Beyond Export-Led Growth', *World Development*, vol. 12 (September 1984) no. 9, pp. 937–49. Concise statements on the role of agriculture in economic growth are found in W. Arthur Lewis, *The Evolution of the International Economic Order* (Princeton University Press, 1978); and World Bank, *World Development Report 1982* (New York: Oxford University Press, 1982).
10. Half of this number are projected to remain underemployed, however. *ECA and Africa's Development 1983–2008* p. 59; other data are from World Bank, *Accelerated Development in Sub-Saharan Africa: An Agenda for Action* (Washington, DC: World Bank, 1981). At current rates of population growth, the absolute size of Africa's agricultural labour force is projected to increase throughout the next century. World Bank, *World Development Report 1984* (New York: Oxford University Press, 1984) p. 89.

11. World Bank, *Toward Sustained Development* p. 4.
12. See also Kenneth Shapiro, 'The Limits of Policy Reform in African Agricultural Development: A Comment on the World Bank's "Accelerated Development in Sub-Saharan Africa"' (mimeo).
13. Here again, *Toward Sustained Development* illustrates the need for extreme caution in interpreting aggregate figures. In a different table it cites an annual growth rate of –0.6 per cent for Nigerian agricultural production in the years 1970–82, and a similar negative rate of –0.4 per cent for the 1960–70 period.
14. Carl K. Eicher, 'West Africa's Agrarian Crisis', (West African Association of Agricultural Economists, 1984). Data in this section, unless otherwise noted, are from World Bank, *Toward Sustained Development*, Statistical Annex.
15. Charles Elliott, 'Equity and Growth: An Unresolved Conflict in Zambian Rural Development Policy', in Dharam Ghai and Samir Radwan (eds), *Agrarian Policies and Rural Poverty in Africa* (Geneva: International Labour Organisation, 1983) p. 161.
16. For an excellent analysis of this issue in historical perspective see John Tosh, 'The Cash-Crop Revolution in Tropical Africa: An Agricultural Reappraisal', *African Affairs*, vol. 79 (January 1980) no. 314, pp. 79–94.
17. *Accelerated Development* p. 6. See also p. 95: 'An agriculture-oriented development strategy with industry in a supporting role does not mean that Africa would forego industrial development. Long-term industrial growth might, in fact, be higher with this approach. Although agriculture would be the driving force, industry would still grow faster than agriculture.'
18. The stridency of tone in *AD* probably again contributed to this over-reaction. Realising this, *Toward Sustained Development* records in a more conciliatory tone: 'There are no panaceas. Policy reform does not, in particular, simply mean "getting prices right"' (p. 5). Elliot Berg, in Chapter 2 acknowledges that there was probably too much emphasis in *AD* on changing agricultural pricing.
19. Robert H. Bates, *Markets and States in Tropical Africa* (Berkeley: University of California Press, 1981); and *Essays on the Political Economy of Africa* (Cambridge University Press, 1983).
20. In the Ivory Coast, for instance, bananas and pineapples, whose production is so capital-intensive that smallholder production is not viable, are not subject to marketing boards and consequent 'taxation'. Robert E. Hecht, 'The Ivory Coast Economic "Miracle": What Benefits for Peasant Farmers?', *Journal of Modern African Studies*, vol. 21 (March 1983) no. 1, p. 50.
21. Bates, *Markets and States in Tropical Africa* p. 40.
22. David K. Leonard, 'What is Rational when Rationality Isn't?: Comments on the Administrative Proposals of the Berg Report' (mimeo). Even in market-oriented Kenya, the share of public employment in total 'formal' employment rose from 29.6 per cent in 1963 to 41.7 per cent in 1977 (*Accelerated Development*, p. 41).
23. See, for instance, Frank Ellis, 'Agricultural Price Policy in Tanzania', *World Development*, vol. 10 (April 1982) no. 4, p. 266.
24. Tanzania provides an excellent example. Ellis notes that the National Milling Corporation, the parastatal responsible for marketing most

domestic food crops, had accumulated an overdraft with the domestic banking system by December 1980 of T.Shs 2.8 billion. At that date the accumulated indebtedness of all crop authorities was T.Shs 5 billion, nearly three times the total producer value of all official crop purchases in 1979/80, and equivalent to 15 per cent of Tanzania's GDP in 1979 (ibid. p. 277). See also Eicher, Chapter 7 of this volume. According to the World Bank (*Accelerated Development*, p. 59, *n.* 17), charges by marketing authorities in Kenya for storage, marketing, transport and administrative overheads amounted to 34 per cent of the f.o.b. price received for maize exports, 23 per cent for wheat, and 49 per cent for rice.

25. For instance, the marketing parastatal in Benin handled a significant percentage of the Nigerian cocoa crop. See Daniel C. Bach, 'The Politics of West African Economic Co-operation: C.E.A.O. and E.C.O.W.A.S.', *Journal of Modern African Studies*, vol. 21 (December 1983) no. 4, p. 615.

26. Marian E. Bond, 'Agricultural Responses to Prices in Sub-Saharan African Countries', *IMF Staff Papers*, vol. 30 (December 1983) no. 4, pp. 710–11.

27. Ibid. p. 724.

28. Shapiro, 'The Limits of Policy Reform'. In this example, if production was initially 100, a 25 per cent increase in producer prices would induce output to rise to 107.5. Government revenue would decline, however, from 34 (100 × 0.34) to 18.3 (107.5 × 0.17). Even these figures are somewhat optimistic in that they assume a perfect market in crop purchasing in order that the full amount of the price increase will actually be passed on to producers. In the Ivory Coast it is estimated that up to 50 per cent of the official price offered by marketing boards is absorbed by middlemen.

29. World Bank, *Sub-Saharan Africa: Progress Report on Development Prospects and Programs* (Washington DC: World Bank, 1983) p. 4.

30. As Green and Allison argue in Chapter 3, there are alternative incentives to rural producers, e.g. improved availability of inputs and consumer goods, which are less costly for governments – both in economic and political terms – than price increases. Leonard similarly notes that basic needs programmes, criticised by Eicher in his contribution to this volume and apparently largely removed from the Bank's new agenda for Africa, provide incentives to rural producers while also increasing the discretionary political resources available to governments. The abolition of pan-territorial pricing, as advocated by Eicher and *Accelerated Development* similarly involves a trade-off between economic efficiency and political rationality (the satisfaction of regional constituencies) which neither discuss.

31. Raj Krishna, 'Some Aspects of Agricultural Growth, Price Policy and Equity in Developing Countries', *Food Research Institute Studies*, vol. XVIII (1982) no. 3, pp. 219–60. Improved prices will of course encourage farmers to invest in technology. But a substantial increase in government investment in the agricultural sector, e.g. on irrigation, Krishna argues, is more likely to lead to a rapid and sustained increase in output.

32. Eicher, 'West Africa's Agrarian Crisis'. For the case of the Ivory Coast see Eddy Lee, 'Export-Led Rural Development, The Ivory Coast', in Ghai and Radwan (eds) *Agrarian Politics and Rural Poverty in Africa*, p. 104. In

Malawi, increases in agricultural output have come solely from the estate sector.

33. *Accelerated Development* p. 69. Data for the Ivory Coast are presented in Lee, 'Export-Led Rural Development'.
34. Quoted in United States Department of Agriculture (USDA), *Food Problems and Prospects in Sub-Saharan Africa*, Foreign Agricultural Research Report No. 166, August 1981 (Washington DC: US Department of Agriculture) p. 13.
35. Goran Hyden, *No Shortcuts to Progress*, (Berkeley: University of California Press, 1983) p. 5.
36. Eicher, 'West Africa's Agrarian Crisis'.
37. Quoted in USDA, *Food Problems and Prospects*, p. 103. See also *World Development Report 1984*, p. 94. Application of fertilisers will be particularly important if Africa is to move from extensive to more intensive agriculture.
38. USDA, *Food Problems and Prospects*, p. 104. Green records that grain storage losses in Tanzania in the 1976–79 period were equivalent to the total volume of maize imported in the years 1979–81, Reginald Green, 'Incentives, Policies, Participation and Response: Reflections on World Bank "Policies and Priorities in Agriculture"', IDS *Bulletin*, vol. 14 (January 1983) no. 1, p. 35. As Green and Allison note, *AD* had very little to say regarding viable rural technological improvements appropriate for peasant producers.
39. Richard E. Stryker, 'The World Bank and Agricultural Development: Food Production and Rural Poverty', *World Development*, vol. 7 (March 1979) no 3, pp. 331–2. The case against smallholder production is argued cogently by Keith Hart, *The Political Economy of West African Agriculture* (Cambridge University Press, 1982).
40. I.M.D. Little, Tibor Scitovsky and M.F.G. Scott, *Industry and Trade in Some Developing Countries* (Oxford University Press, 1971) p. 237. Elsewhere these authors caution explicitly: 'But what if a large number of developing countries were to follow the example of the leading exporters? Is there not a danger, in that case, that they would cut each others' throats? For some important commodities this clearly is a danger. The most obvious examples are coffee, tea, and cocoa' (ibid. p. 270). These three are respectively ranked numbers one, five and two in Africa's agricultural exports.

    Prices of all of Africa's principal food and beverage exports except coffee and cocoa declined in real terms in the period 1970–82. For the period 1980–90, the World Bank projected an annual increase in the value of world trade in food and beverages of only 1.7 per cent. In 1990, the real price of cocoa is projected to be only 75 per cent of the average in the years 1960–70; for tea the figure is only 44 per cent (*AD* p. 23; *Toward Sustained Development* Statistical Annex; *Progress Report* p. 4).

    While *Accelerated Development* asserts the need for Africa to recover its share of its traditional export markets as a short-term measure for improving export earnings, *Toward Sustained Development* notes that 'an increase in imports is unlikely to be possible from improved exports earnings from these commodities in the short run' but adds, curiously, 'although in the medium to longer run that has to be the objective' (p. 7). By focusing on producer incentives and exchange rate policy the Bank implies that the principal problem facing African agricultural exports is one of supply rather than inelastic world demand.

41. OAU, *Lagos Plan of Action for the Economic Development of Africa, 1980-2000* (Geneva: International Institute for Labour Studies, 1981) p. 7.

42. Especially the series of works summarised in Krueger's *Liberalization Attempts and Consequences* (Cambridge, Mass.: Ballinger, for the National Institute of Economic Research, 1978); see also, for example Balassa, 'Structural Adjustment Policies in Developing Economies', *World Development*, vol. 10 (January 1982) no. 1, pp. 23–38.

43. Manfred Bienefeld comments, for instance, on 'the Report's [*AD*] heavy reliance on, and frequent reference to, the N.I.C. experience – to back up the central assertion that African governments should reduce the extent and change (in a specific manner) the nature of their economic involvement.' 'Efficiency, Expertise, NICs and the Accelerated Development Report', IDS *Bulletin*, vol. 14 (January 1983) no. 1, p. 20. There are only about four references to the NICs in *AD*, however, and only one of those (a reference to supply responsiveness to devaluation on p. 30), bears out his argument. The other references are: (a) an explicit denial that African countries are in a position to follow Korea or Taiwan in export-led manufacturing growth (p. 95); (b) a reference (p. 97) to local value-added requirements in Mexico to illustrate the need for African *governments* to bargain more effectively with transnational corporations (TNCs); (c) a reference to an effective *government* programme of family planning in Indonesia (p. 113) – and some would question whether Indonesia can correctly be termed a NIC.

44. See, for example, John Gerard Ruggie, 'Introduction: International Interdependence and National Welfare', in Ruggie (ed.), *The Antinomies of Interdependence* (New York: Columbia University Press, 1983) especially p. 19.

45. For example, in various periods in Brazil and India. *Industry and Trade in Some Developing Countries* p. 180: 'for some products, India lost foreign exchange by exporting (just as foreign exchange may be lost by inappropriate import substitution)'. See also Paul Streeten, 'A Cool Look at "Outward-Looking Strategies for Development" ', *The World Economy*, vol. 5 (September 1982) no. 2, pp. 159–69. The X-efficiency and other arguments are presented in Anne O. Krueger, 'Export-Led Industrial Growth Reconsidered' in Wontack Hong and Lawrence B. Krause (eds), *Trade and Growth of the Advanced Developing Countries in the Pacific Basin* (Seoul: Korea Development Institute, 1981) pp. 3–27.

46. This point is discussed in detail in John Ravenhill, *Collective Clientelism: The Lomé Conventions and North–South Relations* (New York: Columbia Univerity Press, 1985) Chapter 4. It is questionable whether textiles industries in Europe, with the partial exception of France, were in fact pursuing a strategy of looking to Africa as a location for some labour-intensive processes, as Langdon suggests in Chapter 8 of this volume. Few European industries, given the high cost and low productivity of African labour, have seriously considered SSA as a location in their strategy of worldwide sourcing. Langdon's evidence may suggest, rather, that they

perceived Africa primarily as a convenient dumping ground for obsolete machinery.

47. On the overall inelasticity of industrialised countries' demand for LDCs' exports see William R. Cline, 'Can the East Asian Model of Development Be Generalized', *World Development*, vol. 10 (February 1982) no. 2, pp. 81–90.
48. Christopher Stevens and Ann Weston, 'Trade Diversification: Has Lomé Helped?' in Christopher Stevens (ed.), *The EEC and the Third World: A Survey 4. Renegotiating Lomé* (London: Hodder & Stoughton, 1984) Chapter 2.
49. Patrick Low, 'Export Subsidies and Trade Policy: The Case of Kenya', *World Development*, vol. 10 (April 1982) no. 4, p. 301.
50. Albert O. Hirschman, 'The Political Economy of Import-Substituting Industrialization in Latin America' in Hirschman, *A Bias for Hope* (New Haven: Yale University Press, 1971) pp. 117–19.
51. Reginald H. Green, 'African Economies in the Mid-1980's – "Naught for Your Comfort but that the Waves Grow Higher and the Storms Grow Wilder"' in J. Carlsson (ed.), *Recession in Africa* (Uppsala: Scandinavian Institute of African Studies, 1983) pp. 177–9.
52. Carlos F. Diaz-Alejandro, 'On the Import Intensity of Import Substitution', *Kyklos*, vol. 18 (1965) no. 3, pp. 495–509; on the experience of the People's Democratic Republic of Korea see Green, 'African Economies in the Mid-1980's'. Green's comments (pp. 195–6) are particularly relevant to the Lagos Plan: 'to restructure for economic self reliance requires additional imports, these must be paid for, the most self reliant way of paying is from exports, if exports are allowed to stagnate the nation – and its self reliant strategy – will be delivered bound hand and foot into the hands of its creditors'. For data on the early years of import substitution in Tanzania see Ravi Gulhati and Uday Sekhar, 'Industrial Strategy for Late Starters: The Experience of Kenya, Tanzania and Zambia', *World Development*, vol. 10 (November 1982) no. 11, pp. 949–72.
53. 'International Interdependence and National Welfare' p. 18.
54. For instance, Christopher Colclough, 'Are African Governments as Unproductive as the Accelerated Development Report Implies?', IDS *Bulletin*, vol. 14 (January 1983) no. 1, pp. 24–9.
55. Langdon's excellent empirical study of the Kenyan textile industry, besides questioning the feasibilty of export-led growth, also raises the issue of the relative efficiency of domestic and transnational private firms. He finds that local firms have created more employment, have been more profitable, were less capital-intensive, and generated more linkages with the local economy and contributed more towards the development of local technological capacity.

Whether these findings are generalisable to other parts of Africa warrants further investigation. The unique characteristic of these 'local' companies was that they were owned by Kenyan Asians. To the extent that these companies or their management enjoyed close relations with counterparts in India or Pakistan, as is often the case, the companies might almost be conceived of as Third World transnationals – which, the literature indicates, do tend to employ less capital-intensive techniques, generate more backward linkages, etc. Another factor, as Langdon points out, is the general exclusion of Asian capitalists from Kenya's state elite. Unable to depend on a symbiotic relationship with the state, unlike TNCs, and thus more vulnerable to market forces, Asian firms of necessity were forced to be efficient. A different coalition of indigenous capitalists and politicians may prevail elsewhere with significant negative consequences for the efficiency of local enterprise.

56. Green, 'African Economies in the Mid-1980's' p. 183. Cf. *World Development Report 1983*, p. 46, on the 'need to reassess priorities, prune what has become unmanageable, and strengthen the effectiveness of the state's core responsibilities'.

57. Langdon is probably overly charitable towards the Kenyan state in largely absolving it from responsibility for the failure of the export strategy for the textiles industry. Many of the problems that he discusses point to an ineffective bargaining strategy on the part of the state vis-à-vis TNCs. TNCs were allowed to engage in transfer pricing, were granted protection which effectively removed the possibility of domestic competition, and were bailed out when their inefficiencies caused them to suffer sustained losses. There was, to be sure, a symbiotic relationship between some TNCs and some members of the Kenyan political elite; the fact that some were 'bought off' surely does not absolve the state of responsibility. For an examination of the inability of African governments to bargain effectively with TNCs see Donald Rothchild and Robert L. Curry, Jr, *Scarcity, Choice and Public Policy in Middle Africa* (Berkeley: University of California Press, 1978) Chapter 4.

58. Hyden, *No Shortcuts to Progress*, pp. 19, 195.

59. See ibid., especially Chapters 1 and 8, for example. See also Hart, *The Political Economy of West African Agriculture*.

60. Karl Polanyi, *The Great Transformation* (Boston: Beacon, 1944).

61. Sayre P. Schatz, 'Pirate Capitalism and the Inert Economy of Nigeria', *Journal of Modern African Studies*, vol. 22 (March 1984) no. 1, pp. 45–57.

62. In Kenya, for instance, Nicola Swainson noted that 'the use of official positions within the State to advance business interests . . . is indeed the hallmark of the present stage of indigenous capitalism.' (*The Development of Corporate Capitalism in Kenya 1918–1977* (Berkeley: University of California Press, 1980) p. 191).

63. Anne O. Krueger, 'The Political Economy of the Rent-Seeking Society', *American Economic Review*, vol. LXIV (June 1974) no. 3, p. 302.

64. G. K. Helleiner, *The IMF and Africa in the 1980s* Essays in International Finance No. 152, July 1983 (International Finance Section, Department of Economics, Princeton University).

65. Ayres records that the World Bank, in internal assessment papers, notes that while its advice had helped to strengthen the position of reform-minded technocrats, it was unsuccessful in convincing governments to change policy when its recommendations ran counter to 'political realities'. (*Banking on the Poor*, pp. 33–7).

66. Ronald T. Libby, 'External Co-optation of a Less Developed Country's Policy Making: The Case of Ghana, 1969–72', *World Politics*, vol. 29 (1976) no 1, pp. 67–89.

67. See, for instance, Elliott R. Morss, 'Institutional Destruction Resulting from Donor and Project Proliferation in Sub-Saharan African Countries', *World Development*, vol. 12 (April 1984) no. 4, pp. 465–70.
68. Helleiner, *The IMF and Africa in the 1980s*, p. 12.
69. Compensatory financing is particularly important in helping to reduce the negative effects of fluctuating export earnings to which countries like those of Africa, heavily dependent on a limited number of export products, are particularly vulnerable. When linked to the earnings of individual export crops, as is the case with the Lomé Conventions' STABEX scheme, compensatory financing may assist governments to maintain producer prices at a time of (presumably) temporarily declining world prices. This assumes, however, that the compensatory financing will be utilised in the sector suffering export loss. In the experience of STABEX this has not been the case. For compensatory financing to work in this manner, greater conditionality on use of funds would have to be imposed. Despite a decade of attempting this, the EEC has not been successful. See John Ravenhill, 'What is to be Done for Third World Commodity Producers? An Evaluation of the STABEX Scheme', *International Organization*, vol. 38 (Summer 1984) no. 3, pp. 537–74.
70. While the Bank has become more sensitive to African aspirations, African governments, at least to the extent that the ECA is representative of their views, have increasingly recognised the need for domestic reforms. According to *ECA and Africa's Development*, p. 16, 'Africa's domestic order involving unfavourable development perceptions and patterns, static taboos and traditions, political and economic mismanagement, etc., is one of the major contributory factors to the socio-economic malaise in the region.'

# 2 The World Bank's Strategy

## ELLIOT BERG

This chapter sets out, very briefly, the main lines of argument in the report, *Accelerated Development in Sub-Saharan Africa: An Agenda for Action*, treating diagnosis and prescription separately. Consideration is given to the extent to which events have changed the relevance of the arguments, especially the diagnostic part. Some of the main criticisms of the report's prescriptions are then discussed, but no attempt is made to be comprehensive.

## THE DIAGNOSIS

Africa's economic crisis is severe, general and worsening. It has many dimensions. It is, first of all, a crisis of stagnant or declining production. National output – Gross Domestic Product – has been stagnant or in decline in much of the continent since the late 1960s. The African region grew more slowly in the 1970s than any other developing region – half as much as South Asia, for example. And growth in the 1970s was slower than in the 1960s. Some 15 countries (out of 39 for which usable data are at hand) had negative growth during the 1970s. And since 1979 the crisis has worsened.

It is also a crisis in internal and external economic balance. Budgets are tightly squeezed everywhere, with non-salary expenditures cut to the bone. The performance of routine government functions has been severely impaired because of more and more intense scarcities of funds for operation and maintenance of public facilities and services. In the external accounts, growing current account deficits, higher debt-service obligations and shrinking reserves are the rule.

It is also, and above all, an agricultural crisis:

44

(a) Per capita production is falling. In the 1960s, farm output in the continent (39 countries) rose by 2.3 per cent a year, at about the same rate as population. In the 1970s, total output in the farm sector grew only by 1.3 per cent a year, about half as fast as population. The numbers are unreliable, especially for food production, but price rises and the pattern of food-grain imports are indicative of declining local output. Also, the export crop figures, which are more reliable, show a 2 per cent per annum fall in output in the 1970s, compared to a 2 per cent per annum rise in the 1960s.

(b) The African share in world trade of most of the continent's commodities has declined. For African-produced commodities, world trade grew in volume by 1.8 per cent a year between 1960 and 1980, and by 3.3 per cent a year in value. The comparable rates of growth for African exports were zero and 1.8 per cent per annum.

(c) African food dependency has been deepening at an alarming rate. Commercial food-grain imports have grown by about 9 per cent a year for two decades, and on top of this food aid flows have also increased. A sharp rise of food imports need not by itself disturb economists; but what *is* unsettling is the rapid growth of wheat and rice consumption in countries where these crops cannot be economically produced with existing technologies.

(d) Poor agricultural performance is very general in the region. From the late 1960s to the late 1970s, only six countries had agricultural production increases of more than 3 per cent p.a. - Kenya, Malawi, Swaziland, Cameroon, Ivory Coast and Rwanda. And in the early 1980s a number of these high-fliers have fallen.

Finally, it is an institutional crisis. One aspect of this is the fact that government decision-making capacities remained weak or grew weaker over the decade. Investment decisions in the public sector, or private investment decisions requiring government authorisation, were commonly made without proper analysis and careful evaluation. For many reasons, decisions allocating government expenditure – for development projects or other purposes – have been frequently out of line with expressed national priorities. Financial and administrative controls are weak. Knowledge of investment commitments and especially of external debt obligations, is often highly imperfect.

Another element in the institutional crisis is the failure of the industrial sector in most countries to live up to its expectations. Industry is or should be the leading edge in the development process. Its growth should create jobs, provide markets for agriculture and generate surpluses for new investment and future growth. But in much of Africa the industrial sector has delivered on few of these promises. More often than not it is inefficient, high-cost, oversized, and excessively dependent on imported inputs. In many cases it is a net user of national resources rather than a generator of surpluses. This seems to be true especially of those industrial enterprises that are state-owned, but it is true also of numerous privately-owned industries. Both groups suffer some of the same ills: faulty initial planning in many cases, and lacklustre productivity and managerial performance related to the protection from competition these enterprises enjoy. The public sector enterprises suffer additional problems: conflicting objectives, over-manning, inability to recruit enough good managers and skilled people, exposure to too much or too little control; working capital constraints; and others.

Even more far-reaching were institutional failures in agriculture. Throughout the continent, state organisations ('parastatals') were, and largely remain, responsible for much of the marketing of farm crops and the provision of farm inputs. With only a few exceptions these organisations have proved to be costly and inefficient providers of services to small farmers. Like other parastatals they had too often become sources of jobs for political purposes. They lack assured and adequate budgets for operating and maintenance expenses, and they often have a dubious mandate anyway – such as engaging in agricultural extension activities when there are few tested, viable technical packages to extend, and the price/marketing environment is uncongenial.

THE SOURCES OF CRISIS

The Bank report identifies three sets of factors that together explain the African economic crisis. The first is 'structural': the historical, geographical, political and climatic factors. Most African states began their independent existences with some severe handicaps. Trained, educated and experienced manpower was extremely scarce. Knowledge of the resource base, especially the agricultural base, was limited. They were new states, composed of ethnically diverse populations, and hence fragile politically, which guaranteed that priority attention would be given to political integration rather than economic growth in these early years of national existence. Their inherited institutions – in health care, education, administration – were carbon copies of those in the metropoles, and this meant that great energy had to be given to efforts to adapt these institutions to local conditions. Climatic factors are important, both in long- and short-term perspectives. The tropical climate creates special difficulties of rainfall variation, soil conservation, disease and pest control, maintenance of social capital. And in the 1970s, rainfall was well below trend in much of the continent. Finally, the large size of many countries makes for high costs in physical infrastructure construction and maintenance. All of these 'structural' factors contributed to the slow economic growth of the post-independence period.

External factors also played a role. The oil and food price shocks of the early 1970s sharply raised import requirements and strained current account balances in some countries. Minerals exporters, (notably Zambia, Zaire, Liberia, Mauritania and Zimbabwe) fared badly in the 1970s. So, unfavourable terms of trade played a part in causing the poor economic growth performance of the 1970s, but the available data do not indicate that terms of trade declines were a major or general factor. Changes in commodity terms of trade over the 20 years since 1960 and especially in the 1970s, were not systematically negative and were of large magnitude in only a few cases.

The final source of poor performance is domestic policy deficiencies. The report underscores three of these: over-valued exchange rates, inappropriate agricultural policies, and an excessive public sector role in the economy.

Exchange rates in many countries in Africa fell out of line in the 1970s, as African prices tended to rise more rapidly than prices in countries from which Africa imports. Over-valuation was not a problem everywhere; it tended, for example, to be less severe in countries belonging to the Franc zone. But it was acute in some places: Zaire, Tanzania, Ghana, Nigeria, for example. And there were few countries that were not forced to resort to foreign exchange rationing because of the low prices of imports at existing exchange rates.

In African conditions the problem of over-valued exchange rates is not, primarily, that it gives the wrong industrial signals – too much encouragement to domestic markets, not enough to export markets. This is not so important in African countries as it is in more advanced economies, though it operates in Africa too. Three other impacts are more basic: devastating effects on agricultural incentives, moral corrosiveness, and inefficient foreign exchange allocation. These are well known. Over-valued exchange rates make food imports cheap. Producers of domestically grown substitutes are discouraged. Moreover, consumer tastes are shifted in favour of rice and wheat and away from tubers, root crops, millet and maize. Moreover, over-evaluation makes it harder for exporters to pay farmers higher prices. If the Ghanaian cedi were 10 to the dollar instead of 2 to the dollar, for example, each pound of cocoa that sold for $2 would yield 20 cedis instead of 4. The cocoa producer could be paid more cedis for his cocoa.

In addition to discouraging exports and encouraging imports, over-valued exchange rates are especially corrosive in moral and administrative terms. It is true everywhere that the existence of big differentials between official and 'parallel' exchange rates means that people who get access to import licences can get rich overnight, and that this inevitably gives rise to abuses. But the likelihood of these abuses is greater in most African countries because the administrative ability to prevent corrupt practices is especially weak, and the political cohesion needed to punish wrong-doers is often thin. Corruption is therefore more likely.

The large rewards for corrupt behaviour and the limited capacity to control it is one reason why allocation of foreign exchange often takes place with little regard to national economic priorities. But even where this is not a major factor, efficient administration of an exchange control system is under all circumstances extremely difficult. It is easy to go wrong, with far-reaching economic effects. Basic farm inputs can be off the market for months at a time, and retail outlets can have mountains of sandals or shelves full of canned plums, while evaporated milk is lacking and there is no sugar.

Bad agricultural policies are the second set of domestic factors underscored in the report as major explanatory factors. At the risk of some over-generalisations, the main policy actions behind factors explaining Africa's lagging agriculture can be summarised as follows:

(a) Lack of resources. Agricultural sectors have received relatively little in the way of domestic and external development resources in the past 20 years. Budgets for agriculture remain slim and in the 1950s and 1960s aid money was also scarce. The 1970s, however, did see a change: some $5 billion in external assistance was devoted to African rural development projects between 1973 and 1980.

(b) Over-investment in large-scale projects. Much of the investment in agriculture, especially the domestic component, has gone into state farms, big irrigation schemes and similar capital-intensive activities. These have turned out to be largely a waste of money; their impact on output has been negligible in most cases.

(c) In the 1970s a significant share of new spending on rural development went to disfavoured, poorer regions within African countries – most of them areas of low and variable rainfall. However laudable the motivation for these projects (equity, regional balance, poverty elimination), they failed to have much sustainable effect on output. The main reason is that the technology available for raising production in these marginal zones is very thin.

(d) The incentive structure in most countries has not been conducive to expanded effort by farmers. Producer prices have been too low and in some cases too volatile, and marketing systems too heavily controlled by inefficient and sometimes oppressive government monopsonies and monopolies. In some countries, consumer goods have also been too scarce to provide rewards for increased marketing.

(e) The chosen instrument in rural development programming has been the integrated rural development project relying on public sector institutions – notably extension services and 'cooperatives' mostly formed from above. These organisations are too weak in administrative capacity to perform the functions asked of them. In addition, tested, profitable technological packages remain sparse; there has too frequently been little to extend.

(f) There has been misallocation of effort between research and extension – too little on research, too much on extension. The output of the research effort has been slight. Partly this springs from difficulties internal to the research organisations: dispersal of effort, lack of continuity, limited research memory, weak linkage to the farmers. These deficiencies derive from the predominance of expatriate staff and the high turnover of both expatriate and local researchers at country-level research institutions. Part of the problem of weak research impact also derives from the fact that farming system constraints have been too little considered.

Finally, the report argues, the public sector has become over-burdened. It has taken on tasks it cannot perform well instead of concentrating on better performance of those that are central. African governments have to build more roads and maintain them better, extend and maintain existing irrigation systems and other public capital assets. They have to adapt educational and health care systems to national needs, oversee better agricultural research and extension, undertake more manpower training, create better communication systems. Above all, they have to establish equitable and efficient administration throughout their national territories. These are heavy burdens for any LDC government. Yet African governments are almost everywhere engaged in demanding

activities of secondary importance such as selling consumer goods at
the retail level, buying food-grains from peasants, running truck and
bus services – tasks that private agents could easily do as well or better.

## IS THE DIAGNOSIS OF 1981 STILL RELEVANT?

The economic crisis is certainly now more general and more severe. It is
also more apparent in the GDP figures. Total GDP for 38 countries
(excluding Nigeria) was up 1.2 per cent in 1981 and 1.6 per cent in 1982.
Output per capita has thus fallen by about 1.5 per cent a year since 1980.
The output drop is more pronounced for the low-income countries, as
Table 2.1 shows.

TABLE 2.1    *Growth of GDP per capita*

| | Population 1980 (millions) | GDP per capita (1980 dollars) | Average annual growth of GDP per capita (per cent) | | | |
|---|---|---|---|---|---|---|
| | | | *1960–73* | *1973–80* | *1981* | *1982* |
| Low-income countries | 2161 | 252 | 2.0 | 3.2 | 1.8 | 1.8 |
| Africa | **190** | **274** | **1.1** | **–1.4** | **–2.7** | **–2.1** |
| Asia | 1966 | 250 | 2.2 | 3.8 | 2.3 | 1.6 |
| (India) | (673) | (236) | (1.2) | (2.0) | (3.2) | (1.3) |
| (China) | (977) | (290) | (3.6) | (4.5) | (1.5) | (2.5) |
| Middle-income countries | 1139 | 1411 | 4.0 | 2.2 | –1.0 | –0.8 |

SOURCE    The World Bank.

Economic activity in some countries is at a near standstill – Tanzania,
Mozambique and Angola are examples. Harder times have hit some
others that were previously among the fast growers – the Ivory Coast,
Malawi and Kenya, for example. In some cases dramatic new policy
departures are under way – in Mozambique, Somalia and Madagascar
among others. A great many countries are addressing their policy
dilemmas to at least some degree: Senegal, Zaire, Guinea, Mali,
Uganda, Zimbabwe have each adopted reform packages with one or
more of the 'usual' elements: exchange rate adjustments, budget
cutbacks, reduction of subsidies, improvement of parastatal performance, higher agricultural prices, more economically rational energy
pricing.

The international economic environment has become much more unfavourable since 1980 and this of course means that negative external factors play a larger role in the current pattern of deterioration than was true in the 1970s. The analysis of the report, it should be stressed, was focused on the two decades since 1960, and especially the 1970–79 period. It has been argued that terms of trade factors were not generally or substantially unfavourable during that period, and that the export earnings problem originated more on the supply side. As noted earlier, Africa's share of world trade fell in the 1970s, and markedly so. World trade in the products exported by African countries grew by about twice as much in volume as did African exports of those commodities. The worsened world economic situation since 1980 does not change the validity of the diagnosis covering the earlier period. Some have cited the case of the Sudan, where strong increases in cotton production in recent years have been nullified by low international prices, as a denial of the validity of the 1960–80 diagnostic. But this is not correct. Nor can it be interpreted to mean that export promotion is an inappropriate strategy for the Sudan. It does mean that any expansion of export earnings is more difficult in a recession-ridden world economy than in an environment where income and trade are growing fast. In any event, cotton prices have enjoyed a certain rebound recently, from which the Sudan will benefit.

In most key respects, the policy deficiencies underlined in the report persist. For example, in a recent IMF study it is estimated that real effective exchange rates for African countries on average appreciated between 1973 and 1981 by 44 per cent. This average is much influenced by some extreme cases (Ghana, Sudan, Uganda, Tanzania and Zaire) but the majority of currencies appreciated. From 1980 to 1983 the picture worsened. Figures for 32 countries suggest that 12 of the 32 currencies appreciated in nominal terms, and if price levels are taken into account, appreciation occurred in 19 countries. Where depreciation (devaluation) has occurred (in 13 countries) it has been relatively small: in eight cases it was less than 10 per cent and in five cases currencies were still appreciated relative to the mid-1970s.

Thus most of the exchange rate adjustments made in Africa over the past several years have been ineffective because domestic prices increased by more than the currency was devalued. It is the same with changes in agricultural prices paid to producers. In many, probably most cases, the impact on farmer income and incentives has been lost because the prices of the things farmers buy have risen by as much or more.

PRESCRIPTIONS

The report bristles with recommendations; only the main themes are outlined here. For African governments the following agenda is proposed:

(a) Address the exchange rate problem and the need for economic stabilisation to which it is related. This does not apply to all countries, and less to Franc zone members than most others. Nor does it necessarily mean devaluation; other instruments of adjustment exist. Nor, finally, does it say that devaluation alone will solve anything; fiscal, monetary wage and price policies have to be appropriate if any exchange rate adjustment is to stick and an economic stabilisation programme is to work.

(b) Agricultural development has to be given renewed priority. The main focus should be on smallholders – though there are obvious cases where larger farmers are critically important – Zimbabwe, Zambia, Malawi and Cameroon, for example. The stress on smallholders makes especially important a more congenial incentive structure: better prices, more consumer goods and services, better access to inputs, more open and competitive marketing systems, as well as more attention to rural roads and transport policy. Agricultural research should be expanded, to find the new technology so necessary for food production breakthroughs.

(c) Better economic management is a must in the coming period, when new sources of public revenues will be hard to find. This means using better those resources that are at hand – notably by improving project selection procedures and bringing information and analysis more effectively to bear on public sector decision-making. It also means tapping new sources of revenue by wider resort to user fees for government-provided services and by allowing private provision of services where feasible. It requires, indeed, a general mobilisation of private resources and skills by allowing private agents to perform tasks now frequently monopolised by government. The report stresses the point that public sector monopolies in marketing, transport and other services should be opened to competition from private traders and truckers, cooperatives and any other economic agent.

All of the above is addressed to African governments. There is also a set of prescriptions for aid donors. The report notes that donors cannot be viewed as innocent observers of Africa's lagging economic performance. A substantial share of all investment in the region is financed by external assistance – probably over a third for the region as a whole in the 1970s, perhaps three-quarters of the total in the poorest countries. Donor technical assistance drew up plans, designed projects (directly or indirectly) and implemented many of them on the ground. Africa's economic failures are therefore also donor failures.

The report calls for more aid – a doubling during the 1980s – and for aid of better quality, i.e. better suited to African needs. This is defined as aid that is more programme in nature, and less project-based; aid that covers more local and recurrent costs; that is concentrated on rehabilitation and other quick-yielding projects. This increased volume of more flexible assistance should be tied to policy reform; countries that are trying to reorient failed policies need special assistance because of the difficulties and risks of making such reforms. Finally, there is an appeal for better donor coordination; since without coordination reform-related assistance will not be feasible.

CRITICISMS

The report has generated criticism along a wide front, which is not surprising given the range of the recommendations and the intellectual controversy that has always surrounded many of the underlying issues. Five of the principal criticisms that have been levelled against it are considered here. The debate over whether external factors are more important than indicated is left to one side, as is the debate whether the argument over the report is consistent with the *Lagos Plan of Action*, the statement of African development strategy adopted at a meeting of the African heads of state in 1980. These debates are not without interest but are not directly relevant to the substantive issues of appropriate policies and strategies for the future.

**An inferior role for Africa**

The overall strategy recommended in the report involves a fuller integration into the world economy, with renewed attention to exports and a review of the level and nature of industrial protection. Some critics object to this as 'neo-colonial'; they see it as condemning African economy to an intolerable role in the world division of labour – the hewers of wood and drawers of water.

In fact, the recommended strategy specifies no long-term role. The problem for early-stage economies like most of those in Africa is that we do not know what their long-term future will be. We do not know where their long-term comparative advantage will be. The real issue is: how can this future best be discovered? The process of economic development then has to be understood as a process of uncovering options, and the question that counts is how to do this best. Related to this is the simple matter of resource availability. Africans need more and better food, more and better health care, education, roads, communications systems, technology. How can they pay for it without increasing output and income? An outward-looking strategy allows a more effective exploration of options and a higher level of income. Both will prepare the way for a future we cannot now predict.

### Export-led growth is unfeasible

Many observers have made this point; there is something to it. It is true that if all African states (or all LDCs) were to follow this strategy it might backfire: output of coffee, cocoa, timber, metals, etc., would increase so much that world prices would be depressed and export earnings would be smaller, not greater. This is because world demand for these primary products is price inelastic – demand does not greatly rise when prices fall. Much has been made of this 'fallacy of composition'. But it is mainly sophistry. First of all, not all countries will follow counsel to expand primary exports. So those that do will capture the markets of those that do not, regardless of their respective comparative advantages. Given this reality, those who stand on the sidelines and urge African states to shun the export sector are in fact handing over market shares to Brazil or Malaysia or Indonesia. Since it is not clear that better alternatives now exist for the use of African natural resources and labour, rejection of export orientation on the grounds of the 'fallacy of composition' is itself a monstrous fallacy, condemning Africans to lower incomes and reduced access to vital imports.

In any event, the question comes down to one of alternatives. It may not be very rewarding to expand primary product exports in the face of gloomy predictions about future market conditions, but there may be no better option now at hand. In this regard it is worth recalling that we do not know the true range of options available in any country, and these can change overnight. After all, in the late 1950s, Nigerian planners counted on no oil revenues. Uranium came on the scene suddenly in Niger, and transformed that country's export potential. This is not to say that new natural resource discoveries can be everywhere anticipated, or that they will in fact bring sustained long-term development. But they cannot be ruled out, and their existence can certainly smooth the way to a better future.

## The limits of price policy

Many people argue that the report, and World Bank proposals for reform, put too much emphasis on price changes – on adjustment in the rate of exchange, interest rates, wages, and especially agricultural goods. There is some substance to this criticism, especially with respect to agricultural pricing. For example, the stress on changing official producer prices for basic staples is largely irrelevant in many countries. Most transactions in these countries take place in parallel markets at prices well above the government's 'official' prices.

Moreover, there are limits to price policy. In the first place, export crop price increases are severely constrained by the prevalence of low world market prices, high marketing costs often due to the existence of inefficiencies in state monopoly marketing organisations, and by the need for government revenue for financing basic services, or, nowadays, to sustain an economic stabilisation effort.

With respect to food crops, in many countries what really matters is not price policy in the usual sense, but import policy. Large and/or erratic imports of cereals can be and often are decisive factors in the food market. Large inflows can easily discourage local producers of substitute foods. Finally, in all cases, better prices without better technology will sooner or later run into a production constraint. It is true that because of uncongenial incentive environments, many African farmers are producing less for the market than they might otherwise. But unless new technological possibilities appear, a point will be reached where they cannot respond to incentives by higher production.

What often matters more than official price changes is an opening up of markets to competition, i.e., a removal of legal monopolies or monopsonies. Enforcement of the rule that farmers could sell to whomever they wish at whatever price they can get would do more to stimulate food production than the raising of 'official' prices.

All of this said, prices are instruments of considerable power in influencing both producers and consumers. *Effective* producer price changes will induce production responses in part by inducing people to work harder, but mainly by encouraging adoption of existing technology – use of more fertilisers, better ploughs, carts, perhaps animal traction. And on the consumer side, policies that raise prices of wheat and rice and lower costs of millet, maize, and domestic rice will stimulate shifts in consumption in desirable directions.

## Food first

The report has been taken to task for inadequate stress on food self-sufficiency, but this is in most cases a false issue. Exports and food are not normally competitive. The data tend to show that where the export sector in a country is doing well, so too is food production; where exports are declining, food production tends to lag too and this is what one would expect. A dynamic agriculture will progress on all fronts, food and non-food alike.

But the trade-off can and sometimes does arise. And, here, it is suggested that country circumstances, case by case, should determine strategy. Some countries import marginal quantities of grain, or can import-substitute at relatively low opportunity cost. They can attain self-sufficiency in most basic staples at relatively low economic cost, and hence there is little problem. But some countries import large quantities of food and/or are high-cost producers of substitute foods (Senegal, Somalia and Mauritania, for example). For these countries food self-sufficiency would be extremely costly; it would mean significantly lower personal incomes, worse nutrition, fewer public services and slower economic development. If government decision-makers in this type of country wish to opt for food self-sufficiency, and do so in full awareness of the trade-offs involved, then there is no issue. But this is different from the argument that food self-sufficiency should everywhere and always be the first priority.

A related point has to do with comparative advantage. The report says that in many cases, African economies presently have a strong comparative advantage in production of export crops – cocoa, coffee and cotton, for example. This means that output, income and economic welfare is almost certain to be higher if these exports are traded for some food. This has been interpreted as meaning that African governments and their outside partners should reduce efforts to stimulate food production. It means nothing like that. It means only that it would be economically costly to disregard comparative advantage. The operative concept should be food self-reliance rather than food self-sufficiency. African economies should be able to guarantee their food security needs both by domestic food production and by a strong capacity to import. In any case, events are deciding this issue in many parts of Africa. Because of low world prices and other discouraging factors such as lack of inputs, deteriorating transport systems, and heavy taxation, farmers are reducing their commitment to export crops and growing more food. This is the case, for example, in Ghana and the Cameroon. Some will call this progress, and there is no doubt it represents an appropriate response by individual farmers to present circumstances, including relative prices of exports and food. But if the cocoa industry continues to decline, how will Ghana's factories be made to work again, dependent as they are on imported inputs and spare parts? And what will sustain Ghana's need for school slates and imported medicines, for asphalt and cement, for wheat and textiles and cheap iron for tools, for fertilisers and pesticides, and diesel fuel for irrigation pumps and power stations?

### The private–public issue

The recommendations on this issue have generated more heat than any other part of the report. This is no surprise. It touches political and ideological nerves. To some it smacks of 'Reaganomics'. Many argue that there is no genuinely viable private sector that can be turned to – except the foreign private capitalists. But those who read the report will see that there is not much ideology involved, no radical call for privatisation, not even much encouragement to foreign investment. The argument is for marginal changes in the social division of labour – allowing indigenous private agents a larger role in the economic development of the region. President Machel of Mozambique once made a speech in which he observed that Marxism-Leninism nowhere requires that the state sell tomatoes or matches. Yet that is what many African states are doing. The call in the report is for the public sector to concentrate on its major tasks and allow other agents to perform tasks that are not so critical, or that the state sector performs badly.

It also calls for more competition, for allowing individuals and cooperatives to buy and sell grain, medicines, fertilisers, run trucks, taxis and buses, and generally compete with the state monopolies or monopsonies now so dominant.

It does not seem that much has been done in this area since 1980. The grain marketing systems of some countries have been liberalised

(Somalia, Madagascar, Mali, Senegal and Zaire). But there have been backward steps too – for example with respect to urban transport in Sudan and Ivory Coast. A great deal of planning effort is being given to the rehabilitation and improvement of parastatals, but it is not clear how much is actually happening in this area.

## A BLUEPRINT FOR BANK POLICY?

Some observers, unpersuaded by the analysis in the report, fear that the policies proposed in it are becoming the 'blueprint' for the post-McNamara World Bank in its African operations. It is also said that other donor policies towards Africa have been influenced by the report.

The reality is that many of the general arguments of the report reflect the conventional technocratic wisdom as observable in country economic reports, sector analyses, and project appraisals of the World Bank and other donors during the past five years, or longer. By 1980, aware observers throughout the continent could hardly avoid the conclusion that something was awry. This was true on the micro level. Many projects and especially those in rural development, were clearly in difficulty. In a number of cases, established irrigation systems were falling into disrepair faster than new ones were being built. Overall, the $5 billion spent on rural development between 1973 and 1980 was a record amount, but output was falling or stagnant. The report then, did not set down some new and unfamiliar set of diagnoses and policy proposals. It distilled the prevailing reactions of many practitioners. If it is a 'blueprint' in any sense, it is a blueprint whose main component sections already existed. After all, structural adjustment lending was introduced in the World Bank in 1980, and conceived before then.

Moreover, the report is not a blueprint for Bank policy in the sense that it sets down a line of policy to be followed in every African country. In fact, every country situation is unique, and the Bank has insisted since the report came out that it is only by country-level dialogue that appropriate policy changes can be defined. It is thus not readily apparent that the pattern of Bank loans and credits to Africa has changed appreciably in the past three years. Six structural adjustment loans have been introduced, but this is part of the Bank's overall shift toward more conditional programme-type lending in all regions. Some adherents to the report's general orientations in fact say that not only is it no blueprint for all of Africa, it is no blueprint for any country either. Some Bank staff never believed in the basic priorities stressed in the report. Others have sought to sooth critics by arguing that the Bank shares many of the views of the critics – for example that there really is no difference between what the *Lagos Plan of Action* says and what the Bank is in favour of, or that the Bank's position is not far from what at least some 'delinkers' believe.

There is thus no 'blueprint' here, either intellectually or in operation. As we would expect in an organisation as richly diverse in human talent as the World Bank, there are widely different views on most subjects, and varied ideological predilections. And as we should also expect in a complex and diverse world, any set of general prescriptions is inevitably transformed and adapted when it is applied to individual countries.

# 3 The World Bank's Agenda for Accelerated Development: Dialectics, Doubts and Dialogues

REGINALD HERBOLD GREEN and
CAROLINE ALLISON

. . . In the twilight kingdom . . .
Here the stone images
Are raised, here they receive
The supplication of a deadman's hand
Under the twinkle of a fading star.

> (T. S. Eliot, 'The Hollow Men',
> *Selected Poems*, Faber, 1966)

We asked for bread
And they chucked a stone at us.

> Senior African economic analyst
> on *Accelerated Development*)

Economic growth implies using . . . scarce resources more efficiently . . .
policy making inevitably has to embody wider political constraints
and objectives . . . the record of poor growth . . . suggests that
inadequate attention has been given to policies to increase the
efficiency of resource use and that action to correct this situation is
urgently called for.

> (*Accelerated Development*)[1]

People . . . must be able to control their own activities within the
framework of their communities. At present the best intentioned

governments – my own included – too readily move from a conviction of the need for rural development into acting as if the people had no ideas of their own. This is quite wrong . . . people do know what their basic needs are . . . if they have sufficient freedom thay can be relied upon to determine their own priorities for development.

(President J. K. Nyerere)

WHAT DIFFERENCE DOES IT MAKE?

The 1981 appearance of the World Bank's review of and prescription for sub-Saharan Africa (SSA) – *Accelerated Development in Sub-Saharan Africa: An Agenda For Action* (*AD*) – has certainly attracted more attention, discussion and diatribes than any other economic study on Africa. It is perceived by analysts and decision-takers concerned with Africa – African and external, friend and foe – as of critical importance even if their assessments of it range from a new source of revealed wisdom through a secular variant on the Book of Revelation to a recipe for accelerated starvation. Is this amount of attention justified and, if so, why?

The answer must be yes. *AD* rests on a major data collection exercise. Its presentation of the 1960–79 economic history of Africa – even if one doubts its treatment of the 1970s as a homogeneous period rather than as four quite divergent ones (1970–73, 1974–75, 1976–78 and 1979) – is a serious attempt at description and analysis. It is based on a political economic ideology and model of some real analytical bite, political power and past/present capacity to perform for some classes in some countries at some times. It is therefore a significant work from an applied intellectual point of view.

Moreover, it stands – or as of 1981 stood – virtually alone. It was the only major policy-oriented analysis of Africa's economic crises and what might be done about them. The OAU's *Lagos Plan of Action* certainly presented longer-term (and radically different) two-decade strategic proposals but it neither addressed the immediate crises, nor marshalled an articulated set of prescriptions, nor followed an empirical approach. African national strategic documents are – by definition – not regional and rarely present an overall historical and political economic perspective explicitly. Further, like non-official publications by African authors they tend to be viewed as second-rate or unimportant before (and often in substitution for) reading.[2]

Finally, any set of World Bank proposals backed by its influence, technical capacity, funds and influence on other analysts and sources of finance will have a significant impact on events, as well as the way in which they are perceived. This is particularly true for sub-Saharan Africa – the group of countries which are economically weakest, currently most dependent on external resource transfers, with the poorest export–import substitution access to commercial finance prospects,[3] and historically most disposed to accept (and/or least able to reject?) external advice backed by economic influence. Whatever academic and African official analysts think of it – and however cogently they criticise it – *Accelerated Development* is and will remain a substantial force for good or evil – or, more realistically, for a mixture of both.

## IN THE BEGINNING: GENESIS OF A REPORT

*AD* was born out of a 1979 request by the African Governors of the World Bank to President McNamara for the Bank to review the causes and potential cures of the dim economic prospects that they believed confronted their economies. Their perception – which in 1979 was by no means as stark as it was by 1981 – is fairly well reflected in the opening of *AD*:

> Output per person rose more slowly in sub-Saharan Africa than in any other part of the world, particularly in the 1970s and it rose more slowly in the 1970s than in the 1960s . . . The tragedy of this slow growth in the African setting is that incomes are so low and access to basic services so limited . . . Now, against a backdrop of global economic recession, the outlook for all less-developed nations – but especially for the sub-Saharan region – is grim.[4]

The report was prepared over the ensuing two years on the basis of memoranda from a range of invited commentators, a basic consultancy draft by Elliot Berg and a series of in-house papers and review committee meetings.[5] It appeared in the fall of 1981 as the first comprehensive ideological and programmatic manifesto setting out the post-McNamara Bank's response to lagging development (in many cases disintegration) in the context of rising global economic disorder and deepening industrial economy recession.

## AFRICAN RESPONSE AND SOME OF ITS CAUSES

African responses to *AD* were initially mixed – welcoming the call for a doubling of aid, but politely querying whether outside expert advice was always part of the solution rather than the problem; agreeing on the poor record of the 1970s, but wondering whether it was not both less uniformly gloomy and more the result of external shocks than the report presented it; agreeing to put higher priority on production and, in particular, exports, but expressing some scepticism about the rather simplistic market forces, private sector, primary product-led model of the Agenda. The evolution has been toward sharper criticism – by economists and officials who are both serious and moderate[6] – as well as increased opposition to Bank prescriptions and a sharpening of the plaint 'we are where we are because we did what you told us to do', most recently by the Ivory Coast, one of *AD*'s models of prudent policy.

Several characteristics of *AD* have contributed to this reponse. First, its style is *ex cathedra* and minatory. No signs of self-doubt by the authors as to the correctness of the analysis or the wisdom of prescriptions intrude on the reader (even when these contain apparent major internal inconsistencies or are not backed by the 'supporting' data tables). Further, there is a clear implication that the Bank will support only sub-Saharan African states which act on *its* Agenda – and will seek to influence other donors to do likewise. In this regard *AD* does the Bank and its audience less than justice. In face-to-face discussion and dialogue (and internal debates) Bank personnel show far more uncertainty and realisation that actual decisions are complex, imperfect choices with no unique right answers. Furthermore, at least to date, the Bank has shown uneven, but real, flexibility in adapting programmes to actual contexts and 'pure' economic calculations to political economic realities. It has been, to its credit, more prone to use its potential for mobilising other agencies as a carrot rather than as a stick.

Second, the report's analysis and prescriptions are riddled with sweeping generalisations, logical *non* (or non-necessary) *sequiturs* and inconsistencies. This is partly the result of the normal operation of an institutional editing committee dealing with an outside consultant's draft.[7] Professor Berg's economic worldview is of a more robust and free competitive market-allocated, comparative advantage-led, neo-liberal, political-economic world than that portrayed in *AD*. While some changes were presumably softening, most seem to have been additions to safeguard certain existing Bank commitments (e.g. food production, manpower development, population planning) even where these appear to contradict the main thrust of the Agenda. In addition, the Bank's typical style of using general background analyses, broad principles, perhaps derived from or supported by the analysis, and micro-level thumbnail sketches as a means to arrive at concrete policy proposals, lacks any clear articulation from empirical data to analysis to general principles, or down from them to policy proposals.[8] Apart from the omnipresent danger of over-generalisation, this approach gives maximum room for backing initial premises by selective use both of evidence and of explanations which will 'back' the authors' preferred lines of action without ever subjecting them to any rigorous tests as to practicability or prudence.

Third, reading the Agenda is unlikely to suggest that the Bank has ever made mistakes other than those based on inadequate technical data inputs or misplaced faith in the rationality and expertise of recipient governments (and that, somehow, none of these errors cast any doubt on its collective institutional technical competence and wisdom). Yet – to cite two examples in *AD* – in calling for highway project analysis and support to include maintenance costs (pp. 106, 126), and in condemning the creation of parallel, autonomous, expert-staffed policy/ implementation units outside the domestic decision-taking structure (pp. 130, 132), the Bank is reversing its own 1970s advice with a vengeance.[9] This is damaging in two ways: to admit and to analyse – as well as to reverse – past mistakes is often a necessary step in avoiding future ones; to seek to avoid all responsibility for the results of policies and projects in which one is (and is *known* to be) deeply implicated, both undermines the credibility of the new proposals and generates animosity on the part of those who know their case histories, and thus impedes rational consideration of the new proposals. Learning and convincing others requires recognition of fallibility.[10] Further, *ex post facto* criticism of decisions is not the best way to find out how and why they were made. This is especially true of 'good *ex ante*/bad *ex post*' choices – i.e. ones which during the pre-1973 or the 1976–78 recovery seemed to be sound and would have been had the 1960s world economic trends been continued or restored. With much greater economic uncertainty a fact of the 1980s, and with SSA particularly prone to damage from uncertainties because of its externally open economies and limited resource margins,[11] this topic required a specific attention it did not (and does not) receive. Such attention might have led to more prudence and less certainty in respect to a number of projections and recommenda- tions, e.g. that 1981–85 would see a highly positive evolution of the terms of trade of primary agricultural exports.

Fourth, while certain modifications are made in the direction of human investment and basic services (but with higher user charges and partial privatisation advocated) and of selective, public sector incentive-focused state intervention, the basic doctrine of the report is that of economic (and political) neo-liberalism. Economically it resembles 1930s *mise en valeur* strategies and both economically and politically the 1950s, late colonial era, approaches to development.[12] Access to basic needs, elimination of absolute poverty and distribution are not on this Agenda. They are treated, at best, as optional by-products of maximising growth by selective allocation of resources to areas and sectors with high short-term output potential and by over-riding concentration on (also short-term?) profitability. From this perspective, closer integration of SSA's domestic economies (already among the world's most open in terms of import to GDP ratios) into the world economy is seen as self-evidently desirable, because of the poor growth prospects for the major industrial economies and for international trade. The assertion of *AD* (p. 1) that it builds on the *Lagos Plan of Action* which calls for SSA national and regional integration and for relatively less dependence on and vulnerability to the international economic environment, is (with the exception of the report's support, on pp. 118–19, for regional economic integration) not simply inaccurate; the reverse would be much nearer the truth.

These four characteristics are not all of a kind. The first three raise questions as to completeness, consistency and direct applicability to specific cases (a doubt the Bank, on p. v, occasionally shares), but not necessarily on its overall sweep of data, analysis and conclusions. The fourth is rather different. Economic neo-liberalism as a credo (as opposed to a number of the measures contained in neo-liberal programmes) is contentious analytically, disputable empirically and ultimately accepted or rejected on normative, self-interest or theological rather than pragmatic, public-interest or programmatic grounds.[13]

## CENTRAL THEMES BEHIND THE AGENDA

Four central themes link *AD*'s empirical evidence, descriptive examples and interpretative analysis:

(a) Sub-Saharan African economies performed only moderately well in the 1960s and much less well in the 1970s. Prospects for the 1980s were (correctly to date) seen as being even bleaker, and for the 24 low-income countries to include falls in per capita GDP if existing trends continued.

(b) The external economic environment surrounding SSA in the 1970s was mixed with some negative shock effects (e.g. drought, oil and grain price explosions) and some windfall gains (e.g. 1972–74 commodity and 1976–77 beverage booms); 1980s prospects are worse.

(c) Levels of overall economic growth and of export performance in SSA are significantly poorer than in other developing regions and worsened in the 1970s.

(d) The economic policy and practice of SSA governments lies at the root of their deteriorating economic performance. In particular there have been biases against exports, agriculture and the private sector and in favour of the public sector, inward-looking import substitution and (albeit *AD* is self-contradictory on this) food.

To deny that each of these capsulised contentions contains significant elements of truth for the region and for most countries in it would be otiose. In respect of some of them, *AD*'s 'left' critics are almost more vehement than the Bank. None of the contentions, however, are either as clearcut or as applicable to all SSA states as the *Agenda* suggests (nor, as will be suggested later, do they necessarily lead uniquely to the Bank's policy package).

First, growth performances – while generally unimpressive except during 1976–79 when SSA GNP growth rates were of the order of 6 per cent and *above* the developing country average – have been very diverse by country and by time. Only since 1979 have almost all economies seen stagnation or deterioration.

Second, while the need to adjust to a worsened external setting is unquestionable (especially as neither *AD*'s optimistic terms of trade forecasts nor calls for doubling of aid seem particularly 'bankable'), the report understates the weight of external factors in worsened performance (especially for mineral exporters) for the period covered. Even the Bank would agree that during 1979–83 external shocks have tended to overwhelm reform efforts.[14]

Third, the growth performance of SSA in the 1970s was certainly unsatisfactory in absolute terms and below average (for the decade) regionally. However, so was that of 'structurally disadvantaged' ('most severely affected', 'landlocked', 'least developed') economies, in which categories SSA is disproportionately represented. In these classes, in fact, SSA economies have, on average, done somewhat better than those in other regions – at least until the 1980s.

Fourth, *AD* discusses a number of specific policy and management errors but does not show how widespread or critical they were. More important, it does not uniquely demonstrate how or in what direction to change them. For example, the evidence is consistent with asserting that too little state intervention (on, say, Korean lines) to promote exports and too lax or liberal import licensing were the key external balance failures, rather than – as *AD* argues – too much government intervention and too many barriers to imports. Similarly, government expenditure levels and GDP growth do not correlate – as admitted on p. 36 of the report.

Finally, a substantial number of SSA states did adjust their policies radically during 1974–75 and their economies did recover during 1976–79, both in terms of growth and external balance. The general downturn dates from the 'second oil crisis' and industrial economy depression. This record casts doubt on any general interpretation asserting that policy weaknesses were a primary, as opposed to a contributory, factor in all, or most, of SSA. That is hardly surprising given the very wide diversity of actual policies between states – a diversity *AD* seems to skate over except when appearing to hold up implicit models, seemingly, in particular, the Ivory Coast and Malawi. These are rather unlucky choices given the subsequent reinterpretation of their policies following their experience of export, external balance and growth problems in the 1980s.[15] As the overall GNP growth levels (as opposed to distribution patterns and access to public services, which do vary sharply in relation to policies) do not correlate with the policy differences closely, either a managerial or a specific external or internal contextual explanatory hypothesis might seem more powerful.

None of these criticisms alters the need for clearer priorities, more effective coordination, economy in the use of scarce resources and adjustment to a nastier world environment. It certainly does not alter the facts that over 1976–78 many SSA decision-takers wrongly believed (along with the OECD and the Bank) that the 1960s global economic trends had been restored and that over 1979–81 many (again like the OECD, the Bank and the Fund) were slow to realise that they faced a long recession with a need to cut back and to redeploy that was quite different from 1974–75's gap-bridging by temporary austerity cum interim external borrowing requirements. But the criticisms do suggest that the basic nature of policy errors – and *a fortiori* of correctives – is not clearly nor convincingly demonstrated in *AD*.

## PATTERNS OF PRESCRIPTIONS

A positive forest of proposals is presented in *AD*. They vary widely in terms of generality, individual importance and their interaction with other proposals. Many are fairly clearly desirable by almost any criteria; others are either debatable generally or contextually limited in applicability.

However, a clear set of articulated priorities and a coherent presentation of a framework within which to organise (and achieve consistency among) individual proposals is harder to find. The trees do conceal the parameters of the forest (in some cases apparently from the authors). On the basis of how often and how forcefully cases are cited, ten clusters appear to dominate.

*First*, there should be less (or, at the least, less expansion of) state activity in its traditional areas – except for economic infrastructure supporting the private sector. Universal free access to basic services is rejected as an operational goal in favour of partial privatisation and higher user charges for all services (the latter ironically packaged as an appeal to increase local community participation in decision taking!). Related is the *second* focus – curtailment of parastatal activity (especially in directly productive activities and the potentially profitable sub-sectors of commerce and transport).[16] This is to be in favour of making room for dynamic, flexible, lightly (if at all) regulated private sector entrepreneurs (domestic or foreign). There is no actual proposal for wholesale denationalisation but the number of specific proposals for privatisation (e.g. seeds, drugs, basic foodstuffs, medicine) and the clear conviction that the private enterprise can always outcompete and outperform a public enterprise are close to adding up to the same thing.

*Third*, is greater emphasis on export expansion linked to agriculture as a means of raising both real peasant earnings and foreign exchange, and also keyed to industry as a means of increasing competitive tests on efficiency and diversifying exports (apparently based on cheap labour more than local raw materials). This is *not* simply a pragmatic response to the appalling imbalances of payments (which often with minimum necessary imports plus debt-service amounts to two to three times exports) confronting a majority of SSA economies even in 1980 (and to confront all but a handful by 1983). Rather, it is part of the more general *fourth* theme of closer integration into the world market on the basis of short-run comparative advantage unhampered by government restrictions or by measures designed as insurance against uncertainties (except forward sales and purchases to overcome price risks in respect of grain imports and, by extension, primary product exports).

*Fifth* as a necessary corollary (in *AD*'s view although not in pure logic) to export enhancement, reduced emphasis on self-sufficiency in manufactures and food (albeit *AD* either havers or contradicts itself on this) is urged on the region with the highest ratio of imports to GDP growth rates (1.7),[17] the lowest ratio of food production to basic nutritional requirements, and the greatest vulnerability to external shocks. Protection is clearly seen as demonstrating inefficiency, and arguments about building up acquired comparative advantage, ensuring against risk or using otherwise unemployed resources (raw materials, labour), are either petty quibbles or rationalisations of inefficiency. To improve levels and make-up of production, the *sixth* theme calls for economic incentives – basically price incentives to peasant producers and private entrepreneurs mediated by unregulated markets and bolstered by devaluation. Non-economic incentives (including distribution, basic services and, it would seem, real wage rates) are specifically set aside as falling beyond the proper concern (or knowledge?) of development analysts. Other economic incentives – e.g. actual buyers, inputs, goods to buy, transport in the case of peasants – are mentioned but in a way, and with a lack of stress or articulation, which suggests they are either very much secondary to prices or are not analysable at regional versus national or sub-national levels.

The need for more middle- and high-level trained personnel to provide greater 'technical expertise' is at the core of the *seventh* area of stress. Somewhat oddly, given the calls for government spending cuts, so is more primary (but not adult) education. Knowledge creation is the *eighth* area of emphasis. Data and analysis (e.g. applied research, statistics, financial reports) are seen as a *sine qua non* for better management and improved policy decisions. Further they are presented – albeit with no evident articulation or resource priority even, or especially, in the crucial agricultural sector – as needed to make available simple, cost-reducing, output potential enhancing, technical breakthroughs.

A *ninth* heavy stress is on setting priorities, articulating policies and programmes from them in a consistent manner, coordinating implementation, building in review and actually allocating resources in accordance with clear and articulated priorities. Ironically, *AD* itself does not rate very high on these tests.

*Finally*, the necessity of enhanced donor support and involvement in designing/controlling policy design and resource use receives an entire chapter plus repeated references elsewhere. Concessional finance quality should be raised by greater flexibility and programme, as opposed to project, orientation. *De facto* or *de jure* donor/SSA recipient compacts like Fund stabilisation and Bank structural adjustment programmes should be used to enforce policy change by conditionality. The Bank should, preferably, coordinate flows to individual countries and ensure that sizeable ones go only to those SSA states accepting the *AD Agenda*.

Agenda acceptance is not seen in terms of acceptance (often merited) or rejection (also often merited)[18] of the specific proposals. Rather it hinges on acceptance of the main themes and clusters. This is a logical view – if *AD*'s analytical themes and policy cluster stresses are correct, most of the specifics follow. If, however, they are seriously flawed, the *Agenda* requires basic revision before appropriate, articulated, consistent national strategies and priorities can be constructed even if many components, taken separately, are valid.

*First*, it is clear that most SSA states must live more frugally. However, with the basic functions (including maintenance) at dangerously low levels, a strong case exists for higher taxes more effectively collected and better use of revenue rather than straight output cuts. The bland abstraction from distribution, from saying who would provide what services to whom, and from the human cost of cuts already made[19] is breathtaking. The same general criticism applies to the *second* cluster relating to public enterprises whose performance is far more varied than *AD* suggests and by no means uniformly poorer than that of private enterprises, even in pre-tax profit terms. Nor can one simply ignore (as *AD* does) that often the only alternative is private foreign enterprise whose availability, effectiveness and acceptability cannot be generalised. The reduced rates posited for some public enterprises – buyers, sellers, transporters of last resort and guarantors of inter-year food reserves – would, by definition, guarantee that they made losses while private enterprises, choosing profitable businesses, made profits; thus allowing *AD* Mark II once again to criticise public sector 'inefficiency' (defined as enterprise profits).

The *third* cluster – priority to raising exports – is valid. Many African countries lack coherent, articulated export strategies[20] and several of those which exist seem to require review as no longer viable.[21] The problem is, how? *AD*'s targets are not attainable on present or identifiable future export mixes.[22] Country-specific export rehabilitation, pre-export processing, natural-resource linked manufacturing and new-resource based exports *may* afford answers – a general invocation for high growth of the present low elasticity, poor global demand growth primary products, and neo-NICery is doomed. In any event, the *fourth* theme of greater external integration (at least globally *-AD* does not really pursue the regional alternative) via free trade or unhampered comparative advantage is not a necessary consequence of agreement that more exports are a top priority.

Historically, escape from low-level free-trading dependence has usually involved selective partial withdrawal from the world economy and state intervention to promote exports based on different, acquired (developed) comparative advantage, as in Imperial Germany, France, Italy, Japan and South Korea.

Given the poor export prospects for the 1980s; the historic record of new export bases – especially in manufacturing (e.g. Brazil) as cited in *WDR 82*[23] – being built up behind protective barriers; the stultifying effect of the present incremental import to GDP ratio and the present levels of global excess capacity, deprotection seems likely to release resources primarily to unemployment while reduced emphasis on food production appears to be an agenda for accelerated starvation. If so, the *fifth* cluster on generalised reduction of internal orientation of SSA economies (as opposed to more selective choices of instruments and projects) is plainly wrong, indeed wrongheaded. There are many inefficiencies and rationalisations of unsound open or concealed subsidies (including in respect to the private foreign sector, e.g. domestic market textiles in Kenya and export-oriented ones in the Ivory Coast), which are not cost efficient in terms of risk avoidance, nor in building future efficient, nationally integrated economies. These *should* be reduced (preferably rooted out), but their existence does not render Brazilian,[24] South Korean or Japanese experience irrelevant. Nor does it reverse the fact that import liberalisation and attempts to alter industry and agriculture toward global competitiveness (as advised by the Bank) tripled Mexico's ratio of imports to GDP, sharply increased food deficits and played a central (but not the sole) role in causing the country's present crisis.

More incentives – as stressed in the *sixth* cluster – are needed to raise production (of products with plausible domestic or export market prospects). Whether – especially in the conditions of massive imperfections, severe crisis and generalised (private and public) restrictive practices pertaining in SSA – the free market can provide production-efficient incentives without state market management intervention is a very different question, and one to which few analysts, businessmen or consumers would give an unqualified yes. The exclusion of many apparently relevant incentives, e.g. access to health and education, programmes to reduce time spent gathering fuel and water, suggests tunnel vision (and little examination of peasant and worker stated preferences and priorities).

The *seventh* and *eighth* areas of emphasis are clearly correct. The problems arise at micro-proposal level where ill thought-out ideas and gaps can be discerned. Middle-level personpower – usually scarcer than high-level in SSA[25] – is not treated systematically nor is the accounting cadre (surely an enterprise or departmental management-efficiency *sine qua non*) cited as a special priority.

The *ninth* cluster, stressing the need for clearer strategic priorities backed by resource allocations and consistently articulated to policies, programmes and projects, is a crucial one – whatever agenda any African state adopts. To plan *is* to choose and so is to manage. The fact that similar criticisms could be made of most capitalist and socialist states (and of the Bank) does not alter this fact albeit it may temper expectations of how much can be achieved, and how fast.

In respect of the *final* external cooperation cluster, differentiation is needed. The case for flexible, programme-oriented aid (made at least equally cogently by several SSA states and by UNCTAD well before AD) is both compelling and one on which progress is possible. The doubling of real concessional finance flows to Africa over the 1980s, however desirable, is most unlikely to happen and most irresponsible to project in determining available resources and possible growth rates.

The proposal for greater donor policy involvement would be valid if donors would recognise their own past mistakes (and be less dogmatic now) and engage in dialogue with African recipients. Those characteristics are not evident in *AD*. Views on reorganising bilateral and other multinational aid around a core of conditional Bank/Fund programmes will hinge largely on readers' assessments of the accuracy, practicability, political viability and human desirability of their overlapping world-views. However, even supporters of those world-views may doubt whether the Bank's apparent aspiration to become SSA's (and the Third World's) planning ministry and Platonic Guardian cadre (an aspiration it has had at least since 1970 but seems to see as more fully recognisable as its clients became more desperate to secure foreign finance) is in either the Bank's or SSA's best interests.

## SOME SECTORAL GLIMPSES

To review *AD* fully sector by sector would not be practicable in a single chapter – a whole volume is the minimum appropriate length.[26] However it is possible to make certain comments.

In the first place, most of the sectoral analysis and proposals do relate to one or more of the main clusters outlined above and so are subject to the same queries – or defensible on the same logic. For example, the public expenditure proposals rest on an unsubstantiated hypothesis that African state spending is higher than and different in kind from that in other economies, and that viable alternatives to public enterprises are generally available. The available evidence strongly suggests the opposite for SSA as a region, and for most states taken separately.[27] The export targets appear, on disaggregation to be patently unattainable or undesirable.[28] In the case of agricultural products they would trigger price collapses *reducing* earnings. In that of manufactures they are either premature – if one views the Brazilian and Korean pattern of several decades of protected home-market-oriented, pre-export development as relevant – or plainly surreal – if the implicit model is Hong Kong or Singapore with plentiful infrastructure, established business communities, capital surpluses and no rural hinterlands.

The agricultural sector analysis, projections and proposals are particularly critical, and arguably, open to particularly heavy criticism.[29] While they manage to list almost every measure anybody could suggest, they do not set priorities, establish a selection/coherence framework, take the existing state of knowledge much further forward, nor show any historical perspective as to the past failures or side-effects of a number of the proposals (including cases which the Bank must know because it advocated, financed and –negatively – evaluated them). In respect of food/industrial-export crop priorities, the chapter is incoherent or contradictory – presumably because the sections arguing that food has been over-promoted and that food self-sufficiency is a priority needing higher resource allocations and more price incentives, flow from different hands. Arguably, the very heavy concentration on grower prices (at times apparently nominal rather than real) distracts from less costly, more practicable changes in improving access to buyers, speed of payment, and availability of inputs and consumer goods which would be more cost-efficient in respect to short-run production raising. Ignoring the incentive impact of health, education, water access and fuel supply runs against the Bank's own experience as well as against what African peasants say and do.

Finally, it grossly understates the significance of the fact that in field-tested, economically viable, peasant-practicable, rural technological improvements (in seed, fertiliser, small-scale irrigation, etc.), Africa has perhaps a tenth of the stock available to South and South-east Asia, and a much less adequate structure to raise the flow at all levels from local through national and sub-regional to international crops research institutes' programmatic priorities. This is a particularly unfortunate lapse because the Bank is in a position to provide and mobilise resources (financial, personnel, knowledge, institutions) in this sub-sector. The sums required are manageable, comparative experience is critical, because returns are uncertain in amount and not immediate, and SSA states (and most bilateral donors) are likely to under-invest during a crisis – a set of factors creating a context in which Bank leadership would be particularly appropriate.[30]

## UNIVERSAL ACCESS TO BASIC SERVICES, WOMEN AND DISTRIBUTION: OFF THE AGENDA?

Women[31] appear in *AD* largely as a by-product of its advocacy of reducing population growth as a crucial long-term goal. While the simplistic neo-Malthusian tone of the presentation will grate on many readers, the argument that a 2.5–4 per cent annual increase in population would raise employment generation, infrastructure and basic service resource requirements beyond levels available from any likely growth rate is valid. It is, in fact, accepted by at least the majority of SSA governments.

What is less clear is the analysis of, or proposals for, achieving demographic transition. Apparently *AD* views this as a suitable area for state intervention until the process of 'modernisation' itself takes over, since the 'market' for birth control, unlike others, is perceived by *AD* as imperfect and needing state management! The report fails to address the historic evidence that a decline in the birth rate (and with a lag in population growth) usually follows a fall in death rates (especially infant mortality) which is itself usually related to more assured – economically as well as physically – food supplies, access to pure water and to education for the absolutely poor, less favoured (in ecology or location) regions and women. The whole thrust of raising fees for basic services (and reducing growth of supply), privatisation and concentrating incentives on better prices to more efficient (defined as more modern and larger-scale) peasants and enterprises hardly seems well attuned to achieving these normal pre-conditions for demographic transition.

As is standard in works of economic analysis – even, or perhaps especially, when they seek to articulate development targets and policies – women are semi-invisible and fragmented in *AD*. For example, the facts that a high per cent of rural households are headed by women; that these households appear to have disproportionately low access to inputs and extension advice; and that over half of agricultural labour time is worked by women (with different tasks apparently gender specific), are not mentioned in the agricultural section and therefore lead to no policy proposals. That appears to fly in the face of any common sense approach to identifying and removing constraints on production (let alone on absolute poverty reduction which used to be a central Bank goal). True it is a mistake most SSA governments make but that is precisely why the *AD* report should have highlighted it and called it to their attention.

Women have not totally disappeared in *AD*. The education of women (hardly furthered one might suppose by higher fees which have in the past disproportionately reduced female enrolment ratios) is recognised as a means of reducing population growth and (quite how is unclear) of lessening the burden (on time, not on people) of household work such as food processing, fuel gathering and water collection. The latter is seen as critical to raising agricultural productivity by 'freeing' time for work in the field – a point which oddly does *not* appear in the chapter on agriculture but in the section on population.

These fragmentary references are unrelated to – and arguably conflict with – the main body of argument. Overall the low priority attached to basic services, and expansion linked to proposals to raise charges for those which do exist, run directly contrary to facilitating (creating effective incentives for) the contributions to development expected of women. There is no serious analysis of the specific roles women play in economic (directly productive and supporting) structures in Africa. This is especially serious in respect of agriculture where the vision of the smallholding household as 'African economic man' is simplistic (if better than its predecessor as 'African traditional, irrational man' against which *AD* still has to contend). Quite apart from its reductionist economy mysticism, it excludes women. Even a coherent presentation of 'African economic woman' in the report would have been highly welcome, and potentially highly productive on analytical and operational as well as normative grounds, precisely because so little attention has been devoted to the topic in official analysis and policy making.

The *Agenda* does not overtly discuss distribution – a telling shift from a decade of stress on 'absolute poverty eradication' and 'redistribution with growth'. It is basically concerned only with short-term production increases (which no one would deny are a priority), overlooking the fact that – especially in poor countries – who produces how, determines who gets how much, why. Participation in production is the only safe base for participation in distribution and decision-taking.

While the *AD* report does not discuss distribution, its *Agenda* has an implict philosophy about it. That outlook is not 'trickle down' but 'trickle up':

(a) resources are to go to ecologically and infrastructurally favoured zones and to progressive (i.e. richer) peasants;
(b) basic services are to be de-emphasised – certainly not pushed toward universal access;
(c) remaining services are to be on a fee basis – limiting them to the favoured peasant sub-group;
(d) real wages and informal sector incomes for those whose spending is largely on food are to be reduced with the greatest impact on low wage/informal sector people;
(e) the service cuts and selection principle for peasants will intensify excess labour burdens and differential lack of access for women as household heads, producers, mothers, bearers of wood and water.

This *is* 'redistribution with growth' revisited – *and reversed*.[32]

Whether this approach is consistent with development depends on one's definition. For the majority of the people of SSA over the short run (and, in the not very long run, the poor of Africa are dead and Keynes' dictum against ignoring short-run costs [33] applies forcibly): clearly *no*. That poses problems as to whether the *Agenda* is consistent with medium- and long-term growth enhancement. *First*, throwing away the bulk of Africa's plentiful resource, rural labour, may not be efficient. *Second*, lack of access to basic services will worsen the mental and physical capacity of many workers. *Third*, African states do not have the force to operate productionist police states.

Excluding peasants who are in ecologically unfavoured or low infrastructure zones and lowering poor urban real-income levels is hardly consistent with maximum growth in food production or sales. Rural hunger in Africa is largely in poor peasant households and can only be met by making it possible for them to produce more. Urban food demand (at prices encouraging production) will be compressed by cutting real incomes of the poor.[34] A much more serious, complex and specific context-centred approach is needed to work out production/distribution policies to cut food imports, reduce the incidence of severe malnutrition and hunger, and build up markets for foods.[35]

Concentration on large, better-off, best-land peasants may not maximise production even in the short run. Evidence from Kenya and

Malawi suggests that peasants are more scarce-resource efficient producers on average and for most crops than large farmers or plantations. It does *not* show that among peasants larger ones are more efficient – if anything *au contraire*. Exceptions are marginal and submarginal rainfall zones for which substantial resource allocation can be justified only on the principle that human lives matter.[36] Therefore, even on short-term production-boosting grounds, which *AD*'s peasant focus upholds, its 'neo-kulak' preference is empirically dubious. The same type of argument applies in respect to women, thus, if there has been discriminatory lack of access for women farmers to inputs, advice, marketing, etc. then enhanced access should have a high incremental production pay-off.

Somewhat analagous questions arise in respect of urban workers, whether in the modern or informal sectors, employed or self-employed. *AD*'s whole thrust is toward lower real wages to increase competitiveness. If informal sector incomes largely depend on wage-earner's purchases and tend to be related to (on average substantially lower than) modern sector wages – as appears to be the case – this is certainly a prescription for greater inequality and more absolute poverty. Even brief contact with the rapidly growing exurbs of, for instance, Nairobi, Kinshasa, Lagos, Accra, Addis Ababa and Dakar, makes that a humanly chilling prospect. More to the point of *AD*'s concerns, it is not self-evidently efficient in production terms. Workers without access to basic education, health services, pure water and income to meet their household's basic needs are *not* very productive because they are often sick and hungry, have inadequate knowledge to acquire skills easily and are denied economic incentives (such as being able to feed, clothe and house their families decently). Further, one of Africa's more plentiful resources is labour. Investing so as to increase employment and productivity would, therefore, seem likely to be efficient resource allocation from a production viewpoint even if it did require market intervention other than worker income reduction. *AD* simply overlooks the problem and therefore proposes no answers to an admittedly difficult question but one with which the ILO, to its credit, has been wrestling for at least a decade.

## ACCELERATED DISINTEGRATION: THE AGENDA REVISITED

Since 1981 the economic situation in SSA has deteriorated dramatically, as have perceptions about its probable future trajectory.[37] The 1983

*WDR*'s middle projection for low-income SSA over 1985–95[38] is approximate matching of population and GDP growth rates, following a 1979–85 per capita fall of the order of 20 per cent if 1979–81 terms of trade losses are taken into account. That projection assumes sustained moderate to high growth of OECD economies, no increase in their new protectionism, and enhanced investment in Africa half financed out of increased net aid and commercial borrowing flows. The assumptions look – at best – on the optimistic side of realism, the outlook is grim.

As a recent Bank evaluation of progress in SSA reveals[39] this result and these projections are not for any general lack of attempts to consolidate and to adjust. On the one hand, terms of trade shifts, external resource flow contractions, drought and war or economic destabilisation (especially in respect to states unfortunate enough to be South Africa's neighbours) have often overwhelmed positive national initiatives. On the other hand, the short-term costs of adjustment are usually high and early while the gains are gradual and later; thus additional resources are necessary to alleviate early costs if the changes are to be seen as politically feasible or to survive if adopted.

In fact the Bank – never unanimously in support of *AD* – has resiled from a number of its key positions. How fully, how far and why, is obscured by the fact that the Bank rarely (except in its internal memoranda and published evaluations of individual projects) admits to error. However, the list is impressive:[40]

(a) Major sustained terms of trade improvement of African exports is not in sight and generalised increases in growth rates for tropical agricultural exports would be counter-productive.

(b) Efficient import substitution is a real category and is of comparable importance – at least in the medium run – to export expansion. Basic food self-sufficiency and enhanced domestic energy are generally applicable goals, as is a greater range of basic goods (e.g. broad-market consumer goods, construction materials). ECA's statement, 'Unless sound and efficient import-substitution policies are implemented and exports diversified in terms both of products and markets, the projected historic growth of GDP might not materialize',[41] is now cited by the Bank with approval.[42]

(c) 'Price distortion' has been introduced as an index of policy efficiency[43] – an approach somewhat more objective and less ideological than *AD*'s strictures on public sector efficiency. There are three types of problem with this approach: (i) targeted incentives usually involve price distortion, as does almost any attempt to alter existing income distributions; (ii) the judgements on how much distortion is present are basically subjective (and look very odd in some cases – e.g. Malawi and Kenya appear much too low); (iii) the correlation between price distortion and growth, while positive, is not high – other factors appear to have been more critical in at least some cases. However, the concept is more subject to refinement and to application of constraints than the looser intervention/public sector denigration of *AD*.

(d) Better public sector management has become one of the Bank's key operational targets – for governments and enterprises – and one it is trying to articulate.[44] While *WDR 83* is very uneven and breaks less new ground than it supposes, it at least centres squarely on the selectivity and goal-efficiency focus of *AD*, dropping its partly implicit but unmistakeable parallel theme of 'the less public sector activity the better'.

(e) The priority to applied and tested agricultural research appears to be in the process of significant upgrading.

(f) Some concern is again expressed on distribution issues both in terms of political sustainability and human desirability and of production incentives and results.

(g) At least orally – in some negotiations and public discussions, as well as in private – the Bank's staff are much readier than *AD* was to admit they do not know all the answers, nor do they suppose that the same specific answers can apply equally (or in some cases at all) to each of its 40-odd SSA members.

That is a not insignificant set of changes. Unfortunately it leaves the *AD* strategy and agenda seriously undermined without providing a coherent alternative or set of alternatives. Further, it has been reflected only partially and unevenly in Bank relations with SSA members. Some (not all) negotiations still seem based on the premise that *AD* is absolute revealed wisdom.[45]

Efforts toward alternative construction lie outside the scope of this chapter but have begun to appear from several sources: northern applied academic (often linked to advice to aid agencies)[46], African continental bodies[47] and African non-governmental organisations and scholars.[48] These accept *AD*'s premises that structural transformation – following initial consolidation – is needed and that achieving it requires both austerity and clear priorities in resource use. They are, fairly uniformly, critical of *AD*'s emphasis on primary export-led growth, unleashing the private sector (as opposed to providing more incentives and less purposeless regulation) and reducing (rather than prioritising and restructuring) the role of the state and of state-owned enterprises. In particular they seek to look more closely at particular national contexts clearly believing that direct application of regional general principles to specific cases without thorough selection and adaptation will chop societies and economies to fit an externally designed and warped procrustean bed.


A CONCLUSION ADVOCATING MORE DIALOGUE

The preceding assessment of *Accelerated Development* – and particularly of its *Agenda* – may seem highly critical. It is meant to be. The report's political economic world-view is incomplete, contentious, flawed and, in places, internally contradictory. Therefore, it is not – as the preceding section suggests the Bank might now tacitly agree – a complete or safe guide to action. Further, the report's overly self-confident style and tendency to instruct (or hector), rather than inform or advise Africans and African leaders appears radically inconsistent with its own endorsement of participation, with the reality that only Africans are primarily concerned with the well-being of Africa, and with the brutal fact that outsiders can walk away from the results of wrong decisions (including those taken on their advice) while Africans have to live with them. They have the right to take basic decisions about their own destiny and only they can implement *any* agenda no matter how strong its internal logic or the external pressures for its verbal acceptance.

However, *AD* cannot be written off either as trivial or as totally wrong. It has begun to concentrate attention – both in SSA and more generally – on the need to concentrate attention on strategic reformulation. 'Steady as you go' is hardly an adequate navigational policy on a ship demonstrably in danger of sinking; more of the same seems a counsel of despair given the actual results of 1979–80 (both as to attempted accelerated growth on the same lines and in respect of orthodox retrenchment on those advocated by the IMF). Further, as cited above, a number of elements in its analysis and apparent priority lists and many of its specific proposals are both valid and applicable in at least many SSA countries. To deny this and to seek to return to the strategies and policies of 1976–79 (however appropriate some of them may have been then, or however necessary retention of *some* strands in them may be now) would be even more rigidly ideological, pedantic, captious or blind than the most egregious elements in the report.

The pressing need is for further data creation and collection, more analysis and fuller dialogue on what the strategic, programme, policy and project implications of that data and analysis are. The marginal utility of more general critiques of *AD* – except for new, and especially new African, audiences – is probably declining rapidly. What remains critical is to select what is valuable from it and to reconstruct with additional elements to create coherent, viable, economically practicable and humanly acceptable strategies, policies, programmes, and projects for specific SSA countries for particular time periods (beginning with the present, not starting after consolidation is assumed to have been achieved). It should be stressed that for both normative and operational reasons that is a task which must be carried out primarily by Africans in Africa. The problem to date is not so much that there is absolutely too much outside contribution (albeit the tone of some of it is open to grave objections) but that there is too little African or genuinely joint African/outsider contribution. Ultimately that is a weakness only Africans can remedy but more serious attention to their work, cooperation with their efforts (including finance for research and conferences) and full acceptance that well-meaning academic and international agency paternalism or would-be Platonic Guardianship is as normatively indefensible and ultimately damaging to both sides as any other form of colonialism or neo-colonialism, are contributions which they can expect.

NOTES

1. World Bank, *Accelerated Development in Sub-Saharan Africa: An Agenda for Action* (Washington, DC: World Bank, 1981) p. 24.
2. African critics – with an uncomfortable degree of accuracy – say they are viewed with reservation both globally and in Africa because they are African. Whether this is a variant of 'if you are so smart why aren't you rich', is based on cultural or racial prejudice, or/and is simply because Africans (including African writers and their work) are – like women – so often 'invisible' to many analysts and administrators, is less clear, but the results are almost equally unsatisfactory whatever the cause.
3. See World Bank, *World Development Report 1983* (New York: Oxford University Press, 1983) especially p. 38; African Centre for Monetary Studies/UNCTAD, *African External Debt and Development: A Review and Analysis*, Consultancy report by S. Griffith-Jones and R. H. Green (mimeo, 1984).
4. World Bank, *Accelerated Development*, pp. 3–4.

5. A process which is not in itself at all unusual for international agency reports nor about which (as opposed to what changes were made at whose instigation) the Bank makes any secret. Professor Berg has distinct and growing reservations about the final version of his draft.

6. As illustrated by the opening quotation and by P. Ndegwa's paper 'Accelerated Development in Sub-Saharan Africa: A Review Article', in P. Ndegwa, L. P. Mureithi and R. H. Green (eds), *Report of Symposium on Development Options for Africa in the 1980s and Beyond* (Nairobi: Society for International Development (Kenya) Nairobi, 1983).

7. One co-author has experienced this process from both sides – in academia and government and as a consultant to international agencies. It has its virtues in reaching agreed action programmes but substantial costs so far as rigour of analysis, clarity of priorities and internal consistency are incurred.

8. This is to a degree inevitable in attempting to work from concrete analysis to organising principles and back to concrete proposals for a large number of cases within severe space and time constraints. In *AD* it is exacerbated by the Bank's apparent desire to avoid any serious analysis of the nature of the very distinct political, social and economic divergences among African states. This is understandable but leaves the political and the contextual out of political economy in a way that Smith, Ricardo and Mill would have found just as unsatisfactory as Marx and Engels.

9. One co-author has been in several country negotiations with the Bank on precisely these issues. Indeed on one occasion he was – wrongly he now believes – a supporter of its proposal to create a *de facto* parallel administration.

10. This is not to say that the Bank was either alone, careless or ill-intentioned. One co-author must acknowledge having supported advice from the Bank he now perceives as erroneous while in Tanzania (e.g. early 1970s cuts in grower prices for maize, selecting tea and tobacco as 'growth pole' crops). Nor is it to argue that the Bank necessarily has a worse track record than other sources of external advice. However, it has been influential and in a number of cases instrumental in securing the adoption of policies, the creation of institutions and the implementation of projects now severely and rightly criticised.

11. See African Centre for Monetary Studies/UNCTAD, *African External Debt and Development*, Section B-1 for fuller elaboration.

12. See, for example, Z. A. and J. M. Konczacki, *An Economic History of Tropical Africa* (London: Cass, 1977); and E. A. G. Robinson, *Economic Development for Africa South of the Sahara* (London: Macmillan, 1965).

13. This is true of any broad political economic perspective and of strategies derived from them. The same point could be made about Marxian, pragmatic welfare captalist (e.g. Keynesian or Brandtian) and neo-social democratic (e.g. basic needs) perspectives, albeit in these the public interest (or externalities surrounding self-interest) and distribution have greater weight than in neo-liberalism.

14. World Bank, *Sub-Saharan Africa: Progress Report on Development Prospects and Programs* (Washington, DC: World Bank, 1983).

15. For an independent analysis of Malawi see C. Harvey, 'The Case of Malawi', IDS *Bulletin*, vol. 14 (January 1983) no. 1.

16. To define only inherently loss-making functions as appropriate for private enterprise creates logical problems for using profitability as a test of their efficiency.
17. World Bank, *World Development Report 1983*, p. 38.
18. This is hardly a severe criticism – any list of 500 specific proposals (including any by the present authors) will contain some which are not fully thought out, subject to negative side-effects, impracticable, eccentric and/or plain dotty.
19. See United Nations International Children's Emergency Fund (UNICEF), *State of the World's Children Report 1984* (New York: Oxford University Press, 1984) (extended versions of country and continent studies published in *World Development*, March 1984); see especially R. H. Green and H. W. Singer, 'Sub-Saharan Africa in Depression: The Impact on the Welfare of Children' in this issue.
20. An extreme, but not unique example is Tanzania which had fairly clear sectoral priorities and strategies in most sectors from 1969 on, but none in respect of exports until 1981. Before then there was a clutter of micro-initiatives, projections seeking to estimate (not manage or alter) future export earnings and isolated statements neither welded into a coherent, articulated strategy nor receiving serious political backing. This contrasts oddly with very different approaches to import management and foreign exchange budgeting/allocation – a contrast much more widely perceptible than only in Tanzania.
21. For example, the Ivory Coast whose export volume has stagnated since 1979, and Malawi whose plantation-centred strategy is literally starved of resources to the verge of bankruptcy.
22. In respect of manufacturing see M. Godfrey, 'Export orientation and structural adjustment in sub-Saharan Africa', IDS *Bulletin*, vol. 14 (January 1983) no. 1.
23. World Bank, *World Development Report 1982*, (New York: Oxford University Press, 1982) p. 29.
24. World Bank, *World Development Report 1983*, p. 69, *praises* Brazil for having provided uncoordinated special incentives to enterprises in response to their pressures and influence within a broad import-substitution, and subsequently export-promotion, strategy for manufacturing.
25. This is often disguised by the fact that senior personnel have to do their own middle-level work (or fail to function because it is not done) which gives the first impression that the gap is at or near the top, rather than in the middle of the continuum from unskilled worker to senior manager.
26. See, for example, IDS *Bulletin*, vol. 14 (January 1983) no. 1.
27. See C. Colclough, 'Are African Governments as Unproductive as the *Accelerated Development Report* Implies?' IDS *Bulletin*, vol. 14 (January 1983) no. 1.
28. See Godfrey, 'Export orientation and structural adjustment'.
29. R. H. Green, 'Consolidation and Accelerated Development for African Agriculture', African Studies Association 1983 Conference Paper (University of Michigan, microfilm).
30. See M. Lipton, 'African Agricultural Development: the EEC's New Role', *Development Policy Review*, vol. 1 (May 1983) no. 1, for a fuller exposition

albeit in this article he is urging EEC action because of its focus on EEC/ACP Convention issues.

31. See Allison 'What Alternatives for Women in Africa' in Ndegwa, Mureithi and Green (eds), *Report of Symposium*, for a fuller discussion of *AD*'s implications for women.

32. In fairness, it seems unlikely that *AD*'s final editorial group ever explicitly worked out their document's implicit distribution strategy.

33. '... this long run is a misleading guide to current affairs. In the long run we are all dead.' (*A Tract on Monetary Reform*, London: Macmillan, p. 65.) This is a general criticism of all 'turnpike' and Mahalanobis models pushed to long-term growth maximisation conclusions.

34. See I. Livingstone, 'Choices for Rural and Urban Development' in Ndegwa, Mureithi and Green (eds), *Report of Symposium*, for a fuller exposition with special reference to Malawi.

35. For a much fuller exposition see D. de Gaspar, C. Espirito, and R. H. Green (eds), *World Hunger: A Christian Reappraisal* (Geneva: World Council of Chuches, 1982).

36. See Livingstone, 'Choices for Rural and Urban Development'.

37. See J. Carlsson (ed.), *Recession in Africa* (Uppsala: Scandinavian Institute of African Studies, 1983).

38. *World Development Report 1983*, pp. 57–63.

39. World Bank, *Sub-Saharan Africa: Progress Report*.

40. Ibid.; Please and Amoako, Chapter 6 in this volume; *World Development Report 1982* and *1983 passim*; as well as conversations with bank personnel provide the basis for this list.

41. United Nations Economic Commission for Africa, *ECA and Africa's Development 1983*–2008 (Addis Ababa: ECA, 1983).

42. World Bank, *Sub-Saharan Africa: Progress Report*.

43. *World Development Report 1983*, pp. 57–63.

44. Ibid., Part II, 'Management in Development'.

45. This comment is based on direct experience and on discussions with African officials by one of the co-authors.

46. For example, IDS *Bulletin*, vol. 14 (January 1983) no. 1; Carlsson, *Recession in Africa*.

47. For example, *ECA and Africa's Development* and the 1983 Tunis Seminar of the African Centre for Monetary Studies on External Debt, a majority of the papers for which, and all but a handful of the participants in which, were African.

48. For example, Ndegwa, Mureithi and Green (eds), *Report of Symposium*, also with an African majority of papers and participants.

# 4 Collective Self-Reliance or Collective Self-Delusion: Is the Lagos Plan a Viable Alternative?

## JOHN RAVENHILL

Africa's initial official response to the World Bank's *Accelerated Development* (*AD*) was to assert that 'the Report was not only unnecessary but was antagonistic to the Lagos Plan of Action.[1] Claims made in *AD* that it 'builds on' the Lagos Plan (*LPA*) adopted in April 1980 by the Organisation of African Unity (OAU), and that its prescriptions provide the necessary short-run policy foundation for achieving the medium- and long-term goals of the *LPA* have been rejected by academics and representatives of African governments alike.[2] According to the Secretariats of Africa's three principal international organisations – the OAU, the Economic Commission for Africa, and the African Development Bank – the export-oriented and agriculture-based strategy of *AD* is in fundamental conflict with the internally-oriented and inter-sector-based strategy of the *LPA*. Rather than the short-term prescriptions of *AD* supporting the objectives of the *LPA*, the Secretariats asserted that the *LPA* specifies its own alternative 'series of short- to medium-term activities'.[3] For Africa's international organisations, at least, the *LPA* represents an indigenous alternative to the World Bank's report. Whether it is a viable alternative is the subject of this chapter.

In contrast to the Bank's report, the Lagos Plan has been afforded remarkably little critical scrutiny. A number of factors probably have contributed to this. First, there has been an understandable reticence on

85

the part of non-Africans to criticise a document that has been proclaimed as Africa's preferred development strategy and become the flagship of Africa's continental bureaucracies. Commentators are faced by something of a damned-if-you-do, damned-if-you-don't dilemma: a perceived failure to pay serious attention to African plans renders them vulnerable to accusations of paternalism and even racism;[4] similar charges are levelled, however, at those whose criticisms are regarded as displaying a lack of sympathy with African aspirations. Second, there is undoubtedly a perception that the World Bank is better placed than the OAU to influence the course of Africa's development in the remainder of this century given its own substantial resources, its increasingly close working relationship with the IMF, and its influence over other multilateral and national donor agencies. In terms of its potential for effecting change, *AD* simply is, for many, a document of greater import than the *LPA*. Finally, the nature of the Lagos Plan itself tends to deter criticism: its lack of specificity sometimes makes the critic's job a frustrating exercise in shadow-boxing.

If the *LPA* is to be considered a viable alternative to the Bank's report, similar criteria must be applied in evaluating the two documents. As Green and Allison argued in their assessment of the *Agenda*, it is not the acceptance or rejection of one or more specific proposals that is the crucial criterion but an evaluation of the overall themes embodied in the document. As is true of the Bank's report, a number of weaknesses result from the manner in which the *LPA* was drafted. In this instance the usual complexities of committee work were complicated by rivalries between the OAU and ECA that resulted in two separate drafts of the plan being presented to African ministers.[5] Their hurried fusion is evident in the unevenness of the published plan; meanwhile the rivalry between the ECA and OAU is seen in the preoccupation of the ECA in various chapters with asserting that it should be the lead agency in the plan's implementation. And like the World Bank's *Agenda*, the plan suffers from its adoption of the continent as its unit of analysis: applicability of its proposals to any one country inevitably is questionable.[6]

More fundamentally, the *LPA* is vulnerable to four principal lines of criticism: a failure to specify practical policy measures that might make a realistic contribution towards the attainment of its long-term objectives; a failure to consider the implications of a self-reliant strategy -- particularly the question of how such a strategy would be financed; an absence, analogous to that in the Bank's *Agenda* of any consideration of the political obstacles to implementation; and, most importantly, an unjustified faith in the ECA's long-proclaimed objective of establishing an African Common Market as a *deus ex machina* for Africa's economic woes.

The principal theme of the *LPA* is the need for Africa's future development to be based on collective self-reliance. This was a logical response to what the plan's preamble terms the 'unfulfilled promises of global development strategies'. Few African countries are in a position to take effective unilateral action to improve the terms on which they conduct their external economic relations. Action in global fora to engineer a new international economic order has failed to realise the pay-offs that had been anticipated – especially for the world's least developed countries. Meanwhile, the real value of aid from international agencies and national donors has fallen far short of needs and expectations. Strategies based on export-led development appear to have largely failed. And attempts to construct special relationships with the continent's former colonial powers through the Lomé Conventions have not brought the benefits anticipated.[7] Almost by default, collective self-reliance appeared attractive. For economies as open and thus as vulnerable to externally induced disturbances as those of Africa, a greater degree of self-reliance makes good economic as well as political sense.

Few would disagree with the vast majority of the objectives listed in the Lagos Plan, or with its general thrust that greater self-reliance is a worthwhile means and end. As a statement of desirable objectives the plan for the most part is admirable; as a blueprint for guiding African governments towards their attainment it leaves much to be desired. What is at issue is not so much the desirability of the stated goals but their feasibility and the failure of the plan to outline the policies necessary to bring about their realisation. Notably absent from the plan are detailed policy proposals, any discussion of the compatibility of the various objectives listed and linkages between them, and a realistic appraisal of potential costs and possible sources of finance. If Lagos was to provide the credible alternative to the short-term prescriptions of the World Bank that the Secretariats claimed, then it would need to specify explicit short- to medium-term measures on which the ultimate objective of an African Economic Community could be constructed. Despite the Secretariats' statement to the contrary and the fact that at least two of the chapters – agriculture and transport – are primarily concerned with the 1981–85 period, concrete proposals of this type are notably lacking. The plan offers almost no signposts to help Africa escape from its present morass.

Rather than representing a plan of action, a blueprint for Africa's development, the *LPA* too often resembles a mammoth shopping list – ranging from the provision of maternity benefits to the acquisition of nuclear power stations – with no ranking of the various desired objectives, no price tag, and no conception of the possible trade-offs between one sector and another. The plan states (p. 122), for instance, that 'For the 1980s emphasis should be given to the development of agriculture and agro-based industries, development of socio-economic infrastructure, cooperation, eradication of mass poverty, unemployment, underemployment and the satisfaction of basic needs'. How these worthy objectives are to be simultaneously achieved is not spelt out.

Cynics would note that there are obvious reasons why the plan has greater appeal to African governments than the prescriptions of the Bank. Unlike the latter, the plan avoids discussion of most of the difficult policy choices currently faced by African countries. Rather than listing explicit policy measures, it relies instead on exhortation, being replete with vague phrases such as 'Steps should be taken', 'all Member States should adopt necessary measures', and such meaningless and largely tautological statements as, 'The set-up of agricultural production should be based on adequate and realistic agrarian reform programmes consistent with political and social conditions prevailing in the respective countries. An improved organization of agricultural production must be given priority so as to increase agricultural production and productivity' (p. 13). Who could object to this proposal when the content of these agrarian reform programmes is nowhere detailed?

Adopting the exhortations of the plan forces governments to make no hard choices. The very fact that the plan ostensibly covers a long time frame – to the year 2000 – makes it easy for governments to make a nominal commitment to its objectives with little fear of being called upon to take effective action towards their implementation. Also attractive for African leaders is the emphasis that the plan, unlike the Bank's *Agenda*, places on inherited problems and hostile external forces as the primary causes of Africa's economic difficulties. A legacy of exploitation during the colonial period has been compounded, the plan asserts, by continuing exploitation 'carried out through neo-colonialist external forces which seek to influence the economic policies and directions of African states' (p. 7). There is no room here for acknowledgement of faulty domestic policies: 'Africa, despite all efforts made by its leaders, remains the least developed continent' (p. 7). Like many populist documents,[8] the plan misrepresents the development experience of other areas in claiming that Africa is peculiarly disadvantaged: 'The industrialized countries developed smoothly over the centuries' (p. 79).

In a document of over 130 pages there is a staggering absence of discussion of such fundamental issues as exchange rate policy, appropriate tariff levels to encourage efficiency in import-substituting industry, and the need for increased domestic savings in order to finance proposed development expenditure. Indeed, the plan pays little attention to the practical implications of adopting a self-reliant development strategy. Self-reliance, itself, is not defined in any detail beyond the 'basic guidelines' outlined in the preamble to the plan. These state that 'Africa's huge resources must be applied principally to meet the needs and purposes of its people'; development and growth are to be based on 'a combination of Africa's considerable natural resources, her entrepreneurial, managerial and technical resources and her markets (restructured and expanded), to serve her people'. Africa, the plan continues, must map out its own strategy for development and 'cultivate the virtue' of self-reliance: 'This is not to say that the continent should totally cut itself off from outside contributions. However, these outside contributions should only supplement our own effort: they should not be the mainstay of our development' (p. 8).

For the most part, however, the plan appears to be little more than a plea for externally-financed self-reliance. Rather than meeting the costs of development from internally-generated resources, international donors are expected to foot the bill. Readers are informed that 'Member States consider that they are owed a massive and appropriate contribution by the developed countries to the development of Africa' (p. 19). Elsewhere the plan calls for an immediate substantial increase in overseas development assistance, and urges states to seek funding on an increased scale from international agencies (p. 71). Regardless of the desirability of increased international support for Africa, it is surprising that the plan gives no consideration to the potential incompatibility of a greater reliance on international agencies (and probable subjection to some form of conditionality) with self-reliance in general, and internally-determined priorities in particular. Of the two programmes for which the document provides costing estimates, African states are urged to fund 'at least 50 per cent' of the proposed $21.4 billion expenditure on agriculture for the 1980–85 period from local resources – a wildly optimistic proposition especially when viewed in the context of the other sector, transport and communications, for which the plan provides cost estimates. African governments provided only $155 000 (less than 0.002 per cent) of the $6.3 billion pledged for this programme at a conference held in November 1979 (p. 80).

Aid is the plan's preferred method of financing its proposals rather than internally-generated funds through increased exports or domestic savings. There is in fact no discussion in the plan of Africa's urgent need for increased exports. Export, indeed, almost seems to be a taboo word. Besides the statement in the preamble that 'Africa's almost total reliance on the export of raw materials must change' (p. 8), it is difficult to locate the word elsewhere in the document. A section on international trade merely exhorts African countries to diversify trade patterns on both geographical and structural dimensions. Here the *LPA* appears in danger of throwing the proverbial baby out with the bathwater. As Green argues cogently, a self-reliant strategy of development is import-intensive especially in its early years.[9] While this need not necessarily justify the particular path of export-led growth favoured by the *Agenda* it does suggest that if exports are not boosted a self-reliance strategy will at best be vulnerable to all manner of interference from foreign creditors and donors, and in a worst-case scenario will simply collapse as a result of insufficient import capacity.


MUDDLED SECTORAL PRIORITIES

The unevenness of the *LPA* is most obvious in its treatment of the various sectoral programmes. Trade and finance, for instance, is afforded only 7 pages whereas science and technology receives 27. This is a perhaps unavoidable consequence of the plan having been pieced together by various agencies and committees; some of its chapters are simply drawn from existing proposals by international agencies, e.g. that on transport and communications relies heavily on the programme for the United Nations Transport and Communications Decade in Africa. Such unevenness in itself would not necessarily be a problem if all chapters provided a coherent and practical set of policy proposals. Unfortunately, they do not.

Agriculture is one of the best – or worst – examples of this. Although the plan at least tacitly acknowledges the critical importance of the sector to Africa's future by placing this chapter at the beginning of the document, its treatment, afforded only 8 pages, is at best superficial. Although there is reference to the present crisis in African agriculture there is no detailed discussion of its causes or of past policy failures. As noted above, this chapter is particularly prone to tautologies and largely meaningless exhortations. Member States, for example, are recommended to 'formulate and apply effective and coherent policies to ensure that prices of farm inputs and farm produce provide an adequate incentive for increasing food production, particularly by small farmers, while safeguarding the interests of the poorer consumers at the same time' (p. 15). How these potentially incompatible objectives are to be reconciled is, once again, left unaddressed. A similar possible incompatibility between desires to increase real agricultural incomes and to arrest the rural–urban drift is similarly glossed over. The sentence quoted represents the only reference in the plan to farm pricing policies, an area where the necessity for effective change was one of the principal thrusts of the Bank's *Agenda*, a recommendation frequently repeated by agricultural economists. Again the difficult policy dilemmas faced by African governments are sidestepped in a litany of platitudes. This neglect of practical policy measures is all the more damaging in that an agricultural revolution is the essential prerequisite for further progress towards industrial development in Africa.

Industrialisation is very much the plan's panacea. The years 1980–90 are proclaimed 'Industrial Development Decade in Africa'; Member States are urged to achieve the Lima target of raising Africa's share of world industrial production to 2 per cent by the year 2000. A 1 per cent share of world production is targeted for 1985 (again a wildly optimistic projection) with priority to be given to the establishment of food and agro-industries, building, metallurgical, mechanical, electrical and electronic, chemical, forest and energy industries. Once again, few could dispute the desirability of attaining the targets in the chapter's (unpriced) shopping list. But, regrettably, the chapter fails to outline an appropriate policy framework that might help to realise the objectives. Nor is there any discussion of past policies and their contribution (positive or otherwise) to the pursuit of industrial development on the continent. Much is expected once more from external sources: cooperation with developed countries 'should lead . . . to a massive transfer of resources to finance industrial projects'; 'inventions, patents and technical know-how should be made available freely by industrialized countries' (p. 26).

The plan's chapter on transport and communications is one of its most detailed. Twelve sub-sectors – ranging from postal services to air transport – are examined and 550 projects, for which costing is provided, are identified as ready for immediate implementation. This certainly represents an improvement on the vague aspirations expressed elsewhere in the document. Some doubt may be cast on the priorities in this sector, however. Emphasis in the road programme is given to the planned trans-African highway – a project that has come to have the same symbolic import for the ECA as the Cape to Cairo railway had for the British colonial power. Whether this represents the wisest investment of scarce resources in the short term is surely debatable; there are much greater needs for local feeder roads to enable agricultural producers to transport their crops to market. Quite remarkably, the section on roads fails to mention the urgent need for rehabilitation of existing links, which many donor agencies now perceive as the top priority for African countries.

Education and population are two areas in which the plan once again backs away from controversy and the concomitant hard policy choices. In this regard the plan's section on education is certainly no worse than and, arguably, is an improvement on the equivalent part of the Bank's *Agenda*, for it does recognise the need to give priority to scientific and technical education (whereas the *Agenda*'s comments on the inefficiency of technical in comparison with general secondary schooling are ambiguous at best, and potentially damaging in sending the wrong signals – support for a traditional academic curriculum rather than one which is technically-based). Nevertheless, there is virtually nothing in the plan's chapter regarding the specific skills required in African economies over the next two decades, the need for universities to direct their efforts primarily towards meeting these skill shortages rather than continuing to overproduce liberal arts graduates, the type of primary curriculum which provides basic literacy and relevant technical training rather than serving principally to increase demands for secondary education, and the urgent necessity of reducing costs in the educational sector.

All of Africa's development problems are of course exacerbated by the continent's exceptionally high levels of population growth. Populaion is given merely one page in the plan. Although it notes that 'current levels of fertility and mortality are of concern' the plan sidesteps the controversial policy questions by merely commenting that 'resultant high rates of growth have implications for meeting the needs of majority [sic] of the population' (p. 125). Similarly, the plan's chapter on women, although itself to be welcomed as a sign of a new sensitivity to women's issues on the part of the OAU, is silent on the issue of their right of access to birth control.

Running throughout the plan are proposals for new national, regional, and continental institutions and organisations. Indeed, the plan often gives the impression of being primarily a call by planners for more planning. Despite the statement that 'no new multinational institutions should be created unless their creation has been thoroughly examined and after the possibilities offered by national institutions, of existing multinational institutional ones [sic], have been fully considered', few of the chapters refrain from encouraging the establishment of yet more layers of bureaucracy. Proposals include an African Association of State Trade Organisations, an African monetary fund, an African Mutual Guarantee and Solidarity Fund, an African Energy Development Fund, an African Energy Commission, an African Nuclear Energy Agency, an African Regional Centre for Consultancy and Industrial Management Services, in addition to a Regional Solar Energy Centre, a Centre for Science and Technology for Development, National Water Committees, and ministries for Manpower Development.

This call for a proliferation of institutions is put forward despite the plan's acknowledgement that:

> The various institutions that have been established, all at the request of African governments, in fields such as natural resources, science and technology, industry, training and human resources and transport and communications, have all suffered from the ill effects of lack of follow-up in the implementation of political decisions. This lack of effective follow-up finds expression in various ways, the commonest one being that after pressing for the establishment of an institution, many African governments, even after having approved the legal document setting up the institution concerned, either fail to become members of the institution or, if they do, fail to give it adequate financial and material support. The net result is that the growth of such an institution is stifled, disillusion sets in and the collective self-reliance of African countries is undermined. (p. 91)

African governments have clearly been disappointed with achievements of the multitude of regional and continental institutions that have already been established (at least 35 were in existence in 1984). Why they should seriously consider the creation of many more, and why there is any reason to expect that, if created, these would enjoy more support than those currently in existence, is discussed nowhere in the plan. Institutional proliferation on the continent has produced a number of under-funded, ineffective organisations which appear to be regarded by participating governments primarily as a dumping ground for disgruntled national civil servants. Meanwhile, the proliferation of meetings places excessive strain on already stretched resources and frequently diverts attention from the work of the more effective organisations. What is needed is not a further increase in the number of institutions but a qualitative improvement in the workings of existing bodies.

This failure of African governments to go beyond the rhetorical in their support for regional and continental institutions and organisations has obvious implications for the centrepiece of the Lagos strategy: the creation of an African Economic Community by the year 2000.

## AN AFRICAN ECONOMIC COMMUNITY: NEITHER NECESSARY NOR SUFFICIENT

Of all the proposals listed in the Lagos Plan, African governments pledged themselves explicitly in the document's Final Act to the attainment of but one – the establishment of 'an African Common Market as a first step towards the creation of an African Economic Community'. According to the ECA, 'no industrial take-off will be possible unless the envisaged degree of regional and sub-regional economic cooperation is achieved. This means, *inter alia*, that an African Economic Community should materialise by the year 2000, which, in turn, implies that current efforts to forge sub-regional common markets through the MULPOC (Multilateral Programming and Operational Centres) must bear fruit'.[10] So central is the proposed common market to the plan's prescription of collective self-reliance that, as Browne and Cummings note, 'without regional integration the *LPA* collapses as a concept, so no allowance is made for failure in achieving it'.[11] As with so many other elements of the plan, the document fails to provide any rationale for the proposal. Nor is there any reference to the difficulties that past integrative schemes in Africa have encountered or of measures that might be enacted in order to minimise these problems. Continental economic integration remains an act of faith – a throwback to the longstanding ECA ambition of constructing an African scheme to rival that of its Latin American sister, the ECLA.

Much of the faith in regional integration appears to rest on the belief that South–South trade in general, and intra-African trade in particular, can and will occur on a different basis to the 'unequal exchange' that is perceived as a characteristic of contemporary North–South commercial interactions. Biersteker's quotation from an official Tanzanian publication provides an excellent illustration of this aspiration: a call to 'devise methods of international economic exchange and cooperation which are different from those at present operating'.[12] To this is added a more recent argument, popularised by Sir Arthur Lewis, that greater South–South trading is the only means of providing the expanded markets that Southern countries seek now that the industrialised countries of the North face a period of recession and, at best, rates of growth substantially below those experienced before 1970.

Both arguments are of dubious validity. Even if Northern markets expand at a rate that is slower than that of their Southern equivalents, the *absolute size* of the additional import capacity created will in all probability continue to exceed that of new markets in the South. There are few signs of a reversal of the 'widening gap' between North and South except for a handful of newly-industrialising countries. Nor is there any reason to believe that difficulties in their extra-continental trade will necessarily lead African countries to turn to regional self-reliance. Experience from the European Community suggests exactly the opposite: the more difficult the external economic environment, the less willing the member states have been to seek a regional solution to their economic problems.[13]

As for the first argument in favour of South–South trade, it rests on a 'second image' fallacy. There is no more reason to believe that trade between weaker and stronger parties will be any less conflictual merely because the countries concerned are located in the South than that international conflict would be ended should countries come to share a capitalist, socialist, or any other ideology. Why an impoverished African country would feel that trade is less unequal when it imports from its slightly better-off neighbour rather than purchasing the goods (probably at lower cost) from a Northern trading partner is unclear – and certainly unjustified in terms of the history of squabbles over the distribution of gains in Third World integrative schemes.

A World Bank study of South–South trade provides some interesting evidence in support of a sceptical position. First, contrary to some assertions, there has been little increase over the past two decades in the proportion of Southern exports going to other countries in the South, if capital-surplus oil-exporting countries are excluded. South–South trade simply has not grown in significance for most countries. Second, the market share of non-oil developing countries in the total exports of the South's most dynamic sector – manufacturing – has *decreased* steadily over the last two decades. Similarly, an increasing share of exports of capital goods from developing countries has gone to industrialised countries. Third, the most dynamic sector of South–South trade is in primary products – in large part attributable to the rapid industrialisation of a number of resource-poor countries and their growing imports from their less fortunate neighbours.[14]

When the 'South' is disaggregated by income level, a second study found that the countries with a per capita income above $1000 (fewer than one-third of the 90 developing countries included in the study) accounted for approximately two-thirds of South–South trade and more than three-quarters of total Southern exports to other developing countries. Whereas more than half of their exports to other Southern countries consisted of manufactures, for the low-income countries (less than $500 per capita) raw materials and minerals accounted for more than 70 per cent of their exports to other developing countries. As Adams comments: 'seen in relation to differences in the levels of economic development of the countries concerned, the pattern of South–South trade presents a virtual mirror image (if in a reduced form) of the pattern of world trade as a whole'.[15] Inequalities in international trade thus are replicated in South–South trading: the more developed export mainly manufactured goods while the lower income countries remain in their traditional role as suppliers of primary products. Why this pattern of trade should be any less unequal than that conducted on a North–South basis remains to be demonstrated.

A leap of faith is evident in the arguments of some commentators who believe that disillusion with outward-oriented strategies will cause African leaders to look instead to collective self-reliance. In reality, however, few countries currently attempting to pursue an outward-oriented strategy are likely to be convinced that even an enlarged regional market will offer better opportunities for their exports, or even sufficient compensation for the constraints on policy autonomy necessary for successful regional integration. While there is un-doubtedly some residual goodwill arising from the 'spirit' of Pan Africanism, the fate of Nkrumah's proposals for continental unity in the 1960s demonstrated that utilitarian calculations will prevail over emotional appeals. The traditional case in support of regional integration among African countries is as valid as ever – low incomes and small populations make for markets of insufficient size to realise economies of scale. Yet this argument also contains a fallacy – essentially a levels of analysis problem. What is potentially good for the region – or even continent – when taken as a whole need not necessarily be to the advantage, particularly in the short term, of any one of the constituent countries. This is a reflection of the classic international relations dilemma that arises from the divergence of short-term individual rationality from long-term collective rationality. For any single country, the potential benefits to be derived from integration rest not on an *a priori* assertion but on a careful consideration of the merits of any particular scheme.

There are three principal forms that regional cooperation in Africa might take: largely unregulated customs unions/common markets; common markets with industrial planning (and, possibly, explicit counter-dependency objectives); and more limited schemes that focus on one or more areas of functional cooperation. Traditionally, African regional cooperation has taken the first of these forms, unregulated customs unions. Problems that have arisen in these schemes have been extensively documented and need only be briefly summarised here.[16] Foremost among them is the apparently inevitable tendency for benefits arising from regional cooperation, particularly import-substituting industries, to accrue disproportionately to the more developed countries in a region (especially when these countries not only offer an apparently more hospitable political climate for foreign investment but also generous economic incentives). A free market works all too well in allocating resources to the more efficient – intra-union inequalities tend to become intensified. Less favoured countries often find themselves in a position where they are required to replace imports from third countries with more expensive, heavily protected, imports from their neighbours. High levels of tariffs necessary to protect infant industries do nothing to encourage efficient production; the high-cost manufactures consequently are unable to compete on the world market. Free trade within the region leads to a zero-sum situation with the manufactures of one regional producer displacing domestic production in the market of another – a tendency noted by Robson in the West African Economic Community (CEAO) where the Ivory Coast has gained at the expense of Senegalese industry.[17]

Although the less favoured countries might still expect to benefit in the long term from cooperation, no African government can afford to adopt this time horizon. Perceptions that neighbouring countries have gained a disproportionate share of the benefits from integration usually lead to moves that have the consequence, whether intended or not, of restricting the scope of regional cooperation. Demands for exemptions from responsibilities under the regional arrangements tend to multiply. Non-tariff barriers against neighbouring countries' exports are maintained or reinforced – either unilaterally or as a result of regional agreement (as was the case with the transfer taxes introduced into the East African Community). Duplication of even more inefficient import-substituting plants on a national basis is the result.[18]

Two alternative methods for remedying an imbalance of gains from cooperation are available. The first is to provide monetary compensation to less favoured countries, a measure which in the past has often been calculated with reference to estimated customs revenues foregone. Since few regional organisations in Africa (unlike the EEC) have been provided with independent sources of revenue, compensation is dependent on direct contributions from the relatively more privileged governments in the regional grouping. Such compensation payments are not only politically unpopular but, given the perennial situation of scarcity exacerbated by the contemporary crisis, also pose economic difficulties for the governments concerned. Frequently the result has been that governments have fallen behind in their payments. Even if the mechanism worked smoothly, the provision of monetary compensation is seldom regarded as adequate by recipient countries, however, since they have 'lost' not only customs revenue but the various learning and multiplier effects associated with the establishment of industry.

The alternative is to move beyond the 'negative' integration of removing tariff barriers to construct a regional scheme that includes provision for industrial planning. Through this means the benefits of producing for a larger regional market can be maintained while ensuring that all participating countries share in the import-substituting industry that is created. Planning along these lines would require a coordinated approach to foreign investors; this offers the potential for achieving the counter-dependency objective of improving bargaining positions with external economic actors. For most commentators, regional industrial planning is the only viable option if common markets are to be constructed and maintained.

Considerable doubt must arise, however, over the political feasibility of this alternative. For the more developed states in a region, acceptance of industrial planning would depend on a perception that the gains from the maintenance of free access to regional markets outweigh the potential costs imposed – not only in terms of loss of industries but also in constraints on economic policies – that would probably inhibit their pursuit of an outward-oriented strategy. Regional industrial planning would require a harmonisation of industrial incentives: countries that had previously offered generous treatment of foreign investment in the hope that they would be used as export platforms by transnational corporations might well find that maintentance of these provisions was precluded. For the Ivory Coast, the attractions of the expanded CEAO market have not outweighed those of exporting to the EEC. For Nigeria, even the total ECOWAS market offers only a small increment on its own internal market. Again the experience of the East African Community is instructive: Kenya, the most favoured of the three participants, rejected two attempts at industrial planning as a means of resolving regional imbalances – the Kampala Agreement of 1965 and the Maxwell Stamp Report of 1971.

The third approach to regional integration eschews the grand design of the common market in favour of cooperation in one or more areas. Among such schemes already in operation are various agricultural and research organisations, the two commissions dedicated to the development of the Niger and Senegal rivers and, more recently established, the most ambitious and wide-ranging scheme, the Southern African Development Coordination Conference (SADCC). This approach to integration enjoys a number of advantages over the common market alternative. First, while the potential benefits over the long term may be less than those that might be gained from the successful (a powerful qualifier) establishment of a common market, the immediate costs arising are far fewer. Because of the conscious planning of integrative activities, these schemes are less likely to generate the unintended consequences – the 'backwash' effects of polarised development – associated with customs unions and common markets. Similarly, fewer political costs will be involved: while all integration involves some transfer of decision-making authority 'beyond the nation state', the more narrowly delimited the areas of cooperation, the less they are likely to impinge on national sovereignty, a matter that appears to unduly preoccupy many African governments. Secondly, while all forms of regional cooperation are vulnerable to the instability that characterises relations between African countries, more narrowly based schemes appear better insulated than those based on a grand regional design. Finally, there is some evidence in support of the proposition that external donors look more favourably upon the more narrow, functionalist schemes than on grandiose customs unions and common markets.[19]

A particularly distressing feature of the Lagos Plan is the apparent inability of the OAU and ECA to learn from past failures of efforts at regional cooperation in Africa. In criticising the World Bank for its 'superficial treatment of regional cooperation' the OAU does acknowledge that 'Admittedly failures have occurred in previous associations'. It continues, however, 'it must be recalled that these associations were in concept, design and purpose, not aimed at the problems facing the region today. In other words, the conclusion that should be drawn from these experiences is not that the whole concept of economic cooperation as a possible tool for development should be rejected, but rather that there is an urgent need to assess its present and future role, design, objectives, etc.'[20] Unfortunately, these worthy sentiments found no reflection in the Lagos Plan – as far as it is concerned, the optimum form of integration is that so often attempted without success in Africa – a common market. No consideration is given in the plan to the causes of breakdown of previous customs unions or to the types of measures that might be taken to prevent a repetition by effectively tackling the distribution issue. Possibilities for alternative forms of integration are not acknowledged. Africa, it is deemed, must have a common market by the year 2000 if the wider objectives of the plan are to be realised.

Both the OAU and the ECA cling to the outmoded idea that preferential trade can serve as the motor of economic cooperation and development on the continent. The plan's design for an African Common Market represents yet another attempt to force reluctant governments into an ECA-prescribed path and reflects its bureaucratic, top–down approach.[21] According to the ECA:

> one major reason for the present institutional inadequacy has been the failure of African countries to realize that multinational economic cooperation and integration is an absolute imperative, and this has, in turn, led to a lack of political will to support the creation and sustenance of regional and sub-regional cooperation.[22]

'Lack of political will' is an old red herring in the explanation of failed regional integration schemes. Not being able to accept that the breakdown of these schemes has reflected the discontent of participating governments with their design and results, commentators fall back on accusations of irrational behaviour on the part of member states, an alleged inability to perceive their best interests that leads to an absence of political will.[23]

Previous regional schemes in Africa have failed simply because member governments have heavily discounted potential long-term benefits and have focused instead on the short-run balance of costs and benefits. None of the customs unions or common markets created to date in Africa have devised effective measures of 'positive' integration to offset the loss of tariff revenues and employment opportunities suffered by the less favoured members of the arrangements. And such schemes have remained so fragile and so vulnerable to the endemic political instability of the continent that none of the parties have had good grounds to expect that the promised long-term benefits will be realised. Meaningful regional integration inevitably increases not merely the sensitivity of a country's economy to that of its partners but also its vulnerability as it becomes more reliant on its neighbours for essential inputs. Breakdown of well-developed regional arrangements would impose significant adjustment costs. Successful integration demands a considerable element of mutual trust among the parties, otherwise there is little reason to believe in the future security of the arrangements. Little evidence exists of such mutual trust. African groupings remain bedevilled by border disputes (Upper Volta, for instance, has consistently blocked the re-entry of Mali to the Franc zone because of a border dispute), border closures as a result of domestic economic turmoil and fear of smuggling (Ghana and Nigeria in the last two years), the harbouring of political dissidents from neighbouring countries, etc. In the absence of well-founded expectations for future regional stability, African leaders have good reason for not investing their faith or scarce resources in regional arrangements that add to their economic vulnerability.[24]

Nevertheless, the field of regional integration is one area in which there appears to have been progress in implementing the Lagos Plan: with the signature, in October 1983, of the treaty establishing the Economic Community of the States of Central Africa (ECSCA), all but a handful of sub-Saharan African countries have been induced to participate in one of three ECA-inspired groupings (ECOWAS, ECSCA, or the Preferential Trade Area (PTA) intended to link 18 countries in Eastern and Southern Africa).[25] Prospects for translating these schemes into effective action are, however, remote at best.

These preferential trading agreements, all of which are committed to the creation of regional common markets and, eventually, economic unions, represent the realisation of ECA's grand design for African regional cooperation first proposed in the mid-1960s. Close to 20 years elapsed before ECA was able to convince African governments to sign the agreements, and only the most optimistic would believe that they will be fully implemented in the next 15 years so that an African Economic Community will be achieved by the year 2000. The danger is that they will remain paper organisations whose elaborate treaties become nothing more than a memorial to a faulty development strategy. Although the ECA has been successful in gaining the signatures of most sub-Saharan governments to one or another of its treaties, these amount only to frameworks in which the critical details, such as the means and time schedules for the introduction of a customs union, are left unspecified. This may be claimed to have the advantage of producing flexibility; the obverse is that it may become an excuse for inaction. The treaties are themselves, like the Lagos Plan, more of a statement of goals than the provision of a means of realising desired ends. There are a number of major weaknesses with the ECA's strategy of externally-imposed regionalism:

(a) In emphasising free trade as the engine of integration, and by making the creation of a common market the principal goal, the ECA is demanding that participating states follow a strategy that will impose maximum constraints on decision-making autonomy yet one that offers minimal prospects for the realisation of immediate benefits. This is particularly the case since the treaties that have been signed fail to specify the means through which the less favoured partners in the region will be compensated for the inevitable unequal distribution of gains from integration. At best, the weaker parties are assured that their interests will be taken into account in implementing the arrangements. By aiming at a common market, the ECA is asking for a maximalist commitment by the participating states. Not surprisingly, the negotiation of the treaties has been accompanied by demands by weaker states in the regions for exemptions from the obligation to liberalise trade. Both in psychological and tactical terms, this is an unfortunate approach: a less propitious beginning for a regional enterprise can hardly be imagined. Support for member states for a regional organisation is more likely to be maintained in an arrangement like SADCC where negotiations are for the purpose of positive commitments to projects rather than primarily to seek relief from unwanted obligations.

(b) The ECA's vision is of a top-down self-reliance organised around regions defined with little consultation of the governments concerned. Angola, for instance, a member of SADCC and a country that clearly perceives itself as part of Southern Africa, is assigned by the ECA to its Economic Community of the States of Central Africa. By continuing to employ its own definitions of Africa's sub-regions, the ECA has ensured that conflict will occur with existing regional organisations which it expects to adjust their procedures to accord with those of the ECA-sponsored regional bodies. Relatively well-established groupings like the CEAO have already displayed an understandable reluctance to modify their arrangements in order to accommodate to ECOWAS, an ECA-inspired grouping, the benefits from which are far from assured. CEAO has signalled that it is at best willing to co-exist with the plans of ECOWAS but certainly not to subordinate itself for uncertain gain. Similarly, SADCC members have been unwilling to join the PTA. A further problem with the ECA-defined regions is their size (dictated by the location of the ECA MULPOCs) – the already immense problems of negotiating regional cooperation in Africa are compounded when the intended regional unit as, for example, in the case of the PTA, consists of 18 states as diverse as the Comoros and Zimbabwe.

(c) The ECA-sponsored organisations to date have been overly-centralised, expensive, top-heavy bureaucracies. Planning follows the traditional top–down ECA approach with little initiative being afforded the participating states. Once again, this is scarcely likely to encourage support of the regional institutions: the former President of Nigeria, Shagari, bluntly criticised the extravagance of the ECOWAS Secretariat at its sixth summit conference.[26] Similarly there is a marked disparity between the relative budgets of the PTA and SADCC and their respective achievements.[27]

In brief, the ECA, unlike some of its member states, appears to have learnt nothing from Africa's dismal record of economic integration over the past two decades. It continues to worship at the altar of free trade despite overwhelming evidence that African governments have no faith in common markets as a solution to their economic problems. In the current crisis situation, governments are preoccupied with national economic survival. There is nothing in the ECA's ambitious designs to suggest that they will offer a viable short-term contribution to national economic needs. The ECA regional organisations too often have a Nero-like appearance of fiddling with the technicalities of tariff reductions while national economies disintegrate.[28] Economic cooperation can only proceed in Africa, as elsewhere, on the basis of governments' perceptions of their national interests. Anglin notes that SADCC 'merely coordinates national development plans'.[29] If, however, in the present economic environment, SADCC is successful in this, it is no mean achievement. Gains from this form of regional cooperation may be limited but are preferable to the stalemate that characterises the ECA-inspired institutions. The alternative to co-ordinating national development plans is to have one's grandiose design ignored by national decision-makers. This would appear to be the fate of the Lagos Plan, as the ECA has already acknowledged.[30]

CONCLUSION

This critical appraisal of the *Lagos Plan of Action* should not be perceived as an attempt to denigrate Africa's legitimate aspirations to a better future. It is entirely appropriate that a solution to Africa's current economic problems should be internally generated and that reliance on internal resources should have a prominent place in any strategy. The *Lagos Plan of Action* may correctly be described as 'visionary'. In presenting its idea of an African future characterised by reduced dependence on external actors, of utilising Africa's resources primarily for the needs of its people, and of an integrated African economy, it has served as a useful political foil to the World Bank's *Agenda*. The prior existence of the plan with its radically different projection of the African future undoubtedly has assisted African governments in their negotiations with the Bank.

Unfortunately, the plan is 'visionary' in another sense of the word: a document that is utopian, largely lacking in practicable prescriptions. While the plan has merit as a political statement, it is misleading, indeed, counter-productive to suggest, as have Africa's principal international organisations, that it offers a feasible set of short- and medium-term policy prescriptions comparable to those provided in the *Agenda*.[31] Rather than itself being an agenda for action, the Lagos Plan is primarily a statement of hope. By placing excessive blame on external/historical factors, and in expecting massive external contributions to assist the realisation of its goals, the plan is in danger of diverting governments' attention away from the need for radical domestic economic reform.

This chapter has focused on the plan's prescription for self-reliance through regional integration, since this is regarded by the ECA as central to the realisation of the plan's objectives. As Susan Strange has noted, collective self-reliance has become 'yet another woolly buzz-word'.[32] The Lagos Plan does little to clarify the concept. It appears to display faith in a crude Third Worldism – the belief that trade between unequals will be qualitatively different if conducted among Southern or African countries rather than on a North–South basis. The history of regional integration in Africa, as in other 'Southern' areas, belies this optimism. By now, most African governments, as well as the principal international donor agencies, have woken up to the fact that trade liberalisation is not the best motor for economic cooperation in the Third World. Rather, it has all too often proved to be counter-productive to the legitimate aspiration of increasing self-reliance through regional integration. Unfortunately, the ECA has apparently not yet learnt this lesson. With so many resources invested in the promotion of an African common market, the ECA may prejudice not only its own credibility but also the prospects for regional cooperation on the continent by continuing to unquestioningly pursue this vision.

## NOTES

1. Organisation of African Unity, Council of Ministers, Thirty-Eighth Ordinary Session, 22 February–1 March 1982, *Report of the Secretary-General on the World Bank Report* [CM/1117 (XXXVIII)] (Addis Ababa: OAU, 1982) p. 3, reporting the views expressed by the OAU, ECA, and ADB at the fourth meeting held with the Bank on the report.
2. See, for instance, Green and Allison in Chapter 3. The OAU Secretary General's *Report* provides a systematic comparison of the two documents. See also the very useful monograph by Robert S. Browne and Robert J. Cummings, *The Lagos Plan of Action vs. The Berg Report* (Washington, DC: Howard University African Studies and Research Program, 1984).
3. 'Accelerated Development in Sub-Saharan Africa: An Assessment by OAU, ECA and ADB Secretariats', Annex I to OAU, *Report of the Secretary-General on the World Bank Report*, p. 9.
4. See Green and Allison in Chapter 3.
5. See John Ravenhill, 'The OAU and Economic Cooperation: Irresolute Resolutions' in Yassin El-Ayouty and I. William Zartman (eds), *The OAU After Twenty Years* (New York: Praeger, 1984) pp. 173–92.
6. To some extent this might be perceived as less of a problem for the *LPA* since it couches its objectives in terms of the continent as a whole. On the other hand, no attention is paid to the *distribution* of the proposed improvements in economic capacity among African countries. Unlike the Bank's report, the OAU document refers to the entire continent (with potential concomitant difficulties given the different structures of North African economies). Much to the OAU's annoyance, *AD* dealt only with independent majority-ruled, sub-Saharan Africa, this being symbolised by the blacking out of North Africa, Namibia, and South Africa on the map of Africa on the cover of *AD*.
7. For one case of failed export-led development see Langdon in Chapter 8. See also Henrik Secher Marcussen, 'The Ivory Coast Facing the Economic Crisis', in Jerker Carlsson (ed.), *Recession in Africa* (Uppsala: Scandinavian Institute of African Studies, 1983) pp. 1–27; Lynn Krieger Mytelka, 'The Limits of Export-Led Development: The Ivory Coast's Experience with Manufactures', in John Gerard Ruggie (ed.), *The Antinomies of Interdependence* (New York: Columbia University Press, 1983) pp. 239–70; and Charles Harvey, 'The Case of Malawi', IDS *Bulletin*, vol. 14 (January 1983) no. 1, pp. 45–50. On the disappointments of the Lomé relationship see John Ravenhill, *Collective Clientelism: The Lomé Conventions and North–South Relations* (New York: Columbia University Press, 1985).
8. Gavin Kitching, *Development and Underdevelopment in Historical Perspective* (London: Methuen, 1982) especially pp. 162–3.

9. Reginald H. Green, 'African Economies in the Mid-1980s – "Naught For Your Comfort but that the Waves Grow Higher and the Storms Grow Wilder"', in J. Carlsson (ed.), *Recession in Africa* (Uppsala: Scandinavian Institute of African Studies, 1983) pp. 195 ff.

10. Economic Commission for Africa, *ECA and Africa's Development 1983–2008* (Addis Ababa: ECA, April 1983), p. 89.

11. Browne and Cummings, *The Lagos Plan of Action vs. The Berg Report*, p. 37.

12. See Chapter 9 note 6.

13. Steven Langdon and L; nne K. Mytelka, 'Africa in the Changing World Economy' in Colin Legum *et al.*, *Africa in the 1980s* (New York: McGraw-Hill, 1979) express faith that Africa will choose a self-reliant path. Their argument is criticised in John Ravenhill, 'The Future of EurAfrica' in Timothy M. Shaw and O. Aluko (eds), *Africa Projected* (London: Macmillan, 1985) Chapter 6. On the European experience, see Paul Taylor, *The Limits of European Integration* (New York: Columbia University Press, 1983).

14. Oli Havrylyshyn and Martin Wolf, *Trade Among Developing Countries: Theory, Policy Issues and Principal Trends*, Staff Working Paper No. 479 (Washington, DC: World Bank, 1982). A summary of this paper, 'Promoting trade among developing countries: an assessment', appears in *Finance and Development* (March 1982) pp. 17–21.

15. Nassau A. Adams, 'Towards a Global System of Trade Preferences Among Developing Countries', *Trade and Development*, vol. 4 (1982) pp. 183–204; quotation is on p. 199.

16. See, for instance, John Ravenhill, 'Regional Integration and Development in Africa: Lessons from the East African Community', *Journal of Commonwealth and Comparative Politics*, vol. XVII (November, 1979) no. 4, pp. 227–46; Constantine V. Vaitsos, 'Crisis in Regional Economic Cooperation (Integration) among Developing Countries: A Survey', *World Development*, vol. 6 (June 1978) no. 6, pp. 710–69; Lynn K. Mytelka, 'The Salience of Gains in Third-World Integrative Systems', *World Politics*, vol. 25 (January 1973) no. 2, pp. 236–50.

17. Peter Robson, *Integration, Development and Equity* (London: Allen & Unwin, 1983) p. 40.

18. For the case of the Central African Customs and Economic Union see Langdon and Mytelka, 'Africa in the Changing World Economy'.

19. Thomas S. Cox, 'Northern Actors in a South–South Setting: External Aid and East African Integration', *Journal of Common Market Studies*, vol XXI (March 1983) no. 3, p. 310. External actors often have appeared to be more enthusiastic about regional schemes than were the participating member states. See, for instance, the comments of Robert S. Browne, a former Executive Director of the African Development Fund, on the failure of the fund to support multinational projects. Browne and Cummings, *The Lagos Plan of Action vs. The Berg Report*, p. 63.

20. OAU, 'Provisional Reflections, by a Joint Staff Working Group of the OAU, ECA, and ADB, on the World Bank Report "Accelerated Development in Sub-Saharan Africa: An Agenda for Action"', [CM/1177 (XXXVIII)] Appendix 2, p. 4.

21. Others have noted the tendency of ECA to draw up plans largely without reference to their intended consumers and with little attention to 'how and by

whom they will be carried out'. Isebill V. Gruhn, *Regionalism Reconsidered: The Economic Commission for Africa* (Boulder: Westview, 1979), p. 52.

22. ECA, *ECA and Africa's Development 1983–2008*, pp. 14–15.
23. The ECA is by no means the only party guilty of falling back on this explanation. See, for instance, Arthur Hazlewood, 'The End of the East African Community: What are the Lessons for Regional Integration Schemes', in Christian P. Potholm and Richard A. Fredland (eds), *Integration and Disintegration in East Africa* (Lanham, Md.: University Press of America, 1980); this perspective is criticised in John Ravenhill, 'The Theory and Practice of Regional Integration in East Africa' in the same publication.
24. Zimbabwe, for instance, decided to build its own thermal electricity plant rather than rely on Mozambique's Cabora Bassa and Zambia's Kafue projects. This decision to avoid dependence on imported power for more than 15 per cent of domestic consumption needs is blamed by Seidman on the influence of transnational corporations. While, indeed, they may have gained from this, it was also an entirely rational decision on the part of the Mugabe government given the region's past record of failed integrative efforts. Ann Seidman, 'Debt and the Development Options in Central Southern Africa: the Case of Zambia and Zimbabwe' in Carlsson, *Recession in Africa*, p. 96.
25. Not all of the potential members have signed the agreements. As of mid-1984, Angola, Botswana, Madagascar, Mozambique, the Seychelles and Tanzania had refused to join the PTA. Angola also refused to sign the ECSCA Treaty. No equivalent grouping yet exists for North Africa. How the more developed economies of this region can be integrated with their sub-Saharan counterparts is another issue on which the Lagos Plan is silent.
26. *Africa Research Bulletin, Economic, Financial and Technical Series* (15 May–14 June 1983) p. 6867.
27. In 1983 the PTA Secretariat had a budget of $1.8 million in contrast to that of SADCC of $300,000. Anglin notes that SADCC places its emphasis 'on action not institutions', and that in the PTA there is 'nothing comparable to the deliberate diffusion of initiative and responsibility characteristic of SADCC'. Douglas G. Anglin, 'Economic liberation and regional cooperation in Southern Africa: SADCC and the PTA', *International Organization*, vol. 37 (Autumn 1983) no. 4, pp. 691–5. According to *West Africa* (2 January 1984), the ECOWAS Secretariat will have a budget of $69.46 million in 1984. For a comparison of ECOWAS and SADCC see John Ravenhill, 'The Future of Regionalism in Africa', in R. Owuka and A. Sasay (eds), *The Future of Regionalism in Africa* (London: Macmillan, 1985) pp. 205–24.
28. As Robson argues cogently, tariff reductions themselves are inconsequential when – as has often been the case in Africa – they are merely replaced by a variety of non-tariff barriers. Peter Robson, *Integration, Development and Equity*.
29. Anglin, 'Economic liberation and regional cooperation', p. 706.
30. Economic Commission for Africa, *Critical Analysis of the Country Presentations of African Least Developed Countries in the Light of the Lagos Plan of Action and the Final Act of Lagos*, quoted in Browne and Cummings, *The Lagos Plan of Action vs. The Berg Report*, p. 60.
31. The ECA's *ECA and Africa's Development* is a far superior document.
32. Susan Strange, *Cave! hic dragones*: a critique of regime analysis', *International Organization*, vol. 36 (Spring 1982) no. 2, p. 488.

# 5 The African Crisis: Debates and Dialectics Over Alternative Development Strategies for the Continent

## TIMOTHY M. SHAW

Africa is unable to point to any significant growth rate, or satisfactory index of general well-being, in the past 20 years. Faced with this situation, and determined to undertake measures for the basic restructuring of the economic base of our continent, we resolved to adopt a far-reaching regional approach based primarily on *collective self-reliance.*

*Lagos Plan of Action*[1]

. . . the proposed outward-looking, external-oriented concept of development proposed for our countries in the [IBRD] report is indeed a suggestion that we continue to do what we have been doing all these years. The only difference is that we lose the independence to set our goals, adopt our strategy and determine our policies. Added to this is the glaring arrogant paternalism in the report with no concern shown for the need to increase the capacity of our countries to do in the near future what outsiders are doing for them now.

*Report of the Secretary-General on the World Bank Report*[2]

. . . the most fundamental assumptions underlying a significant improvement in Sub-Saharan economic prospects are unrealistic. The implication is for a continuation of economic stagnation and human misery, recurrent crises and stop gap measures.

'Sub-Saharan Africa: an agenda for action'[3]

The vision of a new society in Africa will need to be developed *in* Africa, born out of the African historical experience and the sense of continuity of African history. The African is not yet master of his own fate, but neither is he completely at the mercy of fate.

'Expectations of independence'[4]

The current African crisis, characterised by economic recession, political decline and social tension, poses fundamental problems not only for indigenous regimes and developmental theories but also for extra-continental actors, particularly Western countries and corporations, plus international organisations. The World Bank has now responded to assorted demands from African and non African governments and non-governmental institutions with its *Agenda for Action*. But this overly optimistic restatement of orthodox, extroverted policies (see Bogdanowicz-Bindert's opening citation) has served only to intensify the prior African response – summarised in and symbolised by the *Lagos Plan of Action* – which is antagonistic towards further agricultural exports and private investment.

The contours of the crisis are now quite familiar – Africa has been the hardest hit of all regions in the 1970s – so that, a century after the Treaty of Berlin, the continent is now more marginal economically than ever: the region contributes least to global trade and product in terms of both primary products and manufactured goods. According to estimates from the Economic Commission for Africa (ECA) and elsewhere, this general trend towards marginalisation is likely to continue while any growth will occur in just a few states such as Algeria, Ivory Coast, Kenya, Nigeria and Zimbabwe. And within these and other political economies, of course, it is the relatively rich social formations which suffer least. As Adebayo Adedeji, the energetic Executive-Secretary of the ECA, warns:

Not only are the forecasts for the immediate future gloomy, but the perspectives of development and economic growth in Africa up to the end of this millennium are heart-rending and continue to give cause for increasing uneasiness. Very bleak prospects are foreseen for Africa in global projections . . . the 1960s and the 1970s may by the end of the century appear in retrospect to have been a golden age for Africa!

Projections by the ECA indicate that unless the orientation of the African economy changes, there is a danger that poverty and the attendant problems of political and social instability will become considerably worse in Africa in the next two decades.

Adedeji hopes, however, that something positive can yet come out of such an unpromising scenario: an African cultural and economic revolution:

> Given these portentous prognostications, what can Africans and their governments do to avert the impending doom? . . . Africa has the capacity and capability to change the tide of her economic fortune in her favour and to emerge from her present economic doldrums and lay the foundation of an internally-generated, self-sustaining and self-reliant process of development.[5]

Notwithstanding either the prophecies of economic decline or the potentials of economic renewal, Africa's consensual response has been both cautious and controversial.

## AFRICAN COALITIONS AND CONTRADICTIONS

The urgent and emergent debate over alternative strategies poses challenges not only to African interests but also for extra-African actors: if either *dependent development*, the IBRD preference, or *collective self-reliance*, the OAU's proposal, become the motifs for Africa up to the year 2000 then demands on and implications for external trade, aid and financial interests vary widely. Ironically, the present wave of protectionist pressures in the North may be more compatible with the 'nationalist' orientation of Africa than with the remaining 'internationalist' advocates such as multinational corporations and the World Bank.[6] The reformist and globalist inclinations of the Brandt Report may now be under attack from nationalists in both the North ('mercantilists') and the South ('*independentistas*'): the African crisis has worldwide impact. This chapter overviews the African debate and examines implications in both Africa and the North. Which regimes and classes on the continent are likely to favour continued dependence rather than disengagement? Which African and Northern interests advocate increased external interaction rather than increased intra-regional exchange? What coalitions or coincidences of interest may arise based on 'monetarism' or 'managerialism'?

The concern here is, then, with the set of issues and actors which inform and extend the controversy about the development crisis on the continent. First, Africa is increasingly divided into a minority of 'semi-peripheral' and a majority of truly 'peripheral' – Fourth World – states, which tend to diverge over preferred development orientation: outward-or inward-looking, respectively. Second, the continent is divided by different levels of and emphases on self-reliance – national, regional and/or continental – in part related to distinctive forms of explanation for underdevelopment, and in part related to divergent perceptions of the continent's future. Third, internal inequalities within African political economies have begun to lead to distinctive dominant coalitions, usually under the hegemony of particular bourgeois elements: national, comprador, bureaucratic or military fractions. And finally, such intra-African differences are replicated in and intensified through 'inter-imperial' rivalries. Which Northern (Eastern and Western) countries and corporations favour extroversion or introversion? And which Northern classes – metropolitan, national, bureaucratic or military fractions – favour increased or reduced transnational linkages with elements in African social formations?

## THE CONTEMPORARY AFRICAN CRISIS

The character of the African crisis has become increasingly clear as relentless and exponential setbacks have hit most countries on the continent over the last decade or so (see first quotation from the *LPA*). To cite Adedeji again:

> . . . the African economy today is the most open and the most exposed economy in the world, overly dependent on external trade and other external stimuli, foreign technology, and foreign expertise. The very strategies of development the African governments have been pursuing since independence have come from outside, derived as they were from theories of economic development that were developed during the colonial and neocolonial periods to rationalize the colonial pattern of production in Africa. Not unexpectedly, those foreign theories of development and economic growth reinforce the economic dependence of Africa . . . The cumulative result is that, today, neither high rates of growth or diversification nor an increasing measure of self-reliance and self-sustainment has been achieved in the African economy.[7]

Indeed, as indicated below, when population and inflation are taken into account, probably the majority of African peoples have suffered from negative, not even marginal positive, growth over the last decade. The combination of internal economic mismanagement and external stagflation has produced a crisis of domestic confidence and foreign exchange. As the IMF reports, albeit in rather bland terms:

> In 1981 . . . the adverse consequences of the recession in the industrial countries were much more severe than had generally been foreseen. The weak demand in industrial countries for primary commodities induced shortfalls in African export volumes that were largely unexpected, but have turned out to be substantial.[8]

The result in economistic terms is that 'severe shortages of essential imports of raw materials and consumer goods have arisen, leading to serious under-utilization of plant capacity and problems of productivity and employment.'[9]

The implications – political and social – of the economic crisis have been more strikingly portrayed by Tetteh Kofi who points to the accelerating decay and disorder which it may entail for the majority of states, particularly those at the periphery:

> The deep recession in the industrialized world has plunged the Black African economies into a depression that will increase starvation and social unrest. With demand for primary commodities depressed, even nations that were regarded as success stories in the late 1970s – resource-rich economies such as the Ivory Coast, Kenya and Nigeria – are now sinking fast. The oil importers, of course, are suffering the most . . . [their] per capita GDP growth is expected to be negative for this decade, after dropping to 1.7% per year in the 1970s from 3.7% in the decade of the 1960s.[10]

As Adedeji, a leading author and advocate of the *Lagos Plan of Action*, has indicated in response to this catastrophic (and cumulative?) condition:

> For Africa, the 1980s – the United Nations Development Decade – will be particularly critical. Unless the fundamental strategic changes I have advocated and the alternative policies that flow from such changes are introduced and become effective during the decade, the chances of installing a new national economic order in African countries and a new regional economic order in Africa as a whole – based on an increasing measure of national and collective self-reliance and self-sustained growth – will be permanently aborted.[11]

Since this warning, given the continuity of recession and regression, Adedeji has reluctantly recognised that 'the prospect for future economic development itself, in countries that stand very much in need of it more desperately than any others, are very dim.'[12] Given such a situation, some African scholars have argued that reliance on external exchange and foreign aid was always misplaced in any case because the developmental difficulties of the continent were *sui generis*:

> . . . the Least Developed Countries of Africa are least justified to place much hope on international aid and trade to overcome the problems of development. First, it is readily apparent that the depth of poverty that prevails in these countries calls for a more determined domestic development effort . . . Secondly, past experience regarding international economic relations hardly justifies the expectation of greatly expanded assistance . . . Thirdly . . . the least developed countries of Africa stand to benefit least even if agreement were to be reached on . . . a NIEO.[13]

In response to, (a) the demise of any real prospect of an effective North–South dialogue and, (b) the perpetuation of international recession and competition, African states have been debating the merits of the two contrasting continental diagnoses and prescriptions – the OAU *LPA* and the IBRD *Agenda* (*AD*) – recognising their almost diametrical (dialectical?) characters.[14] In general, they favour the former over the latter; as an assessment by the combined OAU, ECA and ADB Secretariats suggests, 'it is quite clear that the total effect of the [World Bank] recommendations addressed to African governments could very well make Africa more dependent and less self-reliant.'[15] However, as we will see, certain regimes and classes may yet identify with *AD*, while still others may go beyond the reformist self-reliance proposed in the OAU's *LPA*. Moreover, reactions to these alternative proposals are still fluid and may be affected by a revival of international trade or pressure from international interests and institutions: the vagaries of exchange and the 'conditionality' of the IMF.

## ALTERNATIVE RESPONSES TO THE AFRICAN CRISIS

The motif of the collective indigenous response to the crisis – as indicated in the April 1980 Lagos economic summit and in the earlier deliberations at the February 1979 Monrovia symposium – is 'rapid self-reliance and self-sustaining development'. By contrast *AD* advocates a 'growth-oriented program: (i) more suitable trade and exchange rate policies: (ii) increased efficiency of resource use in the public sector; and (iii) improvement in agricultural policies.' While *LPA* calls on Africa to use the crisis to productively utilise its own resources and to 'cultivate the virtue of self-reliance', *AD* advocates a return to agricultural production for export. Not that self-reliance means autarchy; rather it is an assertion of 'Africa first' in economic as well as in strategic and diplomatic matters: 'outside contributions should only supplement our own effort: they should not be the mainstay of our development.'[16]

In an attempt to mediate the growing ECA–IBRD divergencies and disagreements over strategy, as well as to reassure sceptical conservative regimes on and off the continent, Adedeji and others have moved towards a middle ground: no single solution involving introversion, industrialisation and indigenisation is proposed. Instead of a radical definition of self-reliance – public rather than private sector, industry rather than commodities, and intra- rather than extra-continental exchange – Adedeji has come personally to advocate a shift in emphasis only, as indicated in a recent speech to the Western grouping for 'Cooperation for Development in Africa':

> Our requirements are at two levels. We need massive transfer of resources from the developed countries to Africa. But no less important, we need your understanding, your appreciation and your acceptance of our perception of the kind of development that we need in Africa. . . .[17]

Nevertheless, while moderating Africa's economic demands somewhat, Adedeji has continued to emphasise the psychological element and potential of the Lagos Plan: 'If Africa is to develop the necessary self-confidence to pull its economy out of the shadows of backwardness and underdevelopment, it is essential that our partners-in-development respect our priorities, perceptions, goals and strategies.'[18]

Agreement on the Lagos Plan at the first continental economic summit was a singular achievement given Africa's historical, ideological and developmental diversities: a tribute to the tenacity of ECA diplomacy and the persuasiveness (and moderation) of the Monrovia Strategy, as well as an indication of the seriousness of the economic crisis. The continent had already moved towards forms of 'regional self-reliance' through a variety of integration schemes such as the ill-fated

East African Community and the fragile Economic Community of West African States (ECOWAS), but national and continental arrangements were and are more controversial: will there be an African economic community by the year 2000?

At the national level, self-reliance had been adopted as strategy by a group of more radical and peripheral states – Angola, Benin, Mali, Somalia, and Tanzania, for example. It has been avoided assiduously by those countries and regimes at the semi-periphery which still hope to benefit from continued incorporation into the world system – Algeria, Egypt, Ivory Coast, Kenya, and Nigeria, for example. Many others are both ideologically and structurally ambivalent – e.g. Malawi, Senegal and Zambia. And still others have, in many ways, lost whatever they had of a national economy – Chad, Gambia, Ghana, Sudan and Uganda, for instance – because of the combination of black market, smuggling and foreign exchange difficulties. Indeed, the withdrawal of commodities, including labour, from these national economies and the return to self-sufficient subsistence constitutes a dramatic, if uncoordinated, form of intra-national 'self-reliance', not one which most regimes would want to encourage. Not all forms of self-reliance are compatible, then: internal, national, regional and continental strategies need to be carefully coordinated and integrated to avoid conflicts and contradictions in the future. National self-reliance at the real periphery and regional dominance at the semi-periphery, let alone alternative definitions of regions and assorted attempts at continental leadership, pose considerable difficulties for any serious implementation of the *LPA*.

If the more radical and peripheral regimes can identify most readily with the Lagos Plan then the less radical, semi-peripheral regimes may do so least. Notwithstanding the pressures for African consensus, the latter still retain some confidence in orthodox developmentalist approaches because they have experienced rapid growth rates themselves thus far. So the semi-periphery has served not only as a market for OECD capital and technological exports but also, at least until 1980, as an example of 'successful' orthodox growth policies. Even if the majority of people in, say Kenya or the Ivory Coast or Nigeria have not benefited from high rates of growth, at least their ruling classes have kept their confidence in established assumptions. As the retainers of faith in and linkages with OECD interests, such semi-peripheral regimes can come to exert a regional dominance akin to the global hegemony of OECD countries and corporations; perhaps a very distinctive (and incompatible?) form of 'collective self-reliance'.

As we shall see in the final section they are ambivalent about the

Lagos Plan, supporting its regional and industrial development provisions while playing down its disengagement and agricultural goals. Moreover, as their economic position and projection are already relatively assured – even if their regional dominance is a function of African underdevelopment rather than an indication of their equivalence to Newly Industrialising Countries (NICs) like Brazil and South Korea[19] – they can afford to be beneficent and provide support or at least disinterest while retaining close transnational linkages. Further, again noted below, the more 'national' fractions of such indigenous bourgeoisies may themselves use at least the rhetoric of the plan – self-reliance, not socialism – to bolster their claims *vis-à-vis* the more comprador elements.[20] So notwithstanding continuing selective country and class interests concentrated at the semi-periphery in maintaining linkages with the metropole, the OAU membership as a whole, augmented by widespread national bourgeois interests, has espoused the values of the Lagos Plan.

In part, the advocacy of self-reliance and the satisfaction of basic human needs and wants makes good political sense: African leaders are not interested in encouraging antagonistic contradictions – resulting from generated expectations and intensified alienation – which might lead to their downfall. Moreover, even the so-called 'success stories' such as the Ivory Coast and Kenya (and perhaps now Zimbabwe) face structural constraints which the *LPA*, especially its regionalist elements, might help to transcend.[21] For the developmentalist doctrine of the 1960s has run into difficulties even in the semi-periphery, as *AD* indicates:

> Import substitution can be a sound policy and most industrialization has started on that basis. But in many African countries it has been badly implemented . . . For countries that have nearly completed the first stages of import substitution, such as Kenya, Ivory Coast and Tanzania, few import substitution opportunities exist based on the internal market.[22]

Industrialisation, as the *LPA* recognises, is the *sine qua non* of development – hence the designation of the years 1980–90 as the 'Industrial Development Decade in Africa' – so any over-hasty acceptance of *AD*'s priority of agriculture may serve to perpetuate dependence. Conversely, the logic of *laissez-faire* is differentiation: the successful (in the semi-periphery) expand, albeit modestly, while those without resources (i.e. the periphery) are allowed to decline. The growth of inequalities both within and between African states threatens national and continental order; hence the interest of the *LPA* in a form of Keynesian welfarism – 'international managerialism' – at the African level. The continent's unity is already so fragile that structural as well as strategic and diplomatic divergence might shatter any remaining cohesion. By contrast, the implication of *AD* is for renewed differentiation: those with agricultural and mineral exports would survive while those with neither would be abandoned to *triage*. OECD interests lie with the Third rather than Fourth World; ECA is attempting to camouflage and compensate for such an unequal international division of labour.

## WHICH WAY AFRICA? ALTERNATIVE SCENARIOS AND STRATEGIES

The *LPA* and *AD* are both responses to the present continental crisis, yet the former would seem to offer an enhanced prospect of development by contrast with the latter. Both of them are reflective of current intellectual and ideological conditions and of established modes of analysis and praxis.[23] While *AD* adopts an essentially revisionist developmentalist perspective within the modernisation genre in emphasising internal factors as the primary cause of Africa's underdevelopment, the *LPA* with its emphasis on colonial and neo-colonial exploitation falls within the *dependencia* tradition.

The *LPA* sees disengagement as a prerequisite for development[24] whereas *AD* argues still that 'trickle down' will, eventually, generate growth. Ironically, the former blames external conditions and advances an internal solution – a continental common market – whereas the latter situates the causes of underdevelopment internally – inappropriate policies and processes – yet advocates an external solution. Moreover, the World Bank is concerned with individual African states in the world system and with exchange rather than production. By contrast, the OAU deals with the collectivity of African states in the global economy and with production not just trade. Finally, the Bank prefers the privatisation of economic relations, whereas the OAU strategy is compatible with state control over the means of production.

The two plans are not only antithetical in intellectual association and policy direction; they are also advocated by two exclusive coalitions. The more nationalist or 'Africanist' coalition of the OAU under the leadership of Adedeji consists of indigenous and progressive academics, advisers and leaders, whereas the more 'internationalist' IBRD grouping is less cohesive, more conservative and less indigenous: bankers, bureaucrats and economists. As indicated in the second citation at the head of this chapter, the African coalition rejects most of the Bank's assumptions, analysis and prescriptions:

> . . . the goals, objectives and characteristics of the strategy contained in the Report are in many ways inconsistent with those of the Lagos Plan of Action . . .
> The implication of the recommended approach is to make Africa more dependent on external markets for its agricultural and mineral products and for its essential factor inputs. This is contrary to the principles of self-reliant and self-sustaining development of the Lagos Plan of Action.[25]

The African attack on *AD* was maintained between the Addis Ababa and (aborted) Tripoli summits (February, August, and November 1982) by a critique from the very group which, almost three years earlier, had requested the study from the Bank: the African Governors. Meeting in Dakar in early March 1982 they too, (a) rejected its focus on domestic factors, (b) opposed its concentration on agriculture rather than industry, and (c) expressed scepticism about whether it would deliver the envisaged finance.[26] They also lamented its lack of interest in regionalism and its dissatisfaction with the public and parastatal sectors. But their major complaint was about its focus – the attempt to blame Africa for its own condition – which they asserted placed insufficient importance on external, global conditions: Africa 'imports' many of its problems:

> . . . certain questions have not been dealt with in the World Bank Report: problems such as the soaring of interest rates in the international financial markets, global negotiations with a view to establishing a new international economic order, and stabilization of commodity prices.[27]

The consensual, collective adoption and defence of the Lagos Plan derives in part from Pan Africanism redefined as economic nationalism. Unhappily, neither of the two Tripoli non-summits provided an occasion for a restatement of the Lagos Declaration despite the increasing urgency of the situation, with foreign exchange reserves falling to almost desperate levels in many OAU states. An opportunity was missed in 1982 for the continent's leaders to reflect on the latest assessment by Adedeji. As *West Africa* editorialised:

The tone of his statement is indicative of the mounting sense of desperation increasingly found in government circles and elsewhere when contemplating the present condition of the continent. At no time in the past 20 to 25 years of independence has the collective situation of Africa generated so much concentrated pessimism, with considerable evidence of actual decline, such as a negative growth rate of 1.4 per cent.[28]

Although 'political' difficulties prevented Africa's leaders from formally treating their collective 'economic' dilemmas in 1982, the *LPA* is still being discussed and implemented at levels below that of 'high politics'.

Its reformist and welfarist elements reflect the common interest of all of Africa's ruling classes in retaining power. For not only have African states become less equal since the independence period, African classes have become more established and antagonistic. Given prevailing global and national conditions – the African crisis – the ability of regimes to meet basic human needs has decreased. The threat to anarchy and the withdrawal of peasants from the commodity and cash crop sectors, let alone massive un- and under-employment, are all aspects of declining real personal incomes and living standards.

With the receding prospect of a consensual New International Economic Order (NIEO) being created to replace the Bretton Woods system – reflective of IBRD inattention to global rather than continental conditions – African leaders have a collective interest in designing an alternative to either Northern protectionism or Northern paternalism. Aside from the apparent trend towards increasing repression and depoliticisation – an attempt to 'contain' the results of under-development – the *LPA* is one major aspect of the continuing quest by Africa's ruling classes to secure (or, in a few cases, to recapture) high degrees of development and order. The realisation of these objectives would enhance their prospects of surplus production and accumulation. If most projections of insufficient growth materialise, then African leaders will be faced by massive marginalisation and opposition.

If the initial African assertion of its collective self-reliance was a response by the continent's ruling class to Northern *protectionism*, then the subsequent African reaction to World Bank subversion of its self-reliant orientation was a rejection of Northern *paternalism*. Post-independence Africa has endured continual Western attention to its 'developmental' needs, from 'modernisation' to 'mutuality', symbolised by the transition from Pearson to Brandt Commissions.[29] It has tired of being the 'laboratory' for Northern development 'experts' and so is now innately sceptical of Western prescriptions and intentions, as indicated by the second citation at the beginning of this chapter.

In addition, Africa is dubious about whether the West has the resources any longer, given the impact of the world recession, to implement any of its schemes. Mahbub ul Haq expressed this widespread fear – the inability of the Bank to deliver any accelerated assistance as indicated in its *Agenda for Action* – on his resignation from the Bank because of his opposition to its move away from a real concern for poverty, the retreat from McNamara's BHN (Basic Human Needs) to Clausen's or Berg's GNP:

> The major danger is that the Report may well be used to lecture to Africa about its internal policy reforms without providing an increase in financial assistance. It will be very unfortunate if the foreign assistance recommendations of the Report fall through, which looks likely at the moment, and all that remains are generalizations and homilies about Africa's domestic problems.[30]

Notwithstanding such a possibility, and notwithstanding the general preference of the OAU coalition for the *LPA* over *AD*, certain states and class fractions both inside and outside the continent may well still identify with the World Bank perspective. These represent alternative coalitions, either tacit or organised to advance different strategies and policies intended to resolve the continent's crisis.

## ANOTHER DEVELOPMENT? ANOTHER DEBATE? ANOTHER DIALECTIC?

The history of African international relations is replete with alliance formation and interaction: from the innocent and idealistic days of the Monrovia, Casablanca and Brazzaville blocs to the more calculating and intransigent debates over Chad and Polisario, continental diplomacy has been characterised by coalition politics.[31] The latest issue is that of economic rather than strategic or diplomatic direction. Because the controversy involves crucial issues as well as external interests it has tended to be treated as 'high' rather than 'low' politics, i.e. imbued with intensity, intolerance and idealism.

As already indicated, the continent is divided increasingly into semi-periphery as well as periphery: the former, more affluent and capitalist economies expect to gain more from *AD* than from the *LPA*.[32] Likewise, the continent is divided increasingly into more bourgeois as well as more proletarian classes: the former interests, more advantaged and propertied, may prefer the *laissez-faire AD* over the more structured *LPA*. Given such burgeoning interests among the middle powers and middle classes, while the OAU consensus may be maintained at the level of interstate diplomacy, in practice some regimes and fractions may go along with World Bank prescriptions and provisions, with serious implications for African unity and development. The IBRD perspective – after all, why did the African Governors of the Bank ask for such a study in the autumn of 1979, following the February Monrovia symposium? – may be most appropriate for the few successful 'state capitalist' agricultural economies: Ivory Coast, Kenya and Malawi; and for oil-exporting 'semi-industrial' states: Algeria, Gabon and Nigeria.

Reflective of such divergent reactions are the statements of Sierra Leonean and Nigerian representatives respectively at the Governors' Dakar meeting. The former, Dr Sama S. Banya, was quite critical: 'The Report advocates that Africa should adjust to shocks generated by the world economy but says little about the need for restructuring the world economy, i.e. stabilization of commodity prices, reduction of interest rates, and reduction of rates of inflation . . . The Report somewhat lacks balance by failing to give due importance to these issues which like the oil bill affect the region's balance of payments'.[33] The latter, S. A. Ogunleye, was quite positive, even to the point of offering an apologia: 'The Report's analysis of a number of key problems and conclusions it draws are also appropriate.' Whilst moderately decrying the IBRD's attack on the public sector and lamenting its neglect of external forces. Ogunleye still asserted that, 'despite this the Report does have several positive aspects. There are several instances in which priority problems have been appropriately identified, analysed, and appropriate conclusions drawn.'[34]

If the very poor and the middling-rich countries diverge in this manner then we may anticipate a somewhat similar internal reaction, both between different parts of government and between distinct social groups. First, the more orthodox financial ministries (e.g. Treasury, Central Bank, and Finance) may prefer economic orthodoxy whereas the less orthodox developmental ministries (e.g. Planning, Technology, Environment, and Economic Development) may espouse more radical economic ideas. And second, the more bourgeois and least bureaucratic social classes and fractions may prefer more *laissez-faire* whereas less bourgeois and more bureaucratic interests may advocate more radical values. In short, the minority of affluent countries and classes may opt for *AD*, whereas the majority of less affluent countries and classes will tend to stay with the *LPA*. Thereby, the better-endowed states, in going along with IBRD guidelines, will reinforce their claim to a special status with the OECD grouping along the lines of 'trilateralist' preferences. By contrast, the more 'political' and 'national' elements within the indigenous bourgeoisie throughout the continent will tend to favour disengagement while more 'technocratic' and 'comprador' interests will advocate further external incorporation to advance their own interests.

Such 'divide and rule' results (and intentions?) arising from the Bank's report are particularly worrisome for any continent-wide African coalition. For in a period of global recession not all economies can expand: the implications of *AD* are that only cooperative semi-peripheral states will grow while the impoverished periphery will suffer further marginalisation. This is the logic of externally-oriented economies in a period of contraction: growth for the few and *triage* for the many. Hence the charge of 'new paternalism' against the IBRD *AD* and the imperative of collective self-reliance if Africa is not to be subjected again to divide-and-rule tactics in the post-colonial era. Hence, too, the contradictions within as well as between African states as dominant social forces attempt to come to grips with the post-Bretton Woods reality.

If the prospects of division in Africa are worrisome, their incidence is likely to increase because of analogous tensions within the North – the OECD nexus – as well as between eastern and western industrialised states. 'Inter-imperial' rivalries have intensified as the recession has continued: some countries in the East and West have weathered the global depression better than others (e.g. Hungary *v.* Poland or Japan *v.* Britain). Moreover, some international institutions and governmental agencies (e.g. World Bank and trade ministries) are more extroverted in character than others (e.g. OECD and finance ministries). Finally, some countries are home to more multinational corporations and international banks than others and so tend to have more 'internationalist' values.

The latter coalition identifies most closely with the Brandt Report and North–South dialogue whereas a more 'nationalist' and protectionist grouping favours a retreat from global reach and neo-mercantilist, as well as neo-monetarist, positions. While the 'internationalists' would favour *AD*, the 'nationalists' would identify with the *LPA*: an unlikely alliance of self-reliance advocates between northern and southern hemispheres. Notwithstanding problems in the global economy, the internationalists still advance extroverted, exchange-oriented economies, such as those at the semi-periphery, whereas the nationalists exist in a tacit coalition with the periphery in favour of more introverted, self-sufficient economies.

The broader global debate about alternative theories and strategies to treat recession and underdevelopment[35] reinforces, then, the new division of Africa, a prospect which the OAU plan sought to avoid but which extra-continental pressures seek continually to exacerbate. To be sure, this chapter may over-emphasise the binary nature of Africa's emerging place in the world system. Moreover, inter-imperial rivalries will always tend to be dialectical, resulting in attempts to moderate protectionist competitiveness through GATT and economic summits. Nevertheless, alternative responses to recession, debt and decay are generating novel coincidences of interest which may yet provide the basis for new tacit coalitions across the North–South divide, unlike those identified by the Brandt Commission, founded on mutuality of interests:[36] not only the OECD–NIC nexus anticipated by the Trilateral Commission but also a rather unlikely monetarist–nationalist 'alliance' of coincidental common solutions between 'old' industrial economies in the North (eg. UK and USA) and 'new' non-industrial peripheries in the South (e.g. Guinea and Tanzania).

The simple East–West, North–South dichotomies have disappeared in both strategic and economic affairs despite the revival of superpower confrontation:[37] 'proxies' in the former and NICs in the latter axes' issue areas serve to complicate 'bipolarities'. Hence the prospect of, say, a confluence of interest between so-called 'like-minded' middle powers in the West (centred on Scandinavia and Canada) and determined yet undogmatic least developed countries (e.g. Botswana, Tanzania and Zimbabwe within the Southern African Development Coordination Conference (SADCC) – an innovative institutional definition of regional self-reliance). While both of these sides emphasise relative disengagement they also remain staunchly internationalist, seeking the mutuality which the Brandt Commission highlighted.[38] By contrast to protectionist pressures, then, some elements at the 'periphery' of the Western and world systems remain committed to global management à la Keynes rather than revival of the market-place à la Friedman.

One final caveat: the types of latent or tacit coalitions suggested can only arise through protracted negotiation and debate. If global economic dialogue ends – which, despite cynicism and fatigue is unlikely – or if international strategic tensions increase – regrettably a real possibility given socio-economic trends towards conservatism in the North in military matters as well as in economic – then such potential configurations may be obliterated by the imperatives of 'high politics'. The possibilities of renewed extra- and intra-continental strategic 'intervention' are heightened because of, and not despite, Africa's economic crisis. A prerequisite for the successful implementation of the Lagos Plan, or any other development strategy, is peace and time. Unfortunately, precisely because of its condition Africa is unlikely to experience much of either before the end of this century in either national, regional or continental affairs.

## NOTES

1. Organisation of African Unity. *Lagos Plan of Action for the Economic Development of Africa, 1980–2000* (Geneva: International Institute for Labour Studies, 1981) p. 5; emphasis is added.
2. Organisation of African Unity, *Report of the Secretary-General on the World Bank Report*, Council of Ministers Thirty-Eighth Ordinary Session, 22 February to 1 March 1982, [CM/1177 (xxxviii)] (Addis Ababa: OAU, 1982) Appendix ii, p. 3.
3. Christine A. Bogdanowicz-Bindert, 'Sub-Saharan Africa: an agenda for action', *Journal of World Trade Law*, vol. 16 (July–August 1982) no. 4, p. 286.
4. J. F. Ade Ajayi, 'Expectations of independence', *Daedalus* vol. 111, (Spring 1982) no. 2, p. 8.
5. Adebayo Adedeji 'Africa: permanent underdog?' *International Perspectives* (March–April 1981) p. 17. On the human dimensions and rights involved as well as the politico-economic difficulties see Richard Sandbrook, 'Is there hope for Africa?', *International Perspectives* (January–February 1983) pp. 3–8.
6. For an introduction to these conflicts and coalitions see Timothy M. Shaw 'Debates about Africa's future: the Brandt, World Bank and Lagos Plan blueprints', *Third World Quarterly*, vol. 5 (April 1983) no. 2.
7. Adebayo Adedeji, 'Development and economic growth in Africa to the year 2000: alternative projections and policies', in Timothy M. Shaw (ed.), *Alternative Futures for Africa* (Boulder: Westview, 1982) pp. 280–1.
8. IMF, *World Economic Outlook: A Survey by the Staff of the IMF*, Occasional Paper No. 9 (Washington, DC: 1982) p. 96.
9. Ibid.
10. Tetteh A. Kofi, 'Black Africa: bleak prospects and rising unrest', *Business Week*, 1 November 1982, p. 122. See also Sandbrook, 'Is there hope for Africa?'
11. Adedeji, 'Development and economic growth in Africa to the year 2000', p. 301.
12. Adebayo Adedeji, 'The deepening international crisis and its implications for Africa', (Addis Ababa: ECA, April 1982) p. 8.

13. Fassil G. Kiros, 'What is in a NIEO for the least developed countries of Africa?' *Africa Development*, vol. 6, (1981) no. 4, pp. 16–17.
14. Which is not to assert that the Lagos Plan is really radical. It is an essentially 'nationalist' document based on anti-dependence sentiment rather than on anti-bourgeois premises.
15. 'Accelerated Development in Sub-Saharan Africa: an assessment by OAU, ECA and ADB Secretariats', Council of Ministers, Thirty-Eighth Ordinary Session, 22 February to 1 March 1982, [CM/1177 (XXXVIII)] (Addis Ababa: OAU, 1982) Annex 1, p. 29.
16. OAU, *Lagos Plan of Action*, p. 8.
17. Adebayo Adedeji, 'Address at the formal opening of the annual policy meeting of the Cooperation for Development in Africa conference, Washington, 26 October 1982', p. 14.
18. Ibid.
19. On the differences as well as similarities between, say, Brazil and Nigeria, see Peter Evans, *Dependent Development: the alliance of multinational, state, and local capital in Brazil* (Princeton University Press, 1979) especially pp. 308–14. And in terms of the(ir) relevance of/to Bill Warren's thesis to Africa see Alain Lipietz, 'Towards global Fordism?' and 'Marx or Rostow?' *New Left Review*, vol. 132, (March–April 1982) pp. 33–58.
20. On the national bourgeoisie in Nigeria and Zambia see Timothy M. Shaw, 'Nigeria in world politics: contemporary calculations and constraints', in Timothy M. Shaw and Olajide Aluko (eds), *Nigerian Foreign Policy: Alternative Perceptions and Projections* (London: Macmillan, 1983) and 'Dilemmas of dependence and (under) development: conflicts and choices in Zambia's present and prospective foreign policy', *Africa Today*, vol. 26 (Fourth Quarter 1979) no. 4, pp. 43–65.
21. See Chapter 8 by Steven Langdon in this volume.
22. World Bank, *Accelerated Development in Sub-Saharan Africa: An Agenda for Action* (Washington, DC: World Bank, 1981) p. 93.
23. For comparisons between development strategies see, *inter alia*, A. M. Babu, 'Development Strategy – Revolutionary Style', in his *African Socialism or Socialist Africa?* (London: Zed, 1981) pp. 144–64 and Timothy M. Shaw, 'From dependence to self-reliance: Africa's prospects for the next twenty years', *International Journal*, vol. 35 (Autumn 1980) no. 4, pp. 821–44.
24. For a set of case studies of disengagement see Kal Holsti *et al., Why Nations Realign: foreign policy restructuring in the post-war world* (London: Allen & Unwin, 1982). See also Timothy M. Shaw, 'Towards an International Political Economy for the 1980s: from dependence to (inter) dependence', (Halifax: Centre for Foreign Policy Studies, 1980).
25. 'Accelerated Development in Sub-Saharan Africa: an assessment by OAU, ECA and ADB Secretariats' Annex I, pp. 44–5; cf. the rejoinder by IBRD President, Alden Clausen, 'Looking towards a brighter future', *West Africa*, vol. 3378, (3 May 1982) pp. 1194–9.
26. See 'What the World Bank didn't say', *Africa News*, vol. 18 (10 May 1982) no. 19, pp. 3 and 11.
27. 'World economy: Africans respond to World Bank study', ibid. p. 2.
28. 'Editorial, Adedeji's stocktaking', *West Africa*, vol. 3413 (10 January 1983)

p. 63. And for a lament that the proposed 'Tripoli Declaration', reaffirming support for the plan and restating opposition to *AD*, was never made see, Editorial, 'The untouched topic', *West Africa*, vol. 3408 (29 November 1982) p. 3063.

29. For the latest in the series of 'internationalist' statements see *Common Crisis, North–South: Cooperation for World Recovery. The Brandt Commission 1983* (London: Pan, 1983).

30. 'World Bank "stagnant and confused" says former director', *Africa Now*, vol. 13 (May 1982) p. 89. But cf. the positive public relations tone – 'greater involvement will demand a new era of more intense partnership between the peoples of Africa and the Bank' (p. 1194) – set by Alden Clausen in his address at the Nigerian Institute of International Affairs: 'Looking towards a brighter future'.

31. For an overview of the current state of international interaction and investigation about Africa see Timothy M. Shaw, 'Beyond the conventional: towards a political economy of the periphery', *Radcliffe Presidential Conference on Challenging Conventional Wisdom*, Cambridge, Mass., April 1983.

32. On the calculatedness of 'ideological' shifts in Africa as the world system and external opportunities expand and contract see Thandika Mkandawire, 'African state responses to economic cycles and economic crises: a preliminary note', *African Studies Association* Washington, DC, November 1982.

33. 'What the World Bank didn't say', p. 11.

34. 'Agenda for Action: valuable criticism', *West Africa*, vol. 3377 (28 April 1982) pp. 1132 and 1131.

35. For a good current overview see Ankie M. M. Hoogvelt, *The Third World in Global Development* (London: Macmillan, 1982).

36. On the bases and contours of some of these, as well as on the demise of the much-flaunted Afro-Arab relationship, see Paul Hallwood and Stuart Sinclair, *Oil, Debt and Development: OPEC in the Third World* (London: Allen & Unwin, 1981) and Timothy M. Shaw, 'Towards a political economy of the OAU and Arab League: collaboration, conflict or contradiction?' in Dunstan M. Wai *et al.* (eds), *Africa and the Middle East: Relations in Perspective* (forthcoming).

37. See the thoughtful overview of current affairs in terms of these established yet changeable axes by Allen Gotleib and Jeremy Kinsman, 'North–South or East–West?' *International Perspectives* (January/February 1983) pp. 25–8.

38. See Shaw, 'Debates about Africa's future'.

# 6 OAU, ECA and the World Bank: Do They Really Disagree?[1]

## STANLEY PLEASE and K. Y. AMOAKO

### INTRODUCTION

In a recent contribution to the discussion of 'Policy Analysis and Development', Bruce Johnston and William C. Clark regretted the 'inconclusive skirmishes among development advisors' which were leading to the danger that: 'those bent on self-interested efforts to exploit or to ignore the poor can invariably find some advisory recommendation to interpret as support for their favoured programs', and that 'while academic pursuits may thrive on conflict, effective implementation of a social action program requires substantial consensus . . . because policymakers, with their time and attention limited, otherwise find it difficult to make the "right purchases" of policy options'. 'The nay-sayers carry the day'.[2]

All those who have been party to, or observers of, the discussion on sub-Saharan Africa since the publication in September 1981, of the World Bank's Report *Accelerated Development in Sub-Saharan Africa: An Agenda for Action*, (*AD*), cannot but be halted in their tracks by such warnings and reprimands. As the flow of written and spoken words has increased, the crisis has deepened. While this chapter adds to the flow of words, it attempts to find the commonalities upon which agreements on action can be based.

In particular it attempts to clear up some of the widespread misunderstandings that have arisen regarding the position taken on certain key issues in the World Bank Report. Moreover, after two years of intensive discussion of the report, there is a clear need to reflect both on the markedly deteriorated global circumstances within which Africa has

to live and devise its programmes, and on the component parts of the
*Agenda for Action*. There is an attempt here to isolate and contain the
major areas of continuing disagreement; in doing so, perhaps it will be
possible to move the discussion towards action on the issues for which
there is widespread agreement, and towards the mobilisation of
adequate external support by the world community in order to avert the
'nightmare' which the Economic Commission for Africa (ECA) projects
for Africa.[3]

While there is an attempt to address major issues raised by many
commentators on the Bank's report, this chapter focuses on two groups
particularly. Firstly, it focuses on the issues raised by the African
Governors of the World Bank when they met formally to discuss the
report in Dakar in March 1982,[4] and on the Report of the Eighth
Meeting of the Conference of African Ministers responsible for
Economic Development and Planning of the Member States of ECA,
held in Tripoli in April 1982.[5] Secondly, the chapter focuses on the
articles in the special edition of the *Bulletin* of the Institute of
Development Studies (IDS) at the University of Sussex, England, which
reviewed the Bank's report.[6] These present in a systematic and
comprehensive manner most of the important issues raised in other
reviews of the Bank report.

Reginald Green's article in the IDS *Bulletin* provides an excellent
starting point. Green emphasises at the beginning that: 'Precisely
because many aspects of the [World Bank's] Report's agricultural vision
and prescription are controversial, it is important to list areas of fairly
broad agreement which exist among its authors and enthusiasts as well
as its sceptics and critics. *It is*', he continues, '*clear that common ground is
wide, especially in the identification of broad problem areas*' (emphasis
added).[7] He then goes on to list some areas of agreement:

(a) the poor agricultural production record of the region between 1970
    and 1979 both for food and export crops;
(b) the important negative role played by adverse external factors;
(c) the need for price and non-price incentives;
(d) the need for peasant participation in decision-making and policy
    design;
(e) the need for clearer priority setting;
(f) the significance of remedial public policy inefficiencies;
(g) the need for more and better data;
(h) the need for more knowledge on agronomic packages.

Green continues by emphasising that the 'wide range of proposals presented in the Bank's Report *include virtually all those to which the present author* [i.e. Green] *or most critics would give high priority'* (emphasis added). His major criticism is that there is 'no systematic setting of priorities' in the Bank report and 'no coherent presentation of a consistent priority package'. Green's concern on this issue can be welcomed because, contrary to what he says later, there was a genuine recognition in the Bank report that the diversity of African conditions (political and social as well as natural and economic) makes the formulation of a blueprint for each and every African country an unrealistic and undesirable objective. The African Governors of the World Bank at their meeting in Dakar also placed major emphasis on the need to formulate country-specific reform programmes. This emphasis is not in dispute.

If Reginald Green is correct that there is so much substantive agreement on major issues, why is there so much apparent disagreement? The remainder of this chapter attempts to isolate these factors and to put them in perspective.

## EQUITY, POVERTY ALLEVIATION AND THE GENERAL BACKGROUND TO THE BANK'S REPORT

Many commentators on the Bank report have expressed concern about its overwhelming preoccupation with increasing production in Africa and therefore with efficiency considerations rather than with considerations of equity and of poverty alleviation.

The IDS *Bulletin* brooks no hesitation in this regard. It asserts that the *Agenda for Action* is the 'first comprehensive ideological and programmatic manifesto setting out the post-McNamara Bank's response to lagging development (in many cases, disintegration) in the context of rising global economic disorder and deepening industrial economy recession'.[8] In subsequent articles assertions are made about 'changed World Bank priorities' and 'the prescriptions of the Report would involve the heaviest costs being shouldered by the poorest members of the population.'[9]

It is difficult to understand the basis for these concerns. The whole thrust of the World Bank's approach to the poverty problem has always been through the improved provision of efficient and, therefore, sustainable productive income-earning opportunities to the poor – the smallholder, the urban unemployed, etc. Redistribution of low or declining national incomes has never been seen by the World Bank as the answer to the poverty problem. The *AD*, with its emphasis on the actions necessary for raising smallholder production as a pre-condition for the achievement of all the other goals of African development, including the wider provision of goods and services to meet basic needs, is fully consistent with previous World Bank priorities.

Furthermore, the improvement in agricultural incentive prices (about which more is said later) is seen in the Bank's report as a primary condition for achieving an increase in smallholder production. Because the poor in Africa are overwhelmingly in the agricultural sector – unlike, for instance, Asia and Latin America where there is a large landless class of poor people both in the towns and in the countryside – improved internal terms of trade for agricultural producers is both desirable from a production and from an equity point of view.

This point is also missed in another part of the IDS review where it is regretted that the Bank study did not make any more 'than a passing reference to the need for changes in the wage and salary structure' when there is an urgent need for a reduction in real wages and salaries over the next year or two to reduce government budget expenditure.[10] This is a surprising comment on the Bank's report because the whole thrust of the report (as opposed to simply being a 'passing reference') is on the priority that should be accorded to the tradeable sectors in African economies and particularly to agriculture. This priority can only be achieved through a combination of, firstly, a switch in the internal terms of trade in favour of the tradeable sectors and against the service sectors (most obviously in African circumstances this means against government employment) and, secondly, through a switch of government expenditure in favour of agriculture services and against other services such as administration and defence. Education, health, water supply, etc., should, in this connection, be thought of as necessary inputs into agricultural production – both Green and Colclough very correctly emphasise this point. The Bank report does, therefore, approach the problem of real wages and salaries policy but less directly, perhaps, than Colclough would wish. Furthermore, he is, of course, correct to emphasise that if wage and salary earners are able to resist the short-run declines in their real incomes, then inflation will result and the aim of giving greater priority to making real resources available to agricultural producers will be thwarted. This is, of course, the central political issue for development in Africa, raised by the Bank report and others.

It is this political issue which is correctly emphasised by Manfred Bienefeld in his contribution to the IDS review.[11] The consequent changes in real incomes carry implications to which he rightly draws attention in terms of the changed consumption patterns of the urban salaried elites as compared with the smallholder producer, and also the changed (and improved) balance of payments impact which these consumption patterns would have. None of this is in dispute with the Bank's analysis and recommendations. However, Bienefeld concludes on the pessimistic note that usually only governments which are of a different political constitution than those at present in power, could achieve this switch in real incomes in favour of agriculture. The Bank's report did not share this pessimism and, in any case, it would clearly have been inappropriate for it to comment on such matters.

In summary, on this first set of issues, there has been a gross misrepresentation of the priorities which the Bank believes are important for Africa. Poverty alleviation and the provision of basic needs are still seen as the important objectives. However, they are seen, as they always have been seen by the Bank, as dependent on and consistent with a greater concern about what is required to get production, and particularly agricultural production, moving upwards. The only major changes over the past few years or so in Bank perceptions on these matters is an increased concern over what is necessary to achieve a higher rate of growth in agricultural production. Anybody who looks at the record of the past two decades cannot but share this concern.

## THE LAGOS PLAN OF ACTION AND THE WORLD BANK REPORT

The position taken by the Conference of African Ministers responsible for Economic Development and Planning of the Member States of the ECA at their Tripoli meeting was that the strategy recommended by the World Bank 'is in fundamental contradiction with the political, economic and social aspirations of Africa' as reflected in the *Lagos Plan of Action, (LPA)*.[12] In fact, of course, the World Bank has neither the right nor the wish to supplant the objectives for Africa established by the Heads of State of the OAU under the *LPA*. The Bank's responsibility is to give support to member governments individually and collectively to achieve their developmental goals. In doing so, the Bank has a duty to examine whether policies and programmes which it is requested to support have a reasonable probability of achieving the national and regional goals. The Bank's *AD* was designed within this approach. The 'twin principles' of the *LPA* – 'national and collective self-reliance and self-sustaining development' – are developmental goals which are fully eligible for support within the mandate of the Bank.

The question, therefore, is not about objectives, but about how agreed objectives are to be attained and over what time period (the year 2000 was the target date in the *LPA* and the ECA has now taken the year 2008 for its 'Perspective Study', published in March, 1983). The Bank's *AD* represents a contribution to the discussion of this question. Its central theme is that, whatever the advérse nature of past and prospective external factors (weather, terms of trade, market access, etc.), unless African governments adopt policies and programmes which more effectively unlock the productive potentials of their economies – particularly that of their smallholder producers and their small-scale artisans and providers of haulage and other services – then their longer-term development objectives outlined in the *LPA* and in national and sub-regional plans have little hope of being achieved. Greater efficiency in resource use is what the Bank report is about. This is necessary for achieving any set of objectives. While the desirability of 'greater efficiency' in resource use can be criticised as a platitude which has universal validity, the record of growth of output in Africa over the past two decades has clearly demonstrated that it is a platitude which has greater significance for policy-making in Africa than in most other parts of the world.

It is clear, however, that this conception of the Bank report as a contribution to the discussion of what should be done *now and during the next few years* to achieve the *longer-term objectives of the Lagos Plan of Action*, is not accepted by many participants in the discussion of African development strategies. They continue to see the *AD* as inconsistent with the *LPA*. There are several strands to this view. However, the following issues appear to be the most important and will be examined in turn, although they are, of course, interrelated:

(a) food self-sufficiency;
(b) export agriculture;
(c) industrial policy;
(d) pricing policy;
(e) roles of the private sector and of government;
(f) regional and sub-regional development.

## FOOD SELF-SUFFICIENCY

Food self-sufficiency as an objective of African policies is an issue upon which much of the criticism of the World Bank report has focused.

Reginald Green in the IDS *Bulletin* argues that the Bank report is inconsistent on this issue: 'It havers [sic] on food self-sufficiency, intuitively supporting it, almost pulling back on the basis of its commitment to letting short-run global market prices decide and pushing exports, and also arguing that food and export/industrial crops are complementary anyhow'.[13] Rather than try to defend the Bank's report against Green's criticism it would seem preferable to re-state the Bank's position so that discussion and action can proceed further.

Self-sufficiency in staple foodstuffs is an objective which the Bank fully accepts. The fact that this is not recognised by readers of *AD* arises from the emphasis placed in the Bank report on reservations to the definition of the food self-sufficiency objective and to the implications for its achievement. There are three major reservations.

Firstly, the report questioned the desirability of achieving food self-sufficiency in the extreme and absolute sense of meeting from domestic production *all* the food demands from *all* the population irrespective of: (i) the resource costs of so doing; (ii) the fact that some of these food demands are inflated by consumer subsidies; and (iii) that the beneficiaries of such high-cost/consumer-subsidised food demands are typically the relatively well-to-do in the urban areas. These are the cases of the so-called 'imperial grains'. The view that meeting these high-cost food demands should not be given high priority in the allocation of very scarce resources and therefore that the objective of self-sufficiency in food should exclude such requirements is, we believe, widely accepted by both proponents and opponents of the World Bank's *Agenda for Action*, and is, moreover, consistent with the ECA's projections in its 1983 *Perspective Study*.[14]

Secondly, the report noted as a fact that research into basic staples had not progressed very rapidly and certainly not as rapidly as for export crops, either under colonial or post-colonial governments (hybrid maize is an exception). There is, therefore, an existing imbalance in the technical production packages available to agricultural producers. The Bank strongly recommended that this imbalance should be corrected over the next several years through the rapid development of programmes of research including local adaptation into basic foodcrops. In this way the present comparative advantage in export crops could be changed over time into a comparative advantage in food crops. Comparative advantage was clearly seen as a dynamic concept. Furthermore only by the development of such food research programmes could the objective of self-sufficiency in basic foodcrops by the year 2000 for Africa's rising population be achieved (the *LPA* target date). In the meantime, of course, this rising population has to be fed; this means importing the required amounts of food to cover the food deficit. It should be emphasised that part of the import needs of individual food-deficit countries can be met from those African countries which are producing a surplus. In fact, efforts at regional economic integration should probably start with food rather than with manufactured goods. However, from whatever source imported food might come, in the absence of food aid the increased import bill has to be paid for through increased exports. It is in this context of the need for a phased programme to achieve self-sufficiency in basic foodstuffs that the need for increased exports in the short/medium run has to be seen.

Thirdly, and finally, the report was overwhelmingly concerned with the dismal record of the agricultural sector as a whole over the past decade or so and with the prospect that this poor performance would continue unless major policy changes were introduced. In emphasising the sector-wide nature of the problem, the report noted that the evidence suggested that domestic food production and export production appeared to be complements not substitutes; that ʿwhere export agriculture had performed well so also had food production. This suggested two lines for future policy formulation. Firstly, and most importantly, that the shortcomings of policy related less to the balance between food and export agriculture than to policy in relation to the sector as a whole. For instance, the concern should be with the terms of trade of agriculture as against other sectors and only secondarily with the fine-tuning between production incentive prices for food as against exports. Secondly, the apparent complementarity of exports and food suggested that in some circumstances, at least in the short/medium run, if the efficiency of the institutional and other arrangements established to increase export agriculture could be increased, this could, in addition, result in increased food output.

In summary, the Bank report accepts food self-sufficiency in basic foodcrops as a desirable objective for African countries individually and collectively. Its qualifications relate to the definition of food self-sufficiency and to the measures required for achieving the objective and their phasing.

## EXPORT AGRICULTURE

The *AD*'s recommendations on primary product exports in general and agricultural exports in particular have generated controversy along two lines. Firstly, on the relative priority of exports in the *Agenda for Action* and, secondly, on the realistic potential for generating increased income from this source given the prospective terms of trade and the so-called 'fallacy of composition' in the Bank report.

On the first of these issues, it would appear that whatever the rate of growth of industry might be over the next 20 years, and whatever strides Africa might make in 'delinking' itself from the rest of the world – assuming this to be the desired objective under the *LPA* – export agriculture will inevitably have to grow rapidly if development is to be accelerated. There are no feasible alternatives for the provision of the foreign exchange that will be required for providing inputs for industrial growth and the growth of the supporting infrastructure.

A Keynesian-type 'bootstrap' strategy, in which higher levels of output in the industrial and food-producing sectors to meet increased levels of domestic demand are generated without 'leakages' into imports, is not feasible in Africa. Certainly a lot more can and should be done by African governments to make the strategy more feasible than at present – for instance, by developing both appropriate technologies and patterns of consumption which are less import-intensive. The policies that are required in order to achieve this greater 'delinking' or 'reduced leakage of increased economic activity into the balance of payments' are taken up later in this chapter. However, even if these policies were to be acted upon much more rapidly than at present seems likely, increased flows of foreign exchange would be required to meet the import levels generated by an agenda for accelerated development. Thus the characterisation in the IDS articles and elsewhere of the Bank report as recommending 'export-led' growth is a misrepresentation. The appropriate characterisation is that it is a strategy for accelerated development in which increased export earnings are a necessary condition – but also, of course, one which is conditional on many other policies. Furthermore, the Bank strategy is one which aims to minimise the rate of growth of imports associated with any level of overall GNP growth in Africa because of the external constraints on export earnings (see below). The export of many of Africa's traditional primary products is not seen as an 'engine of growth' in the long term, however important they might be seen as a condition for growth over the next ten years or so.

It is in this framework that the second issue of export agriculture has to be examined, namely, the terms of trade problem and the so-called 'fallacy of composition' which underlies the Bank report. A major concern of most reviewers of *AD* has been with the declining terms of trade prospects and market access for primary products of African countries. The African Governors of the Bank very correctly emphasised this concern in the communiqué they issued after reviewing the report. These poor prospects were acknowledged in the Bank report and in other reports of the Bank such as the annual *World Development Report*. They are particularly depressing in relation to those agricultural exports of special interest to African countries, e.g. the tropical beverages (cocoa, coffee and tea). Furthermore, in the years since the Bank report was prepared, both actual and prospective prices have declined further. It is also true that to the extent that many African countries take the action recommended by the Bank and increase their supplies of these exports, the price prospects will deteriorate even further – and *a fortiori* if *all* African countries were to do so. This is the so-called fallacy of composition in the Bank report.

Clearly, the most desirable way to handle the commodity problem for those primary commodities that are produced overwhelmingly in the developing world and consumed overwhelmingly in the developed countries and for which the long-run price and income elasticities are very low, is through commodity agreements which restrict production through quota allocations. This most obviously applies to the tropical beverages but to date such an agreement has only been effective (on and off) for coffee. Such quota agreements one hopes would give preference to both the poorer developing countries and to those having fewer alternative export opportunities. Preference along these lines would favour most African countries as against most of those in Asia and Latin America.

Unfortunately the developing world continues to have difficulty in coordinating its policies and programmes in a manner that would effectively maximise the aggregate income which it derives from trade with the developed world in primary products. The relevant question is then how individual African countries and Africa as a whole should act in these circumstances. To date, Africa's behaviour – deliberately or by default – has been to permit its share of the international market for a whole range of primary products to fall: cocoa, groundnuts, oilseed cake and meal, palm kernels and palm oil, sesame seed, bananas, rubber, sisal, sugar, tobacco. Brazilian cocoa producers, Malaysian palm product and rubber producers, and other non-African primary product producers have not hesitated to increase their shares of the international market for these commodities while those of Africa have fallen. Yet the comparative advantage of African countries is undoubtedly in these commodities and, moreover, the per capita income of African countries and therefore the significance of marginal income losses/gains is greater than for other developing country competitors. It seems strange for opponents of the Bank's *Agenda for Action* to appear to be arguing that Africa should continue to reduce its contribution to supplies reaching primary product markets in order to maintain the foreign exchange earning power of its more wealthy and more economically diversified developing country competitors. While the Bank's critics who draw attention to the fallacy of composition in the Bank report might be correct in arguing that for many products Africa as a whole is a price-setter not a price-taker, they must equally recognise that for these same products the elasticity of supply from frequently richer, non-African developing countries is very high. How can it make sense, for instance, for Ghana, with so few export alternatives in the short run and with its whole economy held at very low levels of economic activity due to its balance of payments constraint, to be handing over its cocoa market to Brazil which has so many alternative foreign exchange earning opportunities? Similar examples exist throughout Africa for other countries and other products.

It is, moreover, also important to emphasise that while the Bank report did, of course, look at Africa as a whole, for which the fallacy of composition has some relevance, decision-making is at the individual country level. In making decisions on primary product export policy, any one African country has to judge to what extent its African neighbours (and other countries around the world) will be seeking to exploit market opportunities for particular products (possibly under encouragement from the World Bank!). In fact experience will suggest to it that many countries are unlikely to respond through effective pricing and other policies to these market opportunities. On the contrary, critics of the Bank who base their criticism on the 'fallacy of composition', assume that all countries will do so (or that many, or most of them, will do so). Of course, the critics can continue to make a debating point of the fact that the Bank's advice on the importance of primary product exports only makes sense if a small number of countries heed the advice. If, however, in the judgement of governments in individual countries this is the realistic assumption for them to make, then the fallacy of composition becomes a fallacy of logic, not of real world national economic decision-making.

But even if the fallacy were a real world possibility, the Bank's recommendation on export policy is simply modified, not irrelevant. Export prices and price prospects would, of course, be even more depressed if all African countries increased their primary product exports. However, given the foreign exchange constraint on their growth, and the probable absence of alternative export-earning opportunities in the short run, African countries need to ensure that they fully exploit their comparative advantage as against other suppliers for whom alternative income-earning opportunities are likely to place a floor on costs of production which is higher than that in countries for which alternatives are not so readily available. However, the depressed market prospects should hasten the determination of African governments to diversify out of such products and into other forms of primary and industrial production in which market opportunities at home and overseas are more buoyant. On this there is no disagreement. The question is the phasing of policy changes which is required to achieve this objective and, in particular, the role of traditional primary-product export earnings within this phased programme. The Bank considers that they have a vital role to play in the short and medium term; the Bank's critics seem content to ignore the transition problem and to concentrate their attention on the ultimate goal of an Africa less dependent on earnings from primary products with limited market opportunities – a goal which is not in dispute.

## INDUSTRIAL POLICY

Africa's intentions in terms of industrial development, as expressed in the *Lagos Plan of Action* and elsewhere, are extremely ambitious. The Bank report shared much of this ambition, recognising in particular that industry should grow more rapidly than agriculture. However, it is central to the Bank's analysis that the growth of agriculture and of industry are complementary;[15] that industry can only grow as rapidly as demand for its products is growing from rising incomes in the agricultural community, supplemented by export demand, and as rapidly as the supply of inputs into industrial activities from the agricultural sector is growing. On the basis of a thriving agricultural sector and appropriate industrial policies, the Bank report envisaged rapid growth in a number of industries – textiles, metal manufactures, building materials, light consumer goods. In the Bank's *AD*, priority to agriculture in the 1980s is not, as suggested by critics, in substitution for industrialisation but as a necessary condition for industrialisation to take place.

Furthermore, the industrialisation process is seen overwhelmingly in terms of the internal needs of African countries individually and collectively. While the report argues that Africa should take every opportunity through policy changes to exploit market opportunities for its manufactured goods, it is a clear distortion to argue that the report proposes an export-oriented strategy for industrial development.[16] In general the Bank would agree with Godfrey's conclusion that the export of manufactured goods is a development which should come 'later rather than sooner'. What is now required is an industrial strategy which will generate such opportunities as 'less late' as possible. Godfrey does not spell out the elements of such a strategy. However, his emphasis on the need for considerations of efficiency to be strongly reflected in the framework of industrial policy is completely in accord with the Bank report. In this respect, like the Bank report, he expresses reservations about direct controls on imports through product-by-product licensing and the indefinite continuation of high tariff levels. In a cryptic footnote, he refers to 'macro import limits enforced other than through product-by-product import licensing'[17] but he fails to elaborate on what is in his mind and whether the role of exchange rate policy is part of his thinking. In fact, like all the IDS contributors and most other commentators on the Bank report, he presumably decided to ignore the issue of the exchange rate regime as a component of policy packages for dealing with agricultural and industrial policy and with the achievement of the developmental objectives of growth and poverty alleviation more generally (about which more will be said later).

## PRICING POLICY

One of the most distinctive features of the contrasting approaches of the World Bank report and of many of its critics is the emphasis given in the Bank report to pricing policy. In the *AD* it emerges as the pervasive policy issue in agriculture, industry, energy, and other sectors. Moreover, it is seen as of equal importance irrespective of the ownership question, i.e. the private sector/public sector issue.

Essentially the Bank report asserts that all micro-economic decision-makers – smallholders, artisans, industrialists, managers of parastatals, families as both consumers and income earners, etc. – are highly responsive to price incentives. Maybe part of this responsiveness will only be in the medium-to-longer run (planting more tree crops, investing in a new factory, etc.) but there will also, so the Bank argues, be more immediate and shorter-term responsiveness. Contrary to the reverse assertions which are often made, the responsiveness of African economies is in many respects likely to be greater in both the short and long run than that of developed countries where established economic structures are frequently strongly defended against changes in technology and patterns of consumer demand by entrenched and powerful institutions. Smallholders both in pre- and post-independent Africa have demonstrated very great responsiveness to changes in price signals and to changing market opportunities.

The *AD* is concerned that too little emphasis has been given by governments in Africa to the need to permit or to mandate price signals which will encourage micro-actions that are consistent with the achievement of national development objectives – increased agricultural output, the earning of foreign exchange, the widening and deepening of the industrial sector based on local inputs and serving domestic consumer needs – and which discourage micro-actions that are contrary to the achievement of national development objectives – discouragement of imports, etc. If improved efficiency in resource use is to be achieved, furthermore, a greater recognition of the pattern of international comparative advantage in a dynamic sense is required. This was not intended in the Bank report to imply a blind allegiance to the structure of international prices, but to emphasise that failure to reflect the present and prospective international pattern of prices in domestic prices has costs in terms of reduced real incomes and rate of growth of real incomes.

In common with *AD*, the *LPA* also stressed one overwhelmingly important aspect of pricing policy when it asserted: 'At the root of the food problem in Africa is the fact that Member States have not usually accorded the necessary priority to agriculture in the allocation of revenue'[18] and it later recommended that, 'Member States formulate and apply effective and coherent policies to ensure that prices of farm inputs and farm produce provide an adequate incentive for increasing food production particularly by small farmers while safeguarding the interests of the poorer consumers at the same time' and, more generally, that 'policies have to emphasize consistently the need not only to improve the living conditions on the farms but also to increase farm real incomes as a means of making agriculture more attractive and remunerative.'[19]

However, in contrast to the Bank report, the *LPA*, as well as the ECA and many other critics of the Bank report have given overwhelming emphasis to the institutional changes that are required to achieve Africa's national, regional and sub-regional objectives. This emphasis is expressed most clearly by the ECA when it states: 'The Plan [i.e. the *Lagos Plan of Action*] places special importance on the establishment and strengthening of various institutional arrangements for regional technical co-operation and economic integration' and it 'underscores the importance of involving all agents of development and change, such as private and public enterprises in agriculture and industry.'[20]

In emphasising the importance which the Bank report believes should be given by African governments to pricing, there has clearly been a danger that the report would be interpreted as suggesting that 'getting the prices right' is all that is required of policy-makers if development is to be accelerated. In fact, of course, the report gives at least equal importance to institutional improvements for achieving accelerated development, e.g. agricultural marketing arrangements, research and extension, parastatal efficiency. Certainly considerably more work is required to ensure that institutional arrangements are modified in ways that are required to ensure that the responsiveness to price changes is maximised.

Likewise it would seem important that more research should also be undertaken to determine the appropriate changes in pricing policy that are required if the objectives of the *LPA* are to be achieved. Self-sufficiency in food, greater weight to industrialisation, African economic integration, etc. cannot be achieved without a pattern of incentives to farmers, consumers, etc. that induce them to behave in ways which will ensure the achievement of the Lagos objectives. We would hazard the guess that when this work is completed its conclusions will be very similar to those on pricing and incentive systems which emerge from the Bank report.

## EXCHANGE RATE POLICY

Of particular significance in this regard would be an examination of the implications for exchange rate policy of a determination to achieve the objectives of the *LPA*. The complete failure of the critics of the Bank report (including the IDS contributors) to address this issue reflects the widespread failure to recognise that exchange rate policy is one of the most pervasive instruments of development policy. On the contrary, it is regarded by many as simply a component part of restrictive demand management programmes. Moreover, its 'active' use by governments as an important instrument of development policy has been replaced by a 'reactive' and negative attitude by governments, most obviously in the context of negotiating with the IMF for use of Fund resources. Yet it is impossible to see how the remuneration of agricultural producers as visualised under the *LPA* can be achieved in many countries without more attention being given to exchange rate policy. More generally it is difficult to see how the Lagos objectives of greater self-reliance and African economic integration can be achieved without an appropriate exchange rate policy being formulated. Self-sufficiency in food or in manufactured goods is going to be difficult if not impossible to achieve if the foreign exchange with which to buy these products from non-African sources continues to be so cheap and, therefore, imported goods are so frequently at a price advantage over domestic output. Why, furthermore, should any individual African country buy its food or its manufactured goods from another African country when they can be purchased more cheaply from the Western world, from Japan or elsewhere? African integration can only be encouraged in an efficient manner by making it more profitable for consumers, farmers, artisans and industrialists within African countries to trade with each other rather than with the rest of the world.

Exchange rate policy, in the Bank's view, has to be a central part of any realistic policy framework to achieve African growth and structural objectives. It should be examined by individual countries and by African regional institutions in this context and in advance of the frenetic and emotionally laden circumstances that typically exist when a financial emergency requires the use of IMF resources. The IDS review could have usefully contributed to such a discussion. Colclough briefly acknowledges the problem of over-valued exchange rates but then immediately proceeds to emphasise the undesirable secondary effects of devaluation on wage and salary levels.[21] In general the silence on the issue of exchange rate policy by all critics of the Bank's report is deafening.

## ROLES OF THE PUBLIC AND PRIVATE SECTORS

In a curious way this is an issue on which there is more agreement among Africans and among observers of African economies, and yet one on which there is more perceived disagreement, than on most other issues.

The World Bank's view was expressed by its President in the Foreword to the Africa study when he stated that a greater role for the private sector 'is not a recommendation which derives from any pre-conceived philosophy of ownership'. Rather:

It derives from considerations of efficiency, which suggest that governments can more effectively achieve their social and development goals by reducing the widespread administrative overcommitment of the public sector and by developing and relying more on the managerial capacities of private individuals and firms, which can respond to local needs and conditions, particularly in small-scale industry, marketing, and service activities.[22]

Other observers are equally balanced and objective in their statements. For instance, the *LPA* emphasises the importance of smallholder production in agriculture and of the 'network of small and medium scale industries' and of the 'informal sector' and 'indigenous entrepreneurs in the industrial sector'.[23] The ECA emphasises that the *LPA* underscores the importance of involving 'all agents of development and change, such as private and public enterprises in agriculture and industry' and more recently in its *Perspective Study* the ECA draws attention to 'the limited rate at which the Government sector can continue to expand and absorb enough labour force' and 'thus the need to expand output and employment opportunities in sectors outside government such as private industries, large scale mining and agriculture'. The ECA continues: 'A large number of entrepreneurs should thus be developed who, in the process of creating employment for themselves, will also provide employment opportunities for others in the critical productive sectors.'[24]

Yet controversy continues: in particular, critics assert that the Bank exaggerates the role and potential of the private sector. Reginald Green, in his contribution to the IDS *Bulletin*, gives the correct lead to governments when, in discussing the public/private issue in the extremely important context of agricultural marketing, he asserts that the: 'Arguments turn on the mix [of public/private roles] and on the real efficiency of the private sector'. He continues by arguing that: 'For some crops the private sector does have lower costs and pays at least the same price to the grower as the public sector'. However, he argues that 'this may not be general' and that the Bank report 'gives a somewhat too general and too roseate picture'.[25]

Green's pragmatic approach based on efficiency and particularly on price and service (e.g. punctuality of payment) to producers, is in complete accord with the approach of the Bank. Maybe he is correct that the Bank's view of the private sector is 'too roseate'. Maybe his fellow contributor, Christopher Colclough, is correct when he asserts that: 'In response to the view that the private sector should take on more of the activities presently conducted by government, the crucial question is: does an indigenous private sector with sufficient resources and experience to do so yet exist?' 'In most cases', he asserts, 'the answer will be in the negative'.[26]

The answer to Green, to Colclough and to others (including the World Bank) would seem to be very simple. Let the African smallholder, artisan, truck driver, consumer, decide. Economists sitting in Sussex, Washington, Oxford, Nova Scotia, Sydney and other places arguing on the basis of grossly inadequate analytical tools and data will never reach agreement.

So the answer should be found by permitting small entrepreneurial activities in marketing, transportation, industry, etc. to develop in 'fair' competition with the public sector. At present, private activities are often illegal (e.g. marketing of crops) or discriminated against: is it likely in many countries that a local artisan wishing to repair tractors will ever be able to buy the required tools and materials and spare parts under present import licensing and marketing arrangements? Similarly public sector organisations are often undertaking services other than the commercial ones with which they would be competing with the private sector. They would, therefore, either have to be relieved of these responsibilities or compensated for their cost, if competition were to lead to a test of the real efficiency cost of supplying a commodity or service. A typical example is where a public marketing agency is bearing the costs of providing marketing services to outlying areas through pan-territorial pricing structures, or of carrying buffer stocks or feeding people in drought-stricken areas or of operating an extension service.

Public sector/private sector competition is not, of course, a panacea for all problems; there are no panaceas, only packages of policy reforms. It is, however, a way forward to provide an objective test of efficiency in certain instances and one that has been used by non-African countries including those which incline to a large government role in their economies. The Bank would hazard the view that whatever might be the final 'mix' of public/private in any activity (i.e. the Reg Green issue), Colclough will come to be seen as markedly off the mark in his view that an indigenous private entrepreneurial sector does not exist in most African countries in respect of the provision of many goods and services supplied by the small-scale and informal private sector.

This conclusion is not, of course, intended to cover the problem of public utilities or of those industrial activities which, because of their technical nature, must be of large or medium size (fertiliser factories and so on). Colclough confuses these two types of activity with the small-scale artisan, service and informal sector activities, and, in so doing, muddies the water of discussion rather than providing greater clarity.

One further issue of public sector activity, as discussed in the Bank report, can be commented upon at this point. Colclough jumps from a correct statement of the support given in the Bank's report to the charging of fees for schools, medicine, irrigation and drinking water, to the preposterous statement that the 'Bank feels that these are the main areas where cuts in government expenditure can be made'. On the contrary it is because the Bank feels these are, and should remain, priority areas for increased expenditure both for consumption and *production reasons*, that it argues for ensuring that the present constraints on their expansion which stem from the actual or perceived constraints on taxable capacity should be addressed through the examination of alternative financing and delivery mechanisms. Furthermore, evidence suggests that when their incomes rise rural families and villages often have *more interest* in meeting their own basic needs than Colclough credits them with and, conversely, that when tax revenues rise many African governments have *less* interest than Colclough credits them with in meeting the basic needs of rural families and more interest in expending revenues on other activities – frequently activities having zero or low developmental priority (defence, increased civil service employment, non-targeted subsidy programmes). As argued earlier in this chapter, there has not been any *volte face* by the Bank on the related issues of growth and development, raising the incomes of the poor, the meeting of basic needs, and so on. Colclough has misread, or is misrepresenting, the position of the Bank on these issues, both during the 1970s and today.

## CONCLUDING COMMENTS

The Johnston/Clark quotation at the beginning of this chapter, emphasised the need for 'substantial consensus' among analysts if policy-makers were to be expected to take action. The message in what has followed in the chapter has been to suggest that substantial consensus does, in fact, exist; and to demonstrate that many, if not most, disagreements have been apparent rather than substantive. This message reinforces Reginald Green's conclusion that the 'proposals in the Bank's Report include all those to which he [Green] and most critics would give high priority'.

The perception of major disagreements, particularly between the recommendations of the *Lagos Plan of Action*, the ECA *Perspective Study* and the World Bank's *Agenda for Action* stem overwhelmingly from the different time frames of the analyses. The *LPA* and the ECA analysis, have been concerned with setting longer-term developmental objectives for Africa within which technological changes, industrial development, food self-sufficiency, human resource development and African integration figure very prominently. The Lagos Plan and the ECA have left for further study at the regional, sub-regional and national levels, the determination of the policy and institutional changes that are required if Africa is to move effectively from its present position to the achievement of its longer-term objectives. The Bank report, on the contrary, was concerned overwhelmingly with the short- and medium-term problems. In particular it was obsessed with the problem that unless the poor and deteriorating record of agricultural production can be reversed, the longer-term developmental objectives that Africa has set itself have little or no chance of being achieved. The *AD* was, therefore, concerned to address the question of what can be done to raise output and improve the efficiency of resource use in the short and medium run when the basic constraints on African development have to be accepted as given – present state of agricultural and industrial technology; the present levels of human resource development (education, training, experience, health standards); the present level of costs in the industrial sector; and so on.

The point at which this contrast between the *LPA* and the *AD* becomes clearest is in respect of the signficance of comparative advantage for the determination of agricultural policy and also of industrial policy. In the short run, comparative advantage is determined not only by natural factors but also by historical factors. For most of Africa this means that export agriculture frequently has a comparative advantage at the margin over food production and industrial production. Hence the emphasis placed by the Bank on ensuring that export agricultural opportunities be more fully exploited during the 1980s than they were during the 1970s. However, comparative advantage can and should be changed over time through technological changes, research, extension and through policy and institutional development. Failure to take a dynamic view of comparative advantage in this manner would imply a failure to respond to the technological and market opportunities that are the basis of long-term development. For Africa, the food self-sufficiency, export diversification and industrialisation objectives of the *LPA* are fully consistent with the emphasis placed on comparative advantage and the efficient use of resources in the Bank's *AD*. This consistency, however, has to be within a realistic time frame and what is realistic will depend on the priority accorded to the factors that determine dynamic comparative advantage. It is in this area that the emphasis given in the *LPA* to the development and transfer of technology, and in the Bank's *AD* to the importance of agricultural research come together.

If this message is accepted, that there is much greater consensus than often assumed at the level not only of broad objectives but also of policy requirements, the priority now is for African governments to determine individually and jointly the precise paths of action which they need to take. These programmes of action need to recognise two over-riding realities. Firstly, there is the reality of the deteriorated global environment of trade and aid within which African development has to take place. At one and the same time this deterioration makes policy reform both more urgent yet more difficult to implement. Secondly, these programmes must honestly recognise the reality of experiences with particular policies and institutional arrangements in each country over the past two decades – bias against agriculture, role of public and private sectors, etc.

Programmes of action, if they are to take Africa out of its pervasive economic crisis, must in this way be responsive to both need and experience. The political challenge to African governments is enormous, but the political challenge is also to the world community, particularly to developed countries, to provide maximum external support on a sustained basis to such programmes of action.

## NOTES

1. This chapter is a modified version of a paper presented to a conference sponsored by the Society for International Development, Kenya Chapter, on 'Development Options for Africa in the 1980s and Beyond', Nairobi, Kenya, 7–9 March 1983.
2. Bruce F. Johnston and William C. Clark, *Redesigning Rural Development, A Strategic Perspective* (Baltimore, Maryland: Johns Hopkins University Press, 1982) Chapter 1 and specifically pp. 20–21.
3.. Economic Commission for Africa, *ECA and Africa's Development 1983–2008: A Preliminary Perspective Study* (Addis Ababa: ECA, 1983)
4. It should be recalled that the World Bank's Report was prepared in response to a request of the Bank's African Governors, in September 1979, for a programme of action for sub-Saharan Africa.
5. See United Nations Information Service (ECA), 'The World Bank and Africa's Development Strategy', Information Sheet No. 4, 29 September 1982.

6. 'Accelerated Development in Sub-Saharan Africa: What Agenda for Action?' IDS *Bulletin*, vol. 14 (January 1983) no. 1.

7. Reginald Green, 'Incentives, Policies, Participation and Response: Reflections on World Bank "Policies and Priorities in Agriculture" ' IDS *Bulletin*, vol. 14 (January 1983) no. 1, p. 30. See also Green and Allison in Chapter 3.

8. IDS *Bulletin*, vol. 14 (January 1983) no. 1, p. 1.

9. Christopher Colclough, 'Are African Governments as Unproductive as the Accelerated Development Report Implies?' IDS *Bulletin*, vol. 14 (January 1983) no. 1, p. 28.

10. Ibid., p. 29.

11. 'Efficiency, Expertise, NICs and the Accelerated Development Report', IDS *Bulletin*, vol. 14 (January 1983) no. 1, pp. 18–23.

12. UN Information Service, 'The World Bank and Africa's Development Strategy', p. 3.

13. Green, 'Incentives, Policies, Participation and Response', p. 31.

14. ECA, *ECA and Africa's Development 1983–2008*. See in particular Table 14. which shows a self-sufficiency ratio of 85 per cent for cereals in the normative scenario for the year 2008 as against ratios of 100 per cent for roots, tubers and pulses.

15. See also World Bank, *World Development Report 1982* (New York: Oxford University Press, 1982).

16. See, for example, Martin Godfrey, 'Export Orientation and Structural Adjustment in Sub-Saharan Africa', IDS *Bulletin*, vol. 14 (January 1983) no. 1, p. 39.

17. Ibid., p. 44 *n*. 6.

18. Organisation of African Unity, *Lagos Plan of Action for the Economic Development of Africa, 1980–2000* (Geneva: International Institute for Labour Studies, 1981) p. 11.

19. Ibid., p. 18.

20. ECA, *ECA and Africa's Development*, p. 2.

21. Colclough, 'Are African Governments as Unproductive . . .?' p. 29.

22. A. W. Clausen, 'Foreword' in World Bank, *Accelerated Development in Sub-Saharan Africa*, (Washington DC: World Bank, 1981) p. v.

23. OAU, *Lagos Plan of Action*, p. 23

24. ECA, *ECA and Africa's Development 1983–2008*, p. 58.

25. Green, 'Incentives, Policies, Participation and Response', p. 34.

26. Colclough, 'Are African Governments as Unproductive . . .?' pp. 26–7.

# 7 Facing Up to Africa's Food Crisis[1]

## CARL K. EICHER

The most intractable food problem facing the world in the 1980s is the food and hunger crisis in the 45 states in sub-Saharan Africa – the poorest part of the world.[2] Although the crisis follows by less than a decade the prolonged drought of the early 1970s in the Sahelian states of West Africa, weather is not the main cause of the current dilemma.[3] Nor is the chief problem imminent famine, mass starvation, or the feeding and resettling of refugees. Improved international disaster assistance programmes can avert mass starvation and famine and assist with refugee resettlement. Rather, Africa's current food crisis is long-term in nature, and it has been building up for two decades; blanketing the entire subcontinent are its two interrelated components – a food production gap and hunger. The food production gap results from an alarming deterioration in food production in the face of a steady increase in the rate of growth of population over the past two decades. The hunger and malnutrition problem is caused by poverty: even in areas where per capita food production is not declining, the poor do not have the income or resources to cope with hunger and malnutrition.

Twenty of the 33 poorest countries in the world are African.[4] After more than two decades of rising commercial food imports and food aid, the region is now experiencing a deep economic malaise, with growing balance-of-payment deficits and external public debts. The world economic recession has imposed a severe constraint on Africa's export-oriented economies. Prospects for meeting Africa's food production deficit through expanded commercial food imports thus appear dismal. Donors have responded to these difficult problems by increasing food aid flows to the point where African countries now lead the list of the world's aid recipients in per capita terms.[5] Furthermore, the World Bank's report *Accelerated Development in Sub-Saharan Africa* advocates a doubling of aid to Africa in real terms by the end of the 1980s. But the crisis cannot be solved through crash food production projects or a doubling of aid. Since the food and hunger crisis has been in the making for 10 to 20 years, solutions to the crisis cannot be found without facing up to a number of difficult political, structural, and technical problems over the next several decades.

Key questions and policies that must be examined include: What is the record of agrarian capitalism and socialism? Why did the Green Revolution by-pass Africa? What lessons have been learned from crash food production projects in the Sahel and the development strategies of the 1970s – integrated rural development, helping the poorest of the poor, and the basic needs approach? Are technical packages available for small farmers to step up food production in the 1980s? Can foreign aid assist in the alleviation of the food production crisis and economic stagnation?

## OVERVIEW OF AFRICA'S ECONOMY

Despite the fact that Africa is an extremely diverse region, several common features frame the boundaries for addressing its food crisis. First, population densities in Africa are extremely low relative to those in Asia. The Sudan, for example, is two-thirds the size of India, but it has only 18 million people as compared with 670 million in India. Zaire is five times the size of France and has only a small percentage of its arable land under cultivation. But some countries are near their maximum sustainable population densities, given present agricultural technology and available expertise on soil fertility. Much of the arable land in Africa is not farmed because of natural constraints such as low rainfall and tsetse flies, which cause human sleeping sickness and virtually preclude the use of approximately one-third of the continent, including some of the best watered and most fertile land.[6]

Second, most of the economies are open, heavily dependent on international trade, and small: 24 of the 45 countries have fewer than 5 million people, and only Nigeria has a gross domestic product larger than that of Hong Kong. Small countries have special problems in assembling a critical mass of scientific talent and in financing colleges of agriculture and national agricultural research systems.

Third, all but two African states – Ethiopia and Liberia – are former colonies.[7] The colonial legacy is embedded in the top-down orientation of agricultural institutions and the priority given to medicine, law, and the arts rather than agriculture in African universities and partially explains the low priority that African states have assigned to agriculture and to increasing food production over the past 25 years.

Fourth, Africa is an agrarian-dominated continent where at least three out of five people work in agriculture and rural off-farm activities. Moreover, since agricultural output accounts for 30–60 per cent of the gross domestic product in most countries, the poor performance of the agricultural sector over the past two decades has been a major cause of poverty and economic stagnation.

Fifth, Africa's human resource base is extremely weak relative to those of Asia and Latin America. In most countries, even after 20 years of independence, there are still only small pools of agricultural scientists and managers because of the token priority that colonial governments gave to educating Africans.

## PROFILE OF AFRICAN AGRICULTURE

Although there are more than one thousand different ethnic groups in Africa and wide differences in farming and livestock systems by agroecological zones, the following overview pinpoints the major features of African agriculture and some of the differences between it and agriculture in Asia and Latin America.[8] For the most part, land ownership in Africa is remarkably egalitarian as contrasted with that in Latin America. The uniform agrarian structure is partially a function of colonial policies that prohibited foreigners from gaining access to land in some parts of the continent, such as West Africa. But in Zambia and Zimbabwe, colonial policies promoted a dual structure of large and small farms.[9]

Empirical research has shown that African farmers, migrants, and traders are responsive to economic opportunities. Although custom, local suspicions, jealousies, ignorance, and fatalism can play a role in inhibiting the introduction of change in a particular situation, these variables do not serve as a general explanation of rural poverty.[10]

Africa is a region of family-operated small farms, in contrast to Latin America, where land ownership is highly concentrated. The typical smallholder has 5 to 15 acres under cultivation in any one year and frequently has as much or more land in fallow in order that soil fertility can be gradually restored. Thus, it is more accurate to describe most

African farming systems as land-extensive farming systems rather than land-surplus systems. The typical smallholder gives first priority in terms of land preparation, planting, and weeding to growing staple foods (such as millet, sorghum, yams, cassava, white maize, and beans) to feed his family and second priority to producing cash crops such as coffee, cotton, and groundnuts for the market.

Family labour supplies the bulk of the energy in farming, unlike in Asia, where the main energy source is oxen. The short-handle hoe and the machete are the main implements used in land preparation and weeding. Rural non-farm activities account for 25–50 per cent of the total time worked by male adults in farm households over the course of a year in Africa. Unlike in Asia, there is no landless labour class in most African countries because of the presence of idle land. .

Land tenure in Africa can be characterised as a communal tenure system of public ownership and private use rights of land.[11] The combination of private use rights and communal control over access to land allows families (a) to continue to farm and graze the same land over time and to transfer these use rights to their descendants and (b) to have the right to buy and sell rights to trees (such as oil palm and cocoa) through a system of pledging. There is no active rural land market in most countries. Land tenure and land use policy issues will be of strategic importance in the 1980s and 1990s as the frontier phase is exhausted, land markets emerge, irrigation is expanded, and herders shift from nomadic to semi-nomadic herding and sedentary farming systems that integrate crops and livestock.

Unlike in Asia, where two or three crops are grown sequentially over a twelve-month period, most African farmers produce only one crop during the rainy season and engage in some form of off-farm work during the dry season. Irrigation is a footnote in most countries because farmers can produce food and cash crops more cheaply in rainfed farming systems.

Rural Africa is at a crossroads. Farming and livestock systems are complex, heterogeneous, and changing. African villages are experiencing major changes in response to the penetration of the market economy, drought, explosive rates of population growth, and the oil boom in countries such as Nigeria and Gabon. For example, the oil boom in Nigeria has escalated rural wage rates, induced migration from northern Cameroon and Niger, and provided a market for livestock and food crops from neighbouring countries.

The subsistence farmer producing entirely for his family's consumption is hard to find in Africa today except in special cases where inadequate transport, rebellion, or political unrest have forced farmers to withdraw from the market and produce for their subsistence needs (such as in Uganda and Guinea in the 1970s and in Tanzania in the early 1980s). In the 1980s and 1990s, village institutions will be under pressure as rural Africa shifts from extensive to intensive farming and livestock systems in response to the decline in the ratio of land to labour. Inequality between countries – for example, Upper Volta and the Ivory Coast – and within countries – for example, southern and northern Sudan – will likely increase in the coming decades.

## UNDERDEVELOPED DATA BASE

Africa has a weak and uneven data base, and there is a need to interpret official statistics with caution. For example, accurate data on acreage under cultivation and yields are available for only a handful of countries. Estimates of land under irrigation vary from 1 per cent to 5 per cent. Estimates of the size of national livestock herds are notoriously suspect because of cattle tax evasion. Even trade data must be carefully examined. For example, official data on cocoa exports from Togo in the 1970s included a large volume of cocoa from Ghana which was smuggled into Togo. Data on rural income distribution are available for only a few countries. Agricultural statistical agents in most countries rely heavily on guesstimates from extension agents, and they have been known to revise their figures to bring them into line with published estimates from international agencies. The combination of underdeveloped data and the case study nature (village studies, for example) of much of the research in the past decade makes it difficult to generalise about the sources of agricultural output and the causes of poverty, malnutrition, and lagging food production.

There is also a need to beware of the pitfalls of studies that present the results of survey research, such as farm management and nutrition surveys, in terms of averages. For example, data showing that farmers produce enough food to feed each family member an average of two thousand calories a day during a given year are meaningless if some family members do not have enough food to survive during the 'hungry season'. Moreover, the use of averages promotes the view that there is a homogeneous or classless rural society and that interventions designed to improve the average incomes in an area will automatically improve the incomes of all people, including those on the lower end of the income scale. Numerous researchers have shown that rural inequality is an integral part of Africa's history, that inequality may increase as a result of technical change, and that assistance to particular groups of people will have to be carefully targeted.

In summary, although a few scholars talk glibly about average sorghum yields for a country, the 'African case', and uncritically use Africa-wide figures (for example, that women produce at least 80 per cent of the food in Africa), serious scholars wisely eschew generalising about even a sub-region such as West Africa – an area as large as the continental United States.

## FOOD AND POPULATION TRENDS

Although Africa's food statistics are unreliable – especially on food production in a given year – the overall pattern of Africa's food and population trends emerges clearly when examined over the 1960–83 period. The data on food imports, population growth and food production show that since independence Africa's historical position of self-sufficiency in staple foods has slowly dissipated.[12] Over the 1960–80 period, aggregate food production in Africa grew very slowly – by about 1.8 per cent per year, a rate below the aggregate growth rate of Asia or Latin America. However, the critical numbers are not statistics on total food production but per capita figures. The US Department of Agriculture statistics show that sub-Saharan Africa is the only region of the world where per capita food production declined in the 1960–78 period. In addition the average per capita calorie intake was below minimum nutritional levels in most countries.[13]

The per capita figures reflect the fact that Africa is the only region of the world where the rate of growth of population actually increased in the 1970s. The annual population growth rate in Africa was 2.1 per cent in the mid-1950s and 2.7 per cent in the late 1970s and is projected to increase throughout the 1980s until it levels off at about 3 per cent by the 1990s. Underlying the upward population trend is a young age structure. The average African woman produces six living children in her reproductive years.

There is little hope for reducing fertility levels in the 1980s because of a complex set of factors, including the economic contribution of children to farming and rural household activities, the pro-fertility cultural environment, the failure of family planning programmes to date, the pro-natal policies of some states, such as Mauritania, and the indifference of most African heads of state and intellectuals to population growth in what they consider to be a land-surplus continent. But explosive rates of population growth cannot be ignored much longer. For example, Kenya's annual rate of population growth of more than 4 per cent implies a doubling of population in about 17 years.[14] In Senegal, where 95 per cent of the population is Muslim and the Muslim leaders have great political power, the government is moving gradually on population intervention as it expands demographic research and quietly opens child and maternal health clinics in urban areas. In sum, for a variety of reasons, it is almost certain that most states will move slowly on population-control policies during this decade. As a result, population growth will press hard on food supplies, forestry reserves, and livestock and wildlife grazing areas throughout the 1980s and beyond.

Food imports are another important dimension of the critical food situation. Many countries that were formerly self-sufficient in food significantly increased their ratio of food imports to total food consumption in the 1960s and 1970s. According to USDA figures, food imports are dominated by grain imports – especially wheat and rice – which have increased from 1.2 million tons a year in 1961–63 to 8 million tons in 1980, at a total cost of $2.1 billion. Significantly, commercial imports of food grain grew more than three times as fast as population over the 1969–79 period. Rising food imports are attributed to many factors: lagging domestic production; structural and sectoral shifts arising from such factors as the oil boom in Nigeria and the increase in minimum wages in Zimbabwe following independence; increasing urbanisation; the accompanying shift of consumer tastes from cassava, yams, millet, and sorghum to rice and wheat; availability of food aid on easy terms; and over-valued foreign exchange rates, which often make imported cereals cheaper than domestic supplies. Although data on food aid are imprecise, food aid represented about 20 per cent of Africa's total food imports in 1982. Wheat, wheat flour and rice dominate overall imports.

Given the intimate linkage of hunger and malnutrition to poverty, economists, nutritionists, and food production speacialists are coming to agree that food and poverty problems should be tackled together. For if rural and urban incomes are increased, a large increment of the increased income of poor people (50–80 per cent) will be spent on food.[15] Unless food production is stepped up, an increase in rural and urban incomes will simply lead to increased food prices and food imports and a hardship on families in absolute poverty. Conversely, while expanded food production should be the centrepiece of food policy in Africa in the

1980s, food policy strategies must go beyond crash food production campaigns to deal with poverty itself because expanded food production by itself will not solve the basic problem of poverty.

Africa's food and poverty problems should not be allowed to overshadow some impressive achievements of the continent over the past 25 years. Foremost is the increase in average life expectancy – from an estimated 38 years in 1950 to almost 50 years in 1980. This 30 per cent increase is often overlooked by those who are mesmerised by rates of economic growth. Moreover, the achievements in education have been impressive in some countries, and there has been a vast improvement in the capacity of countries such as Nigeria, Kenya, the Ivory Coast, Cameroon, and Malawi to organise, plan, and manage their economies.

## HISTORICAL ROOTS OF POVERTY AND THE NEGLECT OF AGRICULTURE

From this overview, one can see that while most Africans are farmers and Africa has enormous physical potential to feed itself, there are substantial barriers to tapping this potential. Experts from academia, donor organisations, and consulting firms emphasise post-independence corruption, mismanagement, repressive pricing of farm commodities, and the urban bias in development strategies. Year after year, African heads of state point to unfavourable weather in their appeal for food aid. In fact, the food production crisis stems from a seamless web of political, technical, and structural constraints which are a product of colonial surplus extraction strategies, misguided development plans and priorities of African states since independence, and faulty advice from many expatriate planning advisers. These complex, deep-rooted constraints can only be understood in historical perspective starting with the pre-colonial and colonial periods.[16]

The colonial period formally began when the colonial powers met at the Berlin Congress in 1884 and decided how Africa should be partitioned among the main European powers. Until the past decade, much of the literature by economists on the colonial period has been pro-colonial. For example, Bauer boldly asserts that 'far from the West having caused the poverty in the Third World, contact with the West has been the principal agent of material progress there'.[17] But empirical research over the past two decades has shown that colonial approaches to development created a dual structure of land ownership in some countries and facilitated the production and extraction of surpluses –

copper, gold, cocoa, coffee, and so on – for external markets while paying little attention to investments in human capital, research on food crops, and strengthening of internal market linkages. For example, colonial governments gave little attention to the training of agricultural scientists and managers. By the time of independence in the early 1960s, there was only one faculty of agriculture in French-speaking tropical Africa. Between 1952 and 1963, only 4 university graduates in agriculture were trained in Francophone Africa, and 150 in English-speaking Africa. In 1964, 3 African scientists were working in research stations in Kenya, Uganda, and Tanzania.[18]

Many colonial regimes focused their research and development programmes on export crops and the needs of commercial farmers and managers of plantations. In fact, Evenson points out that in 1971 cotton was the only crop that enjoyed as much research emphasis in the Third World as in industrial countries.[19] The modest investment in research on food crops could be defended during the colonial period because the rate of population growth was low – 1 per cent to 2 per cent per annum – and surplus land could be 'automatically' brought under cultivation by smallholders. But with annual rates of population growth now approaching 3–4 per cent in some countries, researchers must devote more attention to food crops and the needs of smallholders and herders. Although the debate on colonialism will continue for decades, we have established the simple but important point that contemporary agriculture problems can only be understood by serious analysis of colonial policies and strategies.


FIVE DEBATES ON FOOD AND AGRICULTURE IN THE POST-INDEPENDENCE PERIOD

Africa's food and poverty problems are also a product of misguided policies, strategies, and priorities over the past two decades. In the post-independence period since 1960, African states have engaged in five key debates on food and agriculture. The first was over the priority to be given to industry and agriculture in development plans and budget allocations. As African nations became independent in the late 1950s and early 1960s, most of them pursued mixed economies with a heavy emphasis on foreign aid, industrial development, education, and economic diversification. For example, the late President Kenyatta promoted capitalism and encouraged investors 'to bring prosperity' to Kenya. A small number of countries such as Mali, Ghana, and Guinea shifted abruptly to revolutionary socialism in the early 1960s. But whether political leaders were espousing capitalism or socialism, they generally gave low priority to agriculture. African leaders, like former colonial rulers, thought agricultural development would simply reinforce dependency. They tended to view agriculture as a backward sector that could provide surpluses – in the form of taxes and labour – to finance industrial and urban development. Agricultural policies in many capitalist and socialist countries supported plantations, state farms, land settlement schemes, and the replacement of private traders and moneylenders with government trading corporations, grain boards, and credit agencies. The effects of these policies on agricultural production were typically inhibiting, in some cases highly so.

The second debate was over the relevance of Western neo-classical models versus the 'political economy' (stressing dependency and class structure) and radical models of development. As Western economists assumed important roles in helping to prepare development plans and serve as policy advisers in the early 1960s, Western modernisation and macro-economic models were introduced into Africa. The dominant neo-classical models emphasised the industrial sector as the driving force of development and the need to transfer rural people to the industrial sector. These models had three major shortcomings. First, they assumed that one discipline – economics – could provide the answers on how to slay the dragons of poverty, inequality, and malnutrition. As Hirschman reminds us, development is a historical, social, political, technical, and organisational process which cannot be understood by means of a single discipline.[20] Second, the cities were unable to provide jobs for the rural exodus because of trade union pressure that elevated minimum wages in government and in industry, and capital-intensive techniques in the industrial sector.[21] Third, the neo-classical growth models were unable to provide a convincing micro-understanding of the complexity of the agricultural sector – the sector that employs 50–95 per cent of the labour force in African states. Although these models were technically elegant, they seem remarkably naive today because they assigned a passive role to the agricultural sector.

The vacuity of the Western neo-classical models of development and their failure to come to grips with the broad social, political, and structural issues, as well as the complexities of the agricultural sector, opened the door for the political economy and dependency models to emerge in the 1960s and gain a large following among African intellectuals.[22] The models that emerged in Africa were greatly influenced by Latin American dependency writers. Samir Amin, an Egyptian economist, has been the pre-eminent proponent of the dependency and underdevelopment paradigm of development in Africa over the past two decades.[23] The political economy literature attempts to link rural poverty and underdevelopment to historical forces, world capitalism, and surplus extraction. The political economy models have made a valuable contribution in stressing the need to understand development as a long-term historical process, the need to consider the linkages between national economies and the world economic system, and the importance of structural barriers (for example, land tenure in Zimbabwe and Zambia) to development. But there is little empirical support for many of the assertions made by some of the political economy scholars.

The question remains, can political economy and dependency scholars move beyond their abstract models to develop models based on studies of the behaviour of African farmers and herders, on African institutions, and on micro/macro linkages in order to provide policy guidance in a continent in which the majority of the people are farmers?

The third debate – over agrarian capitalism versus socialism – has been one of the most emotional topics over the past 30 years; it will continue to dominate discussions on politics, development strategies, and foreign aid in the 1980s. Even though it is difficult to define African socialism, about one-fourth of the states now espouse socialism as their official ideology. The experiences of Ghana and Tanzania are well documented. Four years after Ghana became independent, President Nkrumah abruptly shifted from capitalism to a socialist strategy that equated modernisation with industrialisation and large-scale farming and state control over agricultural marketing. Ghana was unable to assemble the technical and managerial skills and incentive structure to operate its vast system of state farms, parastatals, and trading corporations. The failure of agrarian socialism has imposed a heavy toll on the people of Ghana.[24]

Tanzania's shift to socialism in 1967 produced a voluminous literature, international press coverage, massive financial support from international donors – especially Scandinavian countries and the World Bank – and attention from political leaders and intellectuals throughout Africa.[25] The vision of agrarian socialism is set forth in President Nyerere's essay 'Socialism and Rural Development'. But after 17 years of experimentation, it seems fair to examine the balance sheet on socialism in a country where 80 per cent of the population live in rural areas. The Tanzanian experiment is floundering in part because of the quantum jump in oil prices in the mid-1970s and the conflict in Uganda, but basically because of the sharp decline of peasant crop production[26] and production on government-managed coffee, tea, and sisal estates. One cannot overlook Tanzania's gains in literacy and social services, but one may legitimately worry about their sustainability over the longer term without increased rural incomes or exceptionally heavy foreign aid flows. There are many unanswered questions about Tanzania's experiment with agrarian socialism, such as why President Nyerere authorised the use of coercion to round up farmers living in scattered farmsteads and forced them to live in villages. Many pro-Tanzania scholars avoid this topic. But the failure of Tanzania to feed its people explains why Tanzania is no longer taken seriously as a model which other African countries want to emulate.[27]

Agrarian socialism is now under fire throughout Africa: after 20 years of experimentation, presently no African models are performing well. Even Benin, Mozambique, and Guinea are silently retreating from some of the rigid orthodoxy of socialism. What are the reasons for the failure of agrarian socialism to date? First, and most important, socialist agricultural production requires a vast amount of information and managerial and administrative skills in order to cope with the vagaries of weather, seasonable labour bottlenecks, and the need for on-the-spot decision-making authority. In most African countries, the critical shortage of skills and information is the biggest enemy of agrarian socialism. No amount of socialist ideology can substitute for the lack of soil scientists, managers, bookkeepers, mechanics, and an efficient communication system. Second, many parastatals, state farms, and government-operated grain boards have been plagued with over-staffing, corruption, mismanagement, and high operating costs. Because these constraints cannot be easily overcome, it is unlikely that Africa will make much progress with socialist agriculture in this century.

As the pendulum swings from socialism to private farming and private traders in the 1980s, it is important to stress that to put all or most of the weight on ideology – capitalism or socialism – is to ignore the important lesson learned over the past 30 years in the Third World, namely, that ideology is but one variable influencing the outcome of agricultural development projects. The 'correct' choice of ideology cannot in and of itself assure successful development. Examples of failure under both capitalist and socialist models are too numerous to conclude otherwise.

The fourth debate was over the use of pricing and taxation policies to achieve agricultural and food policy objectives. The first issue here is whether Africans are responsive to economic incentives. Empirical research has produced a consensus that African farmers do respond to economic incentives as do farmers in high-income countries but that Africans give priority to producing enough food for their families for the coming one to two years.[28] The next question is whether African states have pursued positive or negative pricing and taxation policies for agriculture.[29] Numerous empirical studies across the continent have provided conclusive evidence that many countries (both capitalist and socialist) are maintaining low official prices for food and livestock in order to placate urban consumers. The impact of these negative policies dampens incentives to produce food and livestock for domestic markets and encourages black market operations and smuggling across borders.

For example, starting in the mid-1960s Tanzania paid farmers throughout the country a uniform price for maize in order to achieve equity objectives. But this policy discouraged regional specialisation, increased transportation costs, and encouraged smuggling across borders. In Mali, the government pricing policy for small farmers in a large irrigated rice production scheme in 1979 could be labelled 'extortion'. A meticulous two-year study has shown that it costs farmers 83 Malian francs to produce a kilo of rice but that the government paid farmers only 60 Malian francs per kilo.[30] Does it seem irrational that farmers smuggled rice across the border into Senegal, Niger and Upper Volta, where they secured 108–28 Malian francs per kilo?

Not only food crops are subjected to negative pricing policies; export crops are also heavily taxed. In an analysis of pricing and taxation policies for major crops in 13 countries over the 1971–80 period, the World Bank concluded that, taking the net tax burden and the effect of over-valued currency into account, producers in the 13 countries received less than half of the real value of their export crops.[31] These examples and other studies carried out over the past two decades provide solid evidence that African states are using negative pricing and taxation policies to pump the economic surplus out of agriculture.[32] A simple but powerful conclusion emerges from this experience: African states should overhaul the incentive structure for farmers and livestock owners and adopt increased farm incomes as an important goal of social policy in the 1980s. Moreover, increasing incentives to farmers and herders is a strategic policy lever for attacking poverty and promoting rural employment.

The fifth debate – about the Green Revolution and the African farmer – concerns what can be done to increase the low cereal yields in Africa. A dominant cause of rural poverty is the fact that 60–80 per cent of the agricultural labour force is producing staple foods at very low levels of productivity. While food-grain yields in Latin America and Asia have increased since 1965, those of Africa have remained stagnant. Over the past 20 years, the Green Revolution debate has focused on whether African states could import high-yielding food-grain varieties directly from International Agricultural Research Centres in Mexico, the Philippines, and other parts of the world or whether improved cereal varieties could be more efficiently developed through investments in regional and national research programmes in Africa.

Twenty years ago, foreign advisers were optimistic about transferring Green Revolution technology to Africa, but after two decades of experimentation the results are disappointing. In fact, the Green Revolution has barely touched Africa. For example, ICRISAT's transfer of hybrid sorghum varieties from India in the late 1970s to Upper Volta, Niger, and Mali was unsuccessful because of unforeseen problems with disease, variability of rainfall, and poor soils.[33] Moreover, the Green Revolution crops – wheat and rice – that produced 40–50 per cent increases in yields in Asia are not staple foods in most of Africa.[34] Knowledgeable observers agree that African farming systems are extremely complex and that the development of suitable technical packages requires location-specific research by multidisciplinary research teams supported by strong national research programmes on the staple foods of each country.[35]

These five debates illustrate the complex set of problems that have preoccupied African states over the past two decades as they have tried to find a meaningful role for their agricultural sector in national development strategies. Throughout much of the post-independence period, most states have viewed agriculture as a backward and low-priority sector, have perpetuated colonial policies of pumping the economic surplus out of agriculture, and have failed to give priority to achieving a reliable food surplus (food security) as a pre-requisite for achieving social and economic goals. The failure of most African states to develop an effective set of agricultural policies to deal with the technical, structural, institutional, and human constraints is at the heart of the present food crisis. Part of the failure must be attributed to the colonial legacy and part to the hundreds of foreign economic advisers who have imported inappropriate models and theories of development from the United States, Europe, Asia, and Latin America. In the final analysis, agricultural stagnation in capitalist Zaire and Senegal, socialist Tanzania and Guinea, and many other countries must also be blamed on heads of state and planners who have promoted premature industrialisation, built government hotels, airlines, and large dams with negative internal rates of return,[36] and spent tens of millions of dollars building large villas for heads of state for the annual meetings of the OAU. Moreover, most African political leaders have also exhibited a fundamental misunderstanding of the role of agriculture in national development when 60–80 per cent of the people are in farming. Unfortunately, these mistakes in dealing with agriculture over the past 20 years cannot easily be overcome through crash production projects and doubling of aid over the 1980–90 period.

POLICY DIRECTION FOR THE 1980s AND 1990s

Africa's inability to feed itself amid vast amounts of unused land and record levels of foreign aid is, on the surface, one of the major paradoxes in Third World development. What should be done? While the several notable recent reports on Africa's food and economic problems agree on the severity of the food and hunger crisis, each of these assessments under-emphasises the mistakes of African states and in a somewhat self-serving fashion over-stresses the need for more foreign aid. Almost all of these reports implicitly assume that capital, rather than human resources, is the most pressing constraint in rural Africa. This preoccupation with capital is understandable because foreign aid institutions such as the International Fund for Agricultural Development (IFAD) and the World Bank have a fixation on capital transfers. Moreover, Third World countries have focused on capital transfers and the need to increase aid in the North/South dialogues, and many donors and African heads of state equate a doubling of aid with an attack on poverty in Africa. The *Lagos Plan of Action* has little new to say about agricultural development except that food production should be accelerated with the aim of achieving self-sufficiency. The World Bank's *Accelerated Development* correctly singles out domestic policy issues as the heart of the crisis, but it also advances an unsupported appeal for donors to double aid to Africa over the 1980–90 period. Further, while the World Bank report criticises large-scale irrigation projects, it does not report the Bank's own difficulties (and those of most of the other donors) in designing sound livestock projects. The World Food Council's report on the African food problem correctly notes the over-emphasis on project-type aid, the excessive number of foreign missions (for example, Upper Volta received 340 official donor missions in 1981), and the small percentage of aid funds for food production projects, but it skirts many of the political and structural barriers to change. The World Food Council's report by the African ministers of agriculture avoids the topic of population growth, the empirical record of agrarian socialism, and the disastrous performance of state grain boards.[37] New approaches are needed. The following discussion spells out a comprehensive approach for the 1980s and 1990s.

## STEPS TO MEET THE CRISIS

Solutions to Africa's food and poverty problems must, first of all, be long term. Second, they require a redirection in thinking about agriculture's role in development at this stage of Africa's economic history and about the need for a reliable food surplus as a precondition for national development. Third, there is a need for both African states and donors to admit that the present crisis is not caused by a lack of foreign aid. In fact, in many countries current aid flows cannot be absorbed with integrity. Hence, donors are part of both the problem and the solution. The Berg report underplays these issues in its unsupported case for doubling aid to Africa by the end of the 1980s. Fourth, there is a need to recognise that the lack of human resources is an overriding constraint on rural change in Africa. In fact, the human resource constraint severely limits the amount of aid that can be effectively absorbed in the short run. In order to buy time to lay a foundation for long-range solutions, it will be necessary to rely on a number of holding actions. Examples include expanded commercial food imports, food aid, and promoting seasonal and international migration until more land is brought under irrigation and higher rainfall areas can be cleared of tsetse flies and river blindness. But these holding actions must not be allowed to substitute for efforts towards long-range solutions.

Three steps should be taken now to start the process of formulating longer-term approaches. First, African states, donors, and economic advisers should jettison ambiguous slogans such as 'National Food Self-Sufficiency', 'Food First', and 'Basic Needs'.[38] Although these have a powerful emotional and political appeal, they offer little help in answering the key question: What blend of food production, food imports, and export crops should be pursued to achieve both growth and equity objectives? The concept of national food self-sufficiency should be scrapped as a rigid target because it promotes autarchy and ignores the historical and the potential role of trade in food and livestock products between African states. In summary, there is a need to return to the basics of agricultural development: investments in human resources and agricultural research, policy and structural reforms that will help small farmers and herders, revamping the incentive structure, changing the role of the state,[39] and strengthening the administrative capacity to design and implement projects and programmes.

The second immediate step should be the phasing out or restructuring of some of the crash food production projects – that is, seed multiplication, irrigated wheat schemes, livestock schemes, and integrated rural development projects – that are floundering. Many of these crash projects were hastily assembled over the past decade without a sound technical package and without being tested in a pilot phase. These unproductive projects consume scarce high-level manpower, perpetuate recurrent cost problems, and create a credibility problem for both African policy-makers and international donors. Particularly important is the reassessment of integrated rural development (IRD) projects. The weakness of most IRD projects – their lack of emphasis on food production and income-generating activities – can be corrected by restructuring some of the projects rather than phasing them out. Other projects that have been implemented in advance of a sound knowledge base, like those in livestock, should be either phased out or scaled down and continued as pilot projects for a 5 to 10 year period. A 5 to 10 year pilot phase is unheard of in Africa, but in projects like those in livestock it is a necessary period for solving technical problems and developing appropriate local institutions to solve such key issues as over-stocking.

The third immediate step is to scale down the state bureaucracy, the state payroll, and state control over private farmers and private traders. After 20 years of experience with parastatals, the record is clear: parastatals (public enterprises) are ineffective in producing food, are no more efficient than private traders in food-grain marketing, are almost all over-staffed,[40] and serve as a sponge for foreign aid. As the number of parastatal employees increases, the pressure intensifies for donors commensurately to increase their contributions to meet the payroll of the expanded bureaucracy. The parastatal disease is well known, but it is not given much attention in the reports cited above, except in the World Bank's *Accelerated Development* report, which should be applauded for its candour on this topic.

The fourth step is to realise that a food policy strategy cannot be pursued in isolation from livestock and export crop policies nor in isolation from policies to deal with rural poverty. A food policy strategy should not rule out the expansion of export crops, because expanded farm income, through food sales, export crops, and off-farm income, and productive rural employment are pre-requisites for solving rural poverty problems. Moreover, although food aid can help the rural poor in the short run, the expansion of productive rural employment is fundamental to coping with rural poverty in the long run.

## FOOD POLICY STRATEGIES

The starting point for food policy analysis in each country should be the development of a food policy strategy with two goals in mind: achieving a reliable food surplus (based on domestic production, grain storage, and international trade) and reducing rural poverty by focusing on measures to help small farmers produce more food for home consumption and more food, cash crops, and livestock for the market so that they can purchase a better diet.[41] But a word of caution is in order: food policy analysis is every bit as complex and as delicate as family planning.[42] The rice riots in Monrovia, which left more than one hundred dead in 1979, and the sugar riots in Khartoum and other major cities in the Sudan following the doubling of sugar prices in 1981 are reminders of the narrow range of options for policy-makers on food policy issues. Consequently, as experiences from the Sudan, Zimbabwe, Nigeria, and Kenya (outlined below) illustrate, most countries will move very slowly on policy reforms unless spurred by famine, a reduction in foregn-exchange earnings from petroleum, or coordinated donor leverage to link long-term food aid with policy reforms.

The Sudan provides a conspicuous example of the difficulty of mobilising the agricultural sector as an engine of growth and expanded food production. In the mid-1970s the international press frequently asserted that the Sudan could become the 'breadbasket of the Middle East' by drawing on several billion dollars of OPEC loans and gifts to develop its vast reserves of idle land. The issue today, however, is not one of exporting food to the Middle East but one of the Sudan's inability to feed its 18 million people. The Sudan was forced to rely heavily on food aid in the early 1980s in order to cope with severe balance-of-payment problems and inflation. Although the Sudan has historically excelled in cotton research, it has devoted only token attention to research on food crops. As long as the Sudan continues to receive food aid and has hopes of striking oil in the southern part of the country, there is little likelihood of policy reforms.

In Zimbabwe, the legacy of the colonial policy of promoting a dual structure of large farms for white farmers and small farms for Africans in poor natural resource regions presents a classic efficiency/equity dilemma for the Mugabe government.[43] In the early 1980s Zimbabwe was a significant maize exporter based largely on the surpluses produced by its 3500 large farmers. But the maize exports were heavily subsidised, and in 1982 the government reconsidered its role as a food security safety net for the southern African region. In 1982 Zimbabwe increased price incentives for soybean oil relative to maize in order to meet the domestic shortage of cooking oil. Although Zimbabwe gains political prestige by exporting maize to black Africa, it realises that it cannot continue to subsidise maize exports at a time when it is facing large budget deficits.

On the eve of independence in 1960, Nigeria was a net exporter of food, mainly oil palm and groundnuts. But during the 1960s Nigeria pursued import-substituting industrialisation, taxed its farmers heavily through export marketing boards, experimented with land settlements, and promoted government plantations. In 1970, ten years after independence, Nigeria was importing food, and by 1981 food imports from the United States alone totalled more than $1 billion. Petroleum exports have enabled Nigeria to pay for food imports and buy time. Although Nigeria is far ahead of most Francophone African countries in trained agricultural manpower, Idachaba reported that more than 40 per cent of the positions for senior agricultural researchers in the eight major research stations were vacant in 1978. The government recently concluded that it will take 10–15 years to achieve self-sufficiency in food production. Nigeria has now formed a high-level Green Revolution Committee to address its food problems.[44]

Although Kenya is widely regarded as an agricultural success story of the 1960s and 1970s, Kenya was confronted with food shortages in 1980 and 1981 and was forced to import maize, wheat, and milk powder. Although adverse growing conditions contributed to the food shortages of the early 1980s, the National Food Policy paper reveals that other factors were undermining Kenya's capacity to feed itself. These included the unprecedented 4 per cent rate of growth of population, the decline in wheat production following the transfer of large farms to smallholders, and a smallholder credit repayment rate of 20 per cent. The message of the National Food Policy paper is clear: Kenya has a major food production constraint that cannot be overcome except through large investments in agricultural research, irrigation, and land reclamation in the 1980s and 1990s. But one wonders why the National Food Policy paper paid lip service to population growth.[45]

The case studies illustrate the complexity of Africa's food problems and the need to analyse each country's problems on a case-by-case basis. Moreover, food policy analysis requires more than the preparation of a National Food Policy strategy paper over a two- to six-month period. Food policy analysis is an ongoing process that will undoubtedly occupy the attention of policy-makers and researchers throughout the 1980s and 1990s.

## Food Aid Leverage

A major issue in achieving policy reforms is whether donor agencies and countries can or should use food aid leverage to promote the required changes. In existence for almost 30 years, food aid is now a topic of growing interest in Africa. Although there is unanimity on using food aid for humanitarian purposes – for example, feeding refugees – food aid for development is more controversial. The opposition to this sort of food aid – where food is sold at concessional terms and extended as grants for food-for-work programmes – comes from evidence that food aid (a) can reduce the pressure on recipient countries to carry out policy reforms; (b) can depress farm prices; (c) is unreliable[46] and (d) can promote an undesirable shift in consumption patterns that will increase rather than reduce dependency or require subsidies (such as wheat production in West Africa) to maintain the Western-acquired consumption pattern.[47]

Food aid programmes are firmly institutionalised with donors. Food aid accounted for approximately 40 per cent of all US economic assistance to Africa over the 1970–80 period. Even Japan started to dispose of some of its surplus rice in Africa in the early 1980s. To date, there has been little solid academic research on the role of food aid for development puposes in Africa. Moreover, the evaluation of food aid is usually assigned to junior officers in many bilateral agencies. Hence, evaluation studies of food aid by donors should be taken with a grain of salt. The food aid experience in Asia and Latin America, however, shows that the availability of food aid can take the pressure off recipient nations to carry out internal policy reforms.

A compelling case can be made for linking food aid with policy reforms in major food-deficit countries in Africa through the development of food policy reform packages. These reform packages will be useless, however, unless there is an agreement by donors to make three- to five-year forward aid commitments in exchange for internal policy reforms. Countries such as Mali and the Sudan would be good test cases for linking food aid to tough domestic policy reforms. But unless donors agree to meet minimum forward food aid levels, African states can easily postpone policy reforms and continue to rely on a patchwork of bilateral food aid programmes.

## Agricultural Research

Beyond policy reforms, a long-range solution to food and hunger problems will depend, to a large degree, on achievements in agricultural research. Authorities on food production and livestock projects in the field now commonly bemoan the lack of proven technical packages for small farmers in dry-land farming systems throughout Africa and the uniformly unfavourable technical conditions (low rates of growth, disease) for livestock production. Significant increases are needed over the next 20 years in research expenditures on dry-land farming systems with emphasis on food crops (white maize, yams, cassava, millet, and sorghum) and on livestock.

An expanded research programme on food and livestock should be viewed in a 20-year time frame because problems such as low soil fertility and livestock diseases cannot be resolved through a series of short-term, *ad hoc* research projects. The US experience, wherein 40 years (1880–1920) were spent developing a productive system of federal and state research programmes, should be heeded by donors who are likely to expect major results in three to five years from new research projects in Africa.

Research on irrigation is particularly important and should be accelerated in the coming decades. The knowledge base for irrigation in Africa is meagre. Irrigation has played a minor role in Africa except in large-scale projects in the Sudan and in Madagascar where there is a history of irrigation by small farmers. The cultivated land under irrigation is probably less that 5 per cent in most other countries (as compared with an estimated 30 per cent in India). Following the 1968–74 drought in the Sahel, there was considerable optimism about the role of irrigated farming in 'drought-proofing' the region. Due to numerous technical and administrative problems and human resource constraints, however, the projected expansion of irrigation in the Sahel is behind schedule, and it is certain that irrigation will not play a significant role in the Sahelian states until early in the next century.

Although research on the economics of irrigation is fragmentary, the limited results provide support for a smallholder irrigation strategy in the 1980s, with priority given to ground-water development with small pumps, land reclamation through drainage and water control, and an increase in small-scale projects that are developed and maintained by groups of farmers with their own family labour. A small-scale irrigation strategy is advocated because the cost of bringing more rainfed land under cultivation is substantially less than the cost of levelling and preparing land for large-scale irrigation. For example, recent irrigation projects in Niger, Mauritania, and northern Nigeria each had costs of more than $10 000 per hectare at 1980 prices.[48] On the other hand, farmers in Seí egal have cleared and prepared their own land for irrigation, expending several hundred hours of family labour per hectare. Although irrigation will not be a panacea for the recovery of the Sahel, nor for feeding Africa in the 1980s and 1990s, a long-term research programme on the human, technical, and institutional dimensions of irrigation should be initiated in the immediate future.

It remains to be seen whether donors will have the courage to view research and graduate training within Africa as a long-term investment and whether they will provide guaranteed funding for a minimum of 10 years. Another important issue is whether country priorities of bilateral donors will remain stable enough to assure African countries of continuity in funding over a 10-year period. A rule of thumb is that an African country should never embark on a long-term programme to upgrade its national agricultural research system with major support from only one bilateral donor. But as we point out below, co-financing by six to eight donors can create as many problems as it solves.

### Investment in Human Resources

A third essential component of a long-range strategy is massive investments in human capital formation, including graduate training of several thousand agricultural scientists and managers. This is necessary to replace the foreign advisers, researchers, managers, and teachers in African universities and to meet the needs of a science-based agriculture in the next century. Since it takes 10 to 15 years of training and experience beyond high school to develop a research scientist, the investments in human capital will not produce pay-offs for Africa until the 1990s.

Building graduate agricultural training programmes within Africa necessitates a re-examination of the role of the African university in national development and the relevance of some of the present undergraduate degree programmes. For example, in 1982 the Faculty of

Law and Economics in the University of Yaoundé in Cameroon was turning out graduates with degrees in law and economics who ended up on the unemployment lines in Yaoundé. The time is propitious for African universities to move from undergraduate to graduate training programmes in science and agriculture. Before graduate education is expanded, however, some questions should be raised about priorities in undergraduate education and the relevance of the curriculum. Undergraduate degree programmes in agriculture in many universities are still embarrassingly under-valued and under-funded when compared with programmes in law, medicine, and history. For example, the University of Dakar in Senegal was formally established in 1957, and in 1960 the Senegalese assumed its administration. In 1982 there were approximately 12 000 students in the University of Dakar, of whom several thousand specialised in law and economics. Not until 1979 was a National School of Agriculture established at Thies, near Dakar, to offer undergraduate training in agriculture. That university-level teaching of agriculture was not initiated until 19 years after Senegal's independence reflects an enduring colonial legacy as well as the government's ambivalence about agriculture's role in national development.

Although the structural reforms entailed in redesigning African universities to serve rural Africa will require decades to resolve, it is time for donors to stop merely paying lip service to African universities. Whereas donors embraced African universities in the 1960s, they generally withdrew their support in the 1970s as they promoted crash food production and IRD projects and invested heavily in international agricultural research centres. Money saved ($100 million to $200 million) from phasing out the floundering crash projects cited above can be reallocated to selected African universities with emphasis on faculties of agriculture. Donors should press for long-term structural reform of the curriculum in universities in exchange for long-term aid commitments of 10 to 20 years.

In 1982 graduate-level education for African students in the United States cost $1 850 per month, or $39 000–$55 000 for a Master's degree over a 20 to 30 month period. Donors should gradually phase out Master's-level training programmes in agriculture and related fields in the United States. Instead, US faculty members should be sent to Africa to help develop regional centres of excellence in graduate training in 8 to 10 African universities over the next 10 to 15 years. In order to achieve this goal, donors will have to give greatly increased priority to aiding African universities, including 10-year authorisations to foreign universities to provide teachers for graduate instruction and research. In the final analysis, the initiative for this second phase – graduate training in agriculture in African universities – will have to come from within Africa.

## Dealing with Rural Poverty

The fourth component of a long-range solution to Africa's food crisis will be an on-going effort to address the hunger/malnutrition/poverty problem. Rural poverty is potentially a much more difficult problem to solve than the food production gap, but self-sufficiency in food production will be a bogus achievement if the poor do not have access to a decent diet. A society cannot expect to move from a low- to a middle-income stage of development if two-thirds of its population are producing millet, sorghum, maize, and yams at stagnant levels of output. Agricultural research on food-grain production is a prerequisite to increasing food production. Moreover, since jobs cannot be created in urban areas for all the unemployed, a rural investment strategy should also facilitate the expansion of rural small-scale industries that are labour-intensive and can provide jobs.[49]

## IMPLICATIONS FOR FOREIGN AID

The implications of all this for the foreign assistance community flow quite clearly from the foregoing analysis. Currently, 40 donors are moving funds and technical assistance through a patchwork of several thousand uncoordinated projects in support of agricultural and rural development throughout Africa. In turn, African states are allocating a high percentage of a scarce resource – trained agricultural professionals – to meet the project-reporting requirements of donors, and African governments are asking donors to pay the recurrent costs – salaries, petrol – of the aid-funded projects. In short, both donors and recipients are prisoners of projects and slogans, and they are caught in a vicious circle. Should aid to Africa be doubled in real terms during this decade? The answer depends on whether donors and African states can replace the short-term approaches with long-term investments and address the following in a consistent manner.

## (a) *Food security policies and strategies*

Donors should urge African policy-makers to focus on policies and strategies to achieve a reliable food surplus (food security) based on local production, storage, and international trade. Despite the pleas of international journalists who urge donors to increase the number of food production projects, a single food policy reform in Mali – raising official farm prices – may be more effective than 20 new food production projects. Donors should concentrate their resources on helping local professionals develop an improved micro-foundation for food policy analysis that addresses the constraints on achieving a reliable food surplus, with emphasis on food production, storage, and international trade.

## (b) *Long-term investments*

Emphasis should be placed on reducing the number of tiny projects (such as producing visual aids for the livestock service in a Sahelian country), increasing the lifetime of aid projects, and increasing the volume of aid in programme grants that are tied to policy reforms. Long-term investment programmes like 10-year research projects, 5 to 10-year pilot livestock projects, 20-year programmes to develop colleges of agriculture, and 5-year food aid/policy reform packages should be perceived not as luxuries but rather as pre-requisites to solving Africa's technical, structural, and human capital constraints.

## (c) *Technology generation within Africa*

Professional agriculturalists in most donor agencies privately concede that there is currently an excess of donor funds in search of agricultural production projects supported by agricultural research findings that have been tested and proven on farmers' fields. In short, the international technology transfer model has failed in the direct transfer of food-grain varieties from Mexico or India to Ghana, Lesotho, and Upper Volta. What can be done? Perhaps it is time for donors to (a) admit that the international technology transfer model is not producing the expected results, (b) maintain but not increase investments (in real terms) in the four International Agricultural Research Centres (IARCs) in Africa, and (c) increase the level of financial assistance to national agricultural research systems and to faculties of agriculture in African universities.

Although the US, Mexican, and Indian food-grain varieties are not directly transferable to Africa, some of the processes these countries used to generate technology appropriate to the needs of their farmers in dry-land areas are applicable in helping to strengthen faculties of agriculture in African universities and national agricultural research services. For example, the US dust-bowl crisis in Kansas and Oklahoma in the 1930s gave rise to the US Soil Conservation Service, research on new varieties, irrigation, and other techniques which transformed the dust bowl into a highly productive area of American agriculture over a 30-year period. In this process, US colleges of agriculture played a strategic role, in cooperation with local and state organisations and with the US Department of Agriculture.

### (d) *Co-financing*

Co-financing of aid projects by donors is a growing problem in Africa because typically six to eight donors each underwrite a piece of an agricultural project. Co-financing is attractive because it spreads the risk for donors and reduces the dependency of African states on one donor. But co-financing is proving to be a liability for institution-building projects such as research institutes and extension schools. The recipient institutions are caught in a cross-fire of imported perspectives from technical advisers, a hodgepodge of buildings, and dubious gifts of equipment from around the world. Moreover, the administrators of these local institutions are overwhelmed by the administrative and reporting requirements of the donors. At most, two donors – one for infrastructure and one for technical assistance and training – should be allowed to assist any one institution. But African states will have trouble getting weaned away from co-financing because they are using this device to pay for part of their recurrent budget deficits and the payroll of the state bureaucracy.[50]

### (e) *Foreign private investment*

A major topic of debate is whether foreign private investment, especially multinational firms, can contribute to the resolution of Africa's food and poverty problem. A related question is whether bilateral aid should assist foreign private firms in establishing fertiliser plants, processing plants, and in some cases large-scale food production projects. Just as the roles of women in African development cannot be analysed in isolation from those of men, the role of the private sector can only be analysed in relation to public investments. The poor record of food and livestock production projects throughout Africa over the past 10 years provides ample proof that many of these projects fail because public-sector investments were not made in agricultural research to develop profitable packages for rainfed farming, prevention and control of animal disease, rural roads, and schools to train agricultural managers. Public sector investments can either facilitate or destroy the conditions for capitalists to function in a market-oriented economy.

In general, inadequate infrastructure, local managerial skills, and technical constraints severely limit the scope for foreign private investment in food production projects and in agro-industries in Africa. Although some foreign firms prospered in colonial periods, when they were given choice land and protected markets, since independence there have been many failures, including the recent efforts of US firms to produce food in Ghana, Liberia, and Senegal. As a rule of thumb, if foreign private firms engaged in food production projects do not receive special subsidies, they cannot compete with African small-holders who have a knowledge of local climate, pests, and soils and are willing to produce food on their own land at rates of return of 75 cents to $3 per day for family labour. Moreover, the large capital-intensive plantations and ranches emphasised by foreign private firms should be questioned on social grounds because they do not produce the badly needed jobs in an area of the world where seasonal unemployment is widespread. Foreign private enterprise, however, can contribute to Africa's food system in countries such as Cameroon, Kenya, the Ivory Coast, and Zimbabwe, which have a good infrastructure and need international managerial skills and capital for investments in food processing and in fertiliser and agriculture input industries. But in the final analysis, the focus of foreign aid should be on making public investments in roads, universities, and research stations to help African capitalists – small farmers and herders – produce food for their families and for urban and rural people.

Aid flows to Africa have grown dramatically in recent years: net official aid in 1980 was $13.70 per capita in Africa, compared with an average of $9.60 for all developing countries. In the Sahelian region of West Africa per capita aid was running from $35 to $50 per person in 1982. In many circles in Africa there is a feeling that the continent is already too heavily dependent on aid and foreign transactions relative to the scarcity of African professionals to implement the projects. In fact, in many countries the critical constraint is not land or capital but human resources. This simple fact is overlooked by many donors – including the World Bank. The World Bank, under Robert McNamara, dramatically increased lending in the 1970s, and it has appealed to donors to double lending to Africa in the 1980s. The unsupported case for doubling aid to Africa in the 1980s, in the light of the acute lack of human resources, is a major flaw in the Berg report. If, however, donors take a broad view of the need for massive, long-term public investments in agricultural research, roads, faculties of agriculture in African universities, and land transfer funds (for example, for Zimbabwe) and if African countries change their agricultural development strategies and priorities and introduce policy reforms, then it may be desirable for donors to double aid to Africa in real terms over the 1980–90 period.

## SUMMARY

To sum up, agricultural development is a slow and evolutionary process, and it is up to African states and donor agencies to jettison the crash project approach and start now to lay the foundation for long-term investments to solve the food production and poverty problems over a 10 to 20 year period. Unless steps are taken in the 1980s to overcome these basic technical, political, structural, and policy constraints, many African states may end up in the 1990s as permanent food-aid clients of the United States, the European Economic Community, and Japan.

## NOTES

1. This chapter has been revised from an article which appeared in *Foreign Affairs*, vol. 61 (Fall 1982) no. 1. It is excerpted and adapted by permission of *Foreign Affairs*, Fall 1982. Copyright 1982 by the Council on Foreign Relations, Inc.
2. Africa is defined here to include the states in sub-Saharan Africa except the Republic of South Africa.
3. Low and unstable rainfall is a common problem in the Sahelian region of West Africa, parts of the Sudan, Ethiopia, Somalia, Kenya, Tanzania, Zimbabwe, and Botswana. But erratic rainfall, like any other single factor, cannot explain the steady erosion of Africa's capacity to feed itself.
4. Per capita GDP ranges from $120 in Chad to $1 150 in the Ivory Coast. Although per capita income is an imperfect measure that is not well suited

to international comparisons, there is no question that rural poverty is a major problem throughout Africa. But because of access to land and the absence of a landless labour class, one does not witness in Africa the grinding poverty that is so pervasive in Haiti, Bangladesh and India.

5.  The average aid flows in the eight Sahelian countries was about $50 per capita in 1982. United States Agency for International Development, *Sahel Development Program: Annual Report to the Congress*, (Washington, DC: Government Printing Office, 1982) p. 5. Kenya received $450 million of the foreign assistance in 1982, or about $25 per person.

6.  Tsetse control is a long-term and costly activity that includes the clearing of vegetation that harbours flies, spraying, release of sterile male flies, and human settlement.

7.  But Ethiopia was under Italian occupation from 1936 to 1941.

8.  For more information see H. Ruthenberg, *Farming Systems in the Tropics*, (Oxford University Press, 1980); and Carl K. Eicher and Doyle C. Baker, *Research on Agricultural Development in Sub-Saharan Africa: A Critical Survey*, International Development Paper No. 1 (East Lansing: Michigan State University, Department of Agricultural Economics, 1982).

9.  Malcolm Blackie, 'A Time to Listen: A Perspective on Agricultural Policy in Zimbabwe', Working Paper 5/81, Mimeo (Harare: University of Zimbabwe Department of Land Management, 1981).

10. William O. Jones, 'Economic Man in Africa', *Food Research Institute Studies*, vol. 1 (1960) pp. 107–34.

11. John Cohen, 'Land Tenure and Rural Development in Africa', in R. H. Bates and M. F. Lofchie (eds), *Agricultural Development in Africa* (Berkeley: University of California Press, 1980), pp. 349–400.

12. Food and Agricultural Organisation of the United Nations, *Regional Food Plan for Africa* (Rome: 1978).

13. The USDA figures on per capita food production trends in Africa over the past two decades should be treated as rough estimates because population and production data for two of the large countries – Nigeria and Ethiopia – are open to question. Since Nigeria and Ethiopia together have about one-third the population of Africa, data distortions in these countries could affect the overall averages for Africa. United States Department of Agriculture, *Food Problems and Prospects in Sub-Saharan Africa*, (Washington, DC: 1981).

14. Republic of Kenya, *Sessional Paper No. 4 of 1981 on National Food Policy* (Nairobi: Government Printer, 1981).

15. John W. Mellor, 'Food Price Policy and Income Distribution in Low Income Countries', *Economic Development and Cultural Change*, vol. 27 (October 1978) no. 1, pp. 1–26 reprinted in Carl K. Eicher and John M. Staatz (eds), *Agricultural Development in the Third World* (Baltimore, Md.: Johns Hopkins University Press, 1984) Chapter 10.

16. Eicher and Baker, *Research on Agricultural Development*.

17. P. T. Bauer, *Equality, The Third World and Economic Delusion* (Cambridge, Mass.: Harvard University Press, 1981) p. 70.

18. See, respectively, J. J. McKelvey, Jr, 'Agricultural Research' in R. A. Lystad (ed.), *The African World* (New York: Praeger, 1965); and B. F. Johnston, 'The Choice of Measures for Increasing Agricultural Produc-

tivity: A Survey of Possibilities in East Africa', *Tropical Agriculture*, vol. 40 (1964) no. 2, pp. 91–113.

19. R. E. Evenson, 'Benefits and Obstacles to Appropriate Agricultural Technology', *Annals of the American Academy of Political and Social Science*, vol. 458 (1981) pp. 54–67, reprinted in Eicher and Staatz (eds), *Agricultural Development in the Third World*, Chapter 24.

20. Albert O. Hirschman, 'The Rise and Decline of Development Economics' in *Essays in Trespassing* (New York: Cambridge University Press, 1981).

21. D. Byerlee, C. K. Eicher, C. Liedholm and D. Spencer, 'Employment-Output Conflicts, Factor Price Distortions and Choice of Technique: Empirical Results for Sierra Leone', *Economic Development and Cultural Change*, vol. 31 (1983) no. 2, pp. 315–36.

22. For an assessment of the modernisation, dependency, and political economy models see Crawford Young, *Ideology and Development in Africa* (New Haven: Yale University Press, 1982); and Colin Leys, 'African Economic Development in Theory and Practice', *Daedalus*, vol. 111 (1982) no. 2, pp. 99–124.

23. See the discussion of Amin's work in Eicher and Staatz, *Agricultural Development in the Third World*, Chapter 1.

24. F. I. Nweke, 'Direct Governmental Production in Agriculture in Ghana: Consequences for Food Production and Consumption, 1960–66 and 1967–75, *Food Policy*, vol. 3 (1978) no. 3, pp. 202–8; and T. Killick, *Development Economics in Action* (New York: St Martins Press, 1978).

25. Tanzania received $2.7 billion of Official Development Assistance – a record in Africa – over the 10-year period 1973–82.

26. The sharp decline in real producer prices in the 1970s was undoubtedly an important contributor to the decline in output. Ellis reports a 35 per cent decline in the price and income terms of trade of peasant crop producers over the 1970–80 period. Frank Ellis, 'Agricultural Price Policy in Tanzania', *World Development*, vol. 10 (1982) no. 4, pp. 263–83.

27. Tanzania is slowly dismantling its state control over agriculture following the 1982 Task Force Report and pressure from donors. The new agricultural policy has reintroduced cooperatives, turned some government estates over to village cooperatives, and has encouraged foreign private investment in tea and sisal production. Tanzania, Ministry of Agriculture, Task Force on National Agricultural Policy, *The Tanzania National Agricultural Policy (Final Report)* (Dar es Salaam: Government Printer, 1982); and *The Agricultural Policy of Tanzania* (Dar es Salaam: Government Printer, 1983).

28. G. K. Helleiner, 'Smallholder Decision Making: Tropical African Evidence', in L. G. Reynolds (ed.), *Agriculture in Development Theory* (New Haven: Yale University Press, 1975) pp. 27–52.

29. Positive and negative pricing and taxation policies are shorthand references to the internal terms of trade between agricultural and non-agricultural products. Negative pricing and taxation policies mean that the terms of trade of agriculture are deliberately depressed by government policies (see Krishna, in Eicher and Staatz, *Agricultural Development in the Third World*, Chapter 11).

30. Mulumba Kamuanga, 'Farm Level Study of the Rice Production System at

the Office du Niger in Mali: An Economic Analysis', unpublished PhD dissertation (Michigan State University, 1982).

31. World Bank, *Accelerated Development in Sub-Saharan Africa: An Agenda for Action* (Washington, DC: World Bank, 1981) p. 55.

32. The following political constraints are partially responsible for the negative policies towards export crops: need for foreign exchange, politically powerful trade unions and urban groups, the demands of the military, and the absence of alternative ways to tax agriculture when land is not registered and the government does not have enough skilled people to collect land or income taxes. The net result of these constraints is that African political leaders have little room to manoeuvre on pricing policies for export crops. Hence, the neo-classical economist who argues that 'getting prices right' is the core of the development problem is overlooking the imperative of political survival in Africa.

33. The International Crops Research Institute for the Semi-Arid Tropics (ICRISAT) has its headquarters in Hyderabad, India. Recently, ICRISAT made a major policy decision to de-emphasise the direct transfer of cereal varieties from Asia to the Sahelian countries and to construct a Sahelian research centre on a site of 500 hectares near Niamey, Niger. The scientific staff of the Sahelian centre will carry out long-term (10 to 20 years) research on cereal production in the Sahel. This is further evidence that agricultural development is a slow and evolutionary process.

34. But wheat and rice consumption are increasing in urban areas throughout Africa.

35. D. W. Norman, *The Farming Systems Approach: Relevancy for the Small Farmer*, Rural Development Paper No. 5 (East Lansing: Michigan State University, Department of Agricultural Economics, 1980).

36. For example, the $900 million Diama and Manantelli dams along the Senegal River are projected to have negative internal rates of return.

37. World Food Council of the United Nations, *The African Food Problem and the Role of the International Agencies: Report of the Executive Director* (Rome: 1982); and *Nairobi Conclusions and Recommendations of the African Ministers of Food and Agriculture at the World Food Council Regional Consultation for Africa* (Nairobi: 1982).

38. Although the World Bank was a staunch advocate of basic needs strategies in the late 1970s, it has recently abandoned its support for this concept. Still the International Labour Organisation continues to confuse African states with recent basic needs missions to Zambia, Tanzania, and Nigeria.

39. The state should play a less direct role in agricultural production and marketing and emphasise indirect approaches such as agricultural research, extension, credit, and educational programmes to help small farmers and herders.

40. Although the government of Senegal dissolved its grain board – ONCAD – in 1980, a large percentage of the employees were transferred to other government agencies.

41. See C. Peter Timmer, 'Developing A Food Strategy', in Eicher and Staatz (eds), *Agricultural Development in the Third World*, Chapter 8.

42. Food policy analysis requires a large amount of micro-information on production, consumption, nutrition, and the functioning of markets, but

this information is not available in most African countries. Although the World Council reported that 19 African countries were preparing national food strategies in 1981, many of these exercises were prepared in capital cities in three to six months, and many of them are likely to be forgotten in three to six months.

43. Republic of Zimbabwe, *Growth with Equity: An Economic Policy Statement* (Salisbury: Government Printer, 1981).

44. F. S. Idachaba, *Agricultural Research Policy in Nigeria*, Research Report No. 17 (Washington, DC: International Food Policy Research Institute, 1980); G.O.I. Abalu, 'Solving Africa's Food Problem', *Food Policy*, vol. 7, (1982) no. 3, pp. 247–56.

45. Republic of Kenya, *Sessional Paper No. 4 of 1981*.

46. For example, US food aid to Mozambique was cut off for six months in 1981. See David Anderson, 'America in Africa, 1981', *Foreign Affairs*, vol. 60 (1981) no. 3, pp. 658–85.

47. The bulk of US food aid – 60 per cent to 70 per cent – is in the form of wheat and wheat flour even though wheat is not a staple food in most of rural Africa.

48. World Bank, *Accelerated Development*, p. 79.

49. For empirical support showing that a rural investment strategy for smallholders and small-scale industry can achieve both growth and employment objectives see the results of a nationwide survey in Sierra Leone. Byerlee *et al.*, 'Employment-Output Conflicts'.

50. For example, the government agency responsible for the development of the Senegal River Valley – SAED – was assisted by 13 donors in 1982. SAED employed 1000 workers and encountered an $8.5 million recurrent budget deficit in 1982. SAED asked the 13 donors to pay two-thirds of the cost of the deficit.

# 8 Industrial Dependence and Export Manufacturing in Kenya[1]

## STEVEN LANGDON

Once the envy of Africa for its thriving economy, Kenya has experienced serious difficulties in recent years. Balance-of-payments pressures have become severe as agricultural growth has fallen, foreign capital inflows have declined and domestic macro-economic management has proved unable to respond efficiently to changed conditions. Underlying these problems has been a serious failure in industrial policy. Despite much rhetorical emphasis on industrial restructuring to achieve export gains (prompted by World Bank Structural Adjustment loans and IMF lending agreements), Kenya's manufacturing sector has remained caught in the import-substitution pattern of the past. Industrial expansion has not been achieved.

This chapter examines Kenyan industrial strategy, and analyses this failure. In particular, it critically reviews the continuing Kenyan reliance on foreign enterprise to initiate and manage industrial expansion. This reliance existed in the post-independence years (1964–74) in the context of the import-substitution policy thrust – and it persisted in the 1974–82 period as official policy shifted toward export promotion. For many analysts this shift to export efforts was to be the solution to Kenya's industrial problems; foreign enterprise would become the vehicle by which Kenya penetrated new markets, reducing industrial inefficiency at home, expanding employment and earning crucial foreign exchange. In fact, Kenya's export record after the policy shift was dismal – by 1979 manufactured exports were only 65 per cent of what they had been in 1972. This policy failure in turn contributed to the high balance-of-payments deficits and growing unemployment that have characterised Kenya in the early 1980s.

What caused this failure? And what lessons are suggested for a more successful industrial strategy in the future? This chapter argues that reliance on foreign enterprise was at the heart of the failure – and that more self-reliance in industrialisation, stressing indigenous entrepreneurship and technological capacity, is essential to future improvement in economic performance. But past dependence has not been a chance occurrence: it has been the reflection of given political and social forces that dominate Kenya. And greater future self-reliance will not be sought by chance; it will require political and social change to initiate such a strategy – and effective and efficient economic planning to implement it.

## TEXTILES IN KENYA

This analysis focuses on the textile industry in Kenya, particularly on yarn and fabric manufacturers. The failure of an export strategy in this sector has been especially clear; some notable gains in Kenyan exports to the European Community had taken place by 1974, and textiles were among the three largest export manufacturing sectors in the country. Yet by the end of the 1970s, despite government plans to expand exports from the industry (via the entry of new foreign enterprise), textile exports were very much *lower* than they had been in 1974 (34 million shillings in 1978 compared to 60 million in 1974).[2] This decline occurred despite the fact that export marketing opportunities in Western Europe were clearly opening up in textiles.

The textile industry in the European Community was retrenching rapidly, moving out of simpler product categories. Measuring employment as one indicator, for instance, levels declined over the 1972–77 period by 32.8 per cent in the Netherlands, 28.4 per cent in Belgium, 26.8 per cent in Germany, 16 per cent in France, 14.5 per cent in Britain and 13.3 per cent in Italy.[3] Various Western European producers and wholesalers were clearly looking for lower-wage locations in which to organise some of their manufacturing processes. Under the terms of the Lomé Convention, most black African countries (including Kenya) enjoyed easier, duty-free entry into the Community than South-east Asia or Latin America, under regulations that in practice also favoured European firms that invested in Africa over their counterparts from Japan or the US. One might well have expected significant growth of European-led textile exporting from Africa back to the Community.

The textile sector in Kenya had also become one of the most important parts of Kenyan manufacturing, accounting by 1977 for some 17–18 per cent of total manufacturing employment in the country.[4] This alone makes the industry an important case study. Such examination, however, must carefully review the historical structuring of the industry and its overall economic performance, before being able to analyse the failure of the export strategy and to suggest better policy directions for the future.

## EVOLUTION AND STRUCTURE OF THE INDUSTRY

'The textile industry in Kenya during the interwar period', suggests Swainson, 'is an example of a branch of manufacturing that was blocked off until after 1945 because of the strength of the metropolitan textiles interests'.[5] Indeed the growth of the industry continued to be closely controlled after the Second World War as well, since it was one of a handful of sectors to be regulated by the East African Licensing Council. One condition for receiving a licence was a commitment to move toward vertical integration; thus once any textile mill reached a weaving output of 3 million square yards annually it had to erect spinning facilities as well.[6] The result of this system was not only to slow any development in Kenya, but to assure that most mills had spinning, weaving and finishing facilities within the one enterprise.

In the 1963–65 period, coinciding with independence, the basis of a textile industry finally did emerge. A series of vertically integrated companies developed. Japanese capital played the central role in two firms – United Textile Industries (UTI) and Kenya Toray Mills (KTM); an India-based textile manufacturer initiated another firm, Kisumu Cotton Mills Ltd (Kicomi); and domestic Asian capital built up several other enterprises – all three of Thika Cloth Mills (TCM), Sunflag and Kenya Rayon Mills had their origins in this period. TCM and Sunflag both began as garment producers, and moved into spinning in 1962 and 1963 respectively, not producing woven fabric until later. Kenya Rayon began in 1964 and was taken over by the Madhvani industrial empire in 1966.

Table 8.1 summarises certain key data regarding these firms, and points out a number of characteristics that the industry came to exhibit as it emerged. There was, first, a significant difference between cotton (Kicomi) and synthetic (KTM) fabric producers in their employment and local linkage effects, with the former generating more jobs and

*Africa in Economic Crisis*

TABLE 8.1 *Foreign enterprises in Kenyan textile manufacturing, 1967–72*

| | Kicomi | UTI | KTM |
|---|---|---|---|
| Shareholding (1972) | 48% Khatau Group (India) 29% DFCK (Kenya State) 9% CDC (British State) Remainder private local interests | 25% Shikishima Spinning Co. (Japan) 25% Nomura Trading Co. (Japan) 33% Hemraj Bharmal (local Asian cloth distributor) 9% DFCK Remainder local Asian residents | 39% Toray Industries (Japan) 20% Mitsui and Co. (Japan) 20% Chori Co. (Japan) 22% ICDC (Kenya State) |
| Activities (1967) | Spinning, weaving and dyeing from cotton | Spinning, weaving and dyeing from rayon | Dyeing and printing of imported nylon cloth |
| (1972) | Moving into printing some synthetics spinning and weaving; 220 semi-automatic looms, 40 automatic | Converting to cotton from rayon; 180 looms | Weaving as well; some automatic printing; 256 looms |
| Capital employed (1967) (1972) | K.Shs 14,769,985 13,546,528 | K.Shs 2,400,000 4,800,000 | K.Shs 16,108,260 29,589,440 |

|  |  |  |  |
|---|---|---|---|
| Sales |  |  |  |
| (1967) | 4,866,159 | 6,000,000 | 15,801,920 |
| (1972) | 18,863,734 | 10,000,000 | 21,235,540 |
| **Profit (loss) after tax** |  |  |  |
| (1967) | (1,323,400) | nil | (2,028,600) |
| (1972) | 1,015,680 | 760,000 | 117,760 |
| Employees |  |  |  |
| (1967) | 448 | 400 | 315 |
| (1972) | 946 | 600 | 620 |
| Product range (1972) | 24–25 varieties of cloth | 15–16 varieties of cloth | 10 different lines, 5 colours each |
| Capacity utilisation (1972) | 70% | 60% | 94% in weaving, low in printing and dyeing |
| Proportion of material inputs imported from outside East Africa (1972) | 20–25% | 65% | 95% |
| Exports as percentage of sales (1972) | nil | nil | 3% |
| Location | Kisumu | Thika | Thika |

SOURCE Company interviews, Kenya, 1973; Companies Registry, Nairobi.

fewer imports than the latter; yet, as Kicomi management indicated in 1973, in the context of import reproduction, that firm had been forced to move more toward synthetics to achieve market success. A second consequence of the import substitution strategy was evident in the considerable product range that each company turned out; this wide range had damaging cost implications. One firm, for instance, suggested its 1972 capacity utilisation was about 20 per cent less than it would be without the changeover problems resulting from product diversity. Another firm noted that 1972 weaving costs would have been 10 per cent less if only one kind of cloth had been produced, while specialisation would have made printing costs 20–30 per cent less.

This points to a third characteristic of the emerging industry. Profits were often marginal or non-existent, capacity utilisation was commonly unsatisfactory, and export performance was quite poor. Parent companies could achieve some return in other ways; subsidiary managers of KTM conceded in 1973 that their operation had been set up so that Toray Industries, a large chemical manufacturer, could supply synthetic fibres and dyes to it – and that Toray did so at prices that were 'more expensive' than available elsewhere.[7] But it remains true that problems were evident in this period. And a fourth characteristic of the industry developed in part in response to this; the state became a source of capital for the industry, via its parastatal bodies active in industrial development – the Development Finance Company of Kenya (DFCK) and the Industrial and Commercial Development Corporation (ICDC).

By the early 1970s, then, an industry had developed which was characterised by much foreign corporate and technological dependence, by considerable import intensity, by small integrated units producing a vast range of output, by consequent production costs at least 40–45 per cent above world prices,[8] by consequent weaknesses in profitability and export capability, and by a growing state role in supporting private firms via equity investment. This unsatisfactory structure was in part a result of the East African Licensing Council's policies of vertical integration. As the Chairman of UTI suggested in a 1973 interview:

> They insist on vertical integration of new projects within three years – you must spin your own goods, process them, etc. This doesn't work. Because the capital requirements for such integration are so great, firms remain small-scale in terms of total output as they integrate. This is all uneconomic. The industry should be rationalized, establishing specialization among firms rather than all reproducing all steps in the production path.

The managing director of KTM made the same point in a 1973 interview. Nevertheless, this particular impediment to specialisation should not be exaggerated so as to overshadow the basic strategy of highly protectionist import substitution, of which it became but one part. As of 1968, evidence shows that nylon dyeing, rayon cloth and cotton cloth production were three of the eight most highly protected industries in Kenya – while ranking 54, 55 and 48 respectively in international competitiveness out of 58 Kenyan industries.[9] By the early 1970s, this heavy protection was taking the form of complete import bans on specific products.

The impetus behind this strong import-substituting strategy should not be misunderstood. The heavy protectionism established was not an autonomous policy simply initiated by state decision-makers. In fact, the approach of the East African Licensing Council aimed to *avoid* high import restrictions. The idea was that by licensing enterprises in the industry, marked domestic competition and over-capacity could be avoided, so that firms could develop as an infant industry with only modest levels of protection against foreign imports. Thus one of the main reasons that the Khatau Group was awarded the licence for Kicomi, over the competing applications of British and Soviet firms, was because it applied no pressure for extra protection and said it was prepared to work within existing tariff levels.[10] Yet, once operating, Kicomi began to apply very strong pressure on government to provide much more protection (in part because, the firm said, transfer taxes by Kenya's partners within the East African Community meant that Kicomi did not have full access to all East African consumers which it had expected). This culminated in 1967 in the firm shutting down two of its three shifts, and declaring many workers redundant in a section of Kenya that was already politically discontented. As the firm reported later:

> It was only then that the government started realizing that restrictions were needed . . . Imports from Pakistan, India and Japan were very strong previously. So protection was given, and only since then have things started to level off. Now all the mills are operating at a fairly reasonable level. (Interview, Kisumu, 1973.)

Both of the other foreign subsidiaries also pushed for increased protection – with KTM insisting that the Minister of Commerce and Industry provide written guarantees of complete import restriction on key competing product lines before the company would proceed with its expansion into weaving (creating 300 new jobs).[11] The pressure of the foreign firms that dominated the development of the textile industry clearly had its impact. They shared a highly protected environment in which their inefficient import reproduction could survive.

A foreign exchange crisis in 1971 made Kenyan authorities quite receptive to the message of the 1972 ILO Employment Report that industrial policy should move towards the promotion of manufactured exports; the textile industry was identified as one of those for which such exports were targeted in the 1974–78 *Development Plan*. Thus, although the plan suggested that there would still be much promotion of import substitution in fabric production during the period, it stressed (p. 289) that one of two new integrated textile units being built 'will specialize in fabrics for export, with capacity of about 13 million square metres'. In part because of this export capability, spinning, weaving and finishing of textiles was projected to absorb more capital investment than any other industry during 1974–78 (16.9 per cent of total industrial investment), and to grow in value-added at a rate of 15.8 per cent annually, compared to 10.2 per cent for industry as a whole.[12]

In the context of this reorientation of policy, a series of new foreign-organised textile projects was initiated in the 1970s. The first of these was a thread and yarn manufacturing firm, East African Fine Spinners, which was founded in 1971 by a German company, Amatex, and began production in 1973. State financing played a key role in the project, with the ICDC contributing 44 per cent of the K.Shs 8 million equity and the state-controlled Kenya Commercial Bank contributing an additional 5 per cent; the Amatex share was 51 per cent. True to the new orientation, the company stressed that half its output was being exported back to West Germany.[13] Meanwhile, the government was shaping its detailed policy towards the integrated textile fabric industry. A policy paper completed in December 1972, set out the criteria by which to assess joint venture proposals to expand the industry; these stressed demonstrated experience and technical expertise, international access to capital, managerial personnel that the foreign partner would provide, and emphasised that the new ventures would be expected to sell 40 per cent or more of their output to overseas markets.[14] On the basis of these criteria, an inter-departmental textile committee assessed three proposals from foreign firms and in late 1974 approved two (Nanyuki Textile Mills, and Rivatex Ltd) while rejecting a third (from the Swiss firm M/S Maurer).

Nanyuki was set up by the David Whitehead textile group in the UK, a subsidiary of Lonrho, in association with a German textile firm which supplied much of the machinery (especially in spinning). Much of the financing came from the German state development finance agency (the DEG), from the DFCK, from another Kenyan parastatal using World Bank funding for industrialisation – the Industrial Development Bank (IDB) – and from the East African Development Bank; only 25 per cent of the capital for the project came from the foreign sponsors in the end. This firm, like Fine Spinners, began its operations in late 1975 by exporting most of its output (the cotton yarn it was spinning before weaving commenced) to other Whitehead companies elsewhere.[15]

Rivatex was directed by a German firm, Seditex, owned by the Seroussi family and having textile investments elsewhere in Africa. This company, too, committed itself to selling on the world market as well as in Kenya. It erected an integrated mill in Eldoret with a capital cost of K.Shs 207 million and an output capacity of 11 500 000 metres.[16] It, too, relied heavily on state funding, both in equity – where ICDC took 36 per cent, the World Bank's International Finance Corporation (IFC) 18 per cent and the DEG 15 per cent – and in loan capital where the IDB, the DFCK and the East African Development Bank added to more ICDC, IFC and DEG contributions.[17] Because it represented the largest foreign project yet initiated in the textile industry, the privileges that Rivatex was able to receive from the government were extensive – including guarantees of import protection, duty-free entry of machinery, free provision of land and infrastructure, right to work permits for expatriates as required, and a generous management/technical agreement for Seditex.[18] These privileges mirror other signs of state–MNC (Multinational Corporation) symbiosis, or mutual inter-dependence, elsewhere in the Kenyan political economy during the 1970s.[19] In that sense, industrial dependence and MNC privileges in the textile industry were only one example of the broader patterns and strategy of industrialisation in Kenya.

Spurred by these new projects and by expansions of existing facilities, the Kenyan textile industry grew very rapidly in the 1970s. Fabric production in particular increased very fast in 1977 and 1978 as the new integrated projects came on-stream. Table 8.2 dissects this fabric production in some detail for the leading firms in the country in 1977, and shows several important characteristics of the industry. First, there were three roughly equal segments: the established foreign subsidiaries begun in the 1960s contributed 30 per cent of overall output; the new European-sponsored projects another 29 per cent, and the larger private domestic firms 29 per cent. Evolving from garment manufacturing and then spinning, locally-owned firms like Thika Cloth Mills and Sunflag had become important parts of the fabric industry by the later 1970s. Second, the output of the industry was becoming quite sophisticated, with 43 per cent of production in printed form and only 6 per cent in unbleached or bleached form. Third, although some specialisation was evident (in the way that some firms did only cotton fabrics or KTM did only synthetics), the basic pattern was one of wide product diversification within firms and considerable competition among firms. This extensive product range within firms continued to lead to high production costs. Managers noted that mills in India or Japan would produce no less than 40 000 metres of one item at a time, while Kenyan mills were often forced by the diversified customer demand within the country to produce 4000–6000 metres in one production run. There was evidence that this problem of lack of scale economies was increasing: one firm, for instance, had gone from 16 varieties in 1972 to 30 in 1980, while another had gone from 25 to 100.

Several other characteristics noted earlier continued to be evident in the industry in the later 1970s. The trend toward synthetic production was maintained, even though Kenya had come to offer ample supplies of local cotton as potential raw material; from 19 per cent of total production, the synthetics' share rose to 26 per cent in 1977, and was projected by the government to rise to 31 per cent in 1978, 36 per cent in 1979 and 40 per cent in 1980.[20] State finance also continued to play an increasing role in the industry. As well as the central financing function it fulfilled in the new projects, the state, via the ICDC, took a 51 per cent share in KTM in 1977; it raised its role in Kicomi via a 26 per cent IDB share (with the DFCK at 17 per cent and CDC at 10 per cent): it took a 12½ per cent share in Thika Cloth Mills to help finance a large 1976 expansion; and it took a share in Kenya Rayon Mills through the East African Development Bank. By 1977 state parastatals held shares in seven of the eight firms given in Table 8.2

This reliance on state financing reflected the problems that, by and large, continued to affect the industry. Capacity utilisation had improved considerably for the established firms in 1977, as a comparison of Tables 8.1 and 8.2 shows (Kicomi up from 70 per cent to 94 per cent and UTI up from 60 per cent to 91 per cent). But profitability remained very low, and the wide swings in economic conditions in Kenya eliminated stability of earnings (1974–75 were very difficult years, then 1977–78 accelerated the economy via coffee price rises, while 1979–80 saw recession conditions re-emerge).[21] Leaving aside the two new fabric projects, which were just underway, Table 8.3 reports on the profitability of four of the remaining seven largest textile firms in Kenya,

TABLE 8.2  *Textile fabric production, Kenya, 1977*

| Firm | | Unbleached | Bleached | Coloured Woven | Dyed Khaki Drill/Twill | Dyed Other | Printed | Total | Estimated Capacity Utilisation (%) |
|---|---|---|---|---|---|---|---|---|---|
| Established Foreign Subsidiaries | | | | | | | | | |
| Kicomi | S | | | | | 964 | 720 } | 8,523 | 94 |
|  | C | | | | | 1,758 | 3,779 } | | |
| KTM | S | | | | | | | 6,360 | 100 |
|  | C | | 360 | | 1,302 | 1,800 | 4,200 } | | |
| UTI | S | | | | | | | 5,000 | 91 |
|  | C | | 300 | 500 | | 400 | 3,800 } | | |
| New Foreign-Led Projects | | | | | | | | | |
| Rivatex | S | | | | | | 2,000 } | 11,500 | 82 |
|  | C | | | 2,250 | | 2,800 | 4,500 } | | |
| Nanyuki | S | | | | | | | 8,000 | 80 |
|  | C | 1,000 | | 1,000 | | 3,000 | 3,000 } | | |
| Private Domestic Firms | | | | | | | | | |
| Thika Cloth Mills | S | | | | | | | 12,050 | 75 |
|  | C | 1,200 | 600 | 8,000 | 2,000 | | 250 } | | |
| Sunflag | S | | | | | 3,700 | | 3,700 | 70 |
|  | C | | | | | | | | |
| Kenya Rayon | S | 100 | | 100 | | 800 | | 3,600 | 75 |
|  | C | | | 600 | | 1,600 | 400 } | | |
| Total* | | 2,442 | 1,260 | 12,450 | 3,302 | 18,597 | 28,849 | 66,900 | 79 |

*State of fabric* (thousand metres)     S=Synthetic, C=Cotton.

*Total includes other smaller firms.

SOURCE  Ministry of Commerce and Industry, *Sector Study – Kenya's Textile Industry*, (Nairobi: 1978) pp. 24–5. This table includes all nine of the largest fabric producers in the industry. Kenwool, the other company surveyed in this study, produced 900 000 metres of dyed synthetic fabrics in 1977, according to the same source.

192        *Africa in Economic Crisis*

and shows how low profit levels were, except in the coffee-boom year of 1977–78. The inclusion of the two new fabric producers, as discussed further below, would make the picture even bleaker. Both were accumulating large losses.

TABLE 8.3   *Profits in the Kenya textile industry, 1976–80*

| Financial Year | Profits (or losses) after tax as a percentage of annual turnover (%) |
|---|---|
| 1974–75* | 6.0 |
| 1975–76* | –9.8 |
| 1976–77 | –3.0 |
| 1977–78 | 11.6 |
| 1978–79 | 2.1 |
| 1979–80 | 2.0 |

*Three firms only
SOURCE   Interviews with TCM, KTM, Kicomi, and East African Fine Spinners, November, 1980; data in Companies Registry, Nairobi.

In the context of these problems, textile manufacturers fought long and hard for yet more import protection. A Textile Manufacturers Association was established and turned itself into one of the most powerful pressure groups in Kenya – 'second in strength only to the vehicle assembly firms', according to a government official who was the object of much of the pressure.[22] That Association mounted a campaign to ban all textile imports, except those for which it would issue a letter of no objection because the item in question was not made in Kenya.[23] The established foreign subsidiaries played a prominent role in this fight, particularly Kicomi; but a strong impetus was added by the new foreign-run projects, especially Rivatex. 'We all owe a big debt to Seroussi', a rival general manager conceded in 1980, 'for his role in getting protection for the industry – because he had a big mouth, and wasn't afraid to fight publicly.'

Seditex used its bargaining position prior to building Rivatex to get written commitments from its state partner, the ICDC, that the latter would

obtain from the Government assurances . . . that imports into Kenya of textiles in general and polyester and polyester blends in particular shall be so rationalized or controlled that such imports shall in no way interfere with or prejudice the production and marketing by Rivatex of all lines of textile and other products to be manufactured by the project upon economical and competitive terms.[24]

After the project was operating, Rivatex and Seroussi used such commitments to push the government very hard, using their state partners. As with Kicomi earlier, however, their most powerful weapon became threatened job losses; in July 1977, Rivatex asked permission from the Minister of Labour to dismiss 1328 workers in Eldoret. In direct response, the government raised *ad valorem* duties on woven fabrics from 45 per cent to 60 per cent, raised specific duties on these items by 20 per cent as well, and also raised *ad valorem* clothing duties from 50 per cent to 70 per cent.[25] Then in December 1977, the Nanyuki project did shut down, at a cost of 1200 jobs. The government committed itself to re-opening the mill, and in February 1978 imposed a total ban on all competing fabric imports which the Textile Manufacturers Association had sought; the state imposed a 100 per cent duty on imported yarn at the same time.[26]

By the end of the 1970s, then, despite the new orthodoxy of MNC export manufacturing, the Kenyan textile industry (under heavy pressure from the foreign-run firms that had originally articulated export goals) was much more protected than ever. Manufacturing continued to take the form of small runs of a wide range of items, aimed at import replacement, rather than specialisation for export. Production costs remained high as a result. And textile exports *dropped* significantly despite the new export policy pronouncements.

What had happened was, on one level, rather clear. The dominant elements in the Kenyan state were concerned about both unemployment pressures and growing foreign exchange shortages in the early 1970s. They identified the textile industry as a source both of jobs (given its relatively labour-intensive character) and of potential foreign exchange (via import savings and export gains). The state thus used its financial resources to assist the industry to expand; this was essential because the industry had already marked itself out as one where competition was considerable (among firms and in relations with textile wholesalers), where production costs were high, and where profits were limited; this meant that private African capital was uninterested in investing (unlike in breweries or cigarette manufacturing, for instance), and that foreign capital would be reluctant to enter except under special conditions. These special conditions included such promises of complete import protection as Seditex extracted. These promises, plus the heavy state investment in the projects, gave foreign entrepreneurs much leverage to obtain even more import protection – lest the state investment be lost along with a great many jobs. The very labour-intensity that made the industry attractive to the state in turn represented a weapon that shutdowns (and the threat thereof) could use to win higher trade barriers.

Yet this case is not just a straightforward example of the inefficiencies shaped by high import protection, nor of the stubborn resilience of such barriers once erected. The question of industrial dependence is closely woven into this Kenyan example. Indeed, this section has shown that it was foreign subsidiaries that exercised the greatest leverage in shaping high import barriers in Kenyan textiles – in both import-substitution and export-emphasis phases. The wider impact of this industrial dependence must now be more carefully probed.

## PERFORMANCE AND OWNERSHIP IN THE INDUSTRY

Three broad segments have been delineated above on the basis of original ownership patterns in Kenyan weaving and spinning. There is, first, that segment established in the 1960s, with financial, technical and managerial inputs being provided by MNCs from Japan and India (Kicomi, UTI and KTM). Second, there is a segment developed by domestic capital on the basis of financial, technical and managerial inputs that local entrepreneurs organised themselves (TCM, Sunflag, Kenya Rayon Mills and Kenwool). Third, there is the new segment established in the 1970s with technical, managerial and some financial inputs being provided by Western European firms (Rivatex, East African Fine Spinners and Nanyuki – reconstituted as Mount Kenya Textiles). Table 8.4 provides an overall profile of these three segments, showing that by 1980 the private domestic category had become the largest in both sales and employment, even though the capital invested in that segment was almost certainly the lowest of the three categories.

This analysis starts with a comparison of the private domestic firms and the established subsidiaries. Perhaps the most important point to stress is that, while both sets of firms have grown significantly, the leading local enterprises have been especially dynamic in their expansion. Figure 8.1 demonstrates this clearly. The largest local firm ($L_1$ on the graph) expanded its turnover by 183 per cent between 1976 and 1980; and another large local firm ($L_2$) also grew very rapidly. Not all local firms were as successful – as the record of $L_4$ shows. But two of

TABLE 8.4   *Kenyan textile spinners and weavers, 1980*

|  | Established as foreign subsidiaries in the 1960s | Private domestic firms | Newly established as European subsidiaries in the 1970s |
|---|---|---|---|
| Number of firms and locations | 3 (2 in Thika, 1 in Kisumu) | 4 (Nairobi, Thika, Mombasa and Kiambaa) | 3 (Nairobi, Nanyuki, Eldoret) |
| Total sales turnover (K.Shs) | 251 million | 380 million | 208 million |
| Employment | 3,730 | 4,300 | 2,343 |
| Looms in use | 880 | 508 | 593 |
| Spindles in use | 24,000 | 40,200 | 21,168* |
| Products manufactured and sold | 25–26 million metres of woven fabric (12 million cotton; 7 million blends; 6–7 million synthetics and nylon); some cotton yarn | 19–21 million metres of woven fabric (11–12 million cotton; 7–9 million blends and synthetics); 1 million kg of yarn; 3–4 million metres of knitted fabrics; some garments | 18–19 million metres of woven fabric (13–14 million cotton; 5 million synthetics); thread and yarn |

*Covers only two of the three firms.
SOURCE  Company interviews, Kenya, 1980; Interview with Industrial Adviser, Ministry of Industry, Nairobi, 1980.

all local firms were as successful – as the record of $L_4$ shows. But two of the subsidiaries ($F_3$ and $F_4$) were also undramatic in their growth; and only one subsidiary ($F_1$) came close to matching the dynamic expansion of the largest local firms. Just as important, the local firms were a good deal more reliant on their own financial resources than the subsidiaries. The largest local firm ($L_1$) had no state investment in it at all; nor had $L_4$, while $L_2$ and the other local firm had no more than minority parastatal shareholdings. Parastatals had provided the majority of equity in all of $F_1$, $F_2$ and $F_4$ by 1980. This reflected, in turn, the differential profitability of the enterprises. Firm $L_1$ made good profits throughout the 1970s, which fuelled its unassisted and rapid growth. And all the other local firms were also generally profitable; enterprise $L_2$ had a period of losses associated with a major new expansion which doubled output in two years, but more than recovered these losses in 1977–78. At the same time, the largest established subsidiary ($F_1$) had marginal profits or losses for five of the six years between 1974 and 1980, and the returns for both $F_2$ and $F_3$ were quite limited, while $F_4$ accumulated large losses. It is

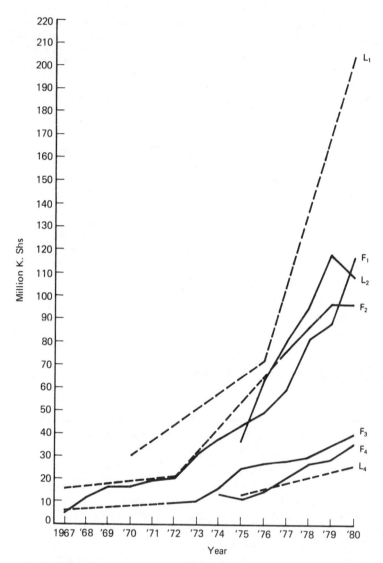

FIGURE 8.1  *Turnover by year in Kenyan textile companies, 1967–80*
(SOURCE: Company interviews 1973 and 1980; *East African Report on Trade and Industry*)

true that $F_1$ and $F_2$ both continued to return management or technical fees to the parent company; but these were not sufficient to offset the better profitability of the domestic private firms.

This dynamic record within the larger local firms suggests that the Kenyan government could very well have relied on and assisted these domestic entrepreneurs to lead the large expansion in the textile industry in the 1970s. Instead, as discussed above, the general orientation of the government to dependence on foreign MNCs and the goal of promoting manufactured exports to Western Europe led to reliance on European firms. The projects these firms established were quite unlike either the private domestic firms or the established foreign subsidiaries. In each of the three cases, the European firms supplied technology that raised serious problems. In each case, they seem to have creamed off returns in their relations with the new subsidiaries that more than covered their financial investment. And in each case, the Kenyan enterprise that resulted was so grossly unprofitable that the state had to intervene to rescue the operation – and to absorb a significant continuing loss. In each case, it is difficult to avoid the conclusion that the Kenyan government, in the words of a senior official, was 'ripped off'.

East African Spinners was the first of these projects.[27] It began operating in 1973, and was supposed to export much of its output back to Germany; this never developed in an on-going way, and (according to the management team that later took over) the parent company Amatex never really had the technical know-how to get the project underway. The result was a loss of 95 per cent of the equity of the firm in the first two years of operation – putting the company into receivership in February 1976. The state, which had held 49 per cent of the original equity, then had to inject K.Shs 13 640 000 in new equity and arrange further financing at 10–13 per cent interest. Coates, a thread manufacturer from the UK, was hired on management contract in May 1976; the operation required three more years until it reached a healthy profitable position in the 1979–80 financial year. By June of 1979 the project had lost K.Shs 27 561 000 on an original equity investment of K.Shs 8 million, of which Amatex had contributed 4.08 million. It is, however, most unlikely that Amatex itself lost money on the project; present management suggests that the German firm got its money out in the first two years, through mark-ups on the machinery sales to Kenya, through purchase of spare parts from the parent company, and through product exports to the parent for which Amatex then refused to pay the full price.

The Nanyuki textile project represented a variation on this pattern. Here the problem was not lack of technical expertise on the part of the UK manufacturer. But the machinery chosen created major difficulties, mainly because it was selected as a function of the decline of the textile industry in Western Europe. The German partner in the project transferred spinning machinery from a factory it was closing in Germany; this machinery was very old and very expensive to maintain (indeed in the reconstruction of the project in 1980, 2500 to 4000 spindles out of 12 000 had to be completely scrapped). The weaving machinery was manufactured by a UK firm that had been closed down, and was re-opened with a government loan expressly to produce 700 looms for this and another African project. The machines, said the present management, 'are automatic looms but on a 25 year old design – they are new but don't look it, and are no competition at all for other automatic European looms now'. Again, this project started off with some low-price exports to associated companies outside Kenya, but did not sustain these. Large losses accumulated, and by the end of 1977 another 100 million shillings was needed to preserve the firm. Lonrho refused to increase their investment and the firm went bankrupt and shut down. Again, the government had to move in to finance a rescue (injecting another K.Shs 50 million), appointed its own management (expatriate experts recruited from Kicomi), and had a reorganised Mount Kenya Textile Mills manufacturing once more by early 1980 – though at a probable loss for the year of K.Shs 17 million. Again the present management suggested that the original foreign partners probably retrieved their investment safely and early – through machinery and input sales as well as intra-company exports.

The biggest disaster, however, was Rivatex. As noted earlier, massive state investments were made in this project and extensive privileges granted in the investment agreements. The company did not begin production until 1977, and yet by 1980 the whole project had collapsed. As a senior Kenyan official described the process:

> I was on the Board of this company for two years. We kept asking for details of the prices of the machines and dyes and chemicals coming from Germany, and we couldn't get these from Hamburg; when we did get these details it was clear we were being much overcharged . . . We were really done in on this project – losses had reached Shs 100 million and all of the equity capital had been lost when we finally threw Seditex out.[28]

Huge sums had been spent on machinery, in a factory that present management asserts was 'overbuilt', without sufficient thought to the interest and depreciation costs that would result. Again the government had to inject yet more funds in its rescue operation, and future losses were certain because of very high debt charges. Once more the state appointed its own management, drawing on the ICDC and on expatriate experts, to try to set things right.

This pattern of government taking responsibility for a faltering foreign firm was also followed in the case of one of the established textile subsidiaries, Kenya Toray Mills. This was a firm, as discussed earlier, that had clearly provided large returns to its parent company through input purchases, while declaring losses or very marginal profits in the subsidiary. Again the state had been forced to take a larger and larger share of equity in the enterprise to keep it going, until finally in late 1978 the ICDC took over completely. In this case, though, the new freedom to purchase inputs completely competitively led to signifiant improvements in profitability, and the new indigenous management of what was now called Kenya Taitex Mills was able to improve the efficiency of production.

By 1980, then, four of the six MNC textile subsidiaries in Kenya had become such problem projects that the state had had to take them over from the original parent; by 1983, a fifth subsidiary – Kicomi – had joined the other four in bankruptcy. Considering just the three projects from the 1970s, and using a conservative estimate of opportunity cost for public capital invested in their equity of 10 per cent annually, the losses absorbed by the Kenyan public sector for these MNC failures reached at least 220 million shillings by 1980 – or about as much as the government's entire development expenditure on education or on health in 1979–80.[29] The financial cost of dependence on MNCs for export manufacturing expansion thus turned out to be immense. Moreover, the government became pre-occupied in its textile policy almost entirely with rescuing these projects so that fundamental strategy questions regarding product choice, specialisation to increase efficiency, or potential export plans, were simply ignored.[30]

What about the wider social externalities associated with the various segments of the industry? Three particularly important social consequences to test in any such assessment are employment effects, linkage effects, and learning effects on a technological level.[31] Table 8.5 provides the data to undertake a comparative analysis of such effects in Kenyan textiles.

It is widely agreed that there are unemployed and under-employed persons in Kenya that make the rapid expansion of employment a social benefit (in that the social opportunity cost of employing such workers in a project is considerably less than the private cost incurred by management in wages for those workers); rapid expansion of industrial

TABLE 8.5   Company data in Kenyan Textiles, 1980

| Firm | (1) Fixed assets per worker (K.Shs 000) | (2) Percentage average annual employment change (years covered) | (3) Number of shifts | (4) Share of cotton goods in output (%) | (5) Percentage of inputs imported | (6) Linkage** investments | (7) Technology source | (8) Percentage expatriates in workforce | (9) Percentage of turnover exported |
|---|---|---|---|---|---|---|---|---|---|
| **Private Domestic Firms** | | | | | | | | | |
| $L_1$ | n.a. | +15 (1978–80) | 3 | over 10 | 60 | G,PFY | Self | 1.4 | 11 |
| $L_2$ | 41 | +13 (1975–80) | 3 | 67 | 30 | no | Self | 1.1 | nil |
| $L_3$ | n.a. | +9 (1976–80) | 3 | 75 | 40–50 | T,C | Self | 1.1 | nil |
| $L_4$ | n.a. | +8 (1975–80) | 3 | 0 | n.a. | no | Foreign suppliers | 2 | nil |
| **Established as Subsidiaries** | | | | | | | | | |
| **1960s** | | | | | | | | | |
| $F_1$ | 60 | +10 (1972–80) | 3 | 50 | 63 | no | Foreign parent +2 licences | 1.1 | 0.1 |
| $F_2$ | 102* | +4 (1972–80) | 3 | 0 | 90–95 | no | Own R&D; licence | 0 | nil |
| $F_3$ | 20 | +4 (1972–80) | 3 | 100 | 25–30 | no | Foreign parent | 1.1 | nil |
| **1970s** | | | | | | | | | |
| $F_4$ | 42 | +8 (1977–80) | 3 | 88 | 42 | no | Foreign management agent | 1.3 | 5.9 |
| $F_5$ | 92† | –46 (1977–80) | 1 | 100 | 15–20 | no | Self | 2† | nil |
| $F_6$ | 140 | +7 (1977–80) | 3 | 67 | 60–65 | no | Self + 2 licences | 0.9 | nil |

*This ratio is based on a revaluation of fixed assets in 1977, unlike the other ratios.
**G=garments, C=carpets, T=towels, PFY=Polyester filament yarn.
†These calculations are based on an assumed 3-shift workforce.
n.a. Not avaiable.
SOURCE   Calculated from company interviews, Kenya, 1980; reports in *East African Trade and Industry*, Nairobi.

employment, too, may have egalitarian distribution effects insofar as it raises demand for simple wage goods like peasant food crops and informal sector output. (The wage levels paid in 1980 in Kenyan textiles, ranging between 450 and 600 shillings per month for machine operators, suggest that it is simple consumer demand which growing textile employment would increase.) Table 8.5 provides some indication of differing employment effects – column (1) providing a very rough measure of the reliance of firms on capital-intensive technology, and column (2) showing how rapidly firms have been expanding their workforce. These columns can in turn be related back to the growth patterns in Figure 8.1.

In doing so, several conclusions emerge clearly. First, the employment-creating success of the private domestic firms stands out; the rapid growth in output of $L_1$ and $L_2$ has been matched by job growth, and even the modest output growth of $L_4$ has produced a higher rate of job expansion than for $F_2$ and $F_3$, which saw their sales grow faster. Second, the older subsidiaries expanded jobs more slowly and were, in the case of a subsidiary like $F_1$, more capital-intensive in their technology than a comparable local firm like $L_2$. Third, the newer subsidiaries were also undynamic in their employment effects, and indeed employed 300 fewer workers in 1980 than in 1977, though this was mainly the result of one firm's performance ($F_5$); the very high capital intensity of $F_6$ points up the problems with machinery choice in certain of the 1970s projects discussed earlier. Overall, then, the employment effects of the larger private domestic firms were particularly great, and those of the new subsidiaries particularly limited.

Linkage effects are another important indicator of the extent and distribution of economic opportunities shaped by an enterprise. One level on which to investigate this question is that of product choice, since cotton is grown by Kenyan peasant farmers (unlike the inputs to synthetic production). Here two of the subsidiary projects ($F_3$ and $F_5$) have advantages as producers exclusively of cotton fabrics (although $F_5$ is planning to follow the general trend in the industry into some production from man-made fibres). In addition, as a comparison of columns (4) and (5) in Table 8.5 shows, product choice is a key element shaping import dependence; enterprises $F_3$ and $F_5$, as producers exclusively from cotton, have the lowest proportion of material inputs imported of all firms surveyed. Nevertheless, ownership differences do seem to be significant in shaping linkage effects, once production patterns are similar among firms. Enterprises $L_2$, $L_3$, $F_1$ and $F_6$ all combine cotton and synthetic fabric production in significant proportions, yet the two domestic private firms import markedly fewer of their inputs. Even $L_1$, which is more oriented to synthetic output, imports slightly lower proportions of inputs than $F_1$ and $F_6$, and much less than the other synthetics-oriented producer $F_2$.

Perhaps most significantly, though, the private domestic firms have been quite active themselves in initiating new linkage investments that either supply inputs to their spinning and weaving, or use their fabric output as inputs for final product manufacturing. Enterprise $L_1$ produces garments that account for 22 per cent of sales turnover, including cotton T-shirts for the Western European export market; enterprise $L_3$ produces towels and carpets in two new associate firms; and $L_1$ has also invested in production of polyester filament yarns. The enterprises that began as subsidiaries have made no such investments – though now that $F_5$ is wholly state-owned, its managment is planning to enter garment manufacturing. State officials have also stressed the efficiency of $L_1$'s linkage investment in synthetic yarn compared to a similar state-funded venture dependent on foreign technology:

> African Synthetics has been another classic problem project. That firm has cost 400 million shillings, received the right to bring in machinery and inputs duty-free, and had government funding from ICDC – yet is not really making it. [Enterprise $L_1$] has quietly gone ahead with exactly the same sort of thing, with no privileges and no government funding, for only 90 million shillings, and is producing better quality output.[32]

What about learning effects? Enterprises were asked where they would turn to for technological know-how for any new investment or product diversification they might undertake. All three of the large private domestic firms indicated they had developed the technological capacity to handle this within their own organisation; only the small domestic firm ($L_4$) suggested that it would have to rely on foreign input suppliers. This firm was planning to move into printing of its fabrics, and had invited three overseas chemical firms to bid as suppliers of the technology; the German firm which had won was to supply the machinery, train local people to use it, and earn its return on the dyes they would then supply. Thus even $L_4$ had developed a shrewd capacity to arrange competing technology bids, though it was still dependent on outside know-how. The other three private domestic firms had all recently demonstrated their technological independence: $L_1$ by establishing its filament yarn production, and $L_2$ and $L_3$ by diversifying into polyester fabric production all on their own. None of these firms had any licensing or trademark agreements with foreign MNCs. Clearly the private domestic firms had 'learned-by-doing' as they developed from small beginnings; and they had also hired individual expatriate technicians to supplement their own skills (as column (8) shows). This development of an independent technological capacity was less evident in the firms that had been established as subsidiaries. The two firms that remained subsidiaries ($F_1$ and $F_3$) still depended on the parent company to supply the know-how for any new initiatives taken. And this was also true for the firm ($F_4$) which was now managed by a foreign textile MNC. All three of these firms had levels of expatriate employment quite similar to those in $L_1$, $L_2$ and $L_3$, yet had not developed the technological independence of those local firms. Licences were also common among the present and former subsidiaries. Two of these were for 'Sanforizing' fabrics, but one was a technology agreement (in $F_2$) with the former parent company, and another provided designs from the Dutch textile MNC, Gamma Holdings-Vlisco, to $F_6$. Several of the former subsidiaries that are now wholly state-run are making significant efforts to expand their own technological capacity, and are stressing company research and development (this is especially true of $F_2$, which now employs no expatriates but spends 8–10 per cent of turnover on a research, design and quality control laboratory). The special need to do this, though, is a commentary on the relative absence of technological learning effects within the firms when they were subsidiaries.

This contrast between the private domestic firms and those established as subsidiaries is not meant to suggest that no learning effects were evident from the latter; training had been carried out by them at a number of levels. But the evidence does suggest that in developing technological capacity, as in employment expansion and linkage initiatives, the record of the private domestic firms was superior.

That points towards the general conclusion of this section. The evidence reviewed here illustrates that a major reason for the unsatisfactory record of the Kenyan textile industry up to 1980 was reliance on foreign MNCs. Private domestic firms have shown that they could grow dramatically, maintain satisfactory profitability, dynamically expand employment, initiate linkages and develop independent technological capacity – all with only limited help from the Kenyan government. The state instead supported a series of disastrous European subsidiary projects – in line with its general reliance on foreign MNCs and its stated goal of MNC-led manufactured exports. The result was financially tragic – a loss in public funds of over 200 million shillings – and socially questionable: the subsidiary projects created fewer jobs, initiated no investment linkages themselves, and developed significantly less technological capacity in Kenya than their private domestic counterparts. On virtually all grounds, the entry of European MNCs into Kenyan textiles had proved a costly mistake.

## EXPORTS FROM THE INDUSTRY

This chapter has emphasised the poor export performance of the Kenyan textile industry. In this section, this failure is analysed in more detail.

Table 8.5 provides a useful starting point. Only two firms in that table have any significant exports, and those of $F_4$ were all to Uganda, from which Kenya cannot earn convertible foreign exchange. Only the cotton T-shirt exports already noted for $L_1$ represent a successful penetration of the Western European market. One of the other private domestic firms ($L_2$) had significant exports to Western Europe (also of T-shirts) in the 1974–75 period, but phased these out when the Kenyan market itself boomed around the coffee price increases. All other firms, in particular those begun with an expressed orientation to exporting to Western Europe ($F_4$, $F_5$ and $F_6$), had absolutely no export market there.

Some European MNCs did expand African export production as part of their adjustment strategy in Western Europe – using as a base facilities they already controlled in countries like Ivory Coast. The European MNC investments in Kenya had different origins; the evidence above suggests they, too, were designed to respond to the decline of the textile industry in Western Europe, but by disposing of excess existing machinery and of the output of excess capacity in textile machinery manufacturing at high prices in Africa. They were aimed at creaming off a quick return, rather than supplying part of some firm's on-going market in the European Community. Thus they generated no continuing exports to Europe. Kenya remained on the margins for any established European textile MNCs looking to base some of their production in the Third World.

Despite this, some significant exports were developed by private domestic firms. Given the competition and instability of the Kenyan market, a local firm that developed in Kenya had some incentive to look abroad for other sources of earnings to cover itself, so as to assure reasonable capacity utilisation even in a Kenyan downturn. To build exports to more than adjacent markets, though, required considerable managerial effort; this is what $L_2$ discovered in its earlier European T-shirt exports, and what held it back from a new export drive – it would take a major new effort to re-establish market contacts within Western Europe. Enterprise $L_1$ had the managerial resources for efforts abroad, and indeed, had established its own subsidiaries in Tanzania, Nigeria, Cameroon, and most recently in the UK (taking over a British firm in order to acquire better know-how to build up exports to Europe). But the basis of $L_1$'s success had also been a highly specialised product mix in Kenya; unlike the dozens of product variations noted earlier for other companies, $L_1$ produced only five to six products, trying (it said) to manufacture as much on a mass production scale as possible. This made it possible for $L_1$ to enter into a long-term contract supplying a West Germany textile manufacturer/wholesaler at a competitive price, and earn a margin of 10 per cent over its own costs even at a time when government export compensation payments were only 10 per cent of export revenues (these later went up to 20 per cent).

As a vertically integrated firm, specialising efficiently, $L_1$ saw a considerable further market for itself in Western Europe; as the company manager stressed:

The demand is there, particularly for cotton piece-goods, and that is where we have the local raw material, that is where we want to expand; we want to have a new spinning mill, which we will integrate forward to garment manufacturing for export . . . this is much harder in fabrics, since the costs of production here are relatively higher.

This perspective has made $L_1$ a strong opponent of high import protection:

All the other textile firms here have been calling for heavy protection; we are the only company saying the opposite. Why? Because we are aggressive and expansionary in outlook, and have strong ties to the international market; also we have the knowledge of how garment exporting can grow, and how considerable the job gains are from such activity – and of how limited the investment is that is needed for each extra job.

The heavy protection in the Kenyan market had to go 'because the inefficiency it caused rebounded on you, and prevented you being competitive for exports'.

This high import protection certainly was a factor evident in the explanation by other firms of their export failure. Enterprise $F_2$, for instance, stressed that the 130 per cent duty on polyester filament yarn (to protect local industry) meant that any fabric produced by it was far higher in price than that from Japan. Companies $F_1$, $F_3$ and $L_3$ all mentioned high import duties on dyes and chemicals as factors making production costs too high for exports. Import protection also underlay the many product variations in most Kenyan mills, and the cost increases tied to this had important export consequences. Enterprise $F_3$, for example, indicated that it could export to Europe competitively if it were producing just one product – though this would require investment to rationalise machinery and manufacturing patterns in the factory, something the parent company would not be willing to do because of the very limited profits it was receiving from the Kenyan subsidiary.

Certain elements of government export policy have also caused problems. Export compensation payments have been subject to long delays in many cases before companies received them. Government has also been slow to move on requests for an export guarantee system to safeguard exporters from losses when overseas purchasers fail to pay. Nor have other industry suggestions been taken up – to allow duty-free machinery entry for export production, to establish a bonding system to provide duty-free inputs for export manufacturing, or to regulate quality specifications for exporting.

Nevertheless, the government cannot be singled out in analysing the export failure. The foreign MNCs investing in Kenya bear much of the responsibility for shaping that failure. Their pressure, as the second section of this chapter has shown, was responsible for the very high import protection that in turn made exports so difficult. Their performance, as shown in the third section, was marked by the limited linkages, limited technological independence and extensive product range that contrast so dramatically with enterprise $L_1$. That firm built a solid export market in Western Europe because it had incentive to diversify its Kenyan base, because it specialised in its product range, and because it was prepared (and able) to carry out linkage investment in garments. The MNC subsidiaries did not do likewise – because some of them were simply cases of predatory fraud, because the strategy of others was aimed at import reproduction behind high barriers for the local market, and because all of them were less interested in direct linkage investments. The cases of predatory fraud have in turn left legacies of high debt burdens that make it very difficult for enterprises like $F_6$ to ever export competitively.

The industrial dependence of Kenyan textiles, and the protected inefficiency that interacted with that dependence, then, were mainly responsible for the textile export failure – just as the firm that defined the pattern was independent, specialised and opposed to the protectionism. But even the counter-pattern carries its dangers. As the Ivory Coast has discovered, export manufacturing expansion can be blocked off by a worried European Community through import quotas (despite the duty-free entry promised to African manufactured goods under the Lomé Convention). Kenya is well under its quota levels but a marked movement in the direction of the $L_1$ model could spur tighter European controls. Another danger is evident in the basis of $L_1$'s exports; they are organised around a contract with a single German firm. If the calculus of profit and loss led that firm to shift to a new source (in Eastern Europe or North Africa, for instance), the disruption for $L_1$ could be considerable. In its case, with its UK investment, $L_1$ could probably find alternative arrangements soon; but that might be less easy for other Kenyan firms that followed the pattern.


CONCLUSION

This chapter has analysed the 'new orthodoxy' of MNC-led export manufacturing growth, assessing its effects in practice in the Kenyan textile industry. Kenya, like many less developed countries, moved toward this new industrial strategy in 1972–74, seeking to take advantage of new export opportunities that seemed to be emerging from a changing international division of labour. Particularly in the early years of the first Lomé Convention, Europe was seen to be shifting out of areas of relatively labour-intensive production based on standardised technology – such as textile spinning and weaving – and aiming to replace such products with imports from the Third World, including Africa. Kenya therefore sought European MNCs as the vehicle to expand its textile industry, with the explicit goal of gaining a share in such trade with Europe.

The result, as this chapter has shown, was a series of disastrous projects, which cost the people of Kenya over 220 million shillings in investment losses. By 1980 the state had been forced to take over all three of the new MNC-led projects; serious technical problems had become evident in each of them; they were doing no exporting back to Europe; and their employment linkage and learning effects within Kenya had been significantly lower than those from private domestic textile firms that were their alternative. Just as important, the bargaining leverage of the new MNCs had been so great during their establishment process that their pressures (and growing losses) had pushed the Kenyan state into more and more protectionism for Kenyan textiles. Behind these massive trade barriers, Kenyan textile firms proliferated their product range, diversified more and more into synthetic production (in which Kenya had cost disadvantages compared to locally grown cotton), therefore experienced higher production costs, and became less and less competitive as potential exporters. Only one textile producer, a private domestic firm without state financial participation, was able to build up a significant European export market (for cotton T-shirts), and this was done on the basis of product specialisation (rather than proliferation), technological independence (rather than MNC-dependence), and investment in garment manufacturing linkages (which the MNC subsidiaries all avoided).

This chapter demonstrates the way in which many African countries have been marginalised in the changing international division of labour. Kenya simply could not force its way into the serious consideration of leading European textile MNCs as they restructured their world activities; Eastern Europe, South-east Asia, Mediterranean North Africa, even parts of West Africa were drawn into particular production roles by Western European textile firms – but Kenya was not. The distance from Europe was too great compared to West Africa; Kenyan tax concessions were much less than those given by the Ivory Coast, for example; Kenyan wages related to productivity were too high compared to South Asia; and in any event none of the European textile MNCs had an earlier import-substitution base in Kenya on which to build (unlike the Ivory Coast where several French and Dutch textile MNCs had invested in the 1960s). Kenya experienced the restructuring of the European textile industry only in the form of predatory attempts to utilise European excess capacity to extract quick profits from the country.

The state moved into a close symbiotic relationship with foreign capital in much of the industrial development that marked Kenya's post-independence history. The Kenyan textile strategy was an unexceptional continuation of this pattern – with impetus added to it by the employment and foreign exchange needs of the early 1970s. The growing failure of the strategy in turn had two effects. First, it led state officials to ignore many broader policy questions affecting the industry, as they increasingly concentrated on how to deal with these particular disasters. Second, the failure ultimately forced the state to intervene directly and take full control of four large textile firms; having finally grown sceptical of foreign dependence in this industry, the state has established its own locally-recruited management in the case of the last three of these takeovers. This resolution of events, though it has not solved the financial problems of the problem projects, has facilitated a new focus on broader policy questions affecting the textile industry, and has given the state considerable leverage, through the firms it now controls, to shape a long-run strategy. Such a strategy could respond to the serious structural problems that have been shown to characterise the Kenyan textile industry.

The first goal of a recovery strategy would have to be to plan much more specialisation within the industry. Such a textile recovery strategy would be based on independent technological capacities in Kenya, rather than MNC-dependence. It might, accordingly, have to allow somewhat more scope to companies to bring in individual expatriate technical personnel (note the higher expatriate levels in the successful enterprise $L_1$). But, most important, a strategy must also be developed to increase indigenous Kenyan technological capacities in textiles. A Textile Institute is being started under the auspices of the National Industrial Training Council, with Dutch assistance and personnel and Indian textile machinery;[33] that will make a contribution in this direction. But the government should also develop more research and development efforts within the textile companies themselves; only one firm ($F_2$) presently devotes significant resources to this.

A broad textile strategy of this sort would mean, in effect, following the $L_1$ model of successful domestic production and export, described in much of the analysis in the third section. But the political realities of Kenya have meant that in the past it was precisely firms like $L_1$ that did *not* receive the privileges and state asssistance that were provided to MNC projects. All four of the private domestic textile firms surveyed during the study were controlled by Kenyan Asian capital; and such firms have traditionally been by-passed in Kenyan state policy in favour of joint ventures that gave the MNCs investment privileges, and generated senior managerial position for Africans within the resulting subsidiaries. In some sectors, this symbiosis has been extended to shared MNC and private African shareholdings in combination with the state – though this has not been true of textiles because of the relatively low profit rates which have characterised the industry. The on-going reality in the wider political economy of this pattern of symbiosis among the MNCs, the state and the well-off Africans who influence much state action, must be recognised in any assessment of the likelihood of a basic new textile strategy being implemented. The easy option for the state may simply be to allow the textile industry to follow the pattern that the

MNCs led it into, of wide product proliferation behind massive import barriers; the indigenous state managers who have now taken over several of the subsidiaries may even be able to argue more persuasively for such a protectionist course, given their close ties with state policy-makers. Companies like $L_1$ may continue to have very limited political leverage in the Kenyan political economy in arguing for a new strategy.

The limited political power of domestic Asian capital in Kenya, then, is one impediment to the state orienting its policies to the $L_1$ model. Another impediment is the power of the political forces within Kenya that support strongly protectionist industrial policies – policies which this analysis has suggested would have to be dismantled to enforce specialisation and export success in the textile industry. Certain elements within the Kenyan state, strongly pushed by the World Bank and the IMF, have tried for some time to reduce protectionism in Kenyan industry; this culminated in the 1980 budget in the abolition of import bans in favour of import duties, and an end to the system of 'letters of no objection' by which local manufacturers had to authorise any imports that could be made. These moves, however, set off major political conflict within Kenya. Dozens of letters and protests flowed into the Treasury; the major economic ministries of Industry and of Commerce fought the changes strongly; the Kenya Association of Manufacturers, the Chamber of Commerce, the ICDC, and its parastatal associate, Kenya Industrial Estates, all proved themselves very powerful – mobilising their member firms to articulate tough protests.[34] Such pressures persuaded 'higher ups outside the Treasury building' against the policy change,[35] and by November 1980, the new moves had been reversed. Letters of no objection were again required for imports, and complete import bans were announced (in textiles, for instance) – and all in the context of a serious foreign exchange crisis. The evidence is clear that the forces behind extreme protectionism are very strong and very resistant to change.

Finally, a third impediment to change exists in the on-going commitment to foreign reliance in wider Kenyan economic policy. Despite the deplorable record of MNC-led textile exporting, official policies in Kenya are still built around industrial dependence; key policy-makers insist they are more likely to expand manufactured exports through new MNC-led projects than by building on existing firms in Kenya, and therefore encourage less-regulated MNC invest-ment in Kenya as one means of achieving such export expansion.[36] These attitudes make such policy-makers sceptical of a self-reliant textile strategy, based on independent Kenyan firms rather than on subsidiaries.

Nevertheless, the evidence suggests that such a strategy could be viable. It would, moreover, help redress the marginalisation of Kenya in world manufacturing, in a way that foreign reliance has in practice failed to do. Given the growing economic pressures experienced by Kenya, such potential may yet enforce policy change. Industrial dependence has brought the Kenyan textile industry to a dead-end; that lesson may spur a new direction, but only in the context of wider political and social change in Kenya.

## NOTES

1. The research on which this chapter is based has been funded by the Social Sciences and Humanities Research Council of Canada. Special thanks are due to David Gachuki for his help in Nairobi. Research assistance has been provided by Benedict Mongula and Colin Jacobs.
2. Kenya, *Statistical Abstract 1979* (Nairobi: 1979) p. 60.
3. This is the result of research undertaken as part of a broader study of international textile restructuring in association with Michael Dolan and Lynn Mytelka.
4. Industrial Survey and Promotion Centre, Ministry of Commerce and Industry, 'Sector Study – Kenya's Textile Industry' (Nairobi: February 1978) p. 3.
5. N. Swainson, *The Development of Corporate Capitalism in Kenya, 1918–1972* (London: Heinemann, 1980) p. 27.
6. Industrial Survey and Promotion Centre, 'Sector Study', p. 8.
7. Company interview, Thika, 1973.
8. Company interview, Nairobi, 1973
9. R. Elgin, 'The Oligopolisitic Structure and Competitive Characteristics of Direct Foreign Investment in Kenya's Manufacturing Sector', in R. Kaplinsky (ed.) *Readings on the Multinational Corporation in Kenya* (Nairobi: Oxford University Press, 1978) pp. 111–12.
10. Company interview, Kisumu, 1973.
11. Company interview, Nairobi, 1973.
12. *Development Plan, 1974–1978*, pp. 286–7.
13. *East African Report on Trade and Industry*, vol. 4 (July 1974).
14. W. Mutunga, 'Kenya: Contract Law and Society – A study of Rivatex's Investment and Management Agreements', Paper presented at the Workshop on Investment and Management Agreements, University of Warwick, UK, 1979 pp. 10–12.
15. Company interview, Nanyuki, 1980.
16. 'Engineering, Technical Services and Management Agreement between Rivatex and Seditex', mimeo (Nairobi: 1975) pp. 2, 14.
17. Mutunga, 'Kenya: Contract Law and Society', pp. 17, 21–2.

18. See 'Engineering, Technical Services and Management Agreement . . .'; also 'Joint Venture Agreement between Seditex, ICDC and Rivatex', mimeo, 1974.

19. See S. W. Langdon, 'The Multinational Corporation in the Kenyan Political Economy', in Kaplinsky, *Readings*; also R. Kaplinsky, 'Capitalist Accumulation in the Periphery – the Kenyan Case Re-examined', *Review of African Political Economy*, vol. 16 (1980).

20. Industrial Survey and Promotion Centre, 'Sector Study', p. 7.

21. A review of relevant economic data from Kenya is presented in S. W. Langdon, 'Industry and Capitalism in Kenya: Contributions to a Debate', paper presented to the Conference on the African Bourgeoisie: The Development of Capitalism in Nigeria, Kenya and the Ivory Coast, Dakar, Senegal, December 1980.

22. Government interview, Treasury, 1980.

23. *East African Report on Trade and Industry*, December 1976, p. 5.

24. 'Joint Venture Agreement', p. 4.

25. *Quarterly Economic Review of Kenya*, Third Quarter, 1977.

26. *Quarterly Economic Review of Kenya*, Second Quarter, 1978.

27. The information in these paragraphs comes mainly from company interviews in Nairobi, Nanyuki and Eldoret, November 1980.

28. Government interview, Treasury, 1980.

29. This calculation is based on the sum of: (a) 10 per cent of the public equity in each of the three subsidiaries for each year in which said subsidiary did not show a profit; (b) the accumulated financial losses for each firm as of 1980. The rough estimates suggest a cost for Rivatex of K.Shs 130 million, for Nanyuki of 55 million, and for East African Fine Spinners of 35 million. The development expenditure data come from Republic of Kenya, *Statistical Abstract 1979*, p. 226.

30. Government interview, Treasury, 1980.

31. See P. Streeten, 'The Multinational Enterprise and the Theory of Development Policy', *World Development*, 1973; such externalities in Kenyan industry as a whole are discussed in S.W. Langdon, *Multinational Corporations in the Political Economy of Kenya* (London: Macmillan, 1981) Chapter 5.

32. Government interview, Treasury, 1980.

33. Information provided by Britha Mikkelsen, Centre for Development Research, Copenhagen, from her research on industrial training in Kenya.

34. Government interview, Treasury, 1980.

35. Government interview, Ministry of Economic Planning and Development, 1980.

36. Ibid.

# 9 Self-Reliance in Theory and Practice in Tanzanian Trade Relations[1]

## THOMAS J. BIERSTEKER

Self-reliance is a logical prescription of Latin American dependency writers and a great many other contemporary critics of the international economic and political order.[2] It is based on assumptions and values shared by contemporary critics, employs the same definitions of central concepts, and most important, identifies specific policies designed to eliminate the bases of dependence and exploitation that critics hold responsible for a distortion of the development process throughout much of the Third World.[3] Despite the significance of self-reliance for dependency and other critical writers, it is rarely defined and even less frequently examined systematically. As a result, self-reliance has too often been dismissed as merely part of the ideological jargon that necessarily accompanies discussions of the new international economic order.

## THE MEANING OF SELF-RELIANCE

As has been discussed at greater length elsewhere,[4] self-reliance should be regarded as a process or a deliberate strategy for obtaining a set of objectives, rather than a condition or an end state. The major objectives of a strategy of national self-reliance are to avoid dependence and to promote development.[5] The strategy of self-reliance is basically dynamic, with a distinct temporal relationship among three discernible components or phases. At the outset, it involves a partial disengagement

213

of a country from the existing pattern of dominant economic and political relationships prevailing in the international system. This disengagement initially induces, and is later accompanied by, a deliberate restructuring of these relationships to alter the basis of international relations. This restructuring of international trade, investment, and monetary relationships is often described as a collective self-reliance. There is also a significant domestic component to the restructuring phase, incorporating the alteration of existing class relationships, the modification of consumption values, the development of new (and 'appropriate') technologies and institutions, the de-centralisation of decision-making, and the increase of political participation. This restructuring of domestic relationships is sometimes discussed as local or individual self-reliance, but it also reinforces the restructuring of international relationships. After the partial disengage-ment and restructuring phases, a partial reassociation or re-establishment of relations with the industrial countries theoretically takes place.[6]

The specific policies associated with such a strategy can be described in greater detail. Disengagement from the present international economic system entails the erection of trade barriers to restrict the magnitude and influence of foreign goods. Comprehensive limitations on the amount of foreign investment and expatriate manpower are also an important part of disengagement, as is the deliberate rejection of aid offers from industrial countries. China employed all three of these policies in varying degrees after 1949. Severing ties to existing global political institutions is also an implicit aspect of disengagement. Rejection of multilateral aid offers or IMF financial transfers eliminates the possibility for foreign political leverage. Disengagement from global political institutions might also involve a refusal to participate in UN peace-keeping forces to avoid potentially costly (or embarrassing) international involvements.

The disengagement process is an integral part of the strategy of self-reliance and is intentionally partial and selective. It is not a call for complete autarchy or absolute national self-sufficiency. Rather, disengagement is a call for a partial reduction in the magnitude of international economic transactions with industrial countries and for the attainment of self-sufficiency only in particular sectors or activities. Self-sufficiency in fulfilling the basic needs of the population (such as food, energy, or national defence) is ordinarily given priority in the selective disengagement process. Agricultural self-sufficiency is the basic need closest to being fulfilled in most countries pursuing a strategy of national self-reliance. The prospects for attaining self-sufficiency in the provision of other basic needs (such as energy or national defence) varies from country to country, according to natural and human resource endowments. In a process of selective disengagement, therefore, self-sufficiency would be attained on a sector-by-sector basis. The development of new technologies, or the adaptation of existing methods, is also an important part of the disengagement process. Foreign expertise is rejected, and emphasis is placed on the local design of equipment and methods of production. Ideally, technological modifications are suggested by the workers and lead to more appropriate methods of production that are better suited to local supplies of labour and capital, or based on more locally available supplies of raw materials.

The disengagement process just described induces or accompanies a restructuring of basic international and domestic relationships, a second component of a strategy of national self-reliance. The restructuring initially induced by disengagement is subsequently extended and implemented as policy by the state in countries pursuing such a strategy.

The restructuring of basic international relationships of under-developed countries away from their traditional ties to industrial countries is generally described as 'collective self-reliance'. Collective self-reliance refers to increased cooperation and exchanges of commodities and skills among developing countries, economic integration at the regional level, and the establishment of permanent Third World institutions. Collective self-reliance is induced by disengagement, as transactions with other underdeveloped countries begin to take the place of many of the previous ties to industrial countries. It is subsequently actively pursued in efforts to 'devise' methods of international economic exchange and cooperation which are different in kind from those at present operating'.[7] Like dependency writers and other critics of the contemporary international order, advocates of self-reliance assume that trade and other exchanges between unequal partners are inherently exploitative in favour of the stronger partner. Hence, it is only through the expansion of exchanges with other underdeveloped countries that the exploitation inherent in the structure of the current world system can be eliminated.

Some of the specific forms of cooperation and exchange that are a part of international restructuring are largely economic, while others are predominantly political and institutional. At base, international restructuring involves an increase in both the frequency and magnitude of economic exchanges between underdeveloped countries, including increased trade, improved communication links, and the expansion of educational and technical exchanges. Economic integration of under-developed countries, involving tariff reductions, industrial planning, technological acquisition, and the exploitation of natural resources on a regional basis can also be an important aspect of international restructuring.

Among the types of political and institutional cooperation associated with international restructuring is joint action in UN negotiations, especially on trade and investment issues. The coordination of negotiating positions *vis-à-vis* multinational corporations (on tax rates and investment incentives) is also important, along the lines of the policy coordination within the Andean Common Market. Finally, the development of Third World institutions, including a permanent secretariat and organisations designed to coordinate research, collect and analyse data, and provide economic consulting services can also be a part of international restructuring.

In addition to inducing a restructuring of international relationships, disengagement also induces a major restructuring of basic relationships, values, and institutions domestically, within a country pursuing self-reliance. The domestic restructuring initially induced by disengagement is subsequently extended and implemented as policy by countries pursuing self-reliance. At the most general level, domestic restructuring theoretically changes what Samir Amin has referred to as a situation common in Third World countries of 'producing what we do not consume and consuming what we do not produce'.[8]

One of the best illustrations of domestic restructuring induced by disengagement is provided by an examination of domestic class structure. Disengagement from trade and investment linkages to multinational corporations would undermine the basis of a comprador class, engaged in export–import trading activities or other pursuits designed to facilitate the access of multinational corporations to the domestic market. The erection of trade and investment barriers would also provide a basis for domestic production which would not only alter the domestic class structure but also provide locally manufactured products better suited to domestic markets and tastes. Rejection of military and other aid offers would also necessarily induce technological innovations within the country pursuing self-reliance in order to maintain national security.

Although disengagement induces a great deal of domestic restructur-ing, it is by no means sufficient to effect or sustain the amount of domestic restructuring required for self-reliance. Active state inter-vention at all levels is also required. For example, although disengagement would severely limit the development of a domestic comprador class, state intervention to eliminate such a class altogether might be accomplished by the nationalisation of all import–export activities. State intervention to alter consumption patterns, change basic consumer values, or redirect domestic production might also be pursued with state subsidies for the production of mass consumer goods or campaigns to encourage the consumption of locally produced goods. Tax incentives and state participation in joint ventures have been used by many countries intent on expanding the domestic production of mass consumer items. The promotion of 'individual self-reliance' (the acceptance of responsibility for one's own basic needs) can also assist in the transformation of consumption patterns by instilling self-confidence in, and respect for, the products of local artisans and manufacturers.

Other aspects of domestic restructuring include the creation of new and 'appropriate' institutions. Appropriate institutions are defined as institutions which support the basic principle of relying on local efforts and initiatives and, therefore, are an important part of domestic restructuring. Tanzania has long been associated with efforts to establish appropriate institutions in the field of education.

Security and national defence is another area in which appropriate institutions can be established. Citizens' militias are important in countries pursuing a national strategy of self-reliance because they encourage reliance on local efforts (an example of 'local self-reliance') and also increase mass participation. More important, citizens' militias enhance national security by decentralising national defence and making it virtually impossible to control the country by occupation of its capital city. China has formed citizens' militias to ensure that 'neither foreign bases nor bombers coming from afar can tip the scales of war against an army which moves among the people as fish in water.'[9] Tanzania, Mozambique, Vietnam, and Nicaragua have also formed citizens' militias to buttress their security needs.

In theory, these newly formed appropriate institutions should be decentralised to ensure maximum participation and to ensure that self-reliance is implemented at all levels of society. Existing institutions should also be transformed along the same lines. China is often presented as an example of a country that has decentralised industrial production:

> provinces, municipalities, and even counties (hsien) seem to be developing along self-sufficient, autonomous lines under the official injunction 'to build small but complete industrial systems by self-reliance.'[10]

In administrative terms, however, the state retains control over many strategic industries such as oil, power, steel, transportation, and communications. Decentralisation of the state administrative bureaucracy is also attempted by many countries pursuing self-reliance. Local or regional control of economic planning, of education, or the distribution of social services are all examples of bureaucratic decentralisation.

One of the objectives of decentralisation is to enhance national security. Decentralisation of the economic and political system makes it more difficult for an enemy to conquer or control a country pursuing self-reliance. Increased public participation is another basic objective of decentralisation. Decentralisation eventually involves everyone in solving problems and is a means of 'democratising' daily life. In theory, decentralisation should lead to more active worker participation in management, and to student participation in decisions which affect them in their educational institutions. Allowing workers and students to make their own decisions should increase their personal satisfaction, encourage their commitment to local institution building, and enable them to learn from their own mistakes.

Increased decentralisation and mass participation should also enhance 'local' or 'individual self-reliance'. That is, they encourage reliance on one's own efforts at the provincial, district, commune, factory, or individual level. Ultimately, individual and local self-reliance reinforce the strategy at the national level. As the Tanzanians proclaimed in the Arusha Declaration:

> If every individual is self-reliant, the ten-house cell will be self-reliant; if all the cells are self-reliant, the whole ward will be self-reliant and if the wards are self-reliant, the district will be self-reliant. If the districts are self-reliant, then the region is self-reliant, and if the regions are self-reliant, then the whole nation is self-reliant and this is our aim.[11]

Johan Galtung makes a similar argument when he stresses that self-reliance is a dynamic movement from the periphery, at all levels, which cannot be led from above.[12]

The international and domestic restructuring initiated by disengagement and sustained by state intervention are mutually reinforcing. For example, the expansion of trade with other underdeveloped countries should reinforce domestic efforts to redirect consumption patterns. In theory, at least, products imported from other underdeveloped countries should be more oriented toward fulfilling the basic needs of the mass population than products imported from industrial countries.

Similarly, the elimination of a comprador class reliant on commercial ties to industrial countries should, in theory, expand the opportunities for increased trade cooperation among underdeveloped countries. Following its disengagement and restructuring of international and domestic relations, a country pursuing a strategy of national self-reliance theoretically begins the reassociation phase, i.e. partial re-establishment of previous relations with the industrial countries. A new international economic order is thus created in which economic and political relations take place on a 'different' basis. The prior basis of dependency relations has been altered. Disengagement and restructuring have transformed countries pursuing self-reliance to such an extent that they can afford to re-establish previous economic and political relationships with industrial countries without fear of the consequences of excessive dependence. It is not clear whether any country has yet reached this stage of self-reliance in practice, although some have suggested that China's 'opening up' in recent years and the expansion of East European trade relations with Western Europe are forms of partial reassociation.

To summarise, a strategy of national self-reliance can be defined as: (a) a deliberate policy of selective disengagement from international transactions (trade, aid, investment, technology, information, and manpower exchanges), replaced by reliance on internal capabilities: (b) a conscious *restructuring* of basic economic and political relationships, values, and institutions: (i) internationally, between the country pursuing self-reliance and other countries in the international system and (ii) domestically, within the country pursuing self-reliance; and (c) reassociation, or partial re-establishment of previous economic and political international transactions with industrial countries on a changed basis.

Both disengagement and restructuring are necessary components of a strategy of national self-reliance. Disengagement without deliberate restructuring cannot be described as self-reliance. Reassociation is also a central component, but cannot be assessed empirically for most countries in the current international system. Rather, reassociation is anticipated as a future phase for countries presently undergoing the disengagement and restructuring processes. Finally, the separation of the restructuring phase into international and domestic components is made for analytical purposes only. In a country pursuing self-reliance, the restructuring of domestic relationships will reinforce the restructuring of international ones, and vice versa, as previously described in the text.

## FROM THEORY TO PRACTICE: TANZANIAN FOREIGN TRADE POLICY

Foreign trade policy is only a part of a comprehensive strategy of self-reliance. It is of critical importance in any assessment of disengagement and international restructuring. As we shall see, it is also important in an assessment of domestic restructuring. This evaluation of Tanzanian foreign trade policy should be considered as only a part of a more comprehensive review of Tanzania's strategy of self-reliance which would include other aspects of its foreign economic policy (e.g. foreign investment and aid), as well as its centrally important agricultural policy. The distinction made between foreign and domestic economic policy is an artificial one, but is employed for analytical purposes in this chapter.

The foreign trade policy of a country includes everything from its tariff structure to its position in North–South negotiations. In the discussion that follows, Tanzania's foreign trade policies will be evaluated in an effort to determine how it has translated the self-reliance proclamation in the 1967 Arusha Declaration into specific institutions and policy measures, and the extent to which these policies have been implemented since 1967.

Prior to the Arusha Declaration the structure of Tanzanian trade was similar to that of most other African underdeveloped countries during the early and mid-1960s. The bulk of its exports consisted of unprocessed or semi-processed raw materials, including (in order of importance) sisal, coffee, cotton, minerals (diamonds, gold, tin, and salt), cashew nuts, and cloves. Great Britain, its former colonial power, received the largest share of these exports and provided the largest share of Tanzanian imports, consisting primarily of manufactured items.

Although some elements of disengagement and self-reliance were evident in Tanzania prior to 1967,[13] the Arusha Declaration issued in February of that year provided its first comprehensive statement of self-reliance. The Arusha Declaration and Tanzania's move to self-reliance emerged in part out of frustration over the minimal response to Tanzania's incentives for foreign investors and its difficulty in obtaining international financial assistance for its first five-year national development plan (1964–69).[14] Since most of its development policy was financed from domestic sources, the 'necessity' for international assistance and foreign investment became less apparent. If anything, the government realised the inadequacies of its colonially inherited institutions for domestic capital formation and realised the need for a more independent development strategy. The Arusha Declaration outlined a general strategy for Tanzania's development and had a number of important implications for its trade policy.

From the Arusha Declaration and subsequent discussions of foreign economic policy in Tanzania's Annual Plans, its Second (1969–74) and Third (1975–80) Five-Year Plans, and other government declarations, it is possible to see how Tanzania has translated its ideology of self-reliance into a trade policy that includes disengagement, international restructuring, and domestic restructuring components.

## DISENGAGEMENT

Selective disengagement from the prevailing pattern of international trade transactions is an essential aspect of a strategy of national self-reliance. It can be seen in a number of specific foreign-trade policy measures in Tanzania.

The Arusha Declaration stated that 'it is essential that all the major means of production and exchange in the nation are controlled and owned by the peasants through the machinery of their government and their cooperatives'.[15] Among the activities included on the list of 'the major means of production and exchange' were import and export trade activities. Accordingly, the Tanzanian government nationalised, with full compensation, the eight major foreign-owned, export–import firms operating in the country in 1967.[16] Policy implementation was both swift and complete in this area, as the nationalisations affected all of the large foreign-owned firms engaged in trade and took place within a week of the promulgation of the declaration. The nationalisation of commerce was extended to other firms in 1978, and by February of 1980 the national trading companies assumed responsibility for nearly all of the import and wholesale trade.

In its Second Five-Year Plan (1969–74) another aspect of Tanzania's disengagement in trade policy was identified. According to the plan:

the excessive dependence on foreign sources of supply for virtually all manufactured goods, and the corresponding dependence of the economy on primary commodity earnings as a source of income meant that the pace of development was set largely by forces outside local control.[17]

Accordingly, President Nyerere announced in the introduction to the plan, 'we are trying gradually to transform our economy so that it is no longer export dominated but is directed to the creation and service of a rising local market'.[18] This did not necessarily mean that Tanzania had to decrease its exports. Rather, it needed to decrease its reliance on export receipts for national income.

To evaluate this second aspect of Tanzanian trade disengagement, statistics were obtained on the total export receipts and the gross domestic product of Tanzania for the years 1955 through 1980. The data are displayed in Table 9.1. By computing a simple ratio of total exports

TABLE 9.1   *Export receipts and gross domestic product (GDP), Tanzania* (All figures in million Tanzanian shillings, at current prices, unless otherwise designated)

| Year | Total exports* | GDP** | Exports as percentage of GDP |
|------|------|------|------|
| 1955 | 748.2 | 3,098 | 24.2 |
| 1956 | 925.8 | 3,200 | 28.9 |
| 1957 | 820.6 | 3,418 | 24.0 |
| 1958 | 876.0 | 3,522 | 24.9 |
| 1959 | 944.4 | 3,752 | 25.2 |
| 1960 | 1,131.6 | 3,920 | 28.9 |
| 1961 | 1,012.0 | 4,102 | 24.7 |
| 1962 | 1,071.4 | 4,454 | 24.1 |
| 1963 | 1,302.6 | 4,932 | 26.4 |
| 1964 | 1,428.4 | 6,030 | 23.7 |
| 1965 | 1,361.4 | 6,140 | 22.2 |
| 1966 | 1,795.0 | 7,042 | 25.5 |
| 1967 | 1,698.1 | 7,343 | 23.1 |
| 1968 | 1,626.8 | 7,874 | 20.7 |
| 1969 | 1,688.8 | 8,271 | 20.4 |
| 1970 | 1,704.0 | 9,173 | 18.6 |
| 1971 | 1,792.0 | 9,814 | 18.3 |
| 1972 | 2,143.0 | 11,172 | 19.2 |
| 1973 | 2,411.0 | 13,103 | 18.4 |
| 1974 | 2,643.0 | 15,994 | 16.5 |
| 1975 | 2,712.0 | 19,011 | 14.3 |
| 1976 | 3,846.0 | 23,139 | 16.6 |
| 1977 | 4,474.0 | 29,420 | 15.2 |
| 1978 | 3,595.8 | 33,580 | 10.7 |
| 1979 | 4,215.0 | 36,839 | 10.4 |
| 1980 | 4,162.0 | 40,426 | 10.3 |

*Includes both merchandise and gold exports. Figures before 1965 refer to Mainland Tanzania (Tanganyika) only. Source: UN Department of Social and Economic Affairs, *Yearbook of International Trade Statistics*, various years.
**IMF, *International Financial Statistics Yearbook*, various years.

to GDP, it is possible to compare the annual figures for the significance of export receipts and look for consistent trends over time. The data in Table 9.1 indicate a long-term secular decline in the significance of exports, beginning after independence in 1961. Before independence, Tanzania's exports averaged approximately 26 per cent of its GDP. During the six years of independence prior to the Arusha Declaration, exports began to decline to an average of approximately 24.4 per cent of total GDP. In the 14 years for which data are available since Arusha, the downward trend continued to an average export share of 16.7 per cent.

This trend suggests that Tanzania has succeeded in reducing its reliance on export receipts for national income. The extent of its disengagement should not be overemphasised, however. The decline in the ratio of exports to GDP began at independence, six years before the Arusha Declaration, and decreased only slightly after 1967. The sharpest downturn appears after 1977, due to a combination of falling world coffee prices and a cyclical decline in clove production on Zanzibar. This reduced Tanzanian export receipts and thereby reduced its export to GDP ratio. Although these two factors explain most of the post-1977 reduction, it is important to note that GDP increased at a rate greater than export receipts most years before 1977 (see Table 9.2). If this trend can be continued for an extended period of time (as it has for seven of the last ten years), it would suggest that Tanzania is beginning to reduce its reliance on export receipts for national income.[19]

TABLE 9.2  *Rates of change of export receipts and GDP*

| Year | Export receipts* (current prices) (%) | GDP** (current prices) (%) | GDP** (constant 1975 prices) (%) |
|---|---|---|---|
| 1970–71 | +5.2 | +7.0 | +4.6 |
| 1971–72 | +19.6 | +13.8 | +6.3 |
| 1972–73 | +12.5 | +17.3 | +3.1 |
| 1973–74 | +9.6 | +22.1 | +2.5 |
| 1974–75 | +2.6 | +18.9 | +5.9 |
| 1975–76 | +41.8 | +21.7 | +4.6 |
| 1976–77 | +16.3 | +27.1 | +6.6 |
| 1977–78 | –19.6 | +14.1 | +5.8 |
| 1978–79 | +17.2 | +9.7 | +5.5 |
| 1979–80 | –1.3 | +9.7 | +3.6 |

*UN Department of Social and Economic Affairs, *Yearbook of International Trade Statistics*, various years.
**IMF, *International Financial Statistics*, various years.

In addition to its nationalisation of export–import firms and its efforts to reduce the significance of export receipts, Tanzania has also attempted to cut back its quantity of luxury consumer imports. Efforts to reduce or eliminate altogether the importation of elite consumer items have figured prominently in Tanzania's trade policy and provide a good illustration of selective disengagement. In theory, this kind of selective disengagement should reduce the influence of foreign goods and induce more appropriate consumption patterns.

When Tanzania nationalised its largest export–import firms in 1967, it created the State Trading Corporation (STC) to handle most of the country's foreign trade, as well as the bulk of its internal wholesale trade. The STC, in cooperation with the Ministry of Commerce, was mandated to reduce drastically or eliminate the importation of luxury consumer goods. As President Nyerere reiterated in his introduction of the Second Plan, 'if the things are not essential, we should do without'.[20]

The Ministry of Commerce is able to impose stringent tariffs to reduce the importation of elite consumer articles. The STC was empowered to regulate the importation of luxury consumer goods through a system of import confinements. Any goods confined to STC could only be imported by the corporation or imported under licence to STC. Confinement assured a state monopoly over the importation of a wide range of items, and hence the ability to ban items not deemed 'essential'. According to official Tanzanian statistics, by mid-1969 the STC had 103 items confined to it, compared with only 30 in mid-1968.[21] The powers to ban 'non-essential' items were taken away from the STC in 1972 and assumed by the Bank of Tanzania, as part of its responsibilities for the operation of Tanzania's foreign exchange controls.[22]

Tanzania has continued the import confinements system in its reconstituted national trading companies, and they have proven relatively successful in reducing, and in some cases eliminating altogether, the importation of certain luxury consumer articles. High tariffs imposed on the importation of private automobiles have induced a dramatic decrease in the rate at which these articles of conspicuous (inappropriate) consumption have entered the country. The data in Table 9.3 indicate the extent to which the importation of passenger cars has been reduced. In 1966, a year before the Arusha Declaration, 3020 automobiles were imported at a cost of 33.5 million Tanzanian shillings, or 2.6 per cent of the value of total imports. That figure has been exceeded in only one year since 1967, and the cost of automobiles as a percentage of total imports has remained under 1 per cent since 1972.

The STC and, more recently, the Bank of Tanzania have employed

TABLE 9.3   *Importation of passenger cars, Tanzania*

| Year | Number of automobiles imported | Value of automobiles imported (million Tanzanian shillings) | Automobile imports as a % of total value of imports |
|------|------|------|------|
| 1961 | 2,359 | 24.8 | 3.1 |
| 1962 | 2,766 | 28.4 | 3.6 |
| 1963 | 3,103 | 32.8 | 4.1 |
| 1964 | 2,613 | 27.2 | 3.1 |
| 1965 | 2,232 | 23.7 | 2.4 |
| 1966 | 3,020 | 33.5 | 2.6 |
| 1967 | 2,263 | 26.1 | 2.0 |
| 1968 | 2,978 | 31.8 | 2.1 |
| 1969 | 3,243 | 34.7 | 2.4 |
| 1970 | 2,752 | 32.8 | 1.7 |
| 1971 | 1,935 | 26.0 | 1.1 |
| 1972 | 568 | 8.6 | 0.3 |
| 1973 | 1,519 | 26.5 | 0.8 |
| 1974 | 1,488 | 28.0 | 0.5 |
| 1975 | 667 | 15.0 | 0.3 |
| 1976 | 558 | 12.5 | 0.3 |
| 1977 | n.a. | 31.8 | 0.5 |
| 1978 | 1,994 | 64.0 | 0.7 |
| 1979 | n.a. | 78.0 | 0.9 |
| 1980 | n.a. | 60.4 | 0.6 |

n.a. Not available.
SOURCE   UN Department of Social and Economic Affairs, *Yearbook of International Trade*, various years. Data for 1961–64 refer to Tanganyika only. After 1964, because of the merger with Zanzibar, data are adjusted to include both territories of Tanzania.

import licensing powers to ban the importation of television sets altogether. The importation of electronic goods and certain 'luxury' textile items has also been actively discouraged. President Nyerere has advocated self-sufficiency in certain areas, particularly in the production of textiles:

> We are nearly self-sufficient in the production of textiles and we cannot continue to indulge our stupid preference for imported cloth. What we cannot produce in Tanzania we should buy from East Africa – or, if the things are not essential, we should do without.[23]

Although the STC, national trading companies, and Bank of Tanzania have had the power to restrict the importation of textile goods to Tanzania, their importation has not been eliminated altogether. The quantity of textile imports, particularly cotton fabrics, has been reduced dramatically, however.

In Table 9.4 textile imports are divided into two groups: luxury and non-luxury goods. Luxury goods consist of synthetic textiles, special textile fabrics, and articles made wholly or chiefly of textile products (blankets, rugs, linen, and other furnishing articles). Non-luxury goods include textile yarn and thread, as well as cotton fabrics. The data suggest that the total quantity of imported textile goods has decreased over time, especially since Arusha. However, most of this decrease has been accounted for by a reduction in the import of non-luxury goods, from a level of around 45 million square metres annually in the early 1960s to only 2.1 million square metres in 1976. The quantity of luxury textile items, on the other hand, has not decreased appreciably over time, but has remained roughly constant. As a percentage of the total quantity of textiles imported, luxury goods have increased from 25 per cent in 1961 to 88 per cent in 1976. As a percentage of the total value of textile imports, luxury goods have risen from 43 per cent in 1961 to just over 50 per cent in 1980.

The increase in the relative importance of luxury textile imports can be explained in part by the growth and development of Tanzania's domestic textile industry. The local textile firms produce primarily cotton textile piece-goods for mass consumption. However, the fact that the importation of luxury consumer textile items has remained roughly constant in volume since the early 1960s does not augur well for a policy of disengagement that emphasises the reduction of luxury consumer imports. Unfortunately, comparable data on the quantity of imported textiles have not been supplied to the United Nations since 1976. The data on the *value* of luxury and non-luxury textile imports suggest that luxury imports may have stabilised or decreased slightly since that year.

Thus, Tanzania has demonstrated its ability to reduce the importation of some luxury articles (automobiles) and eliminate others altogether (television sets). However, whether it is due to an inability or an unwillingness to enforce restrictive tariffs and import confinements, other luxury consumer items (textiles) continue to be imported at previous levels.

A fourth and final aspect of Tanzanian selective disengagement in trade policy involves its efforts to attain self-sufficiency in food production, and to eliminate completely the importation of food and food-related products. Agricultural self-sufficiency is an important objective for most countries pursuing self-reliance, and Tanzania is no exception. The Second Five-Year Plan emphasised the importance of sharply reducing food imports, and this objective was reiterated in subsequent annual plan drafts. Despite recent setbacks with its *ujamaa* and *villagisation* programmes,[24] Tanzania remained strongly committed to the attainment of agricultural self-sufficiency in 1980.[25] However, once again the gap between the policy objectives and policy realities is apparent.

Whether measured as a percentage of total imports or as a percentage of GDP, the data displayed in Table 9.5 and Figure 9.1 reveal only a slight decline in food imports into Tanzania following the Arusha Declaration (the continuation of a trend begun in 1965). The most dramatic decrease in food imports during the period took place even earlier, between 1962 and 1963. The conspicuous increase in food imports in 1974, 1975, and most recently in 1980, is attributable to reduced crop yields due to droughts during those years. However, even when natural disasters have not befallen Tanzania, the country has not been able to increase agricultural productivity, let alone achieve agricultural self-sufficiency. The government remained committed to food self-sufficiency in draft documents for its third five-year plan period (1975–80). However, specific policy measures to achieve this

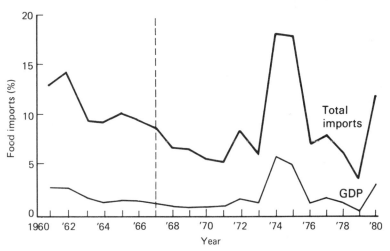

FIGURE 9.1 *Food imports as a percentage of total imports and GDP*

TABLE 9.4  Textile imports, Tanzania, 1961–80*

| Year | (1) Luxury Goods Quantity (million sq. metres) | (2) Luxury Goods Value (million shillings) | (3) Non-Luxury Goods Quantity** (million sq. metres) | (4) Non-Luxury Goods Value (million shillings) | (5) Total Quantity* (million sq. metres) | (6) Total Value (million shillings) | (7) (1) as % of (5) | (8) (2) as % of (6) |
|---|---|---|---|---|---|---|---|---|
| 1961 | 15.2 | 62 | 44.6 | 81 | 59.8 | 143 | 25 | 43 |
| 1962 | 15.6 | 65 | 46.8 | 88 | 62.4 | 153 | 25 | 42 |
| 1963 | 15.6 | 73 | 46.1 | 90 | 61.7 | 163 | 25 | 45 |
| 1964 | 18.6 | 76 | 40.9 | 101 | 59.5 | 177 | 31 | 43 |
| 1965 | 16.9 | 77 | 44.4 | 96 | 61.3 | 173 | 28 | 45 |
| 1966 | 26.3 | 105 | 54.6 | 129 | 80.9 | 234 | 33 | 45 |
| 1967 | 9.8 | 70 | 24.3 | 64 | 34.1 | 134 | 29 | 52 |
| 1968 | 12.0 | 89 | 39.1 | 108 | 51.1 | 197 | 23 | 45 |
| 1969 | 9.4 | 73 | 19.7 | 70 | 29.1 | 143 | 32 | 51 |
| 1970 | n.a. | 69 | 21.3 | 47 | n.a. | 116 | n.a. | 60 |

| | | | | | | | | |
|---|---|---|---|---|---|---|---|---|
| 1971 | n.a. | 73 | 8.1 | 19 | n.a. | 92 | n.a. | 79 |
| 1972 | 11.9 | 102 | 2.0 | 15 | 13.9 | 117 | 86 | 87 |
| 1973 | 22.5 | 160 | 10.6 | 64 | 33.1 | 224 | 68 | 71 |
| 1974 | 16.5 | 213 | 12.8 | 84 | 29.3 | 297 | 56 | 72 |
| 1975 | 10.4 | 134 | 4.1 | 47 | 14.5 | 181 | 72 | 74 |
| 1976 | 14.8 | 151 | 2.1 | 67 | 16.9 | 218 | 88 | 69 |
| 1977 | n.a. | 154 | n.a. | 127† | n.a. | 281 | n.a. | 55 |
| 1978 | n.a. | 170 | n.a. | 183† | n.a. | 353 | n.a. | 48 |
| 1979 | n.a. | 103 | n.a. | 194† | n.a. | 297 | n.a. | 35 |
| 1980 | n.a. | 161 | n.a. | 160† | n.a. | 321 | n.a. | 50 |

*Data before 1966 refer to mainland Tanzania (Tanganyika) only. Zanzibar is included in figures beginning in 1966. Luxury goods consist of synthetic textiles, special textile fabrics, and articles made wholly or chiefly of textile products (blankets, rugs, linen, and other furnishing articles). Non-luxury goods include textile yarn and thread, as well as cotton fabrics.

**Does not include textile yarn and thread import quantities measured in weight rather than volume.

†Most of the increase in the value of non-luxury textile imports after 1976 was accounted for by increases in textile yarns, threads, and other materials employed in the Tanzanian textile industry.

n.a. Not available.

SOURCE  UN Department of Economic and Social Affairs, Statistical Office, *Yearbook of International Trade Statistics* (various years, aggregated by the author).

*Africa in Economic Crisis*

TABLE 9.5 *Tanzanian performance in efforts to attain food self-sufficiency* (All figures in million Tanzanian shillings, at current prices, unless otherwise designated)

| Year | (1) Total imports* | (2) Food, beverages & tobacco imports* | (3) (2) as % of (1) | (4) GDP** | (5) (2) as % of (4) |
|---|---|---|---|---|---|
| 1961 | 903.2 | 120.3 | 13.3 | 4,102 | 2.9 |
| 1962 | 902.1 | 131.0 | 14.5 | 4,454 | 2.9 |
| 1963 | 915.6 | 87.5 | 9.6 | 4,932 | 1.8 |
| 1964 | 952.9 | 90.2 | 9.5 | 6,030 | 1.5 |
| 1965 | 1,082.1 | 112.3 | 10.4 | 6,140 | 1.8 |
| 1966 | 1,360.7 | 133.7 | 9.8 | 7,042 | 1.9 |
| 1967 | 1,359.5 | 121.6 | 8.9 | 7,343 | 1.7 |
| 1968 | 1,531.7 | 108.6 | 7.1 | 7,874 | 1.4 |
| 1969 | 1,418.7 | 99.6 | 7.0 | 8,271 | 1.2 |
| 1970 | 1,939.2 | 109.3 | 5.6 | 9,173 | 1.2 |
| 1971 | 2,412.9 | 127.1 | 5.3 | 9,814 | 1.3 |
| 1972 | 2,595.9 | 227.2 | 8.8 | 11,172 | 2.0 |
| 1973 | 3,141.2 | 197.9 | 6.3 | 13,103 | 1.5 |
| 1974 | 5,429.3 | 990.9 | 18.3 | 15,994 | 6.2 |
| 1975 | 5,324.1 | 955.9 | 18.0 | 19,011 | 5.0 |
| 1976 | 4,738.8 | 334.9 | 7.1 | 23,139 | 1.4 |
| 1977 | 6,041.2 | 520.8 | 8.6 | 29,420 | 1.8 |
| 1978 | 8,775.7 | 495.8 | 5.7 | 33,580 | 1.5 |
| 1979 | 8,882.7 | 307.1 | 3.5 | 36,839 | 0.8 |
| 1980 | 9,927.3 | 1,197.7† | 12.1 | 40,426 | 3.0 |

*UN Department of Social and Economic Affairs, *Yearbook of International Trade Statistics*, various years.
**IMF, *International Financial Statistics Yearbook*, 1979.
†Most of this was accounted for by a major increase of food-grains and cereals.
Data before 1968 are adjusted to include both mainland Tanzania (Tanganyika) and Zanzibar.

objective were never fully worked out. It was not until June of 1981 that some policy changes were introduced, allowing the resumption of private, large-scale farming and reviving some of the regional cooperatives.

## RESTRUCTURING INTERNATIONAL RELATIONS

In theory, Tanzania's disengagement in its trade policy should induce changes in its international economic relations. For example, its nationalisation of major commercial enterprises should encourage a diversification of trading partners that would have been impossible as long as the ties of neo-colonial relationships remained intact. Of course, this tendency would eventually have to be reinforced by deliberate state intervention in order to assure its continuation. Tanzania has adopted a number of specific policy measures designed to restructure its international trade relations.

First, there have been deliberate efforts to diversify the export market destinations of Tanzanian products. The Second Five-Year Plan stated that for commodities affected by limitations in traditional markets, 'there is a need to seek out new trading partners', and emphasised the need 'to diversify away from a few dominant overseas markets.'[26] This position was reiterated in subsequent annual plans[27] and in President Nyerere's review of Tanzania's situation ten years after independence,[28] but was omitted from provisional drafts of the Third Development Plan.[29]

The STC was designated responsible for carrying out much of this export market diversification. STC agencies were established in neighbouring Kenya, Uganda, and Zambia, participation in international trade fairs was increased, and there were efforts to 'pursue expanding trade possibilities through bilateral arrangements with socialist countries'.[30] Parallel trading (making the importation of goods from another country conditional on sales of Tanzanian agricultural products to that country) increasingly became a central concern of official commercial policy and efforts to expand and diversify export markets. In addition to STC activities, commercial attachés were posted to a number of countries (including Zambia, Italy, Egypt, India, and Japan) to promote Tanzanian products, and the Ministry of Commerce established an Export Promotion Bureau. When the STC was gradually dismantled, during 1973 and 1974, the Ministries of Commerce, Treasury, and Economic Affairs, and Development Planning took over its efforts to diversify export markets.

Tanzania has been relatively successful in its efforts to diversity away from a single dominant overseas market. In a country-by-country breakdown of the relative value of Tanzanian exports since 1961 (Table 9.6), it is possible to observe the extent of this diversification. From independence in 1961 until the Arusha Declaration in 1967, between 30 and 35 per cent of Tanzania's exports went to the United Kingdom – historically the primary destination for its exports. Germany, the United States, India, and Hong Kong were the next largest recipients of Tanzanian exports, receiving between 5.1 per cent and 9.8 per cent of its total exports during the 1961–67 period. The British and Commonwealth markets clearly dominated all other national markets for Tanzanian exports in those years. By 1979 the picture was quite different. The value of exports to the United Kingdom had declined in relative terms from 30.1 per cent to 16.8 per cent. West Germany had become the largest recipient of Tanzanian exports (18.3 per cent), followed by Britain (16.8 per cent), Italy (6.3 per cent), and the United States (5.2 per cent). Hence, by the 1970s, no single national market dominated for the exports of Tanzania. This pattern of export diversification is different from the pattern prevailing in some parts of West Africa since decolonisation, where the historical commercial role of the British and French has been largely taken over by the United States (e.g. in Nigeria and Guinea). The consistency of the data before 1967 suggests that export diversification has increased significantly since the Arusha Declaration and is not simply the outgrowth of a longer-term secular trend.

In addition to efforts to diversify export market destinations, Tanzania has also developed policy measures designed to diversify the sources of its imports. This second aspect of its attempt to restructure its international trade relations has received less discussion than export diversification. However, its objective is essentially the same: to reduce

TABLE 9.6  *Value of Tanzanian exports to principal trading partners* (as a percentage of total exports)*

|  | 1961** | 1964** | 1967 | 1970 | 1973 | 1976 | 1979 |
|---|---|---|---|---|---|---|---|
| United Kingdom | 35.8 | 30.6 | 30.1 | 21.9 | 18.8 | 14.3 | 16.8 |
| West Germany | 8.0 | 8.1 | 5.3 | 4.7 | 6.7 | 14.9 | 18.3 |
| USA | 9.8 | 8.5 | 5.1 | 9.6 | 8.3 | 10.1 | 5.2 |
| India | 5.2 | 6.1 | 6.7 | 7.3 | 6.7 | 5.3 | 4.9 |
| Hong Kong | 6.7 | 6.4 | 7.2 | 7.5 | 6.4 | 5.6 | 2.7 |
| Indonesia | n.a. | n.a. | n.a. | 0.1 | 9.4 | 1.5 | 4.5 |
| Singapore | n.a. | n.a. | 0.3 | 5.8 | 1.6 | 7.4 | 0.9 |
| China | 0.0 | 3.3 | 3.6 | 3.5 | 4.4 | 3.0 | 0.5 |
| Italy | 2.5 | 2.4 | 2.7 | 2.7 | 2.1 | 6.7 | 6.3 |
| Netherlands | 6.1 | 5.4 | 4.1 | 3.6 | 3.2 | 4.0 | 4.3 |
| [Japan] |  |  |  |  |  |  | [3.9]† |
| Total value (in millions of Tanzanian shillings) | 1,012 | 1,428.4 | 1,698.1 | 1,704 | 2,411 | 3,846 | 4,215 |

*Does *not* include trade with other members of the East African Community (Kenya and Uganda).
**Includes mainland Tanzania (Tanganyika) only.
†Japan was not always among Tanzania's ten principal trading partners in previous years.
n.a. Not available.
SOURCE  UN Department of Economic and Social Affairs, Statistical Office, *Yearbook of International Trade Statistics* (various years).

Tanzanian reliance on a single trading partner for a large share of its commercial transactions.

Tanzania's Second Five-Year Plan called for a significant increase in the role of the STC in managing imports into the country. It specifically called for 'a complete reappraisal of Tanzania's traditional sources of supply'.[31] According to the Plan:

There will be new opportunities for exporting countries and firms which have been struggling against entrenched brands and agencies, to compete on quality, price, and performance, and rapidly to increase their business with Tanzania.[32]

The STC planned to set up purchasing offices abroad to achieve closer contact with exporting firms and maintain a continuous flow of information on world market availabilities and requirements. The Tanzanian government also made a deliberate effort to shift to China as a major source of imports in 1970. This effort was more a result of Tanzanian commitments to the Chinese for the construction of the TANZAM railway than a result of its general commitment to import diversification, however.

Diversification of Tanzania's import sources appears to have proceeded in much the same way as the diversification of its export markets. The data are presented in Table 9.7. The relative share of its imports from the United Kingdom has decreased from 28.8 per cent in 1967 to 19.7 per cent in 1979. At the time of the Arusha Declaration, Britain provided nearly three times the amount of imports obtained from Tanzania's second most important import source (Italy). By the mid-1970s, the value of imports from the United Kingdom was roughly equivalent to the value of imports from China, Germany, Iran, and Japan. By the end of the decade, China and Iran had faded from the scene (for *very* different reasons), but Germany and Japan continued to rival Britain for a share of the Tanzanian market. As in the case of export destination, no single country has emerged to take the place of Britain. However, the decline of Britain as a major import source may not be due to Tanzania's post-Arusha policies at all. Rather, it appears to be part of a longer-term secular decline in exports from the United Kingdom. The relative share of Tanzania's imports from the United Kingdom has decreased at an average rate of between 1.5 band 2 per cent since 1961, and this seems to be irrespective of specific Tanzanian policy measures.

234 *Africa in Economic Crisis*

TABLE 9.7 *Value of Tanzanian imports from principal trading partners* (as a percentage of total imports)*

| | 1961** | 1964** | 1967 | 1970 | 1973 | 1976 | 1979 |
|---|---|---|---|---|---|---|---|
| United Kingdom | 37.6 | 33.1 | 28.8 | 21.3 | 15.7 | 13.4 | 19.7 |
| China | 0.0 | 0.7 | 4.8 | 13.6 | 22.4 | 7.4 | 3.7 |
| West Germany | 4.7 | 6.4 | 6.5 | 9.4 | 8.2 | 10.2 | 12.8 |
| Iran | 4.6 | 3.0 | 5.8 | 5.6 | 7.8 | 13.0 | 0.1 |
| Japan | 9.9 | 16.6 | 5.1 | 7.4 | 9.7 | 9.0 | 7.7 |
| USA | 5.5 | 6.2 | 7.6 | 8.6 | 3.1 | 6.4 | 4.2 |
| Saudi Arabia | 0.7 | 0.4 | 0.7 | 1.3 | 1.6 | 4.2 | 0.8 |
| Italy | 1.2 | 2.5 | 10.7 | 5.6 | 5.0 | 2.6 | 4.5 |
| Netherlands | 7.0 | 3.9 | 4.1 | 4.3 | 3.5 | 3.7 | 5.2 |
| France | 2.2 | 2.5 | 3.8 | 3.3 | 3.2 | 1.4 | 1.7 |
| [India] | | | | | | | [4.7]† |
| [Iraq] | | | | | | | [2.9]† |
| [Bahrain] | | | | | | | [2.7]† |
| Total value (in millions of Tanzanian shillings) | 794 | 879.4 | 1,359.5 | 1,939.2 | 3,141.2 | 4,738.8 | 8,882.7 |

*Does *not* include trade with other members of the East African Community (Kenya and Uganda).
**Mainland Tanzania (Tanganyika) only.
†These countries were not always among Tanzania's ten principal trading partners in previous years.
SOURCE UN Department of Economic and Social Affairs, Statistical Office, *Yearbook of International Trade Statistics* (various years).

The dramatic increase, and subsequent decline, of imports from China was directly related to the building of the TANZAM railway. It consisted primarily of capital goods and equipment required for the building of the railway and consumer goods (primarily special food and clothing items) required by the Chinese workers involved in the construction of the railway. Despite Tanzanian proclamations to the contrary, the increase in the significance of Chinese imports was not the result of a sustained restructuring of its import sources. Imports from China declined in the late 1970s as quickly as they increased earlier in the decade. The increase in the value of imports from Iran and Saudi Arabia in 1976 was caused by the oil price increases after 1973. Tanzania diversified its sources of petroleum by replacing unstable Iran by Iraq (with 2.9 per cent of total imports) and Bahrain (with 2.7 per cent) in 1979.

A third component of Tanzania's efforts to restructure its international trade relations includes its attempts to expand trans-actions with other underdeveloped countries (i.e. to contribute to collective self-reliance). Specific policy measures have been designed to expand South–South trade linkages, facilitate increased regional integration within East Africa, and coordinate 'southern' negotiating positions in international negotiations.

The expansion of South–South trade has been an important part of Tanzania's foreign-trade policy since 1967. It is based on the assumption that the structure of trade inherited at independence 'means nothing less than the increasing exploitation of the people of the developing world by the industrialized nations'.[33] Accordingly the Second Plan stated:

> Trade possibilities exist with the rest of Africa, the Middle East, Eastern Europe and the Far East. Development of such trading links will further lessen the traditional pattern of dependence upon Western European trading partners, although not leading to decline in absolute size of such traditional trade.[34]

The STC and the Ministries of Commerce and Economic Affairs and Development Planning employed commercial attachés, international trade fairs, special trade missions, and foreign purchasing offices to try to expand Tanzanian trade with other underdeveloped countries after Arusha.

Although Tanzania has been relatively successful in diversifying its trading partners among developed market economies (see Tables 9.6 and 9.7), it has not been notably successful in increasing its trade with other countries, particularly other Third World countries (see Table 9.8). Since the Arusha Declaration, the value of trade with other underdeveloped countries has only increased from 22.5 per cent to 24.5 per cent of Tanzania's total international trade. However, virtually all of this increase in trade has taken place since 1973 and is largely composed of increases in the cost of petroleum imports. Between 1973 and 1976, for example, imports from Iran and Saudi Arabia alone increased from 9.4 per cent to 17.2 per cent of Tanzania's total imports. Tanzania did not significantly increase its exports to other Third World countries during this period, and the volume of its trade with developed market economies has remained virtually unchanged since the Arusha Declaration (the 1967 and 1979 figures are identical). Trade with the centrally planned economies has also remained essentially unchanged or decreased somewhat, except for the interlude in the early 1970s during which China became temporarily important.

In addition to its attemps to expand trade with underdeveloped countries in general, Tanzania has also stated its intent to increase its

TABLE 9.8  *Tanzanian trade with developed, developing, and centrally planned economies*

| | 1961 | 1964 | 1967 | 1970 | 1973 | 1976 | 1979 |
|---|---|---|---|---|---|---|---|
| *Total trade* (percentage) | | | | | | | |
| Developed market economies | 80.6 | 78.7 | 68.9 | 65.0 | 58.0 | 63.7 | 68.9 |
| Developing market economies | 17.3 | 15.5 | 22.5 | 23.3 | 23.2 | 28.1 | 24.2 |
| Centrally planned economies | 0.3 | 4.3 | 6.4 | 10.7 | 17.5 | 6.8 | 3.3 |
| Not distributed | 1.8 | 1.5 | 2.3 | 1.0 | 1.3 | 1.4 | 3.6 |
| Total trade (millions of Tanzanian shillings) | 1,086 | 2,307.8 | 3,057.6 | 3,643.2 | 5,552.2 | 8,584.8 | 13,097.7 |
| *Imports* (percentage) | | | | | | | |
| Developed market economies | 75.9 | 79.3 | 75.4 | 68.2 | 57.7 | 63.7 | 71.5 |
| Developing market economies | 20.3 | 15.2 | 14.7 | 15.0 | 16.0 | 27.3 | 20.1 |
| Centrally planned economies | 0.7 | 2.3 | 6.3 | 15.4 | 24.9 | 8.3 | 4.0 |
| Not distributed | 3.1 | 3.2 | 3.6 | 1.3 | 1.4 | 0.6 | 4.4 |
| Total imports (millions of Tanzanian shillings) | 794 | 879.4 | 1,359.5 | 1,939.2 | 3,141.2 | 4,738.8 | 8,882.7 |
| *Exports* (percentage) | | | | | | | |
| Developed market economies | 83.8 | 78.3 | 63.7 | 61.1 | 58.4 | 63.8 | 63.3 |
| Developing market economies | 15.3 | 15.6 | 28.8 | 32.9 | 33.5 | 29.2 | 32.8 |
| Centrally planned economies | 0.1 | 5.6 | 6.4 | 5.3 | 7.1 | 4.8 | 1.9 |
| Not distributed | 0.8 | 0.5 | 1.2 | 0.7 | 1.1 | 2.2 | 2.0 |
| Total exports (millions of Tanzanian shillings) | 1,012 | 1,428.4 | 1,698.1 | 1,704 | 2,411 | 3,846 | 4,215 |

SOURCE  UN Department of Economic and Social Affairs, Statistical Office, *Yearbook of International Trade Statistics* (various years).
Data before 1965 refer to mainland Tanzania (Tanganyika) only.

trade with the other countries of East Africa. The establishment of the East African Community in 1967 was intended to be a primary vehicle for the expansion of trade with Kenya and Uganda. The Community grew out of discussions about the future of the East African Common

Services Organisation, established by the British during the colonial period to manage transportation and communications facilities on a regional basis. In addition to maintaining the common services, coordinating industrial planning, and creating an East African Development Bank, the Community attempted to establish a common market with a common external tariff and differential tariffs for trade between community members. The differential tariffs were designed to expand trade and assure an equitable distribution of trade surpluses.[35]

Despite its efforts to expand trade within the region, the East African Community was never very successful. The data in Table 9.9 suggests that trade with Kenya and Uganda declined as a percentage of Tanzania's total trade after the establishment of the East African Community. Between 1967 and 1975, the significance of Tanzania's East African trade decreased from 10.7 per cent to 6.9 per cent of its total trade. Tanzania is not entirely blameless for this reduction in trade. Although regional imbalances required some measures to prevent Kenyan domination of the East African Community, Tanzania's insistence on transfer taxes on intra-regional trade did little to encourage an expansion of trade within the Community. Tanzania remained officially committed to regional integration, but it was not consistently integrationist in all of its policy actions.

TABLE 9.9    *Tanzanian trade with Kenya and Uganda as percentage of total value of foreign trade*

| Year | Trade with Kenya and Uganda as a percentage of total trade | Value of total foreign trade (millions of Tanzanian shillings) |
| --- | --- | --- |
| 1962 | 13.2 | 2,320 |
| 1967 | 10.7 | 3,386 |
| 1969 | 11.3 | 3,503 |
| 1971 | 10.8 | 4,714 |
| 1973 | 8.4 | 6,060 |
| 1975 | 6.9 | 8,459 |
| 1977 | 0 | 10,635 |
| 1979 | 1.5 | 13,098 |

SOURCE Tanzania, Bureau of Statistics, *The Economic Survey, 1974–1975*, Table 8, page 15 (for computation of figures for 1962, 1967–74); *The Economic Survey, 1975–1976*, Table 8, page 14 (for computation of 1975 figures only); UN Department of Social and Economic Affairs, *Yearbook of International Trade Statistics*, for 1977 and 1979.

By the late 1970s political disputes between Community members brought Tanzania's regional trade to a halt, first from the closing of its border with Kenya in 1977 and later from its border dispute with (and subsequent invasion of) Uganda in 1979. The Community was also never notably successful in its efforts to maintain a common external tariff. Tanzania charged that Kenya had committed a number of 'unilateral transgressions' of the Treaty provisions, and Kenyans maintained that Tanzania had done the same in its special arrangement with the Chinese in the early 1970s. The East African Community was fully dismantled in 1977, and President Nyerere commented at the time, 'the hope of reviving the East African Community is now a very slight one'.[36] Tanzania began to look south and west for an expansion of regional trade, more than doubling its total trade with Zambia, Mozambique, Burundi, Zaire and Rwanda between 1975 and 1979.

A final aspect of Tanzania's efforts to restructure its international trade relations includes its support of UNCTAD efforts to establish a system of preferential tariffs whereby developed countries would eliminate duties on manufactured products from underdeveloped ones, while maintaining them on imports from other developed countries. Tanzania has been active in coordinating 'Third World solidarity' on this issue and in other international negotiating sessions with industrialised countries.[37] Although the tangible benefits of these sessions remain to be seen (particularly in the case of the Lomé Convention), Tanzania has been an active participant in these forums of collective self-reliance.

Tanzanian trade policy reflects its intention to restructure its international economic relations in a number of key areas. Since the Arusha Declaration, there have been efforts to diversify major trading partners (including both export markets and import sources) and to expand South–South linkages with trade missions, regional integration, and coordinating of Third World negotiating positions. Like its efforts at disengagement, however, the effectiveness of Tanzania's institutions and policy measures in these areas of international restructuring have fallen short of expectations in most cases. Although it has succeeded in diversifying export markets and has been active in coordinating 'Southern solidarity', Tanzanian policy measures since Arusha have not contributed to the diversification of import sources or the expansion of its trade with other underdeveloped countries.

## RESTRUCTURING DOMESTIC RELATIONS

In theory, Tanzanian disengagement in trade policy should also induce changes in its domestic economic relations. For example, its reduction of luxury imports in certain areas should alter its domestic patterns of consumption in ways that would not be possible in the absence of disengagement. Its export promotion efforts should also provide outlets for increased or transformed domestic production. Again, these tendencies would eventually have to be reinforced by deliberate state intervention to assure their continuation. Tanzania has adopted a number of specific policy measures toward this end.

One of the most important aspects of domestic restructuring is the establishment of 'appropriate' institutions. Newly established or recently modified agencies and enterprises designed to implement or reinforce a strategy of self-reliance are often described as 'appropriate institutions'. Tanzania's State Trading Corporation most closely approximates an appropriate institution established for the management of foreign trade policy. It was created in 1967 to control and manage most of the import and export trade, as well as internal wholesale trade after the Arusha Declaration. It took over the operations of nationalised export–import firms and was instrumental in a great many of the specific disengagement and international restructuring policy measures described above. In many ways, the STC was established to implement self-reliance in Tanzania's foreign trade sector.

However, the appropriateness and effectiveness of the STC should not be confused. From its inception the STC was plagued by a number of administrative problems that prevented it from assuming state control over either the export–import trade or the domestic wholesale trade. By 1971 the STC handled only about 5 per cent of the national exports. Most of Tanzania's exports continued to be sold through the relevant crop marketing boards. STC management of imports grew to about 30 per cent in 1970, but most (57 per cent) of the imports purchased by the public sector continued to be purchased directly by government agencies and parastatal enterprises, not the STC.[38] In its attempts to take over domestic wholesale trade, serious mismanagement was evident. Major shortages and overstocking were commonplace, and a large overdraft occurred in 1971.[39]

By 1972 there was a growing consensus within the government that a major reorganisation of the STC would be necessary. During 1973 and 1974 the STC's functions were gradually transferred to a number of smaller, more specialised agencies. Six national import companies were established under the supervision of the Board of Internal Trade. These six companies and eighteen Regional Trading Companies assumed the STC's importing role. The STC's export functions were taken on by the various crop authorities (marketing boards) and by the General Agriculture Products Export Corporation (GAPEX), which handles miscellaneous commodities and by-products of the major ones. As described above, other activities of the STC (import licensing, export market and import source diversification) were assumed directly by the Bank of Tanzania and the Ministries of Commerce, Treasury, and Economic Affairs and Development Planning.

This decentralisation of the STC's export and import functions is consistent with Tanzania's emphasis on decentralisation in other spheres of activity (e.g. in its agricultural and investment location policies). Decentralisation has rendered administration of Tanzania's trade sector more manageable. However, the specialised agencies empowered to administer foreign trade appear to function no more effectively in implementing specific policy measures than did the STC before them, as shown by the evidence presented in the tables elsewhere in this chapter.

In addition to the establishment of appropriate institutions and decentralisation of trade institutions, Tanzania has also made efforts to reorient its internal market. This reorientation involves both the diversification of its exports (hence diversification of domestic production) and also the diversification and restructuring of its import priorities (hence alteration of its consumption patterns). Efforts to diversify export products have historically included both expanding the number and variety of products exported in general, and expanding the share of manufactured exports in particular.

The second plan criticised Tanzania's 'over-dependence' on three major export crops (coffee, cotton, and sisal) and proposed a diversification of agricultural production and, hence, of major commodity exports. Production and export of cashews, tobacco, and tea were to be expanded to diversify the range of primary commodities exported. The Ministries of Commerce and Development Planning formulated an export promotion strategy to diversify Tanzanian exports, and a list of crop priorities was established by the Ministry of Agriculture. The government employed price and tax incentives, extension advice, political exhortation, and direct state investment to expand output in the target areas.[40]

Diversification of the composition of Tanzania's major export commodities, however, has not been very widespread (see Table 9.10). During the mid-1960s, cotton, coffee, and sisal exports accounted for about 53 per cent of the total value of Tanzania's exports. By the late 1970s, exports of the same three items accounted for an average of 61 per

TABLE 9.10  Commodity composition of exports of Tanzania

| Year | Cotton | Coffee | Sisal | Cloves | Cashew nuts | Petroleum products | Minerals | Manufactured products | Others | Total (million shillings)* |
|---|---|---|---|---|---|---|---|---|---|---|
| 1964 | 13.1 | 14.7 | 29.0 | 2.9 | 4.4 | — | 11.1 | 6.0 | 16.2 | 1,506.5 |
| 1965 | 18.0 | 12.6 | 21.0 | 3.4 | 6.1 | — | 13.2 | 7.3 | 16.0 | 1,358.6 |
| 1966 | 19.5 | 16.8 | 13.1 | 4.1 | 5.6 | 0.3 | 11.7 | 7.5 | 15.1 | 1,797.1 |
| 1967 | 14.7 | 13.9 | 11.7 | 5.6 | 5.4 | 7.7 | 14.4 | 8.3 | 16.1 | 1,715.8 |
| 1968 | 17.4 | 16.3 | 9.7 | 3.7 | 6.8 | 10.0 | 9.2 | 7.7 | 16.7 | 1,628.1 |
| 1969 | 14.2 | 15.6 | 9.7 | 9.2 | 8.3 | 6.4 | 9.2 | 8.4 | 17.9 | 1,652.1 |
| 1970 | 15.0 | 18.9 | 10.8 | 6.6 | 8.3 | 6.8 | 6.9 | 7.4 | 18.3 | 1,649.5 |
| 1971 | 13.7 | 12.7 | 7.5 | 10.0 | 8.3 | 8.0 | 7.5 | 7.6 | 17.2 | 1,792.2 |
| 1972 | 15.4 | 17.6 | 6.6 | 11.0 | 7.9 | 9.9 | 6.0 | 7.9 | 12.3 | 2,179.5 |
| 1973 | 13.8 | 20.5 | 9.2 | 9.7 | 7.2 | 3.6 | 7.1 | 8.0 | 13.5 | 2,410.8 |
| 1974 | 17.9 | 14.2 | 17.5 | 3.3 | 9.2 | 4.9 | 4.9 | 10.9 | 13.7 | 2,643.2 |
| 1975 | 11.5 | 18.7 | 11.7 | 12.4 | 8.5 | 5.4 | 7.2 | 9.0 | 14.2 | 2,589.3 |
| 1976 | 15.9 | 33.3 | 6.2 | 6.8 | 5.4 | 4.5 | 4.5 | 5.7 | 16.7 | 3,852.9 |
| 1977 | 12.7 | 40.9 | 17.9 | 5.4 | 6.0 | 3.2 | 0.2 | 6.7 | 7.0 | 4,557.1 |
| 1978 | 11.6 | 35.9 | 17.7 | 1.7 | 6.3 | 2.3 | 0.3 | 11.7 | 12.5 | 3,631.9 |
| 1979 | 9.7 | 29.4 | 15.9 | 5.3 | 5.6 | 3.3 | 0.4 | 16.3 | 14.1 | 4,127.8 |
| 1980 | 9.9 | 26.3 | 15.6 | 9.2 | 5.6 | 4.7 | 5.1 | 13.7 | 9.9 | 4,324.2 |

*Slight differences between these total export figures and those reported in other tables are due to differences in conversion factors employed to standardise amounts originally reported in dollars, pounds and shillings. Unless otherwise specified, official exchange rates are used to standardise figures obtained from the IMF, *International Financial Statistics Yearbook.*

SOURCE  UN Department of Economic and Social Affairs, Statistical Office, *Yearbook of International Trade Statistics* (various years).

cent of that total value of exports (72 per cent in 1977). The value of cashew exports, one of the target priorities, increased only slightly in the early 1970s, and decreased after 1975.[41] The export of tobacco and tea (other priority crops) did not increase sufficiently to be included among Tanzania's major exports during the period.

Most of the changes that have occurred (the decrease in export revenue from sisal, and increases in the value of coffee and clove exports) have been more a function of the vagaries of the primary commodity export markets and cyclical production yields than of deliberate trade policy on Tanzania's part. For example, the decline in the share of sisal in Tanzania's total exports is attributable, to a large extent, to the effects during the 1964–80 period of the declining world market for sisal due to competition from synthetic substitutes. Increases in the importance of coffee exports in 1976 and 1977 were due largely to natural disasters in Central and South America during 1975 that forced up the international prices paid for coffee. The rising share of cloves in total exports is attributable to crop failures in other clove-producing nations and the consequent rise in clove prices. In 1969, for example, a crop failure in Madagascar and a low crop in Zanzibar meant that, although the volume of Tanzania's clove exports fell by 40 per cent, their value rose by 150 per cent. Despite rhetoric to the contrary, therefore, the expansion in the number and variety of primary commodity exports from Tanzania has been due primarily to world market influences and has not been the end result of its deliberate strategy of domestic restructuring.

Tanzania has also tried to increase the share of manufactured goods in its total exports. The Export Promotion Bureau was mandated to increase the export potential of Tanzania's manufacturing sector, and particular emphasis was placed on the processing of raw material commodities prior to export. As President Nyerere commented in his 1977 review of progress since the Arusha Declaration, 'we must make a big effort, so that we have more commodities to sell and can also break into the world market for simple manufactures'.[42] To do this, Tanzania has employed parallel trading arrangements, pressed for non-reciprocal preferential trade agreements in international negotiations, and expanded parastatal investments in low-technology manufacturing activities.

Unlike much of its foreign trade programme, some of these policies appear to have paid off in recent years. Between 1964 and 1976, the share of manufactured goods in Tanzania's exports fluctuated within a limited range of 5.7 to 10.9 per cent. But after 1976, the share of manufactured goods in Tanzania's total exports increased to an impressive annual average of 14 per cent (see Table 9.10).

As part of the reorientation of its internal market, Tanzania has also attempted to restructure its import priorities, thus eventually altering domestic consumption patterns. Holding the values of consumer goods imports constant (and reducing luxury goods imports) has been an important aspect of this restructuring effort. As stated in the Second Plan:

> It is intended to hold consumer goods imports, including durables, constant over the Plan period while both the absolute and relative importance of capital goods and intermediate goods used by domestic manufacturing industry will rise sharply.[43]

This kind of restructuring was to be accomplished through the use of tariffs, import licensing, and expansion of the output of domestic industrial enterprises.

The mixed results of efforts to reduce luxury imports has already been discussed in the section on disengagement. Table 9.11 summarises data on the general composition of Tanzanian imports between 1966 and 1980. The data suggests that Tanzania has had some success in restructuring its import priorities. Imports of consumer goods have declined, and the importation of intermediate and capital goods has increased in both absolute and relative terms since 1967. The changes are variable, however, and not very consistent over time. Unfortunately, comparable data are not available for years prior to 1966 to assess whether the observed changes are simply part of a longer-term trend beginning prior to the post-Arusha trade measures. Although the relative share of consumer imports has declined slightly since 1967, their value has not remained constant, as intended by Tanzanian planners. Rather, the value of consumer goods has increased from 578 million Tanzanian shillings in 1967 to 3,226 million in 1980.[44]

Tanzania has attempted to employ its trade policy to restructure domestic relations with the creation of 'appropriate' decentralised institutions, and with a reorientation of its internal market. Although its trade institutions can be described as 'appropriate' they cannot be described as very effective. Similarly, efforts to diversify export products have been largely unsuccessful. Only its efforts to restructure import priorities since the Arusha Declaration have proven marginally effective.

TABLE 9.11   *Composition of total imports of Tanzania* (percentage by type of goods)

| Year | Consumer goods* | Intermediate goods** | Capital goods† | Total (million shillings) |
|------|------|------|------|------|
| 1966 | 47.3 | 33.5 | 19.2 | 1,691 |
| 1967 | 35.6 | 40.7 | 23.7 | 1,625 |
| 1968 | 39.9 | 37.2 | 22.9 | 1,834 |
| 1969 | 37.5 | 40.6 | 21.8 | 1,710 |
| 1970 | 30.0 | 40.4 | 29.6 | 2,274 |
| 1971 | 25.3 | 44.4 | 30.7 | 2,725 |
| 1972 | 28.8 | 45.9 | 25.4 | 2,878 |
| 1973 | 30.4 | 45.8 | 23.8 | 3,479 |
| 1974 | 37.0 | 42.2 | 20.8 | 5,258 |
| 1975 | 24.2 | 48.4 | 27.3 | 5,694 |
| 1976 | 28.0 | 42.9 | 29.1 | 4,739 |
| 1977 | 24.7 | 42.2 | 33.1 | 6,041 |
| 1978 | 23.5 | 38.8 | 37.7 | 8,776 |
| 1979 | 22.3 | 34.4 | 43.2 | 8,883 |
| 1980 | 32.5 | 35.9 | 31.8 | 9,927 |

* Includes a portion of passenger cars.
** Includes building and construction, and spare parts (i.e. capital goods parts).
† Includes transport equipment and basic machinery.
SOURCE Tanzania, Bureau of Statistics, *The Economic Survey, 1975–1976* (Dar es Salaam: Government Printer, 1975) for 1966 through 1975. UN Department of Social and Economic Affairs, *Yearbook of International Trade Statistics*, for 1976 through 1980.

## CONCLUSIONS: THE NATURE AND LIMITATIONS OF SELF-RELIANCE IN TANZANIAN TRADE POLICY

Tanzania has formulated a number of institutions and policy measures designed to translate self-reliance into practice in its foreign trade sector. These include measures to disengage from dominant economic and political relationships, as well as measures to restructure both international and domestic relations. However, the outcomes of these policy measures have more often than not fallen short of expectations.

Tanzanian trade policy has not been a complete failure. Foreign ownership in the commercial sector has been reduced, export market diversification has increased substantially, and Tanzania has expanded cooperation with other underdeveloped countries in North–South negotiations, all since 1967. In addition, important luxury consumer imports have been reduced, import priorities in general have been altered, manufactured goods have assumed a prominent place in Tanzania's export portfolio, and the significance of export receipts has declined. Despite these accomplishments, however, the insufficiency of policy measures or failures of their implementation have been more striking in Tanzanian foreign trade policy. Food imports have not changed significantly since Arusha, and the imports of certain luxury consumer items have remained largely unchanged. Trade with other underdeveloped countries has not increased in any real sense, inter-regional trade within the former East African Community has virtually been eliminated, and the composition of major primary export commodities remains unchanged. The State Trading Corporation, created to manage Tanzania's post-Arusha trade policy, has been dismantled because of its ineffectiveness and mismanagement. Finally, even the import source diversification that has taken place since 1967 is largely independent of Tanzanian policy measures. Table 9.12 provides a summary of these conclusions. This evaluation is not solely based on criteria derived from abstract theoretical discussions of what self-reliance 'should be'. It is based largely on Tanzanian conceptions of self-reliance and statements of objectives in its trade policy. Despite this fact, Tanzanian foreign trade policy has proven ineffective even on its own somewhat limited terms. If the discussion were extended to consider the performance of Tanzanian trade policy based on criteria derived from theoretical works on the meaning of self-reliance, the policy would appear even less effective.

The sources of Tanzania's policy ineffectiveness are many and complex and can only be alluded to briefly in this conclusion. Several factors stand out prominently, however. Failure of efforts to reduce food imports and alter the composition of major exports results primarily from the recent setbacks in Tanzania's agricultural production. In the early 1970s, Tanzanian production of its principal grain crop (maize) fell precipitously. After reaching an export level of more than 53 000 metric tons of maize during 1970–71, Tanzanian production declined to a level where imports of maize exceeded 317 000 metric tons by 1974–75.[45] Poor rainfall during the 1973 rainy season, followed by droughts in 1974 and 1979 undoubtedly contributed to the problems of agricultural production. However, most observers knowledgeable about Tanzania's agrarian policy contend that the government's use of coercion in its villagisation programme,[46] its insufficient implementation of policy at the local level,[47] or some combination of these two factors[48] provide the best explanation for its recent agricultural crises.

**TABLE 9.12** *Tanzanian trade policy: translating self-reliance into practice*

| Policy objectives | Policy measures | Policy outcomes |
|---|---|---|
| *Disengagement* | | |
| 1. Reduce foreign control and ownership of major means of production | Nationalisation of export–import commercial activities | All large, foreign owned commercial enterprises nationalised in 1967. Subsequent nationalisation of importing enterprises in 1980. |
| 2. Reduce reliance on export receipts for national income | State incentives and investments to transform domestic production | Export receipts begin decreasing shortly after independence. Only significant change in rate of decline after Arusha (during 1977) due to commodity price and cyclical production drops. |
| 3. Reduce luxury consumer imports | Tariffs and STC import confinements applied to targeted luxury commodities | Mixed results: passenger car imports reduced, television sets banned, but luxury textile imports unchanged. |
| 4. Attain self-sufficiency in agricultural production (eliminate food imports) | Considerable state investment in agricultural sector, *ujamaa* and villagisation schemes | Food imports have decreased only slightly since Arusha, and increased dramatically after two drought years. |
| *International restructuring* | | |
| 1. Diversify export market destinations | Establish STC agencies abroad, participate in international trade fairs, employ parallel trading in bilateral trade agreements. | Export market diversification has increased significantly since the Arusha Declaration. |
| 2. Diversify import sources | STC to take control of imports, purchasing offices established abroad | Import source diversification has taken place, but is independent of post-Arusha policy measures. |

| | | |
|---|---|---|
| 3. Expand South–South linkages: | | |
| (a) Expand trade with developing countries | Commercial attachés, special trade missions, foreign purchasing offices | Little success: only increases in trade value due to increased cost of petroleum imports. |
| (b) Expand trade with East Africa | East African Community established (with common external tariff and differential tariff policies) | East African trade decreased after 1967, EAC dismantled in 1977. |
| (c) Cooperate with other developing countries in North–South negotiations | Policy coordination within UNCTAD and Lomé Conventions | Tanzania has been an active participant, but tangible benefits have not yet been received. |
| *Domestic restructuring* | | |
| 1. Establish 'appropriate institutions' to implement self-reliance | STC created to manage trade policy | STC dismantled in 1973 and 1974 due to ineffectiveness and mismanagement. |
| 2. Reorient the internal market: | | |
| (a) Diversify export commodities | Establish crop priorities, employ tax incentives, extension advice, political exhortation, and state investment for diversification efforts | Major primary export commodities remain unchanged, though some progress on export of manufactured goods. Most changes in specific primary commodities due to international market fluctuations, not government policy. |
| (b) Restructure import priorities | Use of tariffs, import licensing, and state investments to expand domestic output | Limited success: consumer imports have declined slightly relative to intermediate and capital goods. |

Because of its sharp decline in domestic agricultural output, Tanzania has been unable to transform its trade relations and attain either agricultural self-sufficiency or alter the composition of its traditional major exports.[49]

Tanzania's inability to reduce certain luxury consumer imports can at least be partially explained by the inept administration of the STC. This is the explanation most popular among Tanzanian government officials,[50] and is similar to the explanation of Tanzania's failure to attain agricultural self-sufficiency. Policy formulation and implementation are held essentially to blame. However, another reason why luxury goods continue to be imported is because of the nature and extent of Tanzanian state participation in the commercial sector. Tanzania never severed a great many of its ties with the international system after the Arusha Declaration. Many commodities were affected by the STC's import confinement procedures, but enforcement of restrictions on luxury imports was difficult because of the size of Tanzania's remaining private commercial sector and the growth of the 'bureaucratic bourgeoisie' within the country.

The 1967 nationalisations affected only the eight largest export-import enterprises. In 1975, nearly 60 per cent of the employees engaged in commerce in Tanzania were still employed in the private sector.[51] A great many of these individuals (perhaps as many as 25 per cent) are non-citizens and have engaged in commerce since the colonial period. Hence, they have developed an extensive network of foreign suppliers and have a history of servicing elite-oriented markets. With the emergence of a bureaucratic bourgeoisie which emulates the consumption patterns of its predecessors,[52] there is a continuing market for these suppliers of luxury imports in Tanzania. Thus, the STC was ineffective not only because of the residual size of the private sector, but also because of the residual size of a market for luxury consumer imports.

The effectiveness of Tanzania's trade policy has also been limited by structural constraints within the international system. It is difficult to expand trade between underdeveloped countries when their export and import profiles are nearly identical. Tanzania will have difficulty expanding its trade with other Third World countries as long as its major exports consist of coffee, sisal, and cotton. South–South trade may be non-exploitative, but in effect there is often very little to trade.

Even the expansion of East African trade prior to the breakup of the EAC was constrained by factors outside the control of Tanzania. Because of its distinct status as a protectorate, Tanzania achieved independence with much less infrastructural and industrial development than either Kenya or Uganda. This inhibited trade expansion because Tanzania feared exploitation and dominance by Kenya, while Kenya was concerned about the burden of carrying Tanzania as a free-rider in any regional cooperative scheme. These concerns are inherent in any regional cooperative scheme which attempts the integration of widely disparate national units.[53] Thus, structural constraints have limited Tanzania's unilateral efforts to expand both South–South and intra-regional trade.

Finally, many of the significant changes that have taken place in Tanzania's trade patterns since 1967 have been entirely independent of its self-reliance policy measures. Tanzania's import source diversification and the fluctuations in the relative value of its major export commodities have been influenced more by changes in the international market than by its deliberate government policy measures.

Ultimately, this evaluation of Tanzania's translation of self-reliance from theory into practice in its foreign trade policy illustrates both the limitations of its specific policy measures, as well as some of the inherent limitations on the extent to which a single country can unilaterally restructure its relations with the rest of the global economy. Tanzania has had difficulty in transforming its trade relations because of the coercive and often highly centralised nature of its implementation of policy from above, the limited extent of its break with the international system, and the existence of structural limitations on its ability to disengage from the world economy. Tanzania has not been entirely successful in its pursuit of self-reliance, as its generally ineffective trade policy demonstrates. Nevertheless, its experiences in this critical area of foreign economic policy help to identify the problems and prospects of self-reliance for other countries contemplating an alternative to conventional approaches to international development.

## NOTES

1. The assistance of Bradley M. Marten and Kitty Kameon with the preparation of an earlier version of this chapter is gratefully acknowledged, as is the research assistance of Christine Kiley and Nancy Gilgosch. David J. Sylvan and Robert Keohane also provided helpful comments and advice. Financial assistance for much of the research was provided by the Yale University Concilium on International and Area Studies. This version of the manuscript (completed in December 1983) is an updated and revised version of a paper by the same title. Reprinted from *International Organization*, vol. 34 (Spring 1980) no. 2, Thomas J. Biersteker, 'Self-

Reliance in Tanzanian Trade Relations', by permission of the MIT Press, Cambridge, Massachusetts.

2. By 'other contemporary critics' I am referring to non-dependency writers like Samir Amin, Arghiri Emmanuel, Johan Galtung, Immanuel Wallerstein and to the groups of scholars that have developed around their respective institutes. Although they are concerned with different regions, different time periods, and often employ different analyses of the contemporary international system, these critics all prescribe variants of disengagement or restructuring that are central components of self-reliance.

3. According to many contemporary critics, free trade disguises unequal exchange, and foreign investment distorts economic development and domestic class structure. Since self-reliance reduces and alters traditional trade and investment relationships, it identifies specific policies designed to eliminate the basis of underdevelopment.

4. For a more extended discussion see T. J. Biersteker, 'Regulation or Self-Reliance? Alternative Strategies for Dealing with Transnational Corporations in Nigeria and Tanzania', paper given at the 1977 Annual Meeting of the American Political Science Association, Washington DC, September 1977.

5. A country's situation of dependence is defined by the extent to which its significant economic, social, and political developments are (and have historically been) conditioned by (or contingent upon) developments in the industrial countries. Since most proponents of self-reliance contend that excessive dependence is the cause of the most significant structural distortions of underdeveloped countries, the reduction of dependence they prescribe in a strategy of self-reliance will necessarily promote development. Development is generally described as 'self-generating' or 'autocentric'. It is defined as the process whereby a highly integrated economy and society is created which is capable of substantially providing for the basic needs of the masses of its population. The dual objectives of avoiding dependence and promoting development are thus integrally related, and self-reliance becomes a logical prescription of the dependency literature from which it is at least partially derived.

6. A comprehensive strategy of national self-reliance need not necessarily follow a strict pattern of disengagement followed by restructuring. Restructuring can also precede disengagement or simultaneously accompany it. The separation between the phases is made in part for analytical purposes and to emphasise the relationship between these essential components of self-reliance. Disengagement usually precedes international and domestic restructuring and is therefore presented first in the text.

7. *Cooperation Against Poverty*, paper submitted by the United Republic of Tanzania at the Conference of Non-aligned States, Lusaka, 1970. Reprinted in *Mbioni*, vol. 9 (1971) p. 6.

8. Samir Amin, 'The Theoretical Model of Capital Accumulation and of the Economic and Social Development of the World Today', mimeo. This paper is a summary of his *L'accumulation et L'échelle mondiale* (Paris: IFAN-ANTHROPOS, 1970).

9. Ross Terrill, 'China and the World: Self-Reliance or Interdependence?' *Foreign Affairs*, vol. 55 (January 1977) no. 2, p. 297.

10. Hans Heymann, Jr, 'Self-Reliance Revisited: China's Technology Dilemma', *Stanford Journal of International Studies* (Spring 1975) p. 34.

11. 'The Arusha Declaration', reprinted in Julius K. Nyerere, *Ujamaa – Essays on Socialism* (Nairobi: Oxford University Press, 1968) p. 34.

12. Johan Galtung, 'Self-Reliance: Concepts, Practice, and Rationale', unpublished manuscript (Geneva: Institut d'études du développement, 1976) p. 8.

13. For example, the First Five-Year Plan (1964–69) emphasised the use of import barriers (disengagement), control of primary product exports, export market diversification, and regional integration (aspects of international restructuring). See Tanganyika, *First Five-Year Plan for Economic and Social Development, 1964–1969* (Dar es Salaam: 1964) vol. 1.

14. Other related factors were also important in Tanzania's transition to national self-reliance. The international reaction to its rejection of West German aid over invocation of the 'Hallstein doctrine' and its break in diplomatic relations with Great Britain over relations with Rhodesia also contributed to Tanzania's decision to alter relations with its traditional trading partners.

15. 'The Arusha Declaration', p. 16.

16. The list of nationalised export–import activities included Smith Mackenzie and Co. Ltd, Dalgety (EA) Ltd, International Trading and Credit Company of Tanganyika, Cooperative Supply Association of Tanganyika Ltd, A. Baumann and Co. (Tanganyika) Ltd, Twentsche Overseas Trading Co. Ltd, African Mercantile Co. (Overseas) Ltd, and Wigglesworth & Co. (Africa) Ltd.

17. Tanzania, *Second Five-Year Plan for Economic and Social Development (1969–1974)*, vol. 1 (Dar es Salaam: 1969) p. 133.

18. Julius K. Nyerere, speech introducing the Second Five-Year Plan, p. xviii.

19. The average growth of GDP (in current prices) exceeded the growth of export receipts (also in current prices) during the 1970–80 period. GDP increased at an average annual rate of 16.1 per cent, while the value of export receipts increased at an average annual rate of 10.4 per cent. In real terms, of course, Tanzania did not exhibit such a significant growth during the period. Real GDP (in constant, 1975 prices) grew in annual terms at a much more modest 4.9 per cent during the same period. See Table 9.2 for further details.

20. Nyerere, speech, p. xix.

21. Tanzania, *The Economic Survey and Annual Plan 1970–71* (Dar es Salaam: Government Printer, 1970) p. 57.

22. John Loxley, 'Financial Planning and Control in Tanzania', Uchumi Editorial Board (eds), *Towards Socialist Planning* (Dar es Salaam: Tanzania Publishing House, 1972) p. 58.

23. Nyerere, speech, p. xix.

24. See especially the discussions of the sources of these setbacks in Joel Samoff and Rachel Samoff, 'The Local Politics of Underdevelopment', *Politics and Society*, 1976, and in Michael F. Lofchie, 'Agrarian Socialism in the Third World', *Comparative Politics*, April 1976.

25. Pius Msekwa, 'Self-Reliance as a Strategy for Development: The Meaning of Self-Reliance', Economic Research Bureau, Paper 76.6 (University of Dar es Salaam, September 1976) p. 21. A continued commitment to agricultural self-sufficiency by 1980 was also emphasised by several high-ranking Tanzanian officials in interviews with the author during June and July of 1977.
26. *Second Five-Year Plan*, p. 141.
27. Tanzania, *The Annual Plan for 1972/73* (Dar es Salaam: Government Printer, 1972) p. 31.
28. Julius K. Nyerere, 'Tanzania Ten Years After Independence', *The African Review*, vol. 1 (June 1972) p. 40
29. Tanzania, *Report by the Government of Tanzania for the East African Consultative Group Meeting on Tanzania* (held in Paris, 23 and 24 May 1977).
30. *Second Five-Year Plan*, p. 136.
31. Ibid., p. 142.
32. Ibid.
33. Ibid., p. 133.
34. Ibid., p. 141.
35. Justinian Rweyemamu, *Underdevelopment and Industrialization in Tanzania* (Nairobi: Oxford University Press, 1973) pp. 45–6.
36. Julius K. Nyerere, *The Arusha Declaration Ten Years After* (Dar es Salaam: Government Printer, 1977) p. 25.
37. Ibid., p. 27.
38. Tanzania, *The Economic Survey 1970–71* pp. 93–6, *n*. 18. See also Ann Seidman, *Comparative Development Strategies in East Africa* (Nairobi: 1972) p. 219.
39. Tanzania, *Annual Plan 1971–72* (Dar es Salaam: Government Printer, 1971) p. 41.
40. *Second Five-Year Plan*, pp. 42–50.
41. The actual production of cashew nuts also increased only slightly during this period. With 1970 as a base year equal to 100 units, the 1966–67 production was 73.7. This compares with a 1975–76 figure of 74.6. Bank of Tanzania, *Economic Bulletin*, vol. IX (December 1976) no. 3.
42. Nyerere, *The Arusha Declaration Ten Years After*, p. 50.
43. *Second Five-Year Plan*, p. 141.
44. This is also an increase in real terms, from about 948 million shillings in 1967 to about 1774 million shillings in 1980.
45. Justin Maeda, 'Popular Participation, Control and Development: A Study of the Nature and Role of Popular Participation in Tanzania's Rural Development', PhD thesis (Department of Political Science, Yale University, 1976).
46. See especially Michael F. Lofchie, 'Agrarian Crisis and Economic Liberalisation in Tanzania', *Journal of Modern African Studies*, vol. 16 (1978) no. 3, pp. 460–75; and David J. Sylvan, 'The Illusion of Autonomy: State "Socialism" and Economic Dependence', PhD thesis (Department of Political Science, Yale University, 1979) pp. 128–33.
47. See especially Maeda, 'Popular Participation'.
48. See especially Andrew Coulson, 'Agricultural Policies in Mainland

Tanzania', *Review of African Political Economy*, vol. 10 (September–December 1977) p. 96.

49. The distinction between foreign and domestic policy is obviously blurred in this case, since the extent of agricultural self-sufficiency and the diversification of export commodities are determined by changes in domestic agricultural output.

50. Research interviews conducted by the author during 1977.

51. Tanzania, Bureau of Statistics, *Analysis of Accounts of Parastatals, 1966–1975* (Dar es Salaam: Government Printer, January 1977) p. 3.

52. Issa G. Shivji, *Class Struggles in Tanzania* (Dar es Salaam: Tanzania Publishing House, 1975) pp. 79–99.

53. This has been shown in numerous empirical studies of regional integration efforts. See especially, Lynn K. Mytelka, 'Regulating Direct Foreign Investment and Technology Transfer in the Andean Group', *Journal of Peace Research*, vol. XIV (1977) no. 2, pp. 155–84.

# 10 Ghana's Economic Decline and Development Strategies

## DONALD ROTHCHILD and E. GYIMAH-BOADI

We need time to reduce our need of the IMF, by seeking alternative ways of production. Small is good, at least for us.
(Flt-Lt Jerry John Rawlings, *Observer*, 13 Feb. 1983, p. 11)

Ghana's political and economic decline is traceable in part at least to the partial delinkage of the 1980s. Contrary to current thought on this subject, however, in this instance the process was not a Third World initiated strategy of 'transformation' (i.e. a reduction of Third World states' connections with Western international capitalism)[1] but rather a steady withdrawal of Western interest in and concern over what the West has come to view as a strategically and economically peripheral country. The recession in the developed countries in the 1980s has led to a decrease in production, entailing less demand for commodities produced by Third World exporters. Tenuous business and financial linkages with Western capitalism have grown weaker as Western-based multinational companies and their governments have pulled back from entangling investments, aid and debt relief programmes in the less stable and strategically unimportant parts of the Third World. Multilateral lending agencies, the logical stopgap, appear somewhat hesitant and aloof – all too parsimonious with their funds and at times insensitive in the conditions they set for the loans they offer. In the face of this partial delinkage by the Western core, states at the periphery, such as Ghana, feel dependent yet neglected, vulnerable while lacking choice, and all this at a time when the world economy seems to be headed into a major crisis of uncertain proportions.

On the domestic level, and to some extent reflecting the contemporary international economic disarray and retrenchment, Ghana is not atypical in encountering a serious problem of governability. Despite the Ghanaian state's utilisation of a high proportion of the country's revenues, it lacks the ability to implement critical public policies.[2] Clearly, task achievement is limited by a combination of relatively high demands and relatively low state capabilities, especially under conditions of greater and greater economic scarcity. Task achievement is further limited by state politics which allocate scarce resources inefficiently, through inadequate attention to smallholder agriculture, an over-centralised state bureaucracy, reliance upon over-staffed state enterprises and parastatal organisations, and so forth. The upshot is a multifaceted problem of governance which is rooted in economic scarcity, and includes the following political elements: social incoherence, over-developed state structures, insufficient state legitimacy, and inadequate state power.

This chapter on Ghanaian development strategies in a context of grave economic constraints focuses on the role of the state in expanding production, managing demands, building political, economic and social infrastructures, and allocating and distributing resources. With the international community disengaging and the indigenous private industrial and commercial sectors too underdeveloped to solve the problems of expanding production and equitable distribution on their own, the tasks of economic leadership fall by default to the state and its institutions.

Yet an examination of the middle African state reveals limitations in its capacity for effective action as well. In contrast to its counterpart in the developed countries, the state in Africa appears hegemonic (a hierarchical military- or civilian-led no-party or one-party system); in actuality, however, it is fragile and lacking in the capacity to implement policies throughout its territory. The typical 'soft state' such as that in Ghana, displays not only a lack of consensus on society's organising principles but an over-centralised state bureaucracy which remains somewhat isolated from its hinterland and unable to enforce compliance from local notables in the rural areas. Hence, from political necessity, state elites enter into exchange relationships with local intermediaries, 'purchasing' their support and compliance through a variety of political concessions involving the sharing of political power, a balanced recruitment of elites, and proportional allocative practices.[3] The state, then, is part of the problem of development: it is soft, isolated, over-staffed and costly, unable to gain agreement on basic principles or to project its policies effectively to the periphery.

Given this broad array of domestic and international constraints, what can a soft state do to increase its options? The forces at work here may be too great for any particular regime caught in the situation in which contemporary Ghana finds itself, yet some insights of a problem-solving nature may be provided by a study of Jerry John Rawlings' strong but very painful policy initiatives. Although the initial years of the Rawlings regime have been characterised by falling standards of living and declining modern sector productivity, some of the Rawlings initiatives, may, if allowed sufficient time for application, provide a basis for increased governability and development under conditions of scarcity. By experimenting with a variety of policies and programmes aimed at enhancing state effectiveness (in part through a reduction in state tasks), the Rawlings government may be able to increase choices under turbulent circumstances.

In order to appreciate the situation which this or any successive regime faces in Ghana, it is necessary to look at the international and domestic environments in which the contemporary Ghanaian state finds itself enmeshed. Such an examination reveals the scope for policy initiative as well as the constraints on development and governability that have persisted since independence. With this environmental setting in mind, the specific initiatives of the Rawlings regime are addressed. Then, after discussing the problems the Ghanaian state is likely to encounter as it attempts to implement Rawlings-type strategies, the conclusion discusses the implications of this approach for a possible 'hardening' of the state. Clearly policy-making under conditions of turbulence is never an easy or smooth process, but it is to be hoped that something is learnt from each attempt to alter reality which proves generalisable.

## THE HARSH ECONOMIC ENVIRONMENT

'The harsh economic conditions which face us today', declares Dr Kwesi Botchwey, the Provisional National Defence Council (PNDC) Secretary for Finance and Economic Planning, 'should leave us in no doubt whatsoever that as a nation, we have reached a make or break point where we must either apply the most effective and necessarily drastic cure or suffer unavoidable disaster. There simply is no middle ground.'[4] The difficult economic conditions that Botchwey refers to arise mainly from structural and policy-based factors and cannot appropriately be attributed to a single regime or development strategy. To lay the entire responsibility for a declining gross domestic product (the real GDP in

1981 has fallen by as much as 15 per cent compared to 1974)[5] upon the operation of the international economic system is fashionable and convenient, for it shifts all blame for the current economic difficulties away from domestic decision elites on to an externalised and impersonal invisible hand. Since this unrealistically denies the local actor's, albeit limited, political autonomy, this chapter views the post-independence economic decline as both structurally and policy based, thereby making a turnaround in the economic situation a matter for Ghanaian as well as international initiative. This element of local responsibility is recognised by Botchwey, who asserts most emphatically that Ghana cannot afford a stance of passivity in the face of what he perceives as an inequitably structured international environment. 'What is required', he has asserted, 'is a complete overhaul of policy in the areas of incomes, and pricing, including the pricing of foreign exchange, to provide a permanent disincentive for these abuses.'[6] Clearly, he seeks ways to moderate the worst effects of what the Rawlings regime refers to as 'neo-colonialism,' and to increase productivity, improve efficiency, and achieve a more equitable distribution of public goods.

Broadly speaking, Ghana, like most countries the world over, is caught in a situation where efforts to achieve autonomous development are complicated by a global economy beyond its control. This is not to argue that international capitalism has an 'interest' in Ghana's impoverishment, for world capitalism is itself obviously weakened by the deterioration of an African state once relatively well-off (at least by the standards of the 1950s).[7] But, a balanced and comprehensive assessment of Ghana's economic decline requires attention to the external limitations that the international economy places on state action before any discussion of the issues of policy failure and mismanagement.

Certainly the neo-Marxists make a useful contribution in emphasising the role of the exogenous variable in Africa's underdevelopment. Africa's structural links to a powerful Europe, which find concrete expression in enduring trade, investment and financial ties, represent the inheritence of colonialism carried over into present times. As Dos Santos asserts, economies such as Ghana's become 'conditioned' by the economic expansion and contraction that occur abroad.[8] A recession in the West, as seen in the early 1980s, is reflected in a declining demand for Ghanaian exports, a situation aggravated by a heavy debt-servicing burden and, in certain periods at least, adverse commodity terms of trade (i.e. the ratio of export to import prices).[9] Oil imports alone account for $1 000 million, or 30 per cent of the country's foreign exchange earnings.[10] Ghana finds itself severely constrained by this combination of factors; the upshot is a reduction in total foreign exchange at a time of steep energy prices and rising costs for chemicals, machinery and other manufactured items.

Many Ghanaians perceive external factors as largely responsible for the country's current economic decline. 'Ghana's engagement in the international capitalist system', Rawlings concludes, 'has contributed in no small measure toward the country's present predicament.'[11] He also points to the wide fluctuations in commodity export prices as well as the decrease in these prices in relation to imported items. Other explanations include the country's small size, its heavy dependence on imports, its continuing reliance upon the agricultural sector, the relative underdevelopment, despite improvements since independence, in the manufacturing sector,[12] and the predominance of a single crop (cocoa) in employment, production, and export earnings.

In conditions of economic scarcity and political instability, it can be anticipated that working out mutually acceptable formulas between state and multinational interests will not be an easy matter. In this, the Ghanaian situation is typical of many. The state, from Nkrumah's time on, has seemed anxious to strike a bargain, even though constrained by public misgivings over the role of foreign multinationals. And, as elsewhere, the multinationals seem determined upon advantageous terms, even if these bring on the very conditions of instability which ultimately threaten the viability of their investment. Many Ghanaians continue to perceive their country, in its relations with multinational companies, as exposed to powerful external forces beyond its control. Ghanaians, have for instance, long been resentful of the relatively low price paid by the Volta Aluminium Company (VALCO) for electricity, the insufficient electricity produced for the country's industrial growth, the company's low tax bills, its failure to process Ghananian bauxite, and Ghana's loss of autonomy under the master agreement.[13] Moreover, they have been deeply disappointed over the agreements signed in the 1970s with Agri-Petco Ghana Inc., Texas Pacific, Phillips and Agip to produce and process petroleum. Under the initial Agri-Petco agreement, only 12 per cent of output need be retained to meet Ghana's domestic requirements, the rest being exported to refineries abroad. As domestic shortages of petroleum products increased, this situation naturally led to heavy criticism, and PNDC officials are known to have been exploring the feasibility of setting up a state oil firm to handle the various stages of the oil business or of shifting from concessions to production-sharing arrangements or service contracts.[14]

If bargaining continues between Ghana and both the oil companies and VALCO, albeit under difficult and unequal circumstances, other Western interests have acted to reduce their involvement in Ghana's economic development. In 1981, for example, at the very time that the administration of Dr Hilla Limann was attempting to attract foreign investors by sponsoring a new investments code bill, the Firestone Company announced its decision to sell its interests in Firestone Ghana Ltd and Ghana Rubber Estates Ltd. Though Ghanaian youth organisations had long criticised the master agreement between the Ghana government and Firestone for including 'fantastic concessions' (reportedly allowing the company broad exemptions from customs duties and from income, sales, and property taxes for a 10-year period)[15] the company contended that in recent years it had not been able to obtain sufficient foreign exchange allocations to import the raw materials required for full production.[16] In this case, the multinational refused to negotiate and, instead, chose the route of corporate delinkage.

Foreign-owned, commercial banks have also disappointed Ghanaians with their highly cautious practices in processing loan requests. The gravity of the situation became public knowledge when international financial institutions, anxious over the fact that Ghana was in arrears in its repayment of short-term loans amounting to ₵1190 million in July 1979, began to refuse the country further credit.[17] In something of a contrast to its behaviour in other, more 'penetrated' economies such as the Ivory Coast, Kenya, and the Cameroon, the international financial community gave clear signs of emphasising prudence, in practice delinking itself from what it perceived as an increasingly unproductive and politically unstable Ghana. Aggregate data on the total net inflow of private and public resources from 1971 to 1980 show Ghana (at $1517 million) well behind the others: Ivory Coast ($3777 million), Kenya ($3375 million), and Cameroon ($2684 million).[18] Nevertheless, as discussed further in the next section, the Rawlings regime, through its harsh programme of reducing budgetary deficits and introducing a complicated multiple exchange rate for the over-valued cedi, has managed to reassure the international lending community, enabling the government to extract new credits and loans from private commercial banks and international lending agencies. In early 1983, the Standard Chartered Bank announced a $100 million loan to the Bank of Ghana. This was followed in the summer by IMF approval of two loans totalling $382 million and an International Development Association loan of $40 million.[19] Although Ghana had no choice but to concede limits on credit, wage increases, foreign borrowing and external payments arrears to secure these multilateral agency loans, the effect was a much-needed boost for the Rawlings regime at a time of general international delinkage from the problems of troubled LDC economies.

If the global international economy has acted to condition and limit domestic economic choice in Ghana, the decline in agricultural and industrial productivity, caused in part by inefficient public policies and bureaucratic mismanagement, has contributed at least as much to the country's economic decline. 'Sluggish growth in Ghana', economist J. Ofori-Atta concludes, 'is due more to policy failures than to any inherent weakness of the economy.'[20] In April 1979 the managing director of Ghana Industrial Holding Corporation (GIHOC) reported that only eight of the 16 divisions of this parastatal body had proved consistently profitable. Although GIHOC's difficulties reflected conditions beyond its control (e.g. obsolete and inefficient plants), the overall effect was to depress any sense of national achievement in the industrial sector. Certainly, growth was negative for many critically important commodities; as shown in Table 10.1, Ghana's major export items fell heavily in the 1975 to 1981 period, some (diamonds, manganese, bauxite) by 50 per cent or more. And despite the incentive of higher export prices for certain items (Table 10.2), Ghanaian producers failed to seize their opportunity by increasing their output. Obviously a large part of the country's economic malaise was attributable to declining productivity.

This downward trend continues to the present. Cocoa output, which normally provided some 60 per cent of export earnings, plummeted from a high of 557 000 long tons in the 1964–65 crop year to 277 000 in 1977–78 and to an estimated 100 000 tons in 1983–84.[21] Many different factors are responsible for this sharp decline in production – the cutting out of cocoa trees in favour of food crops, ageing cocoa trees, bush fires, poor roads and lack of transport, low prices and lack of prompt payment, inadequate labour, ineffective control of pests and diseases, unavailability of inputs, inadequate storage facilities, smuggling, and a decline in the quality of extension services – making no simple solution possible for an incoming regime like Rawlings'. As can be seen from the 1983 budget statement, the cocoa sector, which once contributed 40 per cent of government revenue, made a zero contribution in 1980 and actually incurred a net deficit in the budget in 1981 and 1982.[22] Gold, the dominant factor in the Ghanaian mining industry, has fallen steadily in terms of aggregate output, despite the relatively high price that this metal still fetches in international markets in the 1980s. While 724 100 fine ounces of gold were mined in 1972, production dropped to 402 033

TABLE 10.1 *Major Ghanaian export items, 1975–81 (quantities)*

|  | 1975 | 1976 | 1977 | 1978 | 1979 | 1980 | 1981 |
|---|---|---|---|---|---|---|---|
| Cocoa beans (tonnes '000) | 322 | 328 | 258 | 213 | 204 | 211 | 190 |
| Cocoa products (tonnes '000) | 19 | 22 | 21 | 12 | 25.0 | 23.2 | 14.2 |
| Gold (grams) | 15,973 | 16,416 | 15,208 | 9,747 | 11,818 | 10,820 | 10,764 |
| Timber (cubic metres '000) | 615 | 499 | 539 | 629 |  |  |  |
| Diamonds (carats '000) | 2,372 | 2,308 | 2,079 | 1,476 | 1,007 | 897 | 944 |
| Manganese (tonnes '000) | 373 | 360 | 321 | 287 | n.a. | n.a. | 143 |
| Bauxite (tonnes '000) | 320 | 219 | 250 | 293 | 203 | 223 | 150 |

n.a. Not available.
SOURCE Kodwo Ewusi, *The Ghana Economy in 1981–82: Recent Trends and Prospects for the Future* (Legon: Institute of Statistical, Social and Economic Research, 1982) p. 34.

TABLE 10.2    *Major Ghanaian export items, 1975–81* (Values in million cedis)

|              | 1975  | 1976  | 1977  | 1978  | 1979    | 1980    | 1981    |
|--------------|-------|-------|-------|-------|---------|---------|---------|
| Cocoa beans    | 551.4 | 515.5 | 679.7 | 988.0 | 1,846.3 | 1,949.3 | 1,103.1 |
| Cocoa products | 82.4  | 71.9  | 103.1 | 22.1  | 183.2   | 230.7   | 92.6    |
| Gold           | 83.8  | 70.9  | 72.4  | 91.0  | 208.4   | 522.9   | 435.4   |
| Timber         | 83.7  | 80.0  | 92.2  | 96.9  | 116.6   | 92.5    | 99.0    |
| Diamonds       | 12.7  | 12.7  | 15.5  | 30.0  | 30.1    | 27.6    | 22.6    |
| Manganese      | 17.1  | 19.7  | 18.8  | 24.3  | 29.2    | 26.3    | 21.9    |
| Bauxite        | 4.3   | 3.0   | 3.9   | 7.2   | 7.9     | 8.6     | 7.1     |

SOURCE Ewusi, *The Ghana Economy in 1981–82*, p. 33.

fine ounces in 1978; the Bank of Ghana estimates that 1983 output will have fallen even further, to approximately 260 000 fine ounces.[23]

Commodity production declines are by no means limited to items for export. An already severe food crop crisis has worsened since the latest Rawlings takeover, resulting in sharply rising food prices and widespread hunger. To a considerable extent, these food deficits can be attributed to causes beyond the government's control (drought, bush fires, and the return of one million Ghanaian emigrants from Nigeria), but again a number of policy aspects enter into this equation: for example, low government priority for smallholder farming, neglect of roads and transport, lack of the most basic farm inputs, the inadequacy of agricultural research and disease control, and so forth. The significance, for the time being at least, of this fall-off in food production would be difficult to over-state and is reflected in part in the 1983 budget; commenting on its adverse impact on current public expenditures, Botchwey noted in his 1983 budget statement that the government expected to spend no less than $65 million (or almost the equivalent of the allocations for health and education combined) on the importation of maize, rice, wheat, kako, and other food items.[24] The fall in agricultural and industrial production is an aspect of the larger process of economic decline that has gripped Ghana during the painful period from 1975 onward.

Clearly, Ghana's export-oriented economy is vulnerable not only to constraints beyond its control (e.g. the conditioning effect of the global economy and natural adversites), but also to declines in aggregate production attributable in part at least to policy failure and bureaucratic mismanagement. Even when prices for such basic Ghanaian exports as cocoa and gold are relatively high, the Ghanaian economy has proved slow to seize temporary advantage, largely because of falling production. As the former Minister of Finance and Economic Planning, Dr Amon Nikoi, commented in 1980:

> The structure of the economy remains the same, cocoa still accounts for 60 per cent of foreign revenue, timber has not been doing so well, and gold, which could have earned us a bit more because of the current high prices, has not done so because of an insufficient volume of production. It is safe to say there have been no significant gains in production and employment in the agricultural and export sectors.[25]

Policy, in the sense of guidelines for public action, also bears a responsibility for Ghana's diminished aggregate productivity (defined here as the efficient use of human, material and financial resources employed to produce commodities, goods and services). A heavy responsibility for the economic crisis of the 1970s in Ghana must be attributed to the policies pursued by the regime of General I. K. Acheampong (1972–78). Although drought troubled the country during the second half of the decade, the National Redemption Council/ Supreme Military Council team, under Acheampong's leadership, nonetheless remains responsible for the considerable fiscal and administrative mismanagement that occurred.[26] The government's desire for supplies of low-priced food for the urban dweller and for low-cost export crops to create a foreign exchange surplus led to a worsening of the rural–urban terms of trade. And even though state structures (the bureaucracy, parastatals and marketing boards) remained heavy consumers of scarce fiscal resources, they proved relatively ineffective agencies for delivering the agricultural inputs and infrastructural support needed by the farmers. The results were widespread disaffection and disincentives in the rural area; farmers, particularly those in the cocoa sector, who contributed the largest share of the country's export earnings,[27] turned increasingly away from export crops such as cocoa, which seemed adversely affected by artificially low producer prices. This had grave short- as well as long-term consequences for aggregate output and the country's balance of payments.

The Acheampong fiscal policies led to an expansion of public demand which was not met by increasing output in the domestic economy. The consequence was rapidly escalating inflation rates, a gross imbalance in the external accounts, a steep rise in net credit to the government from the banking system to finance the budget deficits (₵781 million in 1977), sharp increases in unplanned government expenditures, a jump in the money supply from an average of ₵281 million in 1971 to ₵1761 million in 1977, and worsening budget deficits and net foreign exchange reserves.[28] Government expenditures increased more rapidly than revenues, causing public officials to print more and more money to cover budget deficits. By 1978 the economic situation had deteriorated seriously. Inflation was rampant, shortages were widespread, and unemployment was extensive. Compounding this mismanagement, a number of high officials in the Acheampong regime were engaged in a variety of corrupt practices – misusing import licences, awarding contracts to favourites, and taking dubious loans.

In July 1978, as economic mishandling and corruption contributed to a deepening sense of public despair, the Supreme Military Council, taking the government's poor showing in the Union Government referendum as its cue, relieved Acheampong of his position. Lt-Gen. F. W. K. Akuffo, who assumed the duties of Head of State and Chairman of the reconstituted SMC, quickly proclaimed a programme of economic stabilisation. Akuffo sought to restrain Ghana's runaway inflation with a package of policies which included controls on the monetary supply, a reduction in recurrent and development budget expenditures, a 59 per cent devaluation of the currency, an increase in the rates of import duties, a rise for taxation purposes in the minimum chargeable incomes of self-employed persons and companies, an increase in interest rates to encourage savings, a suspension in the use of special unnumbered licences for commercial importation (to limit their abuse), and stringent regulations on overseas travel. Although the IMF supported the Akuffo stabilisation programme and authorised Ghanaian purchases up to the equivalent of 53 million SDRs over a twelve-month period, the general public saw few economic benefits emerging from these harsh economic policies. The rate of inflation remained high and consumer goods, particularly local foodstuffs, continued to be as scarce as ever. As the situation deteriorated and strikes became commonplace, Akuffo in his desperation declared a state of emergency.

On 4 June, 1979, with an IMF team on the scene to monitor the progress of the stabilisation package, Rawlings and his colleagues intervened and toppled the Akuffo regime. Akuffo's austerity plan gave way to an economic populism which displayed elements of idealism and some disdain for long-term consequences. The Armed Forces Revolutionary Council (AFRC) and Rawlings, its chairman, were deeply offended by the corrupt practices of senior military officers and others in the society, and moved swiftly to deal with the worse examples of 'kalabule' (corrupt) behaviour. High-ranking military officers were convicted of corrupt acts and either jailed or executed, hoarders had their houses blown up, market traders charged with exceeding price guidelines were publicly flogged, Accra's Makola Number 1 Market was destroyed on the grounds of being a centre for 'kalabuleism', foreign firms charged with making illegal deals were seized, and the Cocoa Marketing Board and Ministry of Cocoa Affairs were dissolved and a number of their top officials dismissed for alleged gross mismanagement. In addition to this 'housekeeping' exercise, the AFRC increased producer prices for certain commodities and put price controls into effect for a variety of goods. Although the upward adjustment of producer prices, especially for cocoa, can be said to have been overdue, the imposition of price controls had a mixed reception. The enforcement of price controls ensured rapid distribution to hard-pressed consumers, but at the cost of a rapid depletion of existing stocks.[29]

By the time that Dr Hilla Limann was elected to the presidency in 1979, it had become all too apparent that the Ghanaian economy had been reduced to the severest straits of post-independence times. Not only did the incoming Limann administration speak of the country's economy as 'in shambles' and 'bankrupt,'[30] but various other indicators pointed to a continuation of hard times: consumer items were in short supply; inflation was down slightly, but still at an estimated 116 per cent per year; production and imports were at low levels; foreign reserves were negligible; and crude oil prices were rising dramatically. Although there were few promising options to choose from, Limann pragmatically attempted to revive the flagging economy despite powerful domestic and international constraints on decisive action. In the agricultural sector, the Limann regime sought to encourage farmers through a combination of producer price incentives and subsidised inputs and gave assurances to various segments of society that state agricultural enterprises would not be sold to private interests. In an attempt to stimulate the industrial sector, Limann, critical of the former import substitution strategy because it relied upon imported inputs and therefore encouraged an artificial and inefficient industrial base, urged an approach which linked existing and new industries more closely with Ghanaian-produced inputs. In addition, a high priority was placed upon expansion or development of industries tied to Ghana's natural resources, such as the establishment of a pulp and paper industry, the exploitation of the Kibi bauxite deposits, and the increased production and processing of rubber, timber, oil palm and gold. Limann's realism and caution, in part a reflection of his political style and of the constraints of the past, proved inadequate to the task, however. After a brief time in office, this constitutional but immobile regime was toppled by a much more impatient Rawlings.

In sum, Ghana's economic decline cannot be explained by a single factor, but is attributable to a combination of international constraints, policy failures and bureaucratic mismanagement. All past regimes, from Nkrumah to Limann, were alike in finding their economic development conditioned and limited by forces beyond their control. But, despite different policy priorities, they have also found themselves limited in their ability to formulate and apply policies sufficiently effective to arrest the decline and start the process of renewal. Nkrumah's import substitution, Akuffo's austerity, Acheampong's self-reliance, or Rawlings' housekeeping exercise – the resulting programmes seemed partial and inadequate to the challenge. Three broad lines of policy failures seem evident in varying degrees across regimes: inappropriate commodity pricing policies (resulting in adverse, and self-defeating, rural–urban terms of trade), inadequate infrastructural support, and inefficient use of public sector resources. In part, the problem is attributable to the persistence of over-extended state structures that have extracted and consumed extensive public resources while lacking the ability to achieve their own policy objectives. In the face of an ever-deepening scarcity, could any future regime restore governability, accomplishing more while doing less? Clearly, new assumptions and government systems must be explored. These may very well include formulas for decentralisation and a renewed emphasis on rural/agricultural development, both of which might increase the efficiency and reach of the state in Africa.

The second Rawlings regime has in principle adopted a policy approach emphasising a reduced role for the state. Rawlings' commitment to rural development and decentralisation amounts to a willingness to reduce the tasks to be assumed by state agencies. As Rawlings himself summed up his sentiments (and to repeat the quote which begins this chapter): 'small is good, at least for us.' The following section examines this alternative policy approach, with its emphasis on rejuvenating agriculture and on decentralising important functions and powers. There is also an assessment of the utility of such a policy approach in strengthening the Ghanaian state under current conditions of great uncertainty.

RAWLINGS' POLITICAL AND ECONOMIC INITIATIVES: A NEW BALANCE BETWEEN CAPACITY AND LOADS

The broad outlines of the PNDC's policies for economic recovery were set out in the government's 1982 programme for reconstruction and development. This programme included the following objectives:

(a) to eliminate, through planned institutional changes, local and foreign exploitation which manifests itself in rampant malpractice in internal and external trade and in tax evasion and avoidance;
(b) to increase production to modest but realistic targets in a selected number of agricultural products and select manufacturing industries in the first year;
(c) to increase production of food and industrial raw materials to planned levels in the context of the Three-Year Medium-Term Plan;
(d) to lower the rate of inflation;
(e) to improve the distribution of goods, services and incomes.[31]

These policies were to be reiterated and elaborated on in subsequent economic and budget statements. Above all, most of the economic policies being pursued seemed to be geared towards deflating and rationalising the economy – that is, reducing the rate of inflation, supply of money, current expenditures and budget deficits and stabilising the currency. Thus the 1983 budget included a partial, indirect devaluation of the currency, a system of surcharges, taxes on transactions involving the use of foreign exchange, increases in indirect taxes and custom duties, price hikes for several essential goods and services (e.g. soap, milk, meat, baby food, wax prints (textiles), building materials and petroleum products). Such austerity measures resulted in considerable hardships for an already economically hard-pressed public.

Despite the populist air that surrounds the Rawlings regime, these austerity measures nonetheless represent a fairly conventional approach towards dealing with an economy such as Ghana's and have received the stamp of approval of the IMF. Throughout its tenure, the PNDC has not been reluctant to use harsh methods in pursuit of its economic goals. In 1982 it attempted a partial demonitisation of the economy, involving the unpopular method of withdrawing ₡50 notes from circulation. By this method, an estimated ₡800 million to ₡1.36 billion was taken out of the monetary system. The PNDC government has kept tight reins on the supply of money – notably by refusing to print new money and increasing the rate of interest on commercial lending – even at the risk of a liquidity crisis. The first two years of PNDC rulership may well be remembered for the prevalence of acute shortages of essential consumer items, brought on in part, by these austerity measures.

While attempting to keep expenditures down to deflate the economy through monetarist budgetary measures, the PNDC government has shown a keen determination to improve the country's revenue base. Much effort has gone into increasing the government's tax-gathering ability, not only by making better use of existing institutions such as the Central Revenue and the Customs and Excise departments, but also by using new agencies, such as the Citizens Vetting Committee and the National Investigations Committee. As a consequence, collection of direct taxes increased in 1982 by 65.4 per cent over the previous year and in 1983 by another 19.8 per cent. The self-employed sector contributed ₵307 million in taxes in 1982 as compared to ₵52.3 million in 1980. And as current measures for revamping the export sector take effect, additional revenues from this sector can be anticipated.

Apart from these rather short-term monetarist and budgetary measures to reduce public expenditure and improve the revenue base, the PNDC has also taken steps to improve the productive base of the economy. In this, the government looks upon agriculture, and especially food production, as the basis for Ghana's recovery. Agriculture has been declared a priority sector, and available resources have been mobilised to increase farm output. Secondary schools have been directed to manage their own farm and livestock projects, and benefits have been extended to people in their mid-forties to induce them to leave the modern wage sector for various types of agricultural pursuits. An indication of the government's seriousness in this commitment is its allocation of ₵500 million to increase the production of food and export crops.

Not surprisingly, much of the effort made towards improving the productive base in the agricultural sector has been directed at the cocoa industry. To make cocoa farming more attractive, the 1983 budget increased the producer price of cocoa from ₵360 to ₵600 per 30 kg bag. In addition, the government has sought to ensure that consumer goods are available for purchase by farmers, directing its central supply outlet, the Ghana National Procurement Agency, to provide such essential consumer goods as textiles, machetes, and building materials to farmers directly and at government-controlled prices. Moreover, to reduce the incidence of cheating of illiterate cocoa farmers by purchasing clerks, to ensure prompt payment to farmers, to help farmers spread incomes through the off-season, and to encourage them to use the banking system, the government designed the innovative Akuafo Cheque System.[32] A positive spin-off from this system has been an increase in the number of rural banks.

The government has also moved to revive the mining industry. With financial assistance from the World Bank, it plans to rehabilitate the gold mines at Dunkwa, Prestea and Tarkwa. At this time, it remains uncertain whether the PNDC can attract sufficient foreign capital (estimated at over $1.3 billion in 1980) for a comprehensive renovation of the industry. The revival of other segments of the mining industry (such as bauxite, manganese and diamond mines) depends similarly upon capital infusions from outside the country that are not readily available. Hopes for increased offshore oil production also remain tenuous. The two major companies engaged in offshore oil drilling, Agri-Petco and Phillips Petroleum, scaled down their activities in early 1982. However, the government has taken a series of initiatives aimed at improving the country's position as an oil producer and processor. It commissioned a seismic survey by Geophysical Services Inc., at a cost of $7.3 million intended to provide relevant data to serve as a basis for negotiating new oil-prospecting concessions,[33] and it announced plans in November 1982 to set up a Ghana Petroleum Corporation and a National Energy Board under the Ministry of Fuel and Power to handle petroleum contracts, concessions and other related matters.[34] Further initiatives involving international lending agencies include an $11 million IDA/loan project to accelerate petroleum exploration and a $23 million grant for oil and gas exploration from the Canadian International Assistance Corporation.[35]

Rawlings' second coming has brought to the fore a variety of neo-Marxist and dependency perspectives in Ghana that hold imperialism and neo-colonialism ultimately responsible for the Ghanaian economic decline and demodernisation. The PNDC *Policy Guidelines* pointed to 'the continued domination of our economy by foreign financial interests' and vowed to work towards 'a fundamental break from the existing neo-colonial relations' and from 'the existing foreign monopoly control over the economy and social life.'[36] This theme was echoed in various pronouncements by the government and its leading spokesmen and supporters. For instance, the PNDC chairman criticised the Limann administration for allowing Lonrho to exploit Ghana's gold and warned that 'Ghana cannot accept the creation of the monopoly situation for any foreign investors'.[37] And, as noted earlier, calls were made for a review of Ghana's agreements with multinational corporations and for an abrogation of existing investment agreements, denounced by one pro-government group as having 'opened the country to rape'.[38] Various PNDC spokesmen have served notice of the government's intention to renegotiate past agreements with MNCs – in particular, those made with VALCO, Agri-Petco, and Phillips

Petroleum. And the 'December 2nd Programme' with its plans to regulate the foreign banking sector, produced an image of the PNDC as antagonistic to foreign investment.

However, these fears about nationalisation or the harassment of foreign companies by the Rawlings regime have never fitted with reality. PNDC negotiations with VALCO, for instance, appear restrained and cautious, hardly an expression of unremitting hostility. Given its radical public posture, the PNDC government, whose December 1981 coup disrupted negotiations between the Limann regime and the IMF, found itself caught in an awkward position regarding the negotiating process following the takeover. The Limann government–IMF negotiations had been deadlocked on the issue of devaluation.[39] Various interests urged the PNDC not to be like other governments that 'spinelessly yielded to IMF pressures.'[40] And, as the PNDC government entered into negotiations with the IMF itself, it appeared to adopt a more flexible demeanour than its public posturing might have led the casual observer to expect.[41] Rather than rejecting devaluation outright, the government called in 1982 for a 'principled' discussion of the devaluation question.[42] By October 1983, devaluation was made more formal in the budget review, with the cedi devalued by 990 per cent (from ₵2.75 to ₵30 per US dollar). By these actions, the government appears to have won the confidence of the IMF and the World Bank, for the former agreed in August 1983 to lend Ghana SDR 359 million with another SDR 120 million pending, while the Bank, through its IDA soft loan affiliate, has granted $65 million.[43] In light of the Ghana public's reservations over IMF policies generally, the PNDC government deserves credit for its political dexterity in this matter.[44] In brief, the apprehensions that many local and foreign observers have held about the regime's deep hostility toward foreign investment seem exaggerated; in fact, there have been no radical moves against such interests up to this point, and the stabilisation programme put into effect by the PNDC regime seems calculated to allay the worst fears of the international investment community.

Perhaps no PNDC initiative has caught the attention of the international community more than its proposal to decentralise policy-making and implementation responsibilities. The PNDC announced its aim to decentralise the public services in its policy guidelines of May 1982. Viewing decentralisation as complementing its wider efforts to promote 'democratisation' and efficient administration, the new regime outlined a comprehensive and systematic 11-point programme in late 1982 for putting its decentralisation plan into effect. The first phase, which stipulated an intensive education of the general public on the merits of the plan and the modalities of its implementation, was effectively carried out in December 1982 and January 1983. The third point, concerning the appointment of PNDC district secretaries, was also put into effect on schedule. Moreover, the Ministry of Local Government, which was charged under point five with implementing the decentralisation programme, did submit its policy guidelines for the formation of national, regional and district decentralisation implementation committees as required. In its provisional estimates for the last quarter of the 1982 fiscal year, the PNDC sped up the implementation of the decentralisation plan, for the first time specifically allocating funds for running the various regions. This action had the effect of reducing the control exercised by the central service ministries over their regional counterparts.[45] Whether or not the trend toward substantive decentralisation will continue remains unclear. Rawlings, in a speech to the nation in August 1983, felt it necessary to caution the public against expecting parallel structures of government to emerge. 'I want to make it absolutely clear', he stated, 'that without central authority, only confusion and frustration will result from our efforts at national recovery.'[46] Even so, Rawlings seemed to be leaving significant scope for experimentation in decentralising at least limited responsibilities.

## PUBLIC PRESSURES AGAINST GOVERNMENT REFORMS

The Rawlings-initiated reforms have represented a positive attempt to reduce the loads on the state and to increase its capacity to govern.[47] Yet they were not without determined opponents. Although the PNDC's programmes for economic recovery entailed severe hardships for the Ghanaian public, it was the articulate public (or what Karl Deutsch calls the 'politically relevant strata of the population')[48] among the urban middle class and wage earners[49] who gave the government serious cause for concern. The middle class (broadly defined here to include high-status groups such as business people, large traders, managers and bureaucrats) has been adversely affected by and resentful of the PNDC's rigorous and sometimes unconventionally harsh tax collection methods, its 'confiscation' of ₵50 notes, its removal and reduction of subsidies and perquisites, its steep increase in prices of gasoline, air travel, education and medical treatment abroad, and its attempts to isolate this elite from the rest of the public.[50] At times members of the middle class were branded as 'exploiters of the common man', 'quislings' and 'compradors'.

But perhaps a more worrisome constraint upon PNDC leadership has been the creeping disaffection of the urban wage-earning class, initially among the regime's staunchest allies. This relatively deprived socio-economic class has given indications of increasing disillusionment with PNDC economic recovery policies. In particular, it has been disappointed over the regime's inability to repeat the 'miracle' of Rawlings' Armed Forces Revolutionary Council Interregnum of June–September 1979, when retail shops were forced to sell their goods at drastically reduced prices.[51] From the workers' point of view, the PNDC programme of economic rehabilitation – economic ration-alisation and rural development – has imposed decided hardship. Thus the General Transport Petroleum and Chemical Workers Union of the Trade Union Congress voiced its disappointment in a 1983 resolution, declaring that: 'slowly as we move on with the revolution, our confidence began to shake, prices of commodities basic to our needs started surging upwards, while "Kalabule" refused to obey the gun. The purchasing power of workers which was already in bad shape was severely hit and workers in particular were only trying to exist.'[52] More of these feelings of disenchantment came out in the workers' reactions to the austere 1983 budget which they described as 'anti-people; a killer, callous and inhuman'.[53] Clearly, Rawlings' actions have provoked resistance among the ranks of his working class supporters. However, it is also evident that the government has little choice but to pursue austerity policies in the light of the constraints it faces and its rehabilitation objectives.

Although the government responded to these pressures by increasing the daily minimum wage from ₵12 to ₵21.50 (and subsequently to ₵24.20), these actions did very little to placate the workers, who demanded a basic minimum wage of about ₵38 and/or a return to pre-budget prices. Government spokesmen steadfastly maintained that the PNDC's commitment to workers's welfare remained unflinching, yet it was obvious that the high recurrent expenditures (which were rising by some 48 per cent with the new pay increases and other budgetary measures), the still-heavy subsidies on consumer goods and services (calculated at over ₵1300 million), and an over-valued currency were of more pressing concern than the workers' calls for a review of the budget. Thus, despite the government's claim that its measures imposed heavier burdens on wealthier members of the society, workers perceived the budget as an act of betrayal.

In many ways the PNDC has been its own worst enemy. Following the 1981 coup, its rhetoric awakened very high public expectations for economic well-being. In its policy guidelines, the PNDC spoke of an 'important corollary' to the national revolution – 'the struggle for new democracy'. It explained the meaning of this struggle in terms of placing political power in the hands of the people and ensuring their genuine participation in the decision-making process. But most importantly, this 'new democracy' was also to establish 'the material basis for ensuring a democratic and popular education as well as health schemes, housing, food and transportation to ensure the physical, spiritual, moral and cultural quality of life of our people.'[54] Indeed, the regime started on an explicitly populist note, declaring itself to be 'a people's government' and encouraging the use of the symbolic prefix 'people's' for public institutions such as the army and police, retail shops, markets, newspapers, and so forth.

The PNDC sought to institutionalise popular participation and watchfulness in popular groups such as the People's and Workers' Defence Committees (PDCs and WDCs) at local, district, regional and national levels.[55] Rawlings in one on his broadcasts on the day of the 1981 coup, called on his supporters to organise themselves into committees to 'defend' the revolution.[56] Although these committees did provide some critical support to the Rawlings regime in its initial months, they were to prove troublesome as the revolution consolidated its hold. It was the economic sphere that these committees appeared to regard as most significant. They collaborated with army and police personnel in the enforcement of government-imposed price and rent controls, anti-smuggling exercises, and so forth and promoted the idea of people's shops.[57] These were conceived as a 'revolutionary' vehicle for ensuring equitable and popular control over the distribution of essential goods and services. They quickly became an important expression of the new PDC/WDC political order, finding a fervent advocate in the PNDC Secretary for Trade, Ashiboe Mensah. Mensah's retirement some few weeks before the 1983 budget (possibly motivated by Rawlings' desire to remove one source of opposition to the budget from within the government) was widely seen by these popular organisations as a blow to the people's shop idea as well as an effort to accommodate powerful trading interests who felt threatened by Mensah's pro-worker policies. Indeed the PDC statement protesting this move poignantly reminded the government that to remove people's shops was to dismantle the PDC concept.[58] This counter-attack clearly placed the PNDC in a difficult position. On the one hand, it did not want to lose its populist credentials and the loyalty of its working-class supporters; on the other hand, it was concerned over the apparent inefficiencies arising from these hastily organised shops.[59] Its discomfort is best appreciated when one understands that most of the attempts to overthrow the PNDC have been timed to coincide with periods of public dissatisfaction. The abortive coup of 19 June 1983 is a classic example of this pattern.

Similar problems are likely to be encountered as the government moves ahead with plans to redeploy redundant labour from the wage sector to agriculture. The PNDC has recognised the sensitivity of this issue. Militants resisted attempts in November 1982 to lay off workers at the Textile Printing Company at Tema, jointly owned by the government and foreign investors, causing the PNDC to become more cautious than ever in this regard.[60] Indeed, policies that run against the immediate interests of urban workers seem likely to create more disaffection for the PNDC – but then most of the policies being implemented to improve the economy and governance have an anti-urban worker implication. Populism thus exhibits built-in productivity-inhibiting tendencies. The government may respond by calling for greater discipline and sacrifice, but in the circumstances of modern Ghana, persuasion clearly has its limits.

If the PNDC has had some difficulties in its relations with the working class, its greatest opposition comes, without doubt, from the middle class (i.e. the professionals, managers, business people and traders, university teachers, etc.) whose members perceive themselves to be the targets of Rawlings' 'holy war'. In addition to the economic privations discussed above, their grievances include seizures of property without prior investigation, a state of extreme insecurity caused by incidents of kidnapping and murder (most notably the cases of three high court judges and a retired army officer in June 1982),[61] violence by militant pro-government organisations, including the vandalisation of Masonic lodges in the spring of 1982, a night curfew, and the establishment of extra-legal courts administering 'rash and crude' justice (such as the detention without trial of politicians and other citizens). Much resented are the PDCs and WDCs, which are seen as 'instruments of terror, division and antagonism in our society, a haven of corruption, extortion and callousness'. The PNDC is also accused of having created a wedge between 'the people' and the 'non-people'.[62] In addition, Ghana's middle class points to the state media's 'meaningless and irrelevant insults to other countries which could help us'. Here they refer to the anti-Western tirades on the radio and in the newspapers, as well as the courting by some government spokesmen of such countries as Libya, Cuba and North Korea. This leads to a feeling that Ghana's economic hardships are in part the result of the wrath of powerful Western nations, brought on by these slights. Seeing their calls for change and moderation ignored, and the demand for a return to constitutional government ridiculed, the middle class has given evidence of despondency and low morale and has tended to respond by withdrawing or 'exiting' from the country.[63]

By late 1982, the PNDC began to be increasingly conciliatory toward the middle class and its positions. In his August 1983 address to the nation, Rawlings announced plans to review some of the convictions imposed by AFRC and PNDC courts. A step toward implementing these plans was the setting up of a special sub-committee of the National Investigations Committee to review the cases of AFRC convicts, including those sentenced *in absentia*, to facilitate their rehabilitation.[64] The PNDC Secretary for Culture and Tourism, Asiedu Yirenkyi, announced that the government was working out plans to declare a period of national reconciliation. The process of reconciliation could also be seen in the appointments of a traditional chief, the Naandom Na Naa Polkuu Konkuu Chiri IV, as a member of the PNDC, and the Secretary for Defence, Alhaji Tolon Na (vice-presidential candidate for the erstwhile People's Front Party in the 1979 elections) as a member of the Judicial Council, and of such establishment politicians as F. A. Jantuah and J. E. Tandoh as secretaries for Ashanti and Central Regions respectively. The PNDC now appears to recognise that it cannot afford to allow the alienation of the middle class for an indefinite period.[65]

As might be expected, pressures against governmental reforms in Ghana have not disappeared under Rawlings' populist regime. In spite of its outwardly mobilisational appearance, the PNDC in its efforts to redress the imbalances in the Ghanaian economy has been cautious and tentative and, in the light of the gravity of the problems, relatively marginal. For instance, allocations to agriculture remain relatively low. While food imports and manufacturing received $65 million and $15 million respectively, the 1983 budget allocated agriculture only $67 million for its imported inputs. Serious questions may be raised about the adequacy of the incentives being given to farmers under the cocoa replanting exercise. In the inflationary economy of contemporary Ghana ₵600 per acre over a three-year period (or $20 according to the current official exchange rate) seems a rather poor incentive to the farmer. It is not surprising, then, that some farmers refuse to go along with governmental pressures to grow cocoa and instead elect to grow maize. Indeed, the fundamental problems facing Ghana's agriculture (i.e. the lack of social amenities for rural dwellers[66] and inadequate inputs such as seed and fertiliser) are still very much apparent.[67] In spite of the expressed intentions of the PNDC, life in rural areas is still less advantaged with respect to social services and amenities, and the distribution of such goods as soap, matches and rice, etc., continue to leave rural dwellers behind their urban counterparts. There is also an over-reliance on rainfed agriculture with large- and small-scale irrigation remaining manifestly inadequate.[68]

Moreover, it remains unclear whether the PNDC government can resist the pressures of large farming interests (private and parastatal) to pursue policies detrimental to smallholder farmers. Smallholder production has proved relatively efficient under conditions of scarcity.[69] What Bjorn Beckman describes as the dominant strategy for tackling the erosion of the agrarian system – 'bypassing rather than transforming the peasantry' – may remain a fact of life in Rawlings' Ghana unless conscious efforts are made to resist that tendency.[70]

This same lack of decisiveness has characterised the implementation of the much-discussed decentralisation plan. The hopes engendered by the initial flurry of action to implement the 11-point plan discussed above and by the creation of a tenth (Upper West) region out of the former Upper Region have dimmed considerably. It is now apparent that the later, politically more difficult phases of the 11-point plan have become bogged down. The public education programme and appointment of PNDC regional and district secretaries were accomplished swiftly; however, the next phases – the deployment of personnel from the central ministries to the decentralised units and the devolution of the promised financial and administrative authority and autonomy to them – have proven rather more problematic. Taking account of these delays, the government and its spokesmen have blamed the centralised bureaucracy for frustrating the decentralisation programme with their 'characteristic subtle intrigues'.[71] It remains to be seen whether the PNDC can break this impasse and bring decentralisation into existence in Ghana.

## OPPORTUNITIES FOR GOVERNMENTAL REFORMS

While appreciating the difficulties that lie in the way of the reforms discussed above, there are still some prevailing opportunities in the contemporary context. In brief, there is a potential for strategies such as decentralisation and rural/agricultural development to reduce the functional loads on the state. Two forces for changing perceptions can be identified.

First, recent shortages in both imported and locally produced food supplies have given the government and the public a greater understanding than ever of the supreme importance of agriculture. The spirit that motivated the Acheampong regime's Operation Feed Yourself programme is very much alive in Ghana today.[72]

Second, as the resources at the centre of the Ghanaian state have shrunk, individuals who used to derive their welfare from the state have begun to look away from the centre and to the village locale.[73] This has manifested itself in an increasing interest in agricultural activities on the part of the middle class and wage earners. The direct entry of these classes into the rural and agricultural sector might have a beneficial effect on this sector's productivity.[74] Policies relatively favourable to agricultural and rural development may be expected to accompany this shift towards agricultural pursuits.[75]

Survey data collected in 1983 suggest that there is considerable public support for an agricultural and rural development orientation, a potential that the PNDC has not fully exploited thus far.[76] These survey results are admittedly imprecise and unscientific, yet they are useful in giving an insight into public attitudes that cannot be secured from more casual observations. Elite respondents in Legon, Kwabenya and the Achimota School residential area were found to be highly supportive of a development effort concentrating on the rural areas. These university lecturers, professionals, technical and scientific officers and administrators generally recognised that urban areas are relatively advantaged in terms of the quality of life by comparison with the hinterland areas; significantly, they agreed overwhelmingly on the need to change public priorities so as to develop the rural areas and make life in these parts more attractive. Thus 88 per cent of the respondents did not agree that farmers and people living in the rural areas received their fair share of public allocations, and 74 per cent maintained that the development of the rural areas should be given priority over other areas and sectors in setting national priorities. When asked whether they would be willing to deny resources to urban areas in order to undertake development activities in the rural areas, 50 per cent agreed 'strongly' and another 38 per cent agreed 'somewhat' that this should be done. Underlining the extent of their personal commitment to rural development even further, 41 per cent said they would 'readily' and 54 per cent said they would 'reluctantly' go to a rural area if their job required such a transfer. These responses appeared to be in marked contrast to the urban elite's reluctance to leave the comforts of urban life during the mid-1970s; however, whether the current attitudes will translate into actions remains to be seen.

Other survey results indicate that the Ghana government has considerable potential support in the public at large for policies of decentralisation. Here one sees a pattern of considerable continuity over time in the survey results from questionnaires administered in Ghana's Eastern Region in 1973 and in 1982. The 1973 General Public Questionnaire, administered by the Department of Political Science at the University of Ghana, Legon, has been disaggregated for the purposes of this chapter to show results obtained from the Oda District Council Area in Eastern Region alone.[77] What emerges is an impression of a broad public preference for solving developmental problems in the area through local initiative. Although a sizeable proportion of the sample did not respond to a question on the means for dealing with local developmental problems, among those who did, 41 per cent of the total sample answered 'self-help' and 'communal labour'; only 10 per cent of the total sample stated that they looked to the central government for critically needed support. When members of the public were asked where they would go to get something done about specific problems in the areas of housing, sanitation, health services, or educational facilities, 55 per cent of the total sample named the local council, 29 per cent replied the chief and elders, and 1 per cent pointed to the regional commissioner; only 7 per cent of the total sample said they would go to the central government in Accra to secure the necessary support to cope with these local problems.

The 1982 questionnaire administered in the Kwai-Abirem Area of Eastern Region indicated a similar inclination on the part of the general public to depend on local rather than central initiative in dealing with their developmental problems.[78] When asked where the main leadership must come from for village improvement, 54 per cent of respondents replied the town or village development committee and 27 per cent said the central government. The public's high expectations that local leaders would provide the necessary initiative to deal with their developmental problems emerge even more clearly from another question. When asked which agency could be called upon to meet the needs of the village or town, 65 per cent pointed to the town development committee, while only 13 per cent named the central government. Such survey findings suggest that grassroots structures remain important agencies for local development in Ghana.

In the light of the centre's inability to achieve its goals, these results suggest the value of an experiment with decentralisation. Not only will such a development strategy reduce the functional loads on an over-burdened state, but, given the depth of public support for initiatives by local agencies, this strategy may bring about both increased productivity, as it build upon increased public participation in the decision process, and, possibly, a more responsive decision agency. To the extent that such a strategy can create an increased public consensus for its larger developmental goals, it will represent an element of progress in an otherwise depressing situation of economic decline.

## CONCLUSION

In Ghana, a combination of international constraints and domestic policy failures has given birth to desperate measures of rejuvenation. Although the policies of past regimes have varied widely, none have thus far proved effective in arresting the decline in agricultural and industrial productivity or in the general quality of life. Hopes rose as Ghana returned in 1979 to an elected, civilian-led government under President Limann; however, these heady expectations quickly turned to despair as the state proved ineffective and immobile in the face of ever-worsening economic scarcity. As the pace of economic decline quickened, a despondent Ghana, envisaging few options for itself in the period ahead, came generally to accept (or acquiesce in) Rawlings' radical populist alternatives. Not only did Ghana find little choice, but the drama of action seemed more appealing than the continuance of a seemingly directionless drift.

Rawlings received his second chance. As promised, his military-led populism partially insulated the 'soft state' and its institutions from the normally heavy demands of the country's urban middle class. If at times this led to abuses of civil liberties and interference in the operation of the judicial system, it also increased the state's capacity to pursue harsh policies intended to rehabilitate the country's sagging economy. Thus the state invoked some necessarily painful deflationary monetary and economic policies (including a partial devaluation), increased taxes and surcharges, and reduced state subsidies. It even went to the extreme of withdrawing ₵50 notes – an arbitrary measure that had the effect of reducing the amount of money in circulation, even while proving extremely harmful to the interests of the middle class. Rawlings' military-run, hegemonial political system, with its lower costs of decision-making and greater organisational discipline, appeared to have an increased capacity to pursue policies that were likely to prove unpalatable to politically powerful interests in the society. As such, it represented a new – and possibly creative – balance between capacity and loads.

Hence the second Rawlings administration represented something of a paradox. In terms of political style, it presented a picture of tough-minded political populism – intent upon resisting the spread both of domestic class inequalities and of neo-colonial encroachments. The enactment of a net wealth tax upon exorbitant profits by business people is an indication of its commitment to a more equitable distribution of incomes. This radical profile acted as something of a resource, strengthening the regime and enabling it to achieve certain necessary and painful economic reforms long advocated by establishment-minded (if not conservative) policy analysts at home and abroad. In substance, the 1983 budget, with its partial devaluation, reduced subsidies on goods and services, price increases and higher indirect taxes and custom duties, embodied a deflationary programme which effectively courted IMF and World Bank support in exchange for austerity and extensive hardship on the domestic scene.

But such a part-conscious, part-unconscious combination of radical rhetoric and accommodating practice was not without its problems, even in the short term. As noted in the body of this chapter, the Rawlings political style leads to at least four major difficulties.

(a) Over time, a legitimacy crisis seems inevitable where leaders proclaim radical approaches for problem-solving but actually pursue pragmatic, even conservative policies in a number of instances. Although these policies may be calculated to ease international lending agency anxieties, they must be carried out with great sensitivity for domestic majority opinion if they are not to alienate the regime's critically important support base.

(b) A combination of populist rhetoric and accommodating practices inevitably sends ambiguous signals which confuse urban workers as well as the already disaffected middle class. In this case, the regime is acting much as its predecessors have done, denying trade-offs of a policy nature, and consequently proving unable over the long term to achieve either equity or productionist goals.

(c) Not only is the urban basis of Rawlings' power shaky, but it is not easily reconcilable with the objectives of agricultural or rural development. In this regard, the regime's inability to deliver on promises important to rural dwellers (for example, decentralisation, the increased availability of agricultural inputs, significant rises in the prices paid for agricultural commodities, and greater availability of consumer goods) may prove decisive in terms of its ability to stay in power.

(d) Although the Rawlings hegemonial system of governance is in fact limited with regard to its reach and effectiveness under current Ghanaian conditions, it is still rejected by significant elements in society (by no means restricted to the middle class) who remain steadfast in their commitment to constitutional government.

Populism of the Rawlings variety may temporarily strengthen the Ghanaian state and enable it to cope with certain aspects of the problem of scarcity, but, with respect to the four difficulties noted above, it nonetheless remains its own enemy in terms of survival and task achievement.

Nevertheless, to note the transitory nature of the Rawlings phenomenon is not to deny its contribution. For one thing, it has acted to clarify the limits of choice. It must now be apparent to almost all that any regime, radical or conservative, will have little alternative but to put some elements of the current regime's austerity package into effect in order to deal with the mounting economic problems the government must face. For another, it has addressed directly the issue of reducing the heavy functional loads upon the state in order to increase its overall effectiveness. By its willingness to shift responsibilities to the local level (the 'bottom-up' strategy of development), it may be able to free local initiatives as well as to make a leaner and stronger central state more able to tackle the responsibilities remaining in its hands. The evidence presented here on public support for an agricultural and rural development orientation, as well as public preferences for local as opposed to central initiative, indicates that an experiment with decentralisation might facilitate public participation in the decision process, a more responsive decision agency, and, in the light of an increased consensus for regime objectives, a rise in economic productiveness. The 'small is beautiful' theme seems likely to prove of timeless validity – well worth attention in the uncertain times that Ghana is now passing through.

## NOTES

1. On the strategies of development, see Donald Rothchild and Robert L. Curry, Jr, *Scarcity, Choice and Public Policy in Middle Africa* (Berkeley: University of California Press, 1978) Chapter 3.

2.  The political, economic, and social problems of governance are discussed in Donald Rothchild and Michael Foley, 'The Implications of Scarcity for Governance in Africa', *International Political Science Review*, vol. 4 (1983) no. 3, pp. 316–17.
3.  Goran Hyden, 'Problems and Prospects of State Coherence', in Donald Rothchild and Victor A. Olorunsola (eds), *State Versus Ethnic Claims: African Policy Dilemmas* (Boulder, Colorado: Westview Press, 1983) p. 74. Also see Naomi Chazan, *An Anatomy of Ghanaian Politics: Managing Political Recession, 1969–1982* (Boulder, Colorado: Westview Press, 1983) pp. 95–104.
4.  Republic of Ghana, *Summary of PNDC's Budget Statement and Economic Policy for 1983* (Accra: PNDC, 1983) p. 1.
5.  Kodwo Ewusi, *The Ghana Economy in 1981–82: Recent Trends and Prospects for the Future* (Legon: Institute of Statistical, Social and Economic Research, 1982) p. 1.
6.  *Summary of PNDC's Budget Statement*, p. 1.
7.  Richard Jeffries, 'Rawlings and the Political Economy of Underdevelopment in Ghana', *African Affairs*, vol. 81 (July 1982) no. 324, pp. 307–8.
8.  Theotonio Dos Santos, 'The Structure of Dependence', in Charles K. Wilber (ed.) *The Political Economy of Development and Underdevelopment* (New York: Random House, 1973) p. 109.
9.  Tony Killick, *Development Economics in Action: A Study of Economic Policies in Ghana* (London: Heinemann, 1978) p. 109.
10. *West Africa*, 22 July 1981, p. 1659.
11. *Ghana News* (Washington, DC) vol. 12 (February 1983) no. 2, p. 8.
12. On the increase in Ghana's manufacturing sector in the 1960 to 1969 period, see J. Ofori-Atta, 'Sectoral Changes in Income Distribution in the Economies of West African Countries . . .', *Universitas*, vol. 5 (New Series) (November 1975) no. 1, p. 73.
13. *Ghanaian Times*, 29 February 1980, p. 1; and J. A. Peasah, 'Transfer of Technology: Overview of an Issue in the Relations between the Rich and Poor Countries', paper presented at a University of Ghana, Legon, Departmental Seminar, 18 March 1978, pp. 19–20.
14. Howard Schissel, 'Ghana Moves on Oil', *West Africa*, 9 May 1983, p. 1135. In spring 1983, the International Development Association granted an $11 million credit to Ghana to accelerate petroleum exploration. *Ghana News*, vol. 12 (June 1983) no. 6, p. 7.
15. *Ghanaian Times* (Accra), 21 July 1977, p. 1. Also see *Ghanaian Times*, 29 June 1979, p. 1 and 6 July 1979, p. 4. In addition, such leaders as Limann and Rawlings have described the MNCs as operating in an exploitative manner and as being a major source of Ghana's problems. See Robert M. Price, 'Neo-Colonialism and Ghana's Economic Decline: A Critical Assessment', *Canadian Journal of African Studies*, vol. 18 (1984) no. 1, pp. 163–93.
16. As a result of declining capacity, local tyre production fell from 330 000 in 1976 to a low of 63 000 in 1982. *West Africa*, 24 October 1983, p. 2448.
17. *Ghanaian Times*, 8 November 1979, p. 1.
18. Price, 'Neo-Colonialism and Ghana's Economic Decline'.
19. *Africa Now* (London), vol. 27 (July 1983) p. 76; and *African Business* (London) vol. 61 (September 1983) p. 25.

20. J. Ofori-Atta, 'The Stagnation Crisis in Ghana: A Call for Pragmatism', *Universitas*, vol. 4 (New Series) (May 1975) no. 2, p. 29.
21. *West Africa*, 22 August 1983, p. 1967.
22. *The Mirror* (Accra) 30 April 1983, p. 9.
23. *West Africa*, 20 June 1983, p. 1465.
24. *The Mirror*, 30 April 1983, p. 9.
25. Interview, *West Africa*, 11 February 1980, p. 243.
26. Chazan, *An Anatomy of Ghanaian Politics*, Chapter 8; and Donald Rothchild, 'Military Regime Performance: An Appraisal of the Ghana Experience, 1972–1978', *Comparative Politics*, vol. 12 (July 1980) no. 4, pp. 459–79.
27. *Republic of Ghana Five-Year Development Plan 1975/76–1979/80*, Part II (Accra: Ghana Publishing Corporation, 1977) p. 57.
28. Budget Statement 1978/79 as printed in *Legon Observer* (Legon) vol. 10 (29 September 1978) no. 3, p. 67. This and several succeeding paragraphs are drawn from Donald Rothchild, 'Ghana's Economy: An African Test Case for Political Democracy', in Colin Legum (ed.) *Africa Contemporary Record 1979–1980* (New York: Africana Publishing, 1981) pp. A140–5.
29. See Correspondent, 'The Economic Consequences of Rawlings', *Legon Observer*, vol. 11 (16 November 1979) no. 10, pp. 284–7.
30. *Ghanaian Times*, 18 August 1979, p. 1 and 25 September 1979, p. 8; and *West Africa*, 17 September 1979, p. 1714.
31. *PNDC's Programme for Reconstruction and Development* (Accra: Information Services Department, 1982) pp. 5–6.
32. The Akuafo Cheque System involved triplicate cheques with produce weights on them. The produce clerk kept the third copy and gave the original and duplicate to the farmer to be forwarded to his bank. The farmer then went to the bank with his produce passbook bearing his identity number. On the first visit, the farmer opened an account and deposited the cheque into his account. Then the farmer could withdraw a part or all of the money at will. Personal Communication, Kwame Bredu, member of the Akuafo Cheque Monitoring Team, Akim-Oda District, August 1983.
33. *Ghana News*, vol. 11 (November/December 1982) no. 11, p. 7.
34. *West Africa*, 1 November 1982, p. 2859.
35. *West Africa*, 10 October 1983, p. 2376.
36. *People's Daily Graphic* (Accra), 11 April 1983, p. 3.
37. *West Africa*, 22 March 1983, p. 785. Also see *Legon Observer*, vol. 14 (June, 1982) no. 6, p. 143.
38. *West Africa*, 15 February 1982, p. 482.
39. *West Africa*, 14 September 1981, pp. 2093–4.
40. *West Africa*, 15 March 1982, p. 750.
41. There is ample secondary evidence, as revealed by the statements and denials of various government spokesmen, that there was a major split in opinion among members of the government on this issue. See *West Africa*, 25 October 1982, p. 2808, and 8 November 1982, p. 2920.
42. See the statement by Dr Obed Asamoah, *West Africa*, 8 March 1982, p. 682; also the statement by Dr Kwesi Botchwey, *Ghana News*, vol. 11 (November/December 1982) no. 11, p. 11.
43. *Ghana News*, vol. 12 (August 1983) no. 8, p. 8; also see *African Business*, vol. 61 (September 1983) p. 25.

44. These measures were reinforced by the revised budget of October 1983; additional subsidies were removed and the currency was devalued by 30 per cent.
45. *Ghana News*, vol. 11 (November/December 1982) no. 11, p. 10. Significantly, Dr Ansah Asamoah, a member of the National Defence Standing Committee placed the responsibility for delays in implementing the government's decentralisation plan on the shoulders of the central bureaucracy. *People's Daily Graphic*, 14 April 1983, pp. 1, 5.
46. *West Africa*, 12 September 1983, p. 2103.
47. See Rothchild and Foley, 'The Implications of Scarcity for Governance in Africa'.
48. Karl W. Deutsch, 'Social Mobilization and Political Development', *American Political Science Review*, vol. 55 (September 1961) no. 3, pp. 497–8.
49. Following the lead of Max Assimeng, we use the concept of class in the Ghanaian context with all deliberate caution. See his *Social Structure of Ghana* (Accra: Ghana Publishing Corporation, 1981) Chapter 5.
50. For a discussion of the privations of Ghana's middle class under Rawlings, see 'The Respectable Poor', in *West Africa*, 25 July 1983, pp. 1710–11.
51. See 'The Economic Consequences of Rawlings', *Legon Observer*, vol. 11 (16 November 1979) no. 10, pp. 284–7.
52. Excerpts of resolutions in *People's Daily Graphic*, 30 April 1983, p. 5.
53. Among other things, the October 1983 budget review increased the prices of petroleum products, beer, cigarettes, and so forth. See *West Africa*, 17 October 1983, pp. 2415–16.
54. See *Policy Guidelines of the PNDC* (Accra: May 1982) especially pp. 6 and 8.
55. For 'Guidelines for the Proper Functioning and Effectiveness of PDCs', see the insert in *Legon Observer*, vol. 14 (April 1982) no. 4.
56. See *West Africa*, 11 January 1982, p. 23.
57. For a brilliant discussion of the instrumental use of political organisation and power in Ghanaian politics at an earlier time, see Maxwell Owusu, *Uses and Abuses of Political Power* (Chicago: University of Chicago Press, 1970) *passim*.
58. *People's Daily Graphic*, 29 March 1983, p. 1.
59. The PNDC's ambivalence was shown as it gave in to the pressures of its working-class critics and reinstated Ashiboe Mensah, only to quietly drop him in the summer.
60. See accounts in *West Africa*, 29 November 1982, p. 3111, and 6 December 1982, p. 3178.
61. See details on the curtailment of civil liberties under Rawlings in E. Gyimah-Boadi and D. Rothchild, 'Rawlings, Populism and the Civil Liberties Tradition in Ghana', *Issue*, vol. 12 (Fall/Winter 1982) no. 3/4, pp 64–9.
62. See 'Christian Council and the Revolution' (Accra: Presbyterian Press, November 1982) and 'Pastoral Letter from the Heads of Churches of the Christian Council of Ghana to Believers in God and the Lord Jesus Christ', (mimeo), and the statement by Catholic Church of Ghana (Accra: issued on 1 November 1982) (mimeo).
63. A. O. Hirschman, *Exit, Voice and Loyalty* (Cambridge: Harvard University Press, 1981).

64. See *West Africa*, 17 October 1983, p. 2426.
65. *People's Daily Graphic*, 31 August 1983, p. 1.
66. For a micro documentation of rural poverty see K. Ewusi, *Planning for the Neglected Rural Poor in Ghana* (Accra: New Times Corporation, 1978).
67. A summary of problems facing agriculture in Ghana appears in US Agency for International Development, *Ghana: Country Development Strategy Statement*, Fiscal Year 1982.
68. This fact was dramatised in 1983 when a year of severe drought culminated in bush fires estimated to have destroyed over 300 000 acres of farmland. *Ghana News*, vol. 12 (May 1983) no. 5, p. 8.
69. For details of pressures leading to the adoption of large-scale private and/or parastatal agricultural strategies and the disastrous results in Ghana, see R. H. Bates, *Markets and States in Tropical Africa* (Berkeley: University of California Press, 1981); Jack Goody, 'Rice-Burning and the Green Revolution in Northern Ghana', *Journal of Development Studies*, vol. 16 (Winter 1980) pp. 136–55; and Andrew Shepherd, 'Agrarian Change in Northern Ghana: Public Investments, Capitalist Farming and Famine', in Judith Heyer, Pepe Roberts and Gavin Williams, (eds), *Rural Development in Tropical Africa* (London: Macmillan Press, 1981) pp. 168–92. For an analysis of the relative efficiency of smallholder farming, see Polly Hill, *Studies in Rural Capitalism in West Africa* (Cambridge University Press, 1970).
70. Bjorn Beckman, 'Ghana 1951–1978: The Agrarian Basis of the Post Colonial State', in Heyer, Roberts and Williams (eds), *Rural Development in Tropical Africa*, pp. 143–67.
71. See *People's Daily Graphic*, 14 March 1983, p. 1 and 17 April 1983, p. 1.
72. This is discussed in Rothchild, 'Military Regime Performance', pp. 467–72.
73. For a thoughtful discussion of this point, see Chazan, *An Anatomy of Ghanaian Politics*, pp. 66–70.
74. This trend became evident in the mid-1970s, particularly in Northern Ghana. See Goody, 'Rice Burning', p. 153.
75. Bates implies that participation on the part of the politically significant classes in Kenyan and Ivorian agriculture may account for the relatively benign and successful agricultural policies of these countries. See his *Markets and States*, p. 95f.
76. This survey of 50 respondents living and/or working at the Atomic Energy Commission at Kwabenya, the University of Ghana, and Achimota School was conducted on a random sample basis in the summer of 1983. Most of the respondents were university lecturers, administrators, scientific or technical officers and professionals. The survey was administered by E. Gyimah-Boadi with assistance from Kofi Antwi Mintah, Ernest Appiah, Kofi Owusu and Emma Owiredu.
77. For the methodology used and related results of this survey, see Donald Rothchild, 'Comparative Public Demand and Expectation Patterns: The Ghana Experience', *African Studies Review*, vol. 22 (April 1979) no. 1, pp. 127–47.
78. This survey of 228 heads of households was carried out in five villages in the Eastern Region on a random sample basis in the summer of 1982. It was administered by E. Gyimah-Boadi with the assistance of students from the University of Ghana, Legon.

# 11 Africa and the New International Division of Labour

## RICHARD HIGGOTT

Africa is in crisis. The nature of this crisis varies depending on where the observer stands. This chapter looks at the problem from the macro-perspective of the global political economy. Structural changes in train in the global political economy have specific implications for Africa that will shape its destiny for the foreseeable future. In essence, we have seen, and are continuing to see, the evolution of a New International Division of Labour (NIDL). Africa is being drawn into this division in a subordinate manner and this subordination is in turn conditioning the nature of political behaviour in Africa – particularly with regard to the form and functions which characterise the peripheral state in the last quarter of the twentieth century.

## THE EVOLUTION OF THE NEW INTERNATIONAL DIVISION OF LABOUR

The last decade has seen the growth of a dramatic process of structural change in the world's economic order unimagined in that optimistic period of boom and growth in the 1950s and 1960s. The emerging structure has come to be known as the New International Division of Labour – the internationalisation of the production process. In essence this process involve the relocation of entire industries (such as textiles) as well as specific aspects of industrial production (such as component manufacture and assembly) from industrialised to developing countries. This relocation has been enhanced by technological innovation providing for the disaggregation of production so that labour-intensive activities can be carried out in countries providing cheap and largely unskilled and semi-skilled labour.[1] The essence of the new division is greater specialisation in the production process and the ensuing facility of location and relocation of productive activity. The process of refinement still continues with investors now drawing the distinction between varying categories of developing countries. For example, some labour-intensive industrial activities are now being moved from Hong Kong and Singapore into countries of even lower wage costs such as Malaysia or, more recently, Sri Lanka. The increasing sophistication of this international specialisation depends on an on-going supply of new entrants to the cause of export-oriented industrialisation (EOI) to compensate for the rising costs in already established production sites.

It is only since the growth of the 'productionist' critiques of dependency theory in the latter part of the 1970s[2] that the more complex structure of the international division of labour has been recognised. With production as the starting point – as opposed to exchange, or circulation, the essence of dependency theory – the spatial or geographical components of the division of labour, which should not be dismissed entirely, are placed in their proper but secondary perspective. Production is now quite clearly a global, not national, process.[3] As such it is the dynamic of accumulation rather than the logic of unequal exchange which determines the levels of industrialisation in specific Third World countries. The notion of exploitative economic relationships between two countries, or the 'centre' and the 'periphery' in common radical parlance, is replaced by the working assumption of a common subjection of all nations (including the advanced industrial West) to decisions about the movements of capital taken in those decision-making situations which do not draw exclusively on the concept of national interest for their impetus. This is not the same as suggesting that the nation state is no longer the major unit of identity in the international arena. Rather it is to suggest that it is no longer the only one. Within the context of recent international political economy there is now recognised the facility for the location and relocation of international capital into those regions of the world providing the greatest returns.

With its emphasis on capital location for industrial production, the evolution of NIDL has several significant policy implications. One above all, however, stands out. EOI strategies have taken over from Import-Substitution Industrialisation (ISI)[4] strategies as the preferred policy option amongst policy-makers in the major financial institutions and many planning ministries around the Third World. As part of this process, basic needs strategies have been largely jettisoned as we can see in current World Bank policy. If World Bank strategy can be taken as the orthodoxy in development thinking, then growth through trade is the orthodoxy of the 1980s.[5] The way such strategies are to be brought about is through the implementation of structural adjustment policies. In this context national adjustment at the state or sub-state level in the Third World is seen as much more important than global adjustment, or more plainly, movement towards a New International Economic Order.

Arguments for a New International Economic Order might have had currency in a situation where notions of 'unequal exchange' were influential; but in a situation where the utility of comparative advantage is reasserted (rhetorically if not empirically), demands for a radical restructuring of the economic order can be pushed to one side. All that is needed, it is argued, is an 'overhaul' of the existing order. Such an overhaul can best be brought about by the implementation of structural adjustment at both a global and a national level. This proposition has been subjected to scrutiny and criticism elsewhere.[6] The policies are most comprehensively outlined, however, in the *World Development Report, 1981* and the World Bank's *Accelerated Development in Sub-Saharan Africa: An Agenda for Action*, both of which present the detailed argued cases for structural adjustment. In essence, and in keeping with the prevailing economic philosophies of the 1980s, 'adjustment' is a code-word for a variety of overlapping actions such as practising fiscal responsibility, controlling inflation and the money supply, pricing reform (a euphemism for devaluation), having a reasonable balance of payments ratio or, to paraphrase the World Bank, restoring the external accounts of developing countries. There are of course, other aspects of an adjustment package, especially diminishing the role of parastatals and encouraging the private sector, as well as the introduction of a variety of austerity measures geared to cutting down public sector expenditure. In simple terms structural adjustment is really about developing countries 'putting their economic houses in order' in a manner similar to that which seems to preoccupy many Western governments in 1980s. The rationale of adjustment is its supposed facilitation of export-led growth.

The 1981 *World Development Report* points to several countries that are model proponents of these policies and which have benefited accordingly. Of middle-income countries, South Korea is the one above all, though not the only one, that has achieved 'spectacular results through export led growth'. Of the primary producing nations with agriculturally based economies, Ivory Coast and Thailand are prime examples of a fairly successful process of diversification of exports to earn foreign exchange for investment in the development of manufacturing industries.[7] In general terms, 'outward' oriented economies are applauded by the *World Development Report* for having been successful during the last decade in responding to dislocations such as those caused by the rapid increases in the cost of energy during the 1970s. While echoing the general themes of the wider report, *Accelerated Development* identifies what it sees as Africa's major problems and the kinds of strategies required for their alleviation. The report highlights a variety of factors which contribute to Africa's current crisis such as over-valued currencies and other exchange rate problems, too restrictive and protective trade policies and a variety of problems in agriculture. More important for our purposes, however, is the overall assessment of the major cause of such specific problems. Rejecting the views so popular in the 1970s, the report shifts the burden of blame from the international environment to the domestic sector - especially the excessive size, and accompanying institutional decay, of the public sector. Again in keeping with what appear to be the sentiments of the times, the best remedy for many of Africa's problems is to 'get government out of the economy'.

It is not the intention here to suggest that the report is wrong in identifying the inadequacies and deficiencies that it does in the public sector in Africa, but rather to suggest that the report's two major recommendations - in essence economic recovery through export-led growth and a diminution of the role of the state in the process of economic development - are not the 'realistic' proposals the report's coordinator suggests.[8] In fact they are 'utopian' assertions that ignore three factors: firstly, the lessons of history concerning the role of the state in economic development - especially in the recent history of the NICs; secondly, they ignore the political imperatives of government in the Third World in general, but of Africa in particular. To ignore such political imperatives is the paradox and irony of current development 'orthodoxy'. As suggested in this chapter, it is reliant, for a variety of reasons - negative and positive - for the possible success of its strategies on the very sector it likes to criticise most. Thirdly, they ignore Africa's structurally subordinate position in the New International Division of Labour - the subject to which this chapter turns first.

## AFRICA AND THE NEW INTERNATIONAL DIVISION OF LABOUR

Africa's present and future incorporation into NIDL is not comparable with that of the states of Asia and Latin America over the last decade.

The prospect (if that is the correct word) of Africa's incorporation extends at best to only a few states – the ones generally held to be 'semi-industrialising'. Inclusion or exclusion from this category can vary from author to author but a general consensus appears to exist over the right of Nigeria, Ivory Coast, Kenya, Algeria and Egypt to be included in this list.[9] Further, it should not be assumed that the incorporation into NIDL of Africa's semi-industrialising states will approximate to that of the process undergone by the NICs of South-east Asia over the last decade.

There is a variety of reasons why Africa would appear to be marginalised from the mainstream of activitiy in NIDL – especially taking into account that a major component of the emergence of NIDL is the export of capital to industrialising areas of the Third World, in contrast to the more traditional pattern of the industrial revolution when labour migrated to the areas of growing industrial activity. Some of the major reasons are as follows:

(a) Africa's relatively small population, spread in patchwork-quilt fashion over 52 countries – 24 of which have populations of less than 5 million – provides a barrier to the realisation of economies of scale.

(b) Africa's political situation is not conducive to investment. Without elaboration at this stage it may be suggested that the weakness of Africa's state structures; the largely anti-capitalist ideological orientation of most of its governments (at a rhetorical level at least); and the high degree of class, ethnic, regional and religious antagonism, all contribute to a degree of political instability which makes Africa a most unattractive proposition to international capital – especially when contrasted with other areas of the developing world.

(c) Africa's colonial legacies also appear to be inhibitors of anything other than a marginal role in the current international political economy. Africa is geographically and historically still primarily bonded with Europe, arguably the weakest section of the industrial North. By the criterion of economic dynamism, Euro-Africa would clearly rank third in any measurement of the world's regional bondings – behind a North America/Latin America pair-bonding in second place and a Pacific Basin, including Japan and South-east Asia, as the current front-runner.

(d) Africa's attractiveness to the international capital required to spur incorporation into the New International Division of Labour is further inhibited *vis-à-vis* areas such as South-east Asia by the current poor state of its infrastructure (ease of access, existence of free ports, proximity to export markets, etc.); tax factors; business climate (especially business morality, effective administration procedures, etc.) and labour factors (availability of managerial and technical staff, skilled and semi-skilled labour, training facilities, prospects for increased labour supply, etc.)[10]

Most of the literature on Africa in the global political economy to date would tend to suggest that the nature of Africa's incorporation still continues to be of the more traditional pattern – as a provider of raw materials rather than as the provider of a labour force for a global process of industrialisation. Yet even this assertion cannot pass without qualification. Nineteen of the world's 29 'least developed' countries and 26 of the 42 'most seriously affected' countries are in Africa. Only a few African states are really attractive propositions as sources of minerals. Whilst Africa does have vast reserves of resources, the technical and socio-political difficulties of delivering these resources to the global economy are such as to minimise the rate of Africa's incorporation in this role. It is unlikely that there will be any significant growth of exploitation and production of other than Africa's fuel resources before the year 2000. Indeed, of all minerals only energy exploitation has increased since the 1960s. Africa's other mineral reserves are not such attractive exploitation propositions as those of North America, Latin America and Australia. Even with resources like oil, exploration in black Africa is still at a 'pre-development studies' stage. Similarly with coal, this 'pre-development' situation makes the prospect of even moderately successful competition with the world's other major producers (Australia, USA, and South Africa) remote. Further, there is in fact a good deal of mythology concerning the abundance of Africa's resources. Africa is not at a particular advantage *vis-à-vis* the rest of the world and whilst the resources are there to 'make substantial African economic development possible . . . they are not easily exploitable'.[11] It would thus be inappropriate to expect other than a marginal incorporation of Africa into the international division of labour as a provider of raw materials – nor, it should be added, are Africa's resources likely to be used for its own economic development in any significant quantities over the foreseeable future.

This gloomy picture is reinforced when we consider the correlation between economic development and the necessity of improving agricultural performance as a percursor to economic development. As

Eicher points out in Chapter 7, African agricultural production can only be described as at 'crisis point'. Not only is Africa unable to feed itself, it has little prospect for the long-term improvement necessary to allow diversification into the areas of industrialisation currently significant to the New International Division of Labour. More important in understanding Africa's subordinate position in the New International Division of Labour, however, is the establishment of industrialisation as a truly global phenomenon, increasingly located in certain previously non-industrialising areas of the world. This position becomes particularly apparent in any *comparative* examination of the post-colonial era in Africa. In contrast to large parts of Asia and Latin America, as Sandbrook asserts:

> industrialisation in tropical African countries has not affected [*sic*] structural transformations of peripheral capitalism. Industrialisation is typically belated, limited in scope, and dependent upon foreign technologies and knowhow. The capitalist mode of production, though dominant, does not displace petty capitalist and non-capitalist forms with which it is interconnected.[12]

Whilst Sandbrook possibly over-states the case for *all* areas, the general pattern he observes would nevertheless seem accurate – especially when contrasted, for example, with the vast structural changes brought about in the NICs of South-east Asia over the last decade or so.

The obvious specific example of this contrast is the still largely undiversified nature of African economies, in which for example agriculture as the primary means of income for 70 per cent of the population produces only 30 per cent of gross domestic product,[13] whilst Latin American and South-east Asian economies increasingly demonstrate processes of differentiation with, for example, the growth of secondary manufacturing and the utilisation of semi-skilled and skilled technologies. Between 1960 and 1976 manufactures as a percentage of all developing country exports grew from 11 per cent to 27 per cent, representing an increase from 6 per cent to 10 per cent of total world manufactures[14] – a not inconsiderable growth. Africa's share of world manufacturing, however, unlike those other regions of the developing world, has not grown since 1960, and in 1973 stood at only 0.6 per cent.[15] By the year 2000 it is estimated that Africa's share of world manufacturing will still only be approximately 1 per cent of the total.[16] It should, of course, be noted that these figures need to be disaggregated. Just as over 50 per cent of developing country manufactures are produced in six countries, namely Hong Kong, Taiwan, South Korea, Singapore, Brazil and Mexico,[17] so too in Africa several states occupy a position disproportionate to all the rest. The 1973 UN *Survey of Economic Conditions for Africa* saw Morocco, Tunisia, Algeria, Kenya, Zaire and Zambia accounting for 75 per cent of Africa's manufacturing output.[18] As Ake has put it in suitably gloomy fashion:

> A country is said to be industrialising when the share of the manufacturing sector of GDP is between 10 and 20 percent . . . for developing Africa as a whole the share of GDP accountable to manufacturing output is only about 11.8 percent, and if we make allowance for the fact that a large share of the manufacturing output is accounted for by a few countries . . . we find that for all practical purposes, Africa falls into the classification of not having started industrialisation.[19]

There are less gloomy analyses than Ake's, but the difference is a matter of degree rather than substance. The World Bank's *Accelerated Development* suggests that some growth in manufacturing has taken place in absolute terms and that future growth is likely, but it has started from a very small base[20] and represents no real inroad into world manufacturing in a manner comparable to that of Asia or Latin America. The Leontieff study, *The Future of the World Economy*, predicts a growth of Africa's share of world manufacturing between 1970 and 2000 of only 0.3 per cent in contrast to 5 per cent for Latin America and 6 per cent for Asia and the Middle East.[21] The exact accuracy of these figures is of less import than the fairly unchallengeable *general* trends they illustrate – namely the bleak prospect of any industrialisation of real significance in Africa comparable to that which has taken place in other developing regions of the world.

It is perhaps worth stressing that it is the *comparative* performance with other regions of the Third World which is the important factor on which to focus for an understanding of Africa's current and future role in the New International Division of Labour. Only a few African states are likely to find a role in the 'semi-periphery' of popular Wallerstein-ian parlance. Those states that do achieve such a position are likely to fill the role of 'sub-imperial' powers. Industrial production in these semi-peripheral states – Nigeria, South Africa, Kenya, for example – tends to be largely for domestic consumption, or consumption by their regional neighbours. In the short to medium run it will also remain largely dependent in its more skilled phases on imports of technology and machinery from the industrial north. To date, however, as Sandbrook points out: 'Production of finished goods for export or of components for assembly abroad is rare.'[22] Most African manufacturing is of light consumer goods, such as beverages for the home markets, or first and second stage processing of Africa's primary produce in rudimentary installations such as ginneries for cotton, mills for groundnuts or palm oil, sawmills for timber and tanneries for leather. There is little or no advanced-technology production of manufactured goods for export such as that which comes from the rapidly growing industries of South-east Asia. In short, African industrialisation to date has largely been import-substitution oriented, not export-oriented. Further, export orientation has been in agricultural produce or raw materials not in manufactures.

Whilst export-oriented strategies may be the order of the day in development policy circles, the prospects for major growth in the manufacturing and processing of capital goods in Africa should not be over-estimated. The inhibiting nature of the inability to achieve economies of scale has already been noted; such problems become particularly acute in those capital industries such as the technological, engineering and chemical industries which have played such an important role in the industrialisation of the NICs over the last decade or so. Similarly, the level of *risk* is higher in more capital-intensive industries than in many of the less technologically reliant forms of industrial activity – and, as suggested in the last section of this chapter, Africa provides a less favourable political environment for investment in these industries than do most of the states of South-east Asia or Latin America.[23] The particular patterns of political development conducive to international investment in industrialisation for the global market are more highly developed in the states of South-east Asia and Latin America than they are in Africa. No African country can give the guarantees against political turbulence that would reassure multinational corporations in a way that is done in South-east Asia's NICs, for example. Most African states are not ripe for incorporation in a manner comparable to the process that has taken place in the NICs. Africa is neither an area of manufacturing potential nor a market capable of competing in any serious way with South-east Asia or Latin America. Nor is Africa likely in the foreseeable future to be other than marginally involved in the commercial interaction of the global economy – an assertion that is reinforced further by an examination of trade.

Again, in comparative terms the African picture is one of decline *vis-*

*à-vis* the other continents of the developing world. The 1970s saw Africa's share of developing country exports fall by half.[24] Unfortunately, this disastrous performance is rather easily explained. Africa's reliance on the export of primary products, at 70 per cent of total exports, is greater than that of any other region in the world – 35 per cent for the Third World generally, 10 per cent for the world as a whole.[25] Over the decade of the 1970s trade in primary products has grown more slowly than that of manufactures generally and, in addition, Africa's trade in primary products has failed to keep pace with that of the rest of the developing world.[26] Reliance on the export of primary products at a time when such exports are falling as an overall proportion of world trade *vis-à-vis* manufactures pushes Africa into an even weaker and more subordinate role in the global political economy.

Further, the decreasing percentage of world trade provided by Africa is becoming concentrated in only a few states. By the late 1970s half of Africa's exports were produced by five countries; this represented an increase from the 43 per cent concentration in 1960.[27] In the short run (over the decade of the 1980s) some of Africa's major primary exports such as copper, cocoa, cotton, groundnuts, groundnut oil, palm oil, timber, tobacco, etc., can be expected to undergo a process of continuing decline. The notable exception to this trend is petroleum and, to a lesser extent, iron ore.[28] Slightly longer term projections (to the end of the millenium) are similarly bleak. Africa may well be more peripheral, more dependent and in greater economic crisis by the end of the current decade than it was in the 1960s.[29]

Current policy options for alleviating Africa's critical position in the global political economy come out of the same intellectual stable as the strategies that have been so popular in South-east Asia over the last decade, but they have a somewhat different emphasis. The chief characteristic of development policy in South-east Asia and Latin America in the era of the New International Division of Labour has been the advocacy of export-oriented industrialisation (EOI) at the expense of import-substitution strategies (ISI). The current strategies for reform in Africa, as epitomised in *Accelerated Development*, are export oriented but concentrating on the agricultural and primary sectors not the manufacturing sector. This is not to suggest that ISI strategies are still not widely pursued in Africa – but rather that the bulk of policy advice advocates export-oriented approaches.

Yet such policy approaches may well have the effect of tying Africa into the lowest rank of the current international division of labour. For want of an alternative, Africa will remain primarily an agricultural and primary materials producer for the global economy, notwithstanding the inherent problems outlined in this strategy. Such manufacturing as is envisaged will be in those secondary areas from which many of the NICs of the 1970s have now graduated – namely those labour-intensive industries such as textiles, from which they are currently turning to more technological areas of manufacturing epitomised in the microchip industry.

Standing in sharp contrast to the kind of export-oriented strategies that are envisaged for Africa, African governments maintain a fondness for the kind of import-substitution industrialisation that has been pursued to date, and which is a powerful force working against major structural adjustment. Post-independence industrialism in Africa has predominately been a child of the multinational corporation; most of this has mirrored production in the industrial mother countries inasmuch as it has been expensive, capital intensive, only tangentially relevant to general African needs and available almost exclusively to the few.[30] As Langdon and Mytelka evocatively suggest, production ranges from: 'Coca-Cola for the satisfaction of thirst to Mercedes cars for the satisfaction of transport needs'.[31]

These kinds of ISI enterprises force domestic capital to compete on unfavourable terms to produce goods similar, but invariably inferior, to those of the multinational corporation. It does not foster outward oriented production in Africa comparable to that which Fröbel *et al.* see in South-east Asia as a source of manufactured goods for the world market. Rather as Langdon and Mytelka suggest, while Africa *is* incorporated into the world economy it is in a subsidiary manner generating few internal linkages or no significant growth of local entrepreneurs via the need for sub-contracting.[32]

For those few African states that do have some prospect of making the shift from ISI to EOI the difficulties should not be underestimated. Several inhibiting factors have been discussed already that are common to all African states, but there are others that will be particularly acute for Africa's would-be semi-industrialising exporters. For those states that attempt to move from ISI to EOI strategies, the search for markets will be crucial. Semi-peripheral, sub-imperial states must inevitably look to their regional neighbours as an outlet for their manufactures. The recent history of South-east Asia, for example, has seen Hong Kong's exporters making major inroads into its ASEAN neighbours. Nigeria's position in West Africa would seem to be one of the few comparable analogies in Africa for the future. Whilst the dynamics of ECOWAS are obviously not mono-causal, Nigeria's growth to a position in 1980 where it provided 46 per cent of black Africa's total output explains, in part at least, Nigeria's keeness for the organisation. As Shaw and Crone have noted, we may well see a process in Africa of 'involuntary regionalism based on a combination of export led industrialisation in the NICs . . . and decline and dependence in the MSAs.'[33]

The prospects of a smooth path to regional integration are not, however, as much of the literature on integration theory tells us, axiomatic. In consequence, the existing vertical linkage with Europe is likely to prove, in the short run at least, more significant for the pursuit of EOI in Africa's semi-industrialising states than its horizontal linkages with regional neighbours. Such EOI as there has been in Africa is in no small part due to the augmentation of Africa's role as a manufacturer of exports for the European market.

The essence of the New International Division of Labour is the increasingly internationalised nature of production and an accompanying role for developing countries in the provision of secondary manufactures. In this context the Lomé Conventions between the EEC and the African, Caribbean and Pacific states play an important role in the integration of Africa into NIDL. Particularly significant in the process are the STABEX provisions of the agreement which, at one and the same time, preserve elements of an old, extractive, division of labour whilst encouraging manufacturing enclaves, producing structural changes in some, though by no means all, African countries. Lomé also paves the way, through a process of preferential treatment, for European multinational corporations to find a major role for themselves in much of what nascent manufacturing industry there is to be found on the African continent. Lomé then is a bridge. It preserves Africa's role as a provider of primary produce and raw materials for Europe, but it also provides a framework within which the types of structural changes inherent in the new division of labour can emerge.[34]

## THE POLITICAL CORRELATES OF THE NEW INTERNATIONAL DIVISION OF LABOUR: AUTHORITARIANISM AND ORDER IN THE PERIPHERAL STATE

The first two sections of this chapter have dealt with the emergence of the New International Division of Labour, and its policy implications and how they have affected Africa. In this last section, working from the assumption that economic behaviour and policy cannot be isolated from socio-political concerns, their political correlates are considered. Discussion will focus on the nature of the peripheral state – perceived by many strategists as the primary vehicle for successful policy implementation.[35] In so doing, there is, perhaps, not a little irony in the fact that advocates of structural adjustment and export orientation are mostly staunch opponents of growing state involvement in the economics of their own societies, yet are not above using the apparatus of the state to foster the necessary political environment for the implementation of policy in developing countries.

Where EOI strategies have been successful in the Third World, especially in the newly industrialising countries of Asia such as South Korea, Taiwan and Singapore, the state has in fact played a very considerable role. In general terms the role of the state has been to supervise and control the allocation of resources in a manner geared to minimising (and preferably cutting) the costs of production for non-public sector capitalist industrialisation processes. Yet advocates of a return to market-oriented strategies suggest that export-led growth *of itself* has been sufficient to bring about the rapid industrialisation of the NICs whilst completely down-playing the role of the state in this process. The 1981 *World Development Report* in its advocacy of EOI strategies and its use of states like South Korea and Singapore as examples of their successful application, says nothing, for example, about the role of the state in this process. Of late in the African context, however, acknowledgement of the role that the state can play has become much more explicit. Roemer, for example, in setting out the case for an export-oriented strategy for the continent, based on an assessment of the successes of South-east Asia, suggests two main roles for the state. Firstly:

> to liberalise the economy . . . to reduce controls and establish, and then maintain, the market environment in which outward oriented strategy might flourish.[36]

Secondly:

> [to provide] support, through government services or investment, for private activities that form the core of the strategy.[37]

Roemer also suggests, without any apparent concern for the essential tension which might exist with his first role, that '*strong* regimes are essential' (emphasis added).[38] The world is full of economists who have advocated 'strong government' as a means of guaranteeing 'liberalisation' without recognising the prospect of it leading to some form of bureaucratic authoritarianism and the polarisation of society akin to a kind of insider/outsider dichotomy in which the insiders, consisting of that growing politico-technocratic elite, exhibit low levels of tolerance for the political demands emanating from the outsiders. This situation has manifested itself at both the level of the academic literature and, of course, at the practical political level in an emphasis on the importance of order and regime maintenance, accompanied by low levels of political participation, as the necessary prerequisites for efficient and rational policy implementation.[39]

While there might be marginal improvement, there would seem no reason to assume that control over the policy implementation process (implementation capability being the ability to get things done as opposed to simply being able to preserve order) in most African states is likely to increase in any dramatic fashion over the next few years. There are many reasons for this, especially the importance of resources (broadly defined) or, more accurately, the lack of them. Perhaps more important, however, to use Myrdal's old but extremely evocative term, is the 'soft' nature of the African state. The notion of the modern administrative state of popular Weberian image is not apt in the African context despite the fact that the state holds a predominant position in society. Despite this position, control of the policy-making and policy-implementing processes proves elusive, and will in all probability continue to prove elusive for some time to come.

Is this pre-occupation with the state at the expense of a reduction in consideration given to other political concerns justified? At this particular historical instance the answer has to be a qualified yes. The case has been argued for the role that the state plays, for better or worse, in the process of regime maintenance. As important as the state's repressive (negative) role however, is its positive role as a motor or spur to economic development. Only the state, it is commonly argued,[40] especially in countries undergoing the first stages of industrial development, can supply sufficient capital requirements for the industrialisation process. This is not to suggest that the state will be able to satisfy these requirements but rather that private capital on its own will inevitably be insufficient. Above all the state will be required to provide the capital for infrastructural development within which, and very probably only within which, private capital will be prepared to participate in the process of industrial development.

Another major reason for expecting the role of the state to be important in the process of economic development relates to the now familiar argument concerning the differences in 'initial conditions' in which developing countries find themselves when compared with the first industrialisers such as Great Britain. The international economic environment is a much more fiercely competitive arena than it was in the first flushes of the industrial revolution. Further, the global division of labour is now horizontal not vertical as it was in the period prior to its 'transnationalisation' over the last few decades. An international economy which operates *across* national boundaries intensifies competition in a manner inconceivable in an earlier period.

To recognise this situation is not, however, to advocate the kind of social closure or 'exit' from the international economy implicit in much dependency theory in the 1970s. The likelihood of success of such a policy option is decidedly slim. Production for 'self-reliance' may in some ways enhance greater autonomy but it is not likely to act as a spur to economic development. The case for trade, or export-led growth, as a path to development is, as Caporaso suggests, 'compelling', especially for small, weak developing countries.[41] He might also have added that this case is argued as forcefully by Marxists as it is by classical growth theorists.[42] Efforts to achieve 'social closure' or 'self-reliance' also have the added impact of cutting access to the kinds of technology that developing countries cannot provide for themselves. Social closure is not likely to lead to development or overcome dependence.

The alternative to rejecting the excesses of the dependency approach does not, however, mean that benefits from outward-oriented strategies are automatic. Although involvement in international exchange does not lead *per se* into greater dependence, the nature of Africa's incorporation into the New International Division of Labour is likely to be of an increasingly asymmetrical nature for the vast majority of its states. Langdon and Mytelka, whilst recognising the possibility of beneficial developmental outcomes from multinational activity, suggest that the processes to date have been detrimental to African development to the extent that they have been disaggregated and piecemeal. The consequence has been to minimise any flow-on effects from this manufacturing for the greater benefit of particular African economies.[43]

A final reason for 'asserting' the fundamental role of the state in peripheral societies in the era of the New International Division of Labour would appear to be that in any relationship between the state and political ideology, the state appears to be the *independent* variable and particular political ideologies the *dependent* variables. The adoption of ideologies ranging along a continuum from capitalism (whatever the variant) to socialism (whatever the variant) can give rise to a variety of forms of political system ranging from what Richard Falk[44] has called Brazilianisation to Leninisation – both types of regime are characterised by elements, to a lesser or greater extent, of the corporate state. More important than ideology in affecting the strength of the state, however, are its origins and its currently perceived indispensability.

The current African state, for example, is quite clearly the product of a mixed parentage. As Crawford Young has recently argued:

> The colonial state had . . . in its genesis and evolution a vocation of domination; the institutions that developed to accomplish this domination composed the quintessential bureaucratic state, staffed by a foreign mandarinate [while] the African capitalist state achieved sovereignty at a time when all modern politics were committed to the welfare state . . . Thus a heavy commitment of the state to the creation of social infrastructure . . .[45]

The combination of this inheritance with post-colonial nationalist and developmentalist fervour ensures the growth of statism.

African governments are as keen as the World Bank to achieve economic growth, but they are unlikely to adopt the kinds of strategies *Accelerated Development* suggests to minimise the role of the state. Again, as Young puts it, with regards to African development:

> no one believes that it can be left to the beneficent workings of the hidden hand. State intervention and leadership are deemed critical by African capitalists as well as socialists. Only the content and orientation of this intervention are at issue.[46]

When coupled with the recognition that it is control of the apparatus of the state that give African regimes their strength, its role in the development process provokes a consensus on the pivotal role of the contemporary state. Irrespective of ideological persuasion, African governments covet the role of recognised intermediary between the international and domestic arenas. It allows incumbents to bargain with international donors on the one hand, and control (to a greater degree than other groups) the distribution of resources domestically on the other hand. For some incumbent groups, control of the state apparatus can be their sole basis of power. For other groups, and these usually tend to be the more stable regimes, control of state power is supplemented by other forms of support, be they regional, ethnic, economic or other forms of loyalty. Having argued the case for the power of the state, the inherent ambiguity of the situation should not be ignored. The argument for the strength and the role of the state in peripheral societies emerges out of weakness. At the international level it is the weakness of the African state within the international political economy which is compelling. At the domestic level it is the weakness of most other institutions that gives the state its power.

## CONCLUDING REMARKS

Several general conclusions can be drawn from this chapter. Firstly, at a theoretical level, the increasingly important role played by the newly industrialising countries in the New International Division of Labour completely overturns the sense of permanency implicit in the 'development of underdevelopment' hypothesis of the more populist dependency literature of the 1970s. Secondly, at a more practical level, the existence of NIDL is a manifestation of international capital's facility for relocation from areas with declining rates of profitability to areas, such as South-east Asia, where the returns are greater.

Whilst Africa's position in this process to date has been marginal, and whilst most of the evidence presented suggests no major reasons for expecting the pattern to change greatly in the short to medium timespan, the recent history of development studies should by now suggest to us that these patterns are by no means immutable. Some African states will, quite clearly, undergo more rapid and beneficial rates of incorporation into NIDL than others. 'Benefits' in this context for Africa's semi-industrialising states do not necessarily mean, however, a greater share of developed country markets. More likely over the long term will be an increasingly powerful role for such states *vis-à-vis* their regional neighbours, or a role for Africa as a new market for other, more rapidly developing states of the Third World in search of alternative market opportunities lost in a recession-hit West.[47]

From the perspective of most ruling elites in Africa the future path is likely to be one of acquiescence in the incorporation process, justified on the grounds that there is more to be gained from collaboration than confrontation with the global political economy. Most African leaders would subscribe wholeheartedly to Joan Robinson's dictum 'the misery of being exploited by capitalists is nothing compared to the misery of not being exploited at all'.[48] It is in this context of the reasonably beneficial nature of the relationship between African ruling and entrepreneurial elites on the one hand, and international capital on the other that we might expect, without over-stating the case, African governments to look sympathetically at suggestions that they attempt to introduce EOI strategies. Despite all the problems and the limited prospects of substantial success, such strategies offer the emerging national bourgeoisies of Africa's regionally powerful states such as Nigeria and Kenya a prospect of generating surpluses in a way that ISI strategies failed to do.

A final conclusion emanates from a paradox highlighted in the last section of the chapter. While the apparatus of the state in Africa is perhaps the most powerful set of institutional arrangements available to Africa's ruling elites, it is still, for the purposes of Africa's rapid incorporation into the New International Division of Labour, too weak. Ironically Africa is not sufficiently authoritarian to guarantee the socio-political requirements of NIDL. For a variety of reasons, regime change in Africa is accompanied by a degree of regularity and unpredictability that does not exist in states such as Brazil or South Korea. Firstly, the primary characteristic of political change in the so-called NICs is a rotating of personnel from within a relatively advanced bourgeoisie. Secondly, this bourgeoisie as a whole, be it of a military or non-military background, is likely to be committed to the preservation of its state's existing structural relationships in the global political economy. In Africa, by contrast, the infant nature of class formation, particularly with regard to the size and strength (or rather the lack thereof) of its bourgeoisies, does not offer such reassurance. Thirdly, given the weakness of Africa's state structures, regime change is not constrained in a manner similar to the NICs of South-east Asia for example, where substantially developed state structures are in existence. Fourthly, the weakness of these structures in Africa does not auger well for the control of a pliable and accommodating workforce comparable to what Cooper has called the 'disciplined battalions of South Korea, Taiwan and Hong Kong'.[49]

While the evolution of the New International Division of Labour has seen a geographical dispersal around the globe of the physical processes of production, their financial control is still to be found in the increasingly concentrated centres of corporate power. It is, as Fröbel *et al.* have indicated, this corporate power which chooses the locations for the processes of production in the New International Division of Labour and which is currently so influential over the global political economy. This chapter has tried to indicate that, whilst Africa's incorporation into this division of labour is in train, the speed of the process is largely undetermined. In the immediate future, however, it seems likely that Africa's lack of attraction *vis-à-vis* many other parts of the Third World is likely to remain unchanged and its subordinate position in the process of incorporation maintained.

## NOTES

1. See F. Fröbel, J. Heinrichs and O. Krev, 'The New International Division of Labour', *Social Science Information*. vol. 17 (1978) no. 1 and *The New International Division of Labour* (Cambridge University Press, 1980). In addition see: A. Leipietz, 'Towards Global Fordism', *New Left Review*, vol. 132 (March–April 1982).
2. The critiques of dependency theory are now too well known for repetition. For a review see R. A. Higgott *Political Development Theory* (London: Croom Helm, 1983) pp. 52–73.
3. See D. Barkan, 'Internationalisation of Capital: An Alternative Approach', *Latin American Perspectives*, vol. 8 (1981) no. 3/4.
4. For a discussion of the changing fortunes of ISI and EOI see R. Leaver, 'Reformist Capitalist Development and the New International Division of Labour', in R. A. Higgott and R. Robison (eds), *Southeast Asia: The Political Economy of Structural Change* (London: Routledge & Kegan Paul, 1985).
5. World Bank, *World Development Report, 1981* (New York: Oxford University Press, 1981) p. 5.
6. See R. A. Higgott, 'Export Oriented Industrialisation, the New International Division of Labour and the Corporate State in the Third World: an Exploratory Essay on Conceptual Linkage', *Australian Geographical Studies*, October 1983.
7. *World Development Report 1981*, pp. 67–71.
8. The coordinator of the report was Professor Elliot Berg of the University of Michigan. In a presentation to the Harvard Institute of International Development (November 1981) Berg argued that he had selected only 'policy economists' to write the report in order to ensure that its recommendations were 'realistic'.
9. See for example T. Shaw and M. Grieve, 'Africa's Future in the Global Environment', *Journal of Modern African Studies*, vol. 16 (1978) no. 1, p. 81; P. Lemaitre, 'Who Will Rule Africa in the Year 2000?' in H. Kitchen (ed.), *Africa: From Mystery to Maze* (Lexington Books, 1976); and I. Zartman, 'Social and Political Trends in Africa', in C. Legum *et al.*, *Africa in the 1980s: A Continent in Crisis* (New York: McGraw Hill, 1979).
10. For a detailed breakdown of such criteria see the 'Guidelines for Investment' in Fröbel *et al.*, *The New International Division of Labour*, pp. 145–7.
11. A. Kamarck, 'The Resources of Tropical Africa', *Daedalus*, vol. 111 (1982) no. 2, pp. 155–63 discusses these issues.

12. R. Sandbrook, *The Politics of Basic Needs* (London: Heinemann, 1982) p. 50.
13. C. Ake, *A Political Economy of Africa* (London: Longman, 1981) p. 98.
14. A. L. Krueger, 'Newly Industrialising Economies', *Economic Impact*, vol. 4 (1982) p. 26.
15. UN, *Survey of Economic Conditions for Africa* (New York: UN, 1973) p. 3-4.
16. W. Leontieff *et al.*, *The Future of the World Economy: A United Nations Study* (New York: UN, 1977), quoted in Shaw and Grieve, 'Africa's Future in the Global Environment', p. 24.
17. UNCTAD, *Recent Trends and Developments in Trade Manufactures and Semi-Manufactures* (UNCTAD TB/B/C.2/175, 11 May 1977).
18. UN, *Survey of Economic Conditions*.
19. Ake, *A Political Economy of Africa*, p. 102.
20. World Bank, *Accelerated Development in Sub-Saharan Africa: An Agenda for Action* (Washington, DC: World Bank, 1981) p. 94.
21. Leontiff *et al. The Future of the World Economy*, p. 37.
22. Sandbrook, *The Politics of Basic Needs*, p. 52.
23. For a discussion of 'risk levels' in Africa, see L. Rood, 'Foreign Investment in Manufacturing', *Journal of Modern African Studies*, vol. 13 (1975) no. 1, pp. 25-31.
24. *Accelerated Development*, Table 3.4, p. 19.
25. Ibid., p. 20.
26. M. Roemer, 'Economic Development in Africa: Performance since Independence and a Strategy for the Future', *Daedalus*, vol. III (1982) no. 2, p. 129. *Accelerated Development* p. 21ff. offers a variety of reasons for Africa's poor performance.
27. Shaw and Grieve, 'Africa's Future in the Global Environment', pp. 19-20.
28. See *Accelerated Development*, Table 3.5, p. 21.
29. See for example, World Bank, *World Development Report 1983* (New York: Oxford University Press, 1983) p. 125 and T. Shaw and D. Munton, 'Alternative Scenarios for Africa' in T. Shaw (ed.), *Alternative Futures for Africa* (Boulder, Colorado: Westview Press, 1982) p. 78.
30. For an excellent discussion and illustrations from states such as Kenya, Senegal, Ethiopia and Nigeria see S. Langdon and L. Mytelka, 'Africa in the Changing World Economy', in Legum *et al.*, *Africa in the 1980s*.
31. Ibid., p. 170.
32. Ibid., p. 173.
33. D. Crone and T. Shaw 'Industrialisaton and Regionalism in ECOWAS and ASEAN: Nigeria and Indonesia Compared' (Mimeo, n.d.) p. 14.
34. See Langdon and Mytelka, 'Africa in the Changing World Economy', pp. 193-8 for an excellent discussion of this process; and John Ravenhill, *Collective Clientelism: The Lomé Conventions and North-South Relations* (New York: Columbia Unversity Press, 1985).
35. For general discussions of these issues see R. A. Higgott, 'The State in Africa: Some Thoughts on the Future Drawn from the Past', in T. Shaw (ed.), *Africa Projected: From Dependence to Self-Reliance by the Year 2000?* (London: Macmillan, 1984) and J. Caporaso 'The State's Role in Third World Economic Growth', *Annals of the American Academy of Political and Social Science*, vol. 459 (January 1982).

36. Roemer, 'Economic Development in Africa', p. 138
37. Ibid., p. 139.
38. Ibid., p. 138.
39. For a discussion see R. A. Higgott 'From Modernisation Theory to Public Policy: Continuity and Change in the Political Science of Political Development', *Studies in Comparative International Development*, vol. 14 (1980) no. 3, pp. 38-43.
40. Caporaso, 'The State's Role', p. 108.
41. Ibid., p. 110.
42. See the arguments in Geoffrey Kay's *Development and Underdevelopment: A Marxist Analysis* (London: Macmillan, 1975) especially the preface.
43. Langdon and Mytelka, 'Africa in the Changing World Economy', p. 201.
44. Richard Falk, 'A World Order Perspective on Authoritarian Tendencies', *Alternatives* vol. 5 (1979) no. 1.
45. Crawford Young, *Ideology and Development in Africa* (New Haven: Yale University Press, 1982) pp. 187-8.
46. Ibid., p. 188.
47. For a discussion of such possibilities see, 'Africa: The Market Scramble', *South* (November 1983) pp. 24-7.
48. J. Robinson, *Economic Philosophy* (Harmondsworth: Penguin, 1976) p. 46.
49. F. Cooper, 'Africa and the World Economy', *African Studies Review*, vol. 24 (1981) no. 2/3, p. 51.

# 12 The Political Economy of African Debt: The Case of Zaire[1]

## THOMAS M. CALLAGHY

### INTRODUCTION: DEBT AND AFRICA'S ECONOMIC CRISIS

As one shrewd analyst of the international political economy has noted, 'Indebtedness among developing countries generates fierce emotions. Anger, anxiety, fear, resentment, jealousy, disdain and discontent – these are strong feelings often associated with debtors and creditors or (for different reasons) with both at once.'[2] President Nyerere of Tanzania has called the IMF a device by which powerful forces in some rich countries increase their power over poor nations. In late 1982, Ghana state radio referred to the IMF as the arch capitalist institution. Subsequently, however, Ghana came to terms with the IMF and performed relatively well, to the pleasure of both. Rhetoric about the IMF and debt played a major role in the Nigerian elections in 1983, and statements about both were used as justification for the military coup d'état of 31 December 1983 which overthrew an elected civilian government. The new military regime subsequently reopened talks with the banks and the IMF.[3]

This wide range of feelings has lately become more apparent in Africa and among a wide variety of actors dealing with Africa. In the context of the world recession, growth rates are down or negative, per capita income figures are nearly stagnant or actually declining, balance of payments and debt service problems become more severe as many commodity prices remain low while oil prices, despite the 'glut' remain high, and in many countries agricultural production levels are falling while aid levels continue to decline. These problems are often exacerbated by inappropriate policies, lax implementation, limited

307

administrative and technical capabilities, and corruption. Because of these conditions, as another astute analyst has noted:

> the stage is set for a decade of battles between African governments and the IMF. There will undoubtedly be mutual exasperation and fatigue – with charges of foreign interference in domestic affairs on the one hand, and countercharges of policy 'slippage,' 'indiscipline', and failure to abide by the agreements on the other.[4]

Debt is a central feature of this economic crisis for a growing number of African countries. It is in part both cause and effect. By 1983 the total debt of sub-Saharan Africa was about $87 billion. In 1974 the total debt was $14.8 billion. The 1983 debt, owed by nearly 40 African countries, accounted for about 13 per cent of the total non-oil developing country debt. The major debtor countries, listed in descending order by size of total debt, are: Nigeria, Zaire, Sudan, Ivory Coast, Zambia, Kenya, Cameroon, Tanzania, Madagascar, Guinea, Gabon, Congo, Ghana, Senegal and Ethiopia. The International Monetary Fund (IMF) estimated the 1982 average debt service ratio for African countries to be about 29 per cent; it was 8 per cent in 1974. By comparison, the average for Latin American countries for 1982 was 53.2 per cent. Individual debt service ratios were much higher, however. In 1983 Sudan's was about 150 per cent, Togo's was about 80 per cent (both before reschedulings that took place later in the year), and for both Uganda and Guinea it was about 40 per cent. By late 1983 the Ivory Coast's debt service ratio was somewhere between 40 and 50 per cent. It was made worse by the strength of the US dollar *vis-à-vis* the CFA franc. As one banker put it, 'the Ivory Coast is repaying money it hasn't borrowed'.[5] By late 1982 almost all African countries were in arrears on debt payments.

In 1978 only two African countries had agreements with the IMF. Between 1979 and 1982, 28 of 48 African countries had at least one standby agreement or extended fund facility (EFF) with the IMF, for a total of 54 programmes. Of these, 45 were standby agreements and nine were EFFs. Eight other countries drew resources from other IMF facilities, bringing the total number of African countries which drew upon IMF resources to 36. In mid-1983 the IMF had 15 programmes in Africa and four under negotiation. Between 1970 and 1978 African countries accounted for 3 per cent of total IMF assistance from standby agreements and EFFs. Africa's share of the total number of IMF programmes during the same period was 17 per cent; it rose to 55 per cent in 1979. African countries have the highest number of repeat agreements with the IMF of any region in the world. In the 1979 to 1982 period, 12 countries had one programme; eight had two programmes; six had three programmes; and two had four programmes. In discussing these programmes, one African IMF official noted that 'in many cases, the performance fell considerably short of the targets' set as the condition for IMF assistance. In some cases, programmes were suspended temporarily or permanently. The same official noted several reasons for poor performance: unforeseen developments, insufficient political commitment, limitations in administrative performance, overoptimistic targets, and delays in inflows of development assistance.[6]

The size of a given country's debt is not the important issue; the ability to service that debt is. Although African debt is very small by world standards, the ability of these countries to service it is very low. Africa's total debt in 1983 was less than that of Brazil alone and only slightly larger than that of Mexico. The low capability of African countries to service their debt loads is clearly reflected in the number and frequency of Paris Club reschedulings, which cover public debt and publicly-insured private bank debt. In 1979 three of the four Paris Club reschedulings were for African countries (Togo, Sudan, and Zaire*); for 1980 two of the three (Sierra Leone*, and Liberia). In 1981 seven African countries rescheduled with the Paris Club: Central African Republic, Liberia*, Madagascar, Senegal, Togo*, Uganda, and Zaire*. In 1982 five countries rescheduled: Madagascar*, Malawi, Senegal*, Sudan*, and Uganda*. For 1983 eight countries went through the process: Central African Republic*, Liberia*, Niger, Senegal*, Sudan*, Togo*, Zaire*, and Zambia [*indicates repeat rescheduling]. Ghana has also rescheduled repeatedly – in 1966, 1968, 1970, and 1974, and may have to do so again in the near future. Zaire has now rescheduled with the Paris Club five times – 1976, 1977, 1979, 1981, and 1983. As a result of the high percentage of repeat reschedulings, the Paris Club countries have quietly, both formally and informally, bent or stretched a number of long-standing norms of the process, particularly in regard to amounts and types of debt rescheduled, the period of debt service covered, the length of grace and repayment periods, and the treatment of previously rescheduled debt. In addition, a number of countries have had to reschedule their uninsured private bank debt, for example: Togo and Zaire in 1980, Sudan in 1981, and Liberia in 1982. As one British banker put it, World Bank structural adjustment lending can also be 'a form of rescheduling without saying so'.[7]

Private bank lending to Africa is way down. Commercial debt has always been a much smaller percentage of total borrowing by African countries than for countries in other regions, ranging on the average from 10 to 40 per cent. In addition, much of this lending has been publicly insured and thus comes under the auspices of the Paris Club for rescheduling purposes. Given the world recession, continued lending to major Latin American debtors, the low level of economic development of most African countries, and their limited administrative capabilities, bankers have not shown a great interest in Africa in recent years. As one American banker put it, 'Africa's not a good risk now. Most US banks are taking a conservative stand.' He also noted that in the past 'we were giving money without paying attention to how it was used.'[8]

The credit ratings of African countries are very much at the bottom end of the world scale. In its September 1982 ratings, *Institutional Investor* ranked Nigeria highest among African states, at 46th out of 107. Next came the Ivory Coast, Gabon, and Cameroon at 61st, 66th, and 68th respectively. Of those countries between 95th and 107th, eight were African. Zaire was 105th, and Uganda last at 107th. For comparative purposes, Mexico was 37th, Brazil 42nd, and Poland 101st. Trade lending by commercial banks continues for most countries, although at a reduced rate, as does well prepared project lending, but general borrowing is very scarce indeed. In addition, the terms of the loans are shorter, the spreads above LIBOR and fees are higher, and much of the lending is at variable interest rates. In 1981 Africa's share of the Euroloan market was only 3 per cent.[9]

Zaire's debt and economic crisis has a long history by now; its situation is much less atypical than many observers originally believed. As a result, the case of Zaire is interesting because of the nature and causes of the crisis, its duration and persistence, the range of external and internal actors involved, and the diverse and often unusual measures that have been attempted to cope with it. The results of these efforts reveal a good deal about the nature of the regime, the ability of external actors to influence it, and the nature of the current international political economy. It also has relevance to various theoretical efforts to understand the nature of international political economy phenomena and the character of political, economic, and social processes in Africa.

## THE POLITICAL ECONOMY OF ZAIRE'S DEBT CRISIS

Zaire was born in the international arena, and it has remained there. International assistance has been a continuous and pervasive factor supporting the emergence, consolidation, and survival of the Mobutu regime in Zaire. Such support was crucial to Mobutu's control of the armed forces from the earliest days, crucial to his first 'coup' in September 1960, and crucial to his seizure of full power in 1965 as an African *caudillo*. It was also important to the emergence and consolidation of a heavily patrimonial authoritarian state with a political aristocracy and to its ability to survive a severe debt crisis and two external invasions in 1977 and 1978. A word of caution is necessary, however, for although external assistance has been essential, it has not been all-determining. The Mobutu regime *would not* exist today without external support, past and present, but its ruler and his political aristocracy have successfully fought off important challenges to their relative autonomy. This chapter focuses on the causes and nature of Zaire's debt crisis, external efforts to cope with it, and how the character of the Mobutu regime has affected these efforts.

Since his earliest days in the turbulent crucible of Zairian politics Mobutu has shown a Machiavellian flare for establishing and manipulating shifting coalitions of support, both internally and externally. Other states and business interests within them, international organisations such as the IMF and the World Bank, private international banks, transnational corporations, and groups such as the Catholic Church all have complex, shifting, and often competing sets of economic, politico-strategic, and normative interests to pursue in the Zairian arena. The interstices created by these multiple sets of interests often permit some room for manoeuvre, some autonomy for the ruler and his political aristocracy. Thus Mobutu and his ruling class have maintained a significant degree of relative autonomy; external influence clearly has its limits.

Therefore, there is first a need to posit theoretically the relative autonomy of the African state, not to deny its possibility. Then it is imperative to investigate the degree to which it exists in each case, especially since the degree of autonomy will vary over time as a result of a complex interplay of internal *and* external socio-economic *and* politico-strategic forces. Both the importance *and* the limits of external influence and action need to be stressed, as well as the complex interrelationships between the politics of sovereignty and statecraft, class formation, and the behaviour of external actors. Despite its great dependence on powerful external actors, it is argued here that the Mobutu regime has been able to maintain an amazing degree of relative autonomy, and that this is possible due to the patrimonial nature of the Zairian state, the non-productive characteristics of its ruling class, the way various external actors define their interests, and their inability to coordinate their positions sufficiently and over a long enough timespan to make a real difference.

The Zairian regime is an authoritarian state organised around a presidential monarch who adopted the Belgian colonial state structure and patrimonialised it by creating an administrative monarchy which was then used to recentralise power. In this state, patriarchal patrimonialism, which Weber defined as mass domination by one individual, and patrimonial forms of administration, mixed with bureaucratic ones, are both salient characteristics. But Mobutu's kingdom has distinctly limited capabilities. Old forms and structures of authority continue to operate. Mobutu has increased his personal discretion beyond the confines of both traditional (pre-colonial) restraints and modern, legal ones, but has used elements of both for legitimation purposes. He has appropriated the coercive, administrative, and financial means to increase his power. He has used police and military forces and a cadre of territorial administrators or prefects to control all key societal groups via the corporatist elements of the single party, the Popular Movement of the Revolution (MPR), and to emasculate the power of all traditional and quasi-traditional intermediary authorities.

Mobutu's ruling group in Zaire is a political aristocracy because its basic values, its power, and its economic base result from its relationship to the state. The term 'political aristocracy' is preferred, rather than the more common 'national bourgeoisie' or 'bureaucratic bourgeoisie', because, in its historical sense, the term bourgeoisie connotes a productive social class which most African ruling classes are not. The ruling class in Zaire certainly is not, and, as a result, it badly needs external resources and assistance to stay in power. Nor is it a 'national middle class'; it is the top class, the ruling, dominating one. In its style of life and actions, it more closely resembles a political aristocracy.

The patrimonial nature of this state and the unproductive character of its political aristocracy make the regime both more dependent on external actors *and* more able to resist their demands and intrusions. Zaire's severe debt crisis illustrates that Mobutu and his political aristocracy can fend off significant efforts by external actors to change the policies and very structure of the regime without foregoing continued support. Likewise, the failure of externally-induced political liberalisation and military reorganisation efforts after Shaba I in 1977 indicates that Mobutu and his political aristocracy can also fend off political and military demands by external actors, again without jeopardising crucial support to the regime.

The international system operates to maintain the basic integrity and boundaries of a state as they were agreed upon at the time of independence. Powerful actors in the international system can also work to maintain a particular leadership in power or to work to replace it, but the power of actors in the international system is much more restricted at the level of state structure and process, that is, the total set of operative norms and structures that characterise the polity. In short, it is possible to keep a state together; it is even possible to dictate who rules it; but it is very difficult to effectively dictate, even influence in *major* ways the structure and process of a country. The Mobutu regime emerged in Zaire as a result of the complex interplay of internal and external political, economic, socio-cultural, historical, personal, and idiosyncratic factors. Altering its basic structure is extremely difficult.

Mobutu has, however, acquiesced, at least superficially, to a number of externally-oriented changes in order to increase his external legitimacy with Western states (and *their* domestic and international constituencies), international organisations, and banks and to acquire additional resource flows from them. But he has gone only as far as was necessary to obtain such support, and when events changed or the composition of the support coalition could be altered, he has backed off from changes that did not suit his needs or desires. In the process his regime has remained intact and in power, at least so far. The core of the absolutist state – Mobutu's personal discretion and the power of the political aristocracy – remains. It does so in large part due to the assistance of external supporters, but despite their efforts to induce change in the nature and structure of this state. The interplay of a multiplicity of economic and political factors and actors at multiple levels may provide interstices within which individual regimes can manoeuvre and achieve relative, but fluctuating, autonomy from both internal and external groups.

This authoritarian and rather ineffective patrimonial regime clearly served many of what might be called neo-colonial economic interests (but also politico-strategic ones) from 1965 until the onset of the severe economic and fiscal crisis in 1975. Since then several different types of actors in the international system have attempted to change the very nature of the regime, with minimal results so far. At the same time, and for a variety of reasons, some of the major actors fear the politico-strategic and economic consequences of any attempt to replace the current authorities. From the logic of the neo-colonial position, it might be possible to argue that if 'foreign capital' – merchant, industrial, financial or whatever – had been able to structure the Zairian regime freely, it would have designed something quite different from the regime that now exists, or that it would be able to restructure the regime now. The Soviets may now be learning some of these same lessons in Africa, particularly in regard to the difficulties of creating viable Leninist transformation regimes in Angola, Mozambique, and Ethiopia.[10]

## Patrimonial Rule and Financial Crisis

The Achilles' heel of the Mobutu regime is finance. This issue is directly linked to the existence of patriarchal patrimonial rule, the activities of the political aristocracy, and the early modern nature of the state and economy. Financial chaos highlights the distinct limits, precarious nature, and intensely patrimonial character of this regime. It also reveals a good deal about the way external actors relate to it. The Zairian financial system is the weakest point of the regime; in fact, 'system' is too strong a word because Zairian finances have very little order and clarity, even approximate. 'Systematic disorder' is more the norm. Zaire is a wealthy country, one of the most well-endowed in Africa, but it is now on the verge of financial collapse – an increasingly common condition for African regimes.[11]

The Zairian state has a large 'royal' revenue, but it has a weak, inefficient, and massively corrupt financial structure, especially its revenue collection and distribution system. Zaire's rulers cannot understand how they can be in such desperate financial straits when such large sums of money pass through their hands. The country also has an early modern economy. Its economic health varies greatly over time, and, like most of the patrimonial administrative states of early modern Europe, it operates in a period of great 'economic difficulties, suffering both from sudden, violent crises and from phases of stagnation, and of deep depression'.[12]

Mobutu and his political aristocracy have an insatiable desire for more revenue, but they also have a basic ambivalence to this crucial resource. The revenue collected by the state belongs to them, and they should be able to spend it as they see fit. Mobutu is a political, not an economic man. He knows that power and glory depend on money, but for much of the time he is willing to leave the 'details' of acquiring and managing it to others. This ambivalence toward the practical realities of finance is another core chracteristic of patrimonialism and in large part accounts for the shakiness of this crucial pillar of the Zairian state. The costs of power, order, defence, glory, grandiose projects and life styles, and the inherent corruption and largesse of a patriarchal patrimonial regime have proved to be almost too much for Zaire, especially its mass of 'citizens' – subjects, in fact.

Two major things happen as a result of these characteristics: (a) reliance on extraordinary financial measures, and (b) rash and extensive borrowing leading to huge debts and near bankruptcy. The extraordinary measures, numerous and often quite intensive, include shady forms of borrowing, extortion, confiscation, debasing currency, and the operations of foreign businesses and financiers. In fact, the extraordinary measures are almost 'normal' practice. In this regard Weber noted that:

> The patrimonial state offers the whole realm of the ruler's discretion as a hunting ground for accumulating wealth. Wherever traditional or stereotyped prescription does not impose strict limitations, patrimonialism gives free reign to the enrichment of the ruler himself, the court officials, favorites, governors, mandarins, tax collectors, influence peddlers, and the great merchants, and financiers who function as purveyors and creditors.[13]

'Corruption', as Vansina notes, 'is the prime mover in shaping both differences of wealth and class attitudes.' This 'economy of grabbing' has its roots in the horrors of King Leopold's Congo Free State and has been aided and abetted by many of the expatriates who have dealt with the Mobutu regime. One result of these activities, especially in conjunction with structural economic difficulties, is financial crisis. One high state official, speaking of Mobutu, has noted that 'when you are head or leader of a dictatorship, a regime like his, you have to make some corruptions inside and abroad to maintain people loyal, and for that you need some money.' He also pointed out that 'the big victim of this institutionalised corruption remains, without a doubt, the Zairian people.' In 1982, for example, malnutrition for infants under five years was reportedly as high as 45 per cent. Some Zairians refer to the children in Kinshasa's Cité as the 'lost generation', particularly in reference to nutrition levels, quality and availability of health care and education, and any likelihood of eventual employment.[14]

The financial condition of the Zairian state in the late 1960s and early 1970s was excellent, particularly because of the high price of copper which accounted for about two-thirds of Zaire's foreign exchange. The price of copper peaked at $1.40 per pound in April 1974, but began to turn down in May and June. It declined to as low as $0.53 by late 1975; in 1976 it had stabilised in the mid-sixties. By early 1976 Zaire was in the middle of a grave economic and financial crisis which 'pushed the state to the brink of international bankruptcy, and the Mobutu regime to the brink of disaster'.[15] As the 1980s approached, Zaire was nearly $5 billion in debt and on the verge of economic collapse. The percentage breakdown by category was as follows: IMF, 3.1 per cent; World Bank and other international organisations, 8.7 per cent; bilateral credits, *including* publicly-insured private bank loans, 75.8 per cent; uninsured bank debt, 11 per cent; and uninsured commercial debt, 1.4 per cent.[16] Due to their non-productive nature, Mobutu and his political aristocracy need the resources and assistance provided to them by Western governments, the International Monetary Fund, the World Bank and private international banks but cannot afford to comply fully with their demands to reform. To implement the bureaucratic changes demanded by these actors would undermine the very basis of their power – access to and free use of the state's resources. As a result, Mobutu and his political aristocracy use their control of the state apparatus to sabotage change while manipulating the external actors' partially competing interests and fears about the consequences of a collapse of the regime to fend off effective and sustained cooperation between them.

There were multiple causes of this crisis: the dramatic fall in copper and other commodity prices; the closure of the Benguela Railroad since the Angolan civil war in 1975–76; the disastrous economic effects of the Zairianisation moves (1973–75); rising oil costs, and a world recession. This situation was compounded by the Shaba invasions in 1977 and 1978. As serious as these factors were, however, they are far from the whole story. All of these conditions were made far worse by other factors. Political factors were very important, and they relate directly to the patrimonial nature of the state: massive and rash spending and borrowing when revenues were high, rampant corruption and fiscal mismanagement, grandiose and unproductive development schemes such as the Inga-Shaba powerline and the Maluku steel mill, the almost total neglect of agriculture and of the transportation and productive infrastructure, and lack of understanding and concern about the rapidly deteriorating situation by Mobutu and the political aristocracy. As one observer puts it, 'the top government leadership has traditionally known nothing of or cared little for economics, and this shows.'[17] And, of course, the effects of Zairianisation and the massive pre-1974 borrowing can be considered the result of political factors as well.

Mobutu has borrowed extensively and often rashly, and he has been able to do so because of Zaire's vast potential wealth. The debt of the

Zairian patrimonial administrative state has reached important proportions by African standards, and the country is on the verge of bankruptcy. Between 1967 and 1973, Zaire's external public debt quintupled; in 1972 alone it doubled to $1.5 billion. At first the government tried to hide the actual amount of debt service payments, but in the first half of 1973, actual payments exceeded 80 per cent of the budget estimates for such payments for the entire year.[18]

In early 1975, an American embassy economic officer reported that Zaire did not even have a roughly accurate list of how much it owed and to whom.[19] The World Bank and the United Nations finally provided personnel to try to sort things out. The figures were staggering. By 1977 the total debt was estimated at over $3 billion; debt service payments were the equivalent of 43.4 per cent of export earnings and 49.5 per cent of total state revenue.[20]

Mobutu goes to great lengths not to repay his debts, except with new debts. Borrowing *and* non-payment of debts are central features of the Zairian state. Mobutu knows that lending is a two-way street, and he has shrewdly played the debt repayment game by attempting to manipulate slightly shifting coalitions of external actors, and the financial, economic and politico-strategic interests they seek to protect and expand. One observer notes that 'once banks have extended substantial sums to borrowers, they are, for all practical purposes, committed to the borrower through thick and thin . . . traditionally, when nations were unable to meet their payments they have rescheduled their public debts and refinanced their private ones.'[21] Mobutu is managing his dependence for survival, however, not for economic development or the welfare of the mass of Zairians. Given the severity of Zaire's situation, Mobutu and his political aristocracy have done amazingly well so far in this game of brinkmanship. They may not understand the finer technicalities of the international financial system, but they do understand the politics of international finance:

> The very bonds of economic dependency have been used with virtuosity. The regime adroitly trades on the premise that its creditors cannot afford either to see it fall, or to see Mobutu fall. Bankruptcy would be as inconvenient for the banks (and Western governments) as for Zaire; at each negotiating brink, a temporizing formula is found, the debt rolled over one more time, while all await the millenium of higher copper prices.[22]

Thus far, the Zairian political aristocracy has adroitly blocked all efforts by international lenders to control its financial practice. The record on this point is very clear.

Under the International Monetary Fund and other external pressure and guidance, Mobutu and his government put together five stabilisation plans, the 'Mobutu Plans', the first in March 1976, the second in November 1977, the third in August 1979, the fourth in July 1981, and the fifth in December 1983. In each case, Zaire entered into a standby or EFF agreement with the IMF which pledged substantial standby credit (SDR 912 million, about $1.2 billion, for the fourth one, a three-year EFF). The plans reflected the IMF's conditions and aimed to cut corruption, rationalise expenditures, increase tax revenues, limit imports, boost production in all sectors, improve the transportation infrastructure, eliminate arrears on interest payments, make principal payments on time, and generally improve financial management and economic planning. Zaire's public and publicly-insured debt has also been rescheduled by the Paris Club countries five times, in 1976, 1977, 1979, 1981, and 1983. Zaire's private creditors rescheduled their part of the debt in April 1980, and eight World Bank and Western country aid consortia meetings were held to generate larger official assistance (one in 1977, two in 1978, and one each in 1979, 1980, 1981, 1982, and 1983).[23] Without this international support the regime might well have collapsed, but the countries and the banks felt they could not afford to let it do so for both economic and politico-strategic reasons.

### Actors: The Government of Zaire

The government of Zaire had no clear understanding of what it had agreed to do when it signed the first two standby agreements with the IMF in 1976 and 1977, and no intention of living up to the agreements. Given the gravity of Zaire's situation, the degree to which the government could have fully lived up to the agreements is not clear; but since no real effort was made, it is impossible to tell. President Mobutu and his political aristocracy do not view international organisations and aid agencies as sources of development assistance but rather as channels for access to more resources, particularly foreign exchange.

In an assessment of this early period, the World Bank noted that 'through 1978, the Government's response to the crisis was for the most part *ad hoc*'. It pointed to 'the inherent weaknesses of Zairian institutions' which 'interfered with investment selection, debt management, allocation of foreign exchange, implementation of projects, distribution of commodity assistance, and monitoring of the economy.' Corruption was identified as a primary factor. The Bank noted 'the spread of corruption despite condemnation by the highest political authorities' and that 'many government employees are neglecting their official duties in order to pursue other work to supplement their income.' This included 'the incentive to smuggle' which 'outweighed the ability to control such practices.' One crucial consequence of these phenomena was that 'the crisis has seriously aggravated the economic and social conditions of the Zairian population.' The Bank concluded that 'the enormous constraints demand nothing less than a fundamental revamping of institutions and of the system of incentives.'[24]

In addition to the issue of political will, there remains the question of the administrative capability of the regime. It has been plagued by intra-governmental disorganisation, lack of coordination, political and personality conflicts, massive corruption, and a lack of sizeable numbers of technically qualified personnel. The government takes many policy decisions, but they are rarely implemented coherently or for any length of time, if at all. There have been major jurisdictional and policy squabbles between the Presidency, the Central Bank, Finance, and OGEDEP (the debt administration office created in 1976). Zaire did not have any rational debt service policy. Early on even very basic debt data often did not exist, was inconsistent, or uncoordinated. For example, principal and interest figures were often confused or one administrative unit's figures did not match those of another or did not add up, and there was no idea what the total of the debt was or to whom money was owed.

There was never any coherent advance planning concerning debt payments; payment policy was *ad hoc* and uncoordinated. Payments were rarely made on time or in the complete amount. Much debt service was the result of the *ad hoc* exercise of personal discretion by key regime officials. The efforts of external actors at improving the government's 'managerial' capabilities, including such basic things as determining how much is owed, to whom, and when it is due, have had a marginal positive impact. In 1976 the World Bank provided personnel who attempted to compile relatively accurate debt figures; in 1979 Zaire's newly-hired investment bank advisors undertook a similar effort and discovered substantial additional debt. OGEDEP and other administrative units use computers, but their use has made no major headway in overwhelming the practices of patrimonial administration. In fact the computers have been used creatively in several major pay scandals. Putting patrimonial data into computers produces patrimonial rather than bureaucratic results.

*Africa in Economic Crisis*

Zaire does have a number of competent and dedicated people who, with proper political will and protection, could work to *ameliorate* Zaire's situation. There are clear indications, however, that these people, for good political and personal reasons, are not willing to take 'sensitive' actions. The word ameliorate is used intentionally here because the severity of Zaire's situation especially when combined with the effects of the world recession, is such that there are distinct limits to what can be done under current conditions, even assuming political will.[25]

Beyond the short-term financial and debt servicing difficulties of the regime lie some even more severe problems. The Mobutu regime appears to have a neo-mercantilist 'bullion' fixation, i.e. a pre-occupation with foreign exchange and how to get it quickly and in large amounts. Linked with this is a lack of understanding of the real long-term underpinnings of the economy and, above all, of the necessity of patterned, sustained, substantial, and serious medium- and long-term investment in key sectors of the economy to maintain current levels of production, much less increase and diversify them. In 1981, the IMF noted that 'Zaire's present economic and financial difficulties stem largely from inadequate economic management ... In particular, investment policies tended to neglect agricultural development as well as much-needed improvement in transportation and other supporting infrastructure.'[26] It is a fixation on money as a source of wealth, a failure to see savings, investment, and production as the ultimate sources of wealth and growth. These perspectives have been readily apparent in the on-going discussions on the relationship between SOZACOM and GECAMINES, especially over the control of the latter's foreign exchange earnings. Similar characteristics have been common to patrimonial regimes historically, a topic discussed in more detail below.

### Actors: Expatriate Teams

Since the results of the first two stabilisation plans were so meagre, the IMF and the World Bank decided in 1978 to send their own teams of experts to Zaire to take over key financial positions in the Bank of Zaire, the Finance Ministry, the Customs Office, and Planning. As one Zairian commentator dryly put it, 'Certain of the economc policy measures that were taken curiously produced results other than those anticipated.'[27] In December 1978, the head of the Bank of Zaire team, Erwin Blumenthal, a retired German central banker, took dramatic measures which struck at the heart of the power of the political aristocracy. He cut off credit and exchange facilities to firms of key members of the political nobility, including several of Mobutu's closest collaborators, and imposed very strict foreign exchange quotas. Since President Mobutu needs the foreign exchange to keep the warring elements of the political aristocracy in line, this appeared to be a major threat. Foreign exchange and other financial resources constitute the glue that holds the system together.

Many Zairians viewed the expatriate teams as a crude form of neo-colonialism, and they began to refer to Blumenthal as *Bula Matari* – 'he who breaks rocks'. It was a term used during the colonial period for Belgian administrators. From the side of international capitalism, the teams were an attempt to bring some rational order to the chaos of Zairian 'mismanagement'. In large measure, the teams were an effort to create and 'buffer' from political pressure a 'technocratic core' of competent Zairian officials. In this regard, Weber noted that 'in general we can say about capitalism only that, since its opportunities for expansion are limited under . . . patrimonialism, its champions usually attempt to substitute bureaucratization.'[28] The bureaucratic was to do battle with the patrimonial.

Efforts to impose budgetary control over the Presidency and the military have been for the most part delayed or circumvented, however, and ways were usually found around the foreign exchange controls. As Blumenthal noted, 'There just is no effective control over the financial transactions of the Presidency; one does not differentiate between official and personal expenses in this office . . . All endeavors to improve budgetary control in Zaire had to stop short before the operations of the central governing authority: la Presidence!'[29] In addition, Nguza Karl-i-Bond, a former prime minister, charged from exile that Mobutu himself had siphoned off substantial amounts of IMF and World Bank assistance. After his return to power in 1979, largely at the behest of Western creditor countries and banks, Nguza quickly discovered that 'any effort to implement the IMF program of reforms would inevitably lead to confrontation with the personal interests of the President'. He said, 'I found Mr Blumenthal totally discouraged' and asserted that 'Mobutu intentionally undermined my efforts and those of my colleagues.'[30] Blumenthal himself described 'how gradually the possibilities of control, of intervention were wrested from the IMF team, its cooperation with honest Zaireans inside the bank destroyed, my personal influence diminished, the position of the Central Bank within the administration damaged, its independence threatened.'[31]

The valiant efforts of the various internationally-sponsored teams at the Bank of Zaire, the Office of Debt Management, Customs, Finance, and Planning have been distinctly limited in their impact. The manoeuvres of Mobutu and his political aristocracy to detour the controls have been creative, persistent and, to a substantial degree, successful. After Blumenthal's attempt to impose controls on foreign exchange, Mobutu and those around him put substantial pressure on a variety of foreign and domestic actors to provide foreign exchange, legally or illegally. They included local and foreign banks, expatriate businessmen of a variety of nationalities, and SOZACOM (the parastatal minerals marketing organisation) and GECAMINES. In regard to the latter two, Belgian bankers played a particularly important role.[32]

The political aristocracy has both systematically harassed and 'worn down' the teams over time. For example, Blumenthal recounted how 'at the end of January 1979 one evening (around 7 p.m.), when I was still in the bank, soldiers of General Tukuzu (father-in-law of Bofossa), threatened me with submachine guns when they could not get their hands anymore on the head of the foreign department where they wanted to demand foreign exchange for their general.'[33] Toward the end of his one year stay in Zaire, Blumenthal reportedly slept with a shotgun under his bed and had a radio that kept him in contact with the West German and American embassies, with the US Marines in particular. The teams change composition frequently and are often difficult to recruit, and the personnel are few in number. They are not substitutes for domestic political will and administrative capability. As one expatriate banker told me, 'The leakages of foreign exchange have simply been pushed further upstream.'[34] At best the expatriate teams are supplements. Blumenthal stated that it is:

> alarmingly clear that the corruptive system in Zaire with all its wicked and ugly manifestations, its mismanagement and fraud will destroy all endeavors of international institutions, of friendly governments, and of the commercial banks towards recovery and rehabilitation of Zaire's economy. Sure, there will be new promises by Mobutu, by members of his government, rescheduling and rescheduling again of a growing external public debt, but no (repeat: no) prospect for Zaire's creditors to get their money back in any foreseeable future.[35]

The patrimonial was giving the bureaucratic a good drubbing. After Blumenthal's departure in 1979, the expatriate teams were more careful to avoid the 'political hot spots', as one expatriate official put it.[36] It was a way of keeping the level of harassment at manageable levels, particularly in regard to the Presidency and the military.

## Actors: The Western Governments

The Western governments only began to realise the seriousness and structural nature of Zaire's economic and fiscal crises after Shaba I in 1977. The early preoccupation had been with politico-strategic concerns, particularly in regard to the situation in Angola. The economic and fiscal crises were, of course, aggravated by the two invasions of Shaba Region and their aftermath. The proper economic and fiscal information and analysis was apparently being reported to Western governments, but the perceptual frameworks of those making policy tended to play down the seriousness of the situation, in particular by seeing it as merely another of the periodic downswings which would be ameliorated by a rise in commodity prices and other factors. This perspective was also held by the government of Zaire and the banks.

Western governments have partially and often fitfully coordinated their efforts to get Zaire to service its debts, control its expenditures, diminish corruption, take hard economic decisions and implement them, and undertake badly needed 'managerial' reforms. They have rescheduled its public and publicly-insured debt five times via the Paris Club mechanism. They have also helped to generate additional assistance for Zaire from a variety of sources. Given their influence on the IMF and the World Bank, their constant diplomatic presence in Kinshasa, and the fact that 43 per cent of the roughly $3 billion debt rescheduled under Paris Club auspices is guaranteed private bank debt, Western governments are very dominant actors in the external efforts to cope with Zaire's debt crisis. The other major actor is the IMF, with the banks playing a much more minor role.

Charles Lipson has asserted that 'the most distinctive element of the debt regime is the peripheral role played by capital-exporting states', and, thus, that 'the supervision of debt has largely been a function of commercial banking arrangements and the IMF's conditional lending'. He claims that the apparatus for 'the supervision of sovereign debt' is 'a structure built not on state power but on private sanction and multinational oversight' and that 'these arrangements are distinctive among international economic regimes'.[37] As the case of Zaire shows, however, state actors play a central role in the debt regime *vis-à-vis* African, and arguably, other Third World states. This results from their control of the Paris Club mechanism, participation in consultative group meetings, and direct and indirect influence with the IMF, World Bank, and the private banks. This is not to say an international debt regime is state-dominated in all cases, but it is certainly heavily influenced by state actors. Interestingly enough, Lipson's characterisation is similar to some Marxist views of LDC debt which also play down the role of the state, seeing the banks as the prime movers on their own and as the key force behind the IMF. This greatly under-estimates the complex interplay of actors and of politico-strategic, economic, public, and private interests in debt cases. In Latin America, state actors appeared more peripheral until real systemic interests came into play in 1982, at which point they directly asserted their influence.

The Western governments, however, have also on occasion worked at cross purposes, as their interests and perceptions are not identical. For example, there was a major battle between the Belgian and French governments over the choice of Blumenthal's successor at the Bank of Zaire, with the IMF caught in the middle; it was an important battle over potential influence.[38] This holds true between elements of each Western government as well, as it does with the IMF, the World Bank, the private banks, and between each of them. This fact has given Mobutu and those around him some room to manoeuvre. The desire for and commitment to change and reform varies from government to government, and ebbs and flows within each Western government as administrators and policy-makers change. Mobutu has taken good advantage of these changes and lapses of attention.

### Actors: The Investment Bank Advisors

In August 1979 Zaire hired a multinational 'triumvirate' of investment banking firms – Lazard Frères, Lehman Brothers, Kuhn Loeb, and S. G. Warburg. For very high fees, they performed the following tasks: assessed the actual size and structure of Zaire's debt; compiled a series of useful information memoranda; assisted Zaire in two Paris Club reschedulings (1979 and 1981) and in several consultative group or donor club meetings; advised on and helped to guide the complex negotiations for the London Club private bank rescheduling in 1980; and dealt with the IMF, the World Bank, Western governments and private banks in an on-going, albeit informal, way.

Given this broad and important list of functions, it is not surprising that the 'triumvirate' or 'holy trinity' occasionally became involved in sensitive political issues, both in Zaire and at the international level, and that, in the process of carrying out its tasks, it created tensions with a number of Zairian and external actors. At one point, the triumvirate, in conjunction with Central Bank Governor Emony, proposed removing the IMF-sponsored expatriate teams and replacing them with French teams under the supervision of Lazard Frères. President Mobutu reportedly agreed to the scheme and actually drafted a letter to the IMF. Western governments found out about the scheme, including the French government which apparently had not been consulted, and it was never implemented. The Belgians in particular viewed the triumvirate as a 'Trojan horse' for French interests, and to a lesser extent American and British ones.[39]

Many private bankers also viewed the triumvirate sceptically, particularly because of the possible abuse by the three firms of sensitive inside information. The banks also felt that the triumvirate did not give the banks enough information to enable them to make sound decisions and that it tried to play them off against each other in regard to efforts to refinance missed payments on the London Club agreement. Some tension was also generated because the triumvirate apparently advised Zaire to delay payments on the London Club agreement. As one banker put it in reference to Zaire's payment situation. 'It's like trying to squeeze blood from a turnip.'[40]

Tension between Western governments and the triumvirate arose over the negotiation of bilateral agreements following the 1979 and 1981 Paris Club rescheduling. Several Zairian officials and members of the expatriate teams also believed that the triumvirate's presence stunted the development of trained Zairian cadre to cope with the debt crisis. Because of incidents such as these, some governments, private banks and officials of international organisations resented its role, influence, and fees. On the whole, however, the triumvirate was seen to fulfill useful functions.[41]

In October 1982, several months after the IMF had suspended its 1981 EFF with Zaire for non-compliance, the triumvirate severed its contract with Zaire in large part because of the intransigence of its ruler and key elements of the political aristocracy. It felt that the task was too daunting and that its reputation was being damaged. One can argue that Mobutu and the political aristocracy used the triumvirate quite consciously to provide international 'management' cover or legitimacy behind which they could continue to pursue their own narrow personal and class interests. There certainly were many instances when the Zairians did not accept or follow the advice of their investment bank advisers.

## Actors: The Commercial Banks

There is general agreement, even by many bankers themselves, that the banks loaned money to Zaire unwisely, in too large amounts, and without any clear indication of what they were getting into. General agreement also exists that a 1976 Memorandum of Understanding with Zaire, which was essentially a Citibank-led rollover effort that eventually failed, was a mistake. Despite the fact that it, at least temporarily, preserved Zaire's credit-worthiness, it helped to delay driving home the seriousness of the country's situation to the government of Zaire (and to the bankers themselves, for that matter). In the end, the bankers had to reschedule Zaire's uninsured private debt in the April 1980 London Club agreement. The delay in arriving at this point resulted in part from the banks' desire to let the Western governments and international organisations reschedule Zaire's public debt (including the publicly-insured private bank debt) and provide much-needed 'adjustment' assistance, thereby leaving more foreign exchange available to service the uninsured private debt. In fact, the banks' repayment ratio has been ten times that of the public creditors. This tendency was reinforced by the banks holding out the enticement of further lending – much of it to individual members of the political aristocracy, however, rather than to the state.

Zaire's problems have been with the banks (and all the other actors) for quite some time now, and since the summer of 1982 the attention of the bankers has been distracted by much more serious situations, such as those of Brazil, Mexico, Argentina, and Poland. This is reinforced by the fact that the *uninsured* private bank debt, which is divided among 122 banks, totalled only about $513 million in early 1982, quite small compared to the uninsured amounts owed by Brazil, Mexico, Poland, etc., and the London Club agreement in April 1982 rescheduled $402 million of this amount. The bankers' concern for the overall health of the international financial system is much more apparent now than it was in April 1980 when they wanted to make an example out of Zaire. Most of the bankers are now bored with Zaire. After listing the various efforts to help Zaire sort out its problems, one European banker declared, 'What more can we do?'[42] What they have been doing is keeping the pressure on Zaire to stay current with the London Club payments, but being quietly flexible when circumstances dictate. And, since the April 1980 agreement, many of the banks have been quietly writing-down Zaire's debt. American banks have been under some pressure by the bank examiners to reclassify the loans. Some of the big banks, Belgolaise and Citibank, for example, are still making money in Zaire via private and correspondence banking transactions, 'access maintenance' lending to key members of the political aristocracy, loans for various trading ventures, and real estate. But no major balance of payments, project, or medium-term trade lending is being extended to Zaire.[43]

## A Patrimonial Regime and External Reform Efforts

The formal or expressed willingness of Mobutu and his political aristocracy to take effective measures comes and goes. It comes only with substantial and coordinated external pressure and when regime officials perceive that, for the moment at least, they have no other alternatives. It ebbs dramatically when external pressure eases or is worn down, when disputes between external actors can be manipulated, or when a crisis of a politico-strategic or military nature can be used to 'delay' reforms.

In 1982 several high American officials admitted that their reform aspirations had simply been too high and that the Western governments had not sufficiently coordinated and sustained their efforts. As one American official put it, 'It was clearly a gamble – a gamble that didn't work. It was bound to fail from the beginning.' In particular, the European governments had a much more real-politik view of the Zairian situation. Furthermore, certain Belgian business and banking interests had a good deal to lose in 'grey area' profits, especially in minerals marketing and pre-financing arrangements, if reforms went too far. Many foreign business and banking interests, together with some European officials, believed that Mobutu would outlast the IMF, World Bank, and Western government reform efforts and, therefore, the issue became one of maintaining continued access to the regime. The major way of ensuring this was to pursue business as usual while paying lip-service to the reform efforts. Another weak link in the reform effort was the assumption that there would be a major influx of new capital, both public and private.

It is possible to construct two views as to why the reform efforts were attempted. First, there were those who believed that the reforms had some chance of success. Second, there were others who believed from the beginning that the reform efforts had no or very little chance of success, but realised that they were a convenient way of continuing to support the Mobutu regime for whatever personal, organisational, politico-strategic, or economic reasons. The first group clearly misperceived the nature of the regime and thus the chances for success; the second group used the misperceptions of the first for their own ends.

One Western official characterised the Zairian regime's response as Mobutu's 'continued farce' for the benefit of external actors; a second referred to it as a 'policy of mirrors'; and a third said it was like attacking the arm of a monster rather than its head. The Zairians know that they only have to make partial and temporary changes, that they can out-flank, circumvent, or wear down the reform efforts. They know that external actors are unable to watch all areas, all arenas at the same time, and consistently over time. One expatriate official described it as a video game in which the reformers have one ship and sequential shots and the Zairians have wave after wave of invaders coming at and around the reformers; not all the invaders get through, but a good number of them do.[44]

Mobutu and his political aristocracy are constantly scheming to acquire new access to internal and external resources. Among other things this involves budgetary tampering, barter deals with cobalt and other minerals, manipulation of pre-financing arrangements and the relation-ship between GECAMINES and SOZACOM, smuggling, and fraud in the administration of foreign assistance programmes. One of the most infamous examples of the latter involved the administration of the American PL 480 programme. American officials undertook elaborate measures to ensure proper administration of the programme which worked for a while. External actors, however, are simply unable to maintain constant monitoring, even of reform efforts they helped to initiate. Reforms that are ostensibly in progress can, in fact, be easily manipulated.[45]

A classic example involved Western-initiated efforts to eliminate fraud in the payment of teachers. Thousands of mythical teachers were on the payrolls while thousands of real teachers never received their salaries regularly or at all. As part of an effort to restrain both budgetary expenditure and eliminate fraud, the government agreed to eliminate 15 000 teachers from the rolls. Rather than removing the mythical teachers, however, many of the real teachers were removed from the rolls, and the fraud continued. One Western official admitted that they eventually gave up monitoring the situation.[46] Efforts to restrain budgetary expenditure had a very marginal impact. In 1981 the projected budget total for the year was about Z850 million while the actual expenditure was between Z1.5 and Z1.7 billion. For 1982 the budget total was to be about Z1 billion; by June, Z1.6 billion had been spent and one estimate put the projected year-end total at about Z2.5

billion. Lastly, one of the most worrisome problems was the inability of external actors, despite considerable effort, to stop Mobutu and those around him from pillaging GECAMINES, thereby threatening its future productive capacity.

What are the chances for reform? The chances are very slim indeed. To carry out the externally-demanded reforms effectively would undermine the very core of this patrimonial administrative state – the personal discretion of its ruler and the fiscal largesse and corruption which constitute the glue holding the system together. Such reforms are a direct threat to the patrimonial administrative state. Here the imperatives of calculability, of rationality, come into direct conflict with personal and class interests. When the bureaucratic clashes with the patrimonial, the latter will most likely win out:

A review of the Government's control over the entire economy during this time belies the assumption that problems of economic management were solely those of skill rather than of political will. When a large portion of a national budget is dispensed at the discretion of an agency, such as the President's Office, without effective limits on use or cost overruns, then the problems multiply for those technicians who are trying to develop the economy according to some set of rationalistic principles.[47]

Because of the non-productive nature of the political aristocracy, any threat to the viability of the patrimonial patron–client networks that are so central to the regime's survival, especially to the financial resources holding them together, must be avoided at all costs. The degree of external acquiescence is critical. External pressure for reform may only be able to slow the rate of decline of the downward sloping economic curve, to dampen the pillage.

In discussing 'the sociology of world-system stabilization' in Zaire, Guy Gran notes that the 'principal institutional response' used by the 'system managers, the financial and political elite of the core powers' is the IMF. It is 'first and foremost the policeman of international capitalism'. He argues that the IMF imposes the structural changes that are needed to protect the interests of the dominant actors in the 'world system'. According to Gran, 'the Mobutu government has allied itself with international capital, accepted the central teachings of the world-system agencies, and significantly inhibited local capital'. In discussing the 1976–77 stabilisation efforts, he notes, however, that 'Zaire's continued failure even to approach the agreed targets discouragd IMF officials'. As a result, the 'system managers' broadened their efforts to include 'a small team of expatriates at the helm of the Central Bank' and 'an overall coordinating mechanism' – 'a general Consultative Group'. Gran attempts to show the enormous power of the world system managers, but his data about Zaire do not fit his thesis. He copes with this problem by an interesting sleight of hand. He notes that because 'the resulting contraditions are impossible .. the IMF must, to survive, lie to its mandators'! Thus, 'the IMF accommodates the contradictions and produces a mystification the world-system mandators will accept' and 'reveals the bankruptcy of the organization from the perspective *both* of the mandators and of mass human welfare.'[48]

R. Peter DeWitt and James Petras have presented a 'radical' analysis of the 'dynamics of international debt peonage' in which expansion of global debt injures true development prospects while possibly increasing the stability of the global economic system. The developed capitalist states and their international banks manipulate regimes and attempt to 'restructure political power and economic systems'. They use the case of Zaire with its customs-house takeover aspects as a key example of this process. In fact, however, the Zairian case demonstrates *both* the significance of international influence *and* its limits. Manipulating regimes is more difficult than DeWitt and Petras assumed; debt is after all a two-way street. Zaire no longer performs its neo-colonial functions properly, and external actors are finding it difficult to make it do so. In addition, they believe that they cannot just walk away from the problem either, for geo-political and strategic reasons as well as economic ones. According to DeWitt and Petras, 'These Western interventions in Zaire illustrate the banks' and developed nations' ability to restructure LDC debtors.'[49] In fact, they illustrate quite the reverse. How the nature of Third World regimes and the international system can frustrate external control and restructuring efforts remains one of the largest lacunae of the growing debt literature.

A leading Zairian analyst, Nzongola-Ntalaja, flatly asserts that Zaire is a neo-colonial state – one that serves 'the interests of Mobutu, his class, and foreign corporations': 'There is no doubt that the principal beneficiaries of Mobutu's rule are the two social classes controlling the neo-colonial state: the international bourgeoisie and its *junior partner*, the Zairian bourgeoisie' (emphasis added). Having made these claims, however, Nzongola then immediately notes that Zaire has sunk into near total economic disaster brought on by Mobutu and his ruling class, points to 'the futility of internationally-imposed controls and reforms in the face of the struggle of the Zairian *kleptocracy* to defend and promote its own vested interests', and avers, probably correctly, that this state cannot be reformed in any meaningful way. According to Nzongola, Zaire is 'a neo-colonial state whose ruling class helps *to block economic growth and development* as well as the normal functioning of the state apparatus by depriving the state of those essential means and capabilities with which it may improve the living conditions of the population as a whole' (emphasis added). He notes that despite its vast potential wealth, the Zairian state is unable to satisfy even the vital minimum needs of its people, 'unlike neo-colonial states in other resource-rich countries like the Ivory Coast, Nigeria, and Gabon'. He points to Zaire's huge debt owed to 'the barons of international finance capital seeking to recover their loans' and to the fact that 'the social and economic services left behind by the colonialists have deteriorated to the point where most of them exist in name only'.[50]

Nzongola asserts that this economic and moral debacle of Zaire – '*le mal Zairois*' – is 'a function of the *embourgeoisement* of the country's leadership group, its insertion in the import–export economy, *its execution of the neo-colonial tasks of the post-colonial state*, and its mismanagement of public resources' (emphasis added). Is the Zairian neo-colonial state thus serving the interests of 'its senior partners', the 'international bourgeoisie'? Hardly. What in fact exists is an African patrimonial administrative state controlled by a patriarchal patrimonial ruler, a presidential monarch, and his political aristocracy which pursues its own class project of self-aggrandisement despite the persistent efforts of external actors to reform it. To cope with these contradictions in his argument, Nzongola also resorts to an interesting sleight of hand. The ruling 'African bourgeoisie' controls the neo-colonial state and 'serves principally its interests as well as those of its senior partner, the metropolitan bourgeoise' and 'these two sets of interests are *contradictory* in a *non-antagonistic manner*' (emphasis added)! There are a good number of Western officials, bankers and business people who would not agree.[51]

In this case, who is more dependent on whom? Only time will tell, but the patrimonial element is most likely to dominate for now. Mobutu's ability to control Zaire depends in large part on the existence of adequate fiscal resources, of sufficient financial 'slack'. The existence of these resources is greatly dependent on the fluctuating prices of copper and cobalt and Zaire's international debt situation. Externally, Mobutu and his political aristocracy will continue their attempts to reschedule the debt, extract additional resources from friendly Western powers, banks, and international organisations, and hope that the prices of copper, cobalt, diamonds and so on, will rise dramatically, or that a major oil discovery will be made. They will also try to extract more resources from internal groups through higher taxes, new taxes, and more effective tax collection, but only from some of the 'citizens', not all. With the collapse of Zaire's relationship with the IMF in 1982 and continued missed public and private debt service payments, there were those within the highest reaches of the political aristocracy who counselled that Zaire need not make any serious efforts to service the debt or institute reforms because its external 'patrons' or 'kin' in the international 'extended family' or 'lineage group' will have to bail them out. This is truly patrimonial imagery. In one sense this argument is a new and rather different version of the concept of a 'neo-colonial state' – that is, that Western actors are responsible for bailing out regimes that they support. It is almost a form of 'reverse neo-colonialism'. On the other side, there were those in Western circles who argued that Mobutu and his political aristocracy should be allowed to stew in their own juices. After a brief lapse, however, the logic of the interests on both sides dictated that the ritual dances of the debt game begin again.

## PATRIMONIALISM AND CAPITALISM IN AFRICA

So, despite the fact that Zaire was failing to perform most of its neo-colonial functions, Mobutu's regime continues to survive in an international context largely controlled by advanced capitalist states. The performance of this African patrimonial administrative state clearly highlights what Weber called 'the negative anti-capitalist effect of patrimonial arbitrariness':

> The patrimonial state lacks the political and procedural *predictability*, indispensible for capitalist *development*, which is provided by the rational rules of modern bureaucratic administration. Instead we find unpredictability and inconsistency on the part of court and local officials, and variously benevolence and disfavor on the part of the ruler and his servants.[52]

As Weber pointed out, however, patrimonialism is differentially amenable to various types of capitalism: 'Under the dominance of a patrimonial regime only certain types of capitalism are able to develop fully ... the individual variants of capitalism have a differential sensitivity toward such unpredictable factors.' For Weber, the opportunites of expansion are limited for 'production-oriented modern capitalism, based on the rational enterprise, the division of labor and fixed capital, whereas politically oriented capitalism, just as capitalist wholesale trade, is very much compatible with patrimonialism.' Patrimonial rulers need the 'treasure' from trade 'above all for the maintenance of their following, the body-guards, patrimonial armies, mercenaries and especially officials.' The result is what Weber called 'patrimonial capitalism'.[53]

According to Weber, industrial capitalism 'is altogether too sensitive to all sorts of irrationalities in the administration of law, administration and taxation, for these upset the basis of *calculability*.' On the other hand, 'it is quite possible that a private individual, by skilfully taking advantage of the given circumstances and of personal relations, obtains a privileged position which offers him nearly unlimited acquisition opportunities. But a capitalist economic *system* is obviously greatly handicapped by these factors.' The two major forms of this 'patrimonial capitalism' are 'monopolies of their own' for the rulers and 'direct privileges for capital'. Both are heavily politically determined as 'the important openings for profit are in the hands of the ruler and of his administrative staff':[54]

Members and favorites of the royal family, courtiers, military men and officials grown rich, great speculators and adventurous investors of 'systems' of political economy . . . made up the economically interested groups behind the royal monopolies and the industries which were imported, founded or protected on that basis.[55]

Another characteristic 'which tends to restrict the development of rational economic activity' in 'political privileged capitalism' is that 'there is wide scope for actual arbitrariness and the expression of purely personal whims on the part of the ruler and the members of his adminstrative staff.' Weber also mentioned 'the opening for bribery and corruption', especially since 'it tends to be a matter which is settled from case to case with every individual official and thus highly variable.' A final important constraint on the development of a fully capitalist system is that 'in the interest of his domination, the patrimonial ruler must oppose . . . the economic independence of the bourgeoisie', as every potentially autonomous group 'must be suspected of hostility to authority.'[56] As the history of modern capitalism shows, patrimonial rulers have ultimately been unable to prevent the emergence of this independence. Many, however, have been able to slow or skew the development of an autonomous bourgeoisie. This is clearly the case in Zaire and there are many other examples both in Africa and elsewhere in the Third World.

Centralising patrimonial states then are at best linked to emerging capitalism of a political character, historically the type associated with 'the age of mercantilism, when the incipient capitalist organization of trades, the bureaucratic rationalization of patrimonial rulership and the growing financial needs of the military, external and internal administration revolutionized the financial techniques of the European states.' Weber cautioned, however, that the 'bureaucracy' of such states 'was still as patrimonial as was the basic conception of the "state" on which it rested'. The apparent economic nationalism of the early Mobutu period turned out to be heavily patrimonial and statecraft-centred rather than a manifestation of a bureaucratic statist developmentalism. When the rational imperatives of bureaucratic statist development came into conflict with the patrimonial core of the administrative state and its consolidating political class, the former gave way to the latter. The result is what has been characterised elsewhere as a form of African neo-mercantilism.[57]

The notion here of the patrimonial administrative state is similar to Richard Higgott's stress on 'the "soft" nature of the African state'. He correctly stresses that 'the notion of the modern [bureaucratic] administrative state of popular Weberian image is not apt in the African context despite the fact that the state holds a predominant position in society.'[58] Thus, African countries, Zaire included, are not necessarily less state-centric than other Third World countries; they are just much less developed administratively and economically. In this sense, the new World Bank structural adjustment orthodoxy about the minimalist role for the state fails to remember the historical lesson that classical economic and political liberalism fought its early battles against the mercantilist statism of early modern European governments. That this argument applies to more African countries than Zaire is made very plain by Rothchild and Gyimah-Boadi in their discussion of Ghana in Chapter 10. They note that 'the state in Africa appears hegemonic . . .; in actuality, however, it is fragile and lacking in the capacity to implement policies throughout its territory. The typical "soft state", such as that in Ghana, displays not only a lack of consensus on society's organising principles but an over-centralised state bureaucracy' (patrimonial administration, actually).[59] In this sense, Zaire is not atypical in the African context. It is possibly more extreme, but it is the same species as countries such as Zambia, Kenya, the Ivory Coast, even Nigeria.

As Cooper has nicely phrased it, 'Capital has not invariably won the battles it fought in the first and second occupations of Africa – to make production predictable and orderly throughout the continent . . . the march of Africans into the world economy does not appear to follow a straight line.'[60] The argument above about the differential sensitivity of various forms of capitalism is not meant to be a deterministic one. Surely capitalist development in Africa is not out of the question; it is just difficult and takes place slowly, incrementally, and unevenly. This is reinforced by the fact that external corporations and investors have a choice where they go in the on-going changes in the international division of labour, especially in the context of the world recession and comparative advantage calculations which often tend to favour Africa the least:

> Multinational corporations have considerable power, above all, to choose the kind of state they need to cooperate with . . . they do exercise some choice over the battleground. Africa's guerrilla army of the underemployed may well appear less attractive than the more disciplined battalions of South Korea, Taiwan, and Hong Kong, or even the foot soldiers of Brazil or South Africa, who are anything but footloose. Whether Africa plays a significant role in the shift in manufacturing markets in Europe and North America is doubtful, and within Africa concentration is likely in a very limited number of places, such as Zimbabwe and South Africa, where effective state services and a labor force that is well socialized and dependable as well as cheap as available.[61]

This argument holds equally well for the commercial banks or 'finance capital' as it does for 'industrial capital.'

In this sense, there is a real economic marginalisation of Africa underway, a 'delinking' and 'a steady withdrawal of Western interest'. As Higgott notes, 'Africa may well be more peripheral, more dependent and in greater economic crisis by the end of the current decade than it was in the 1960s.'[62] It is a potential peripheralisation rather different from the one the world system theoreticians have had in mind. Rather than maintaining or increasing the level of integration into the world capitalist economy, the reverse may be taking place for a sizeable number of countries. Most African countries with debt problems will find it difficult to export themselves into a stable and manageable debt situation, much less out of debt. In order to earn the foreign exchange necessary to service current debt levels, these countries will most likely continue to concentrate for the moment on agricultural and mineral primary commodity production, thus maintaining the nature, if not the extent of their position in the international division of labour.

In addition, because of the current economic and fiscal crisis and the nature of the state and its administrative capabilities, local capital, where it exists, will not be inclined to make important medium- and long-term investment in new productive capacity for eventual profit. There are even indications that the money economy is shrinking in a number of countries and/or that 'magendo' economic activity is becoming significantly more important. The availability of an 'exit option' varies considerably from country to country, but, unlike most of the major Latin American countries with debt problems, it is a viable if not preferred option for African rural populations. It may also play an important role in reducing the tensions created by recession, austerity measures, infrastructure decline, and domestic political repression and economic extraction, both formal and informal. In the case of Zaire, the shrinking of the money economy, the rise of magendo activity, and the exit option are all present to varying degrees in many parts of the country. These processes are accompanied and in part caused by a progressive patrimonialisation and functional contraction of the inherited colonial state structure.[63]

## AFRICAN AND LATIN AMERICAN DEBT

It is important to disaggregate the nature and consequences of Third World debt. Latin American experience, for example, may not be applicable to Africa in any significant way. The major Latin American countries with debt problems are not peripheral to the world economy. The NIC strategy of debt-fuelled export-oriented industrialisation has more fully integrated these countries into the world economy. As a result, they cannot be ignored or 'marginalised' as much of Africa can be. This fact, combined with the large size of Latin American debt and its heavily private character (often over 80 per cent), means that these countries pose important threats to the stability and character of the international economic and financial system. They thus have been the recipients of large-scale, multi-billion dollar 'rescue packages'.

The political and administrative character of these Latin American states is also an important factor. Most of the major Latin American debtors are bureaucratic and authoritarian or quasi-authoritarian states in the third stage of what O'Donnell and others have called the 'delayed-dependent development syndrome'. The third stage is that of 'deepening capitalism' in which the transfer from import-substitution to capital goods industrialisation takes place. This process is characterised by an increase in the multi-sector complexity and depth of the economy, by rapidly increasing bureaucratisation of patrimonial administrative structures resulting in increased technocratic and administrative capability, by an increased coercive capacity of the state, and by an increased, but tightly controlled, mobilisation of socio-economic groups and classes.[64]

The African situation, with its patrimonial administrative states and patrimonial forms of capitalism, is dramatically different. Most African states are in the first stage of the delayed-dependent development syndrome, that of primary-product, export-oriented economies with much less multi-sector sophistication and depth. This certainly is not the 'deepening capitalism' of most of the major Latin American debtors. As a result, the issues of political will and administrative capacity aside, the ability of most African states to adjust economically is much lower; the economic complexity is just not there. In addition, the money they borrowed has been used much less productively than has been the case in Latin America. The countries are weak and heavily patrimonial administrative states with distinctly limited coercive capacity. Most of them are clearly authoritarian. Yet the authoritarian characteristics of African states are of a rather different order than the bureaucratic authoritarianism of the major Latin American states. African ruling groups or classes are not as well organised and integrated as their Latin American counterparts. Administratively, African states are much less bureaucratised, technically-oriented and capable than is the case in Latin America. Professionalised technocratic groups are significantly smaller and much less important politically. As a result, socio-economic and financial policy formulation and implementation capabilities are much less developed. Patrimonial forms of both politics and administration are dominant. Lastly, the existence of previously mobilised and widely differentiated socio-economic groups is not an important factor for most African states. Class formation processes are simply at a much more incipient stage. In particular, African 'working classes' are much smaller, less organised, and less politically conscious than those of Latin America. Interclass conflict is also significantly less important.

The economic adjustment process and norms established by and evolving out of the post-war Bretton Woods system implied the capacity to adjust, that is to understand, formulate, and implement such policies on the part of the target state. The political will did not always exist, but the administrative capacity usually did exist. Coping with Third World debt crises in the 1980s is by nature interventionist, but to varying degrees depending on the nature of the target state and its economic and politico-strategic importance. In Africa, by definition, it is very interventionist.

There are three major issues in regard to adjustment: (a) political will, (b) administrative capacity, and (c) economic capacity. The first two deal with the nature of the regime; the third is a question of the level of overall economic development. Because of their much higher level of economic development, greater administrative capabilities, and more developed coercive capabilities, most major Latin American debtor countries are more able to take *and* implement painful adjustment policies. In Africa, drift (what one analyst has called 'chaotic adjustment') and externally-imposed and dictated adjustment are more common, but, as we have seen in the case of Zaire, the latter has encountered distinct limitations to its effectiveness. As Gerald Helleiner has pointed out, 'the most important limitation of IMF analytic approaches to African and other low-income countries' macro-economic problems is . . . its inadequate consideration of these countries' limited *adjustment* capacity'. He delineates four factors which constrain short-term adjustment capacity:

(i) limited economic flexibility and limited short-term responsiveness to price incentives; (ii) low and recently falling per capita income and urban real wages; (iii) limited technical and administrative capacity within government economic policy-making institutions; (iv) fragility of political support for many governments of the day.[65]

His first two factors relate directly to the level and type of economic development, and the last two relate to the nature of the regimes.

Helleiner puts particular stress on the issue of technical and adminstrative capacity and notes that 'this can lend a comic-opera character to some of the international squabbling, wherein virtually all of the local memoranda are in fact drafted by foreign advisors'.[66] As we have seen in the case of Zaire, this has led to an important role for merchant bank advisors. In addition to Zaire, the 'holy trinity' of Lazard Frères, Lehman Brothers Kuhn Loeb and S. G. Warburg has advised the governments of Gabon, the Ivory Coast, Senegal, Togo, Congo, Mozambique, and Nigeria. Morgan Grenfell has advised the Sudan, Uganda, and Zimbabwe, and Samuel Montague has advised Zambia. Nowhere else in the world has such private bank advice played such a major and public role. As with the literature on the impact of capitalist production or extraction enclaves in Africa, it is questionable how effective the forward and backward linkages of these 'technocratic enclaves' are likely to be. Bureaucratic rescue personnei in little rubber boats are not going to have a major impact on the patrimonial sea of African political economy.

CONCLUSION

What does the future hold for African debtor countries and their creditors? Modest expectations are in order on both sides. African states cannot expect any major beneficial structural or procedural reforms in the international political economy on the part of their Western creditors; likewise, the latter cannot expect any significant restructuring of African regimes and economies or substantial improvement in their economic and debt service performance. Western actors clearly determine most of the rules of the game and shape the parameters of the field of action, but ruling groups in African patrimonial administrative states have some autonomy, some fluctuating, but nonetheless real, room for manoeuvre.

The New International Economic Order is stillborn. The North has no intention of bargaining about across-the-board structural and behavioural reforms, much less actually making them. Major northern actors, whether they be pure 'rejectionists', or rejectionists posing as 'bring them into the system', 'global agenda', or 'global equity' types, simply do not believe that there is any need to grant such reforms, or even to take part in multilateral negotiations about them.[67] Very few northern policy-makers believe, with Roger Hansen, that 'continued postponement of a significant reorientation of U.S. foreign policy toward the South is becoming costlier with each passing year'.[68] Few share the perception that postponement, delay, and stall tactics will lead to crises which, in turn, will 'force' significant changes down the line, In fact, one of the most striking things about the financial crisis of late 1982, set off by Mexico and kept going by Brazil, Argentina, Poland, and others, is that it has been dealt with without the adoption, or even the serious consideration, of any of the major debt and finance proposals from the NIEO package.

The 'panic of 1982' showed that such a crisis, or at least this one, could be handled by the direct action of dominant Western states, their banks, and the key multilateral organisations and fora which they influence (the IMF, the World Bank, the Bank for International Settlements, the Group of 5, the Group of 10, and so on). At least this is the way they perceived it, and it may have been a correct perception this time. It will not necessarily always be so. The important analytic fact, however, is that the perception existed, not that it was correct or incorrect. The underlying state-centric nature of the finance and debt regimes clearly manifested itself when systematic and crucial individual-country interests were threatened. The financial crisis forced the dominant states to take a direct and public leadership role in the crisis management efforts.

This is not at all to say, however, that 'concessions', changes in norms and rules, have not been made or will not continue to be made. It is rather a question of who makes them, how, in what context, their nature, and the degree to which they are applicable in any general way. Important concessions have been made by northern states, banks and multilateral organisations, particularly to key Latin American debtors, but they have been made quietly, on an *ad hoc* and case-by-case basis, and in arenas, both multilateral and bilateral, that are controlled largely by northern actors. There have not been any debtors' OPECs, general, regional, NIC, less developed, least developed, or whatever. This crisis and the way it was dealt with has greatly affected the mood and desires of southern states, African ones included. One only has to compare the early debt and finance related 'demands' for reform by UNCTAD, the Group of 77, and others with the mild, almost meek 'requests' or 'invitations' of UNCTAD VI in mid-1983.[69]

Since the onset of the financial crisis in 1982, a whole host of debt and financial reform proposals have been made, both generally and in regard to African issues specifically. They range from moratoria, partial write-offs, the creation of new multilateral organisations to assume large portions of the debt, to generalised rescheduling procedures, 'rescheduling markets', new credit, aid, investment, and trade schemes, increased IMF flexibility and low conditionality, and formal arbitration mechanisms.[70] Such proposals are not likely to be discussed seriously, much less acted upon. Rather the debt problems of African countries will continue to be treated on a case-by-case basis within existing multilateral (IMF, Paris Club, and World Bank consultative group mechanisms) and bilateral channels. Quietly, rules will be 'bent' and 'stretched' as reschedulings and IMF programmes follow each other in a semi-continuous fashion. There will be longer terms and grace periods; previously rescheduled debt (PRD) will be rescheduled again and again; there will be some flexibility on interest rates, fees, initial payments, percentages of debt and periods covered, and so on, but no major generalised changes or reforms. And the changes that are made will be affected by the perceptions of the northern actors of their politico-strategic, economic, organisational, class, and individual interests. John Ruggie has nicely conceptualised the northern or Western industrialised order as one of 'embedded liberalism' based on the tension-wrought co-existence of both multilateralism and a significant mediating and interventionist role of the northern state in order to foster the domestic welfare of its population. He notes, however, that 'the compromise of embedded liberalism has never been fully extended to the developing countries' and that, in fact, 'a central ingredient in the success of embedded liberalism to date has been its ability to accommodate and even facilitate the externalizing of adjustment costs.'[71] He has also stressed that 'the impetus for change remains with the regime-making states' and that 'the core regimes in general may be particularly inhospitable to Third World demands for fundamental change, precisely because these regimes matter to the regime-making states.'[72] This is clearly the case in regard to African debt issues. Nonetheless, the *operation*, as opposed to the structure and norms, of these international political economy regimes is directly affected by the nature of African states, societies, and economies.

On the other side of the debt divide then, northern actors will find it difficult to 'restructure' African states and economies or to increase economic and debt service performance. This chapter argues that the nature of authority or domination in African states, both in terms of rulership/statecraft and forms of administration, greatly affects the relations between ruling groups or classes and external actors and that these charcteristics may be as important in determining the form of these relations as the nature of international exchange, position in the world system, or even the nature of production and other economic activity. Patrimonial administrative states and patrimonial forms of capitalism are clearly dominant in most of Africa today.

Western efforts to cope with African debt crises and their economic and administrative roots and consequences will continue, but with only modest results. Repeated reschedulings, IMF programmes, and private bank negotiations will be required in most cases, accompanied by a slow, but quiet manipulation of the norms. These efforts will be carried out in the context of extensive and increasing mass hardship, continued economic marginalisation of much of the continent, slow growth or actual decline of GDP, minimal external and internal development of a long-term productive nature, on-going capacity destruction and infrastructure disintegration, and some political and social instability with occasional change of ruling groups (if not directly caused by economic and debt adjustment pressures, at least justified by them). Many of these processes were underway before the onset of significant debt problems, but they have been further aggravated by them and by factors such as drought, increasing refugee problems, and regional political and military struggles, particularly in southern Africa.[73]

Very few African countries are likely to succeed in exporting themselves out of debt, or even into stable and productive debt, much less into a higher level of development. Under current world conditions, the replication of NIC export-oriented development strategies is in serious doubt in much of the Third World; it certainly is for most of Africa. In this and most other regards, Zaire has not proved to be all that atypical. In slightly exaggerated form, it highlights key processes and relationships clearly present in many other African countries, and, thus, as they have in Zaire, the ritual dances of the debt game will continue for much of the rest of the continent.

## NOTES

1. The research upon which this paper is based was funded by the National Science Foundation under Grant No. SES 80–13453, 'Third World Debt and the International System: The Case of Zaire'. Any opinions, findings, and conclusions or recommendations are those of the author and do not necessarily reflect the views of the National Science Foundation. The bulk of the data comes from confidential interviews with officials of Western governments, the government of Zaire, international organisations, and from private bankers and business people which were conducted in Washington, DC, New York, Boston, San Francisco, London, Brussels, Paris, and Kinshasa from 1980 to early 1984. The author would like to thank Sheila Smith, Sandra Aviles, and the wonderful staff of Columbia University's Research Institute on International Change and the Institute of African Studies for their invaluable help on this project.
2. Susan Strange, 'Debt and Default in the International Political Economy', in Jonathan Aronson (ed.), *Debt and Less Developed Countries* (Boulder, Colorado: Westview Press, 1979) p. 7.
3. On Nigeria, see Margaret Hughes, 'Nigerian Pledge Calms Banker's Fears', *The Financial Times*, 9 January 1984.
4. G. K. Helleiner, 'The IMF and Africa in the 1980s', *Canadian Journal of African Studies*, vol. 17 (1983) no. 1, p. 23.
5. *Africa Economic Digest*, 19 September 1983. The debt data are derived or compiled from the following sources: World Bank, *World Debt Tables* (1981); World Bank, *World Development Report, 1983*; World Bank, *Accelerated Development in Sub-Saharan Africa* (1981) IMF, *World*

*Economic Outlook* (1982); IMF, Current Studies Division; *Financial Times*, 9 May 1983; *African Business*, May 1983; and bank estimates.

6. S. C. Nana-Sinkam, 'The International Monetary Fund in Africa', unpublished paper, New York, October 1983, pp. 34, 36. IMF programme data were derived from: IMF, Treasurer's Department and Bureau of Statistics; *Africa Economic Digest*, 16 September 1983; and Nana-Sinkam, 'The IMF in Africa', p. 1 and tables.

7. *Africa Economic Digest*, 16 September 1983. The rescheduling data were derived from: Department of State personnel; Helleiner, 'The IMF'; World Bank, *World Development Report, 1983*; *Euromoney*, June 1983; and *African Business*, May 1983.

8. *Africa Economic Digest*, 20 May 1983; also see issue of 16 September 1983.

9. *Institutional Investor*, September 1982, p. 284.

10. For a more detailed version of the argument in this section, see Thomas M. Callaghy, *The State–Society Struggle: Zaire in Comparative Perspective* (New York: Columbia University Press, 1984) especially Chapters 1 and 4.

11. See Thomas M. Callaghy, 'External Actors and the Relative Autonomy of the Political Aristocracy in Zaire', *Journal of Commonwealth and Comparative Politics*, vol. 21 (November 1983) no. 3, pp. 287–309.

12. Pierre Goubert, *Louis XIV and Twenty Million Frenchmen* (New York: Random House, Vintage: 1970) p. 310.

13. Max Weber, *Economy and Society*, Guenther Roth and Claus Wittich (eds), (Berkeley: University of California Press, 1978) p. 1099.

14. Jan Vansina, 'Mwasi's Trials', *Daedalus*, vol. 111 (Spring 1982) no. 2, p. 57. On the 'economy of grabbing', see Frederick Cooper, 'Africa and the World Economy', *African Studies Review*, vol. 24 (June/September 1981) no. 2/3, p. 33. The former high regime official is Nguza Karl-i-Bond, 'Current Political and Economic Situation in Zaire', testimony, US House of Representatives, Foreign Affairs Committee, Sub-committee on Africa, Washington, DC, 15 September 1981, p. 38; also see his *Mobutu ou l'incarnation du mal Zairois* (London: Rex Collings, 1982). Also, confidential interview with expatriate official, Kinshasa, 28 July 1982.

15. Kenneth Adelman, 'Zaire's Year of Crisis', *African Affairs*, vol. 77 (1978) p. 37.

16. Calculated from data in Bank of Zaire, 'The Republic of Zaire: Recent Economic and Financial Developments', June 1982. This report is one of a series of information memoranda produced by Zaire's investment bank adviser triumvirate of Lazard Frères, Lehman Brothers Kuhn Loeb, and S. G. Warburg.

17. Adelman, 'Zaire's Year of Crisis'.

18. P. A. Wellons, *Borrowing by Developing Countries on the Euro-Currency Market* (Paris: OECD, 1977) pp. 119–20.

19. Confidential interview, Kinshasa, 21 February 1975.

20. Crawford Young, 'Zaire: The Unending Crisis', *Foreign Affairs*, vol. 57 (1978) no. 1, p. 177.

21. Jonathan D. Aronson, 'The Politics of Bank Lending and Debt Rescheduling in Zaire, Indonesia, Brazil, and Mexico', paper presented at the joint meetings of the Latin American and African Studies Associations, Houston, 1977, p. 6.

22. Young, 'Zaire: The Unending Crisis', p. 117.
23. For a detailed participant–observer look at the 1979 Paris Club and the 1980 London Club reschedulings, see Jeffrey E. Garten, 'Rescheduling Third World Debt: The Case of Zaire', PhD dissertation (School of Advanced International Studies, Johns Hopkins University, 1981).
24. World Bank, 'From Economic Stabilization to Recovery: An Appraisal of the Mobutu Plan', unpublished report, 15 May, 1980, pp. 3, 4, 14, 27; it was distributed to the participants of the 1980 consultative group meeting.
25. Confidential interviews: Kinshasa, 29 July and 5, 6, 10 August 1982; Brussels, 14 January 1982; Paris, 21 January 1982; and Washington, DC, 16 December 1981, 9 July 1982.
26. IMF, 'Zaire: Report for Extended Fund Facility', unpublished report (EBS/81/126, 8 June 1981) p. 3.
27. Kabuya Kalala, 'La relance économique du Zaire: souhaits d'hier et problèmes d'aujourd'hui', *Zaire-Afrique*, no. 160 (December 1981) p. 620.
28. Weber, *Economy and Society*, p. 1091. On *Bula Matari*, see Crawford Young, 'Patterns of Social Conflict: State, Class, and Ethnicity', *Daedalus*, vol. 111 (Spring 1982) no. 2, p. 95 *n*.11.
29. Erwin Blumenthal, 'Zaire – Report on her international financial credibility', typed manuscript, 7 April 1982, p. 19.
30. Nguza, 'Current Political and Economic Situation', pp. 13, 15; for his participant–observer view of the external reform efforts, see *Mobutu*, pp. 143–6, 165.
31. Blumenthal, 'Zaire – Report', p. 9.
32. Confidential interviews: Kinshasa, 29 July and 6 August 1982; Brussels, 22 July 1982, 13 and 14 January 1982; Paris, 20 January 1982; and Washington, DC, 5 August 1981.
33. Blumenthal, 'Zaire – Report', p. 13.
34. Confidential interview, London, 7 January 1982.
35. Blumenthal, 'Zaire – Report', p. 19.
36. Confidential interview, Kinshasa, 29 July 1982.
37. Charles Lipson, 'The International Organization of Third World Debt', *International Organization*, vol. 34 (Autumn 1981) no. 4, pp. 607, 628, 630, abstract.
38. Confidential interviews, Kinshasa, 29 July 1982; Brussels, 13 January 1982; Washington, DC, 3 March 1981.
39. Confidential interviews, Paris, 20 and 21 January 1982; New York, 3 July 1982, 28 June 1982; Washington, DC, 2 March 1981.
40. Confidential interview, London, 17 August 1982; also London, 18 August 1982; New York, 13 June 1983, 30 June 1982.
41. Confidential interviews, Kinshasa, 29 July 1982, 5 and 10 August 1982; Washington, DC, 9 July 1982; Paris, 20 and 21 January 1982; New York, 28 June 1982.
42. Confidential interview, London, 7 January 1982.
43. Confidential interviews, London, 17 and 18 August 1982; Paris, 20 and 21 January 1982; New York, 15 September 1983; Washington, DC, 24 August 1982.
44. This section is based on the following confidential interviews: Kinshasa, 5, 6, and 9 August 1982; Brussels, 22 July 1982, 13 and 14 January 1982; and Washington, DC, 2 and 3 March, 16 December 1981, 9 August 1982.

45. Confidential interviews, Kinshasa, 29 July and 6 August 1982; Washington, DC, 9 July 1982.
46. Confidential interview, Kinshasa, 29 July 1982.
47. Wellons, *Borrowing by Developing Countries*, p. 120.
48. Guy Gran, *Development by People: Citizen Construction of a Just World* (New York: Praeger, 1983) pp. 117, 124, 128, 130–2, 134; also see his introductory chapter in Guy Gran (ed.), *Zaire: The Political Economy of Underdevelopment* (New York: Praeger, 1979).
49. R. Peter DeWitt and James Petras, 'Political Economy of International Debt: The Dynamics of Finance Capital', in Aronson (ed.) *Debt and Less Developed Countries*, p. 190.
50. Nzongola-Ntalaja, *Class Struggles and National Liberation in Africa* (Roxbury, Mass.: Omenana, 1982), pp. 44, 45, 49, 75.
51. Ibid., pp. 44, 45 and 62.
52. Weber, *Economy and Society*, p. 1095.
53. Ibid., pp. 240, 1029, 1095 and 1091.
54. Ibid., pp. 238, 240, 1095 and 1098.
55. Ibid., p. 1098.
56. Ibid., pp. 239–40, 1103 and 1107.
57. Ibid., p. 1098; also see the discussion of African neo-mercantilism in Thomas M. Callaghy, 'The Difficulties of Implementing Socialist Strategies of Development in Africa: The "First Wave"', in Carl G. Rosberg and Thomas M. Callaghy (eds), *Socialism in Sub-Saharan Africa: A New Assessment* (Berkeley: Institute of International Studies, 1979) pp. 112–29 and in Callaghy, *The State–Society Struggle*, Chapter 1.
58. Richard Higgott, Chapter 11, p. 299.
59. Donald Rothchild and E. Gyimah-Boadi, Chapter 10, p. 255.
60. Cooper, 'Africa and the World Economy', p. 51.
61. Ibid.
62. Richard Higgott, Chapter 11, p. 295.
63. On the 'exit option,' see Goran Hyden, *Beyond Ujamaa: Underdevelopment and an Uncaptured Peasantry* (Berkeley: University of California Press, 1980); on the existence of these processes in Africa, see the following recent dissertations: Bianga Waruzi, 'Peasant, State and Rural Development in Postindependent Zaire: A Case Study of "Reforme Rurale" 1970–1980', (University of Wisconsin, 1982); Janet MacGaffey, 'Class Relations in a Dependent Economy: Businessmen and Businesswomen in Kisangani, Zaire', (Bryn Mawr College, 1981); and Vwakyanakazi Mukohya, 'African Traders in Butembo, Eastern Zaire: A Case Study of Informal Entrepreneurship in a Cultural Context of Central Africa', (University of Wisconsin, 1982).
64. In particular, see Guillermo O'Donnell, *Modernization and Bureaucratic-Authoritarianism: Studies in South American Politics* (Berkeley: Institute of International Studies, 1973); 'Reflections on the Patterns of Change in the Bureaucratic-Authoritarian State', *Latin American Studies Review*, vol. 13 (1978) no. 1, pp. 3–38; 'Corporatism and the Question of the State' and 'Tensions in the Bureaucratic-Authoritarian State and the Question of Democracy', both in David Collier (ed.), *The New Authoritarianism in Latin America* (Princeton University Press, 1979), pp. 47–88 and 285–318. For an assessment of this argument and research, see the Collier volume generally.

65. Helleiner, 'The IMF and Africa', pp. 28-9.
66. Ibid., p. 30.
67. On these categories, see Roger Hansen, *Beyond the North–South Stalemate* (New York: McGraw-Hill, 1979) pp. 55–80.
68. Roger Hansen, 'North–South Policy – What's the Problem?', *Foreign Affairs*, vol. 58 (Summer 1980) no. 5, p. 1105.
69. See UNCTAD, 'Resolutions, recommendations and decisions of the sixth session, Belgrade, Yugoslavia, 6 June to 2 July 1983' (UNCTAD/CA/2168 GE.52652, 15 July 1983) pp. 61–3.
70. On the various debt proposals, see: Helleiner, 'The IMF and Africa in the 1980s'; C. Bogdanowicz-Bindert, 'Debt: Beyond the Quick Fix', *Third World Quarterly*, vol. 5 (October 1983) no. 4, pp. 828–38; Reginald H. Green, ' "Things Fall Apart": World Economy in the 1980s', *Third World Quarterly*, vol. 5 (January 1983) no. 1, pp. 72–94; F. Rohatyn, 'The State of the Banks', *The New York Review of Books*, 4 November 1982 and 'A Plan for Stretching Out Global Debt', *Business Week*, 28 February 1983; B. J. Feder, 'The World Banking Crisis: Phase Two', *New York Times*, 27 March 1983, and 'A Debt Partnership', *The Economist*, 2 April 1983; R. S. Weinert, 'Banks and Bankruptcy', *Foreign Policy*, vol. 50 (Spring 1983) pp. 138–49; P. Kenan, 'A Bailout Plan for the Banks', *New York Times*, 6 March 1983; G. Magnifico, 'A New Role for the World Bank', *Financial Times*, 15 December 1982; William A. Colby, 'Moritorium on Debt: A Strategy for Growth', *The Journal of Commerce*, 30 December 1982; 'The International Debt Threat: A Concerted Way Out', *The Economist*, 9 July 1983; Samuel Brittan, 'A World Lender of Last Resort', *Financial Times*, 8 September 1983; and Andrew Lycett, 'Finding a Way Out of the Debt Crisis', *African Business*, June 1983.
71. John G. Ruggie, 'International Regimes, Transactions, and Change: Embedded Liberalism in the Postwar Economic Order', *International Organization*, vol. 36 (Spring 1982) no. 2, p. 413.
72. John G. Ruggie, 'Political Structure and Change in the International Economic Order: The North–South Dimension', in J. G. Ruggie (ed.), *The Antinomies of Interdependence: National Welfare and the International Division of Labor* (New York: Columbia University Press, 1983) pp. 464–5.
73. See Thomas M. Callaghy (ed.), *South Africa in Southern Africa: The Intensifying Vortex of Violence* (New York: Praeger, 1983).

# Index